ENGLISH SURNAMES SERIES

THE SURNAMES OF
LEICESTERSHIRE AND RUTLAND

ENGLISH SURNAMES SERIES

Edited by D. A. Postles

Department of English Local History
University of Leicester

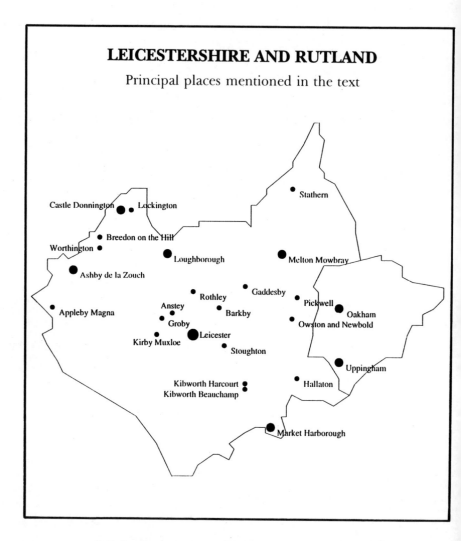

LEICESTERSHIRE AND RUTLAND

Principal places mentioned in the text

- Stathern
- Castle Donnington
- Lockington
- Breedon on the Hill
- Worthington
- Loughborough
- Melton Mowbray
- Ashby de la Zouch
- Rothley
- Gaddesby
- Anstey
- Barkby
- Pickwell
- Appleby Magna
- Groby
- Oakham
- Owston and Newbold
- Kirby Muxloe
- Leicester
- Stoughton
- Uppingham
- Kibworth Harcourt
- Kibworth Beauchamp
- Hallaton
- Market Harborough

Small spheres indicate large towns, whereas large circles refer to "small towns" i.e. Melton Mowbray, Ashby de la Zouch, and Market Harborough

ENGLISH SURNAMES SERIES

VII
The Surnames of
Leicestershire and Rutland

by
David Postles

LEOPARD'S HEAD PRESS

1998
Published by
LEOPARD'S HEAD PRESS LIMITED
1–5 Broad Street, Oxford OX1 3AW

© David Postles

ISBN 0 904920 34 8

*This is the seventh volume in the
English Surnames Series
which is published for the
Marc Fitch Fund*

Typeset by Denham House, Yapton, West Sussex
and printed in Great Britain by
Progressive Printing (UK) Limited, Leigh-on-Sea, Essex

Contents

List of Figures

List of Figures

List of Tables

List of Tables

List of Tables

List of Tables

Abbreviations

Essentially, abbreviations have been employed consistently in the text only for printed primary sources which recur constantly. Otherwise, the practice is to give the full bibliographical details of a work in the first reference to it in each chapter and thereafter, within the chapter, to use a short title. Where the analysis depends on the entire record source, no reference is given. In cases where specific places within the record sources are used, prcise references are given. In preference to using Farnham's *Medieval Village Notes*, I have returned to the original sources for reasons of precise orthography. I have used H. Hartopp, *Register of the Freemen of Leicester, 1196-1770*, (Leicester, 1927), only in conjunction with *RBL*.

AASR	*Associated Architectural Society Reports.*
AASR (1888-89)	W G D Fletcher, 'The earliest Leicestershire lay subsidy roll, 1327', *Associated Architectural Society Reports, 19 (1888-89), 130-78, 209-312.*
Berkeley	I H Jeayes, ed., *A Descriptive Catalogue of the Charters and Muniments . . . at Berkeley Castle*, (Bristol, 1892).
BL	British Library, London.
Bodl.	Bodleian Library, Oxford.
Burton Surveys	G C O Bridgman, ed., 'The Burton Abbey twelfth-century surveys' in *Collections for a History of Staffordshire*, (William Salt Archaeological Society, London, 1918 for 1916), 244-6 (for Appleby Magna only).
HAM	Huntington Library, San Marino, California, Hastings MSS.
Hastings MSS	*Historical Manuscripts Commission Report on the MSS of the late Reginald Rawdon Hastings, Esq.*, vol. 1, (London, 1928).

ME	Middle English.
MM	Merton College, Oxford, Merton, Muniments.
Oakham Survey	**G Chinnery *et al.*, eds., *The Oakham Survey of 1305*, (Rutland Record Society, Oakham,** 1989).
OE	Old English.
PRO	Public Record Office, London.
PRS	Pipe Roll Society.
RBL	M Bateson, ed., *Records of the Borough of Leicester*, vol. I, *1103–1327*, (London, 1899) and vol. II, *1327–1509*, (London, 1901).
Rothley	G T Clark, 'The customary of the manor and soke of Rothley in the county of Leicestershire', *Archaeologia*, 47, (1882), 80–130.
Rutland Hearth Tax	J Bourne and A Goode, eds., *Rutland Hearth Tax, 1665*, (Rutland Record Society, Oakham, 1991).
Rutland MSS	*Historical Manuscripts Commission Report on the MSS of the Duke of Rutland*, vol. 4, (London, **1905).**
Templars	B A Lees, ed., *Records of the Templars in England in the Twelfth Century*, (British Academy Records of the Social and Economic History of England, 9, 1935), ('Inquest' of 1185).
Tudor Rutland	J Cornwall, ed., *Tudor Rutland. The County Community under Henry VIII. The Military Survey, 1522, and Lay Subsidy, 1524–5, for Rutland*, (Rutland Record Society, Oakham, 1980).

Acknowledgements

Without the kindness and assistance of colleagues in many archives and record offices, this book could not have been produced. In particular, however, I would like to acknowledge the following for very kindly arranging for microfilm copies of material: Mary Robertson of the Huntington Library and the staff of the Public Record Office and British Library. Despite his monumental other commitments, Richard Smith has constantly been a considerate and enthusiastic chairperson of the Surnames Sub-Committee of the Council of the Marc Fitch Fund, but more than that has inspired and motivated my research and lent to it his formidable knowledge. I only hope that I have not misrepresented him. My fortitude has been helped in the Department by Alasdair Crockett, who has also very patiently borne my enquiries about IT, but also provided stimulating new perceptions. From afar, now, Paul Ell has been a constant companion, just like in the old days, and to him I owe what little ability I have in IT. I have also latterly become especially grateful to those working in the area of genealogy who have made available their researches through electronic media, not least on the Genuki World Wide Web (WWW) site hosted by the Manchester Computing Centre (Midas). I have to confess that my wife introduced me to this source and I would not have discovered it without her clever advice. The sections on Nottingham would not have been written without it. I do hope that this trend will flourish. I would also wish to mention Judith Bennett, who has always been encouraging and responded helpfully to preliminary thoughts. Finally, my sincerest gratitude is extended to two people, who have supported me, despite my idiosyncracies and irritability: Roy Stephens, a model employer, and Suella, a sharing partner. Nevertheless, I dedicate the book to my late parents and to my brother and sister.

Leicester, 1998   D.A.P.

CHAPTER 1

INTRODUCTION

Onomastic terms

Since its inception, the English Surnames Survey (ESS) has developed a distinctive terminology for naming patterns and processes. In recent years, however, an increasing amount of interest in and research into personal naming, particularly medieval, and especially into naming in countries of continental Europe, has suggested not only new lines of research, but also perhaps a more appropriate onomastic lexicon for personal names.[1] As long ago as 1979, it was recognized that some form of standardization of terms would be necessary to avoid confusion, but that standardization has hardly ensued, not least in the English language.[2] Here, then, are explained the terms employed in this study in relationship to the conventional terms of the ESS and recent other research.

The adjective toponymic has been accepted to replace the previous use of 'locative' by the ESS. Toponymic has a venerable usage, applied to this form of name by, for example, Holt in his discussion of the bynames and surnames of the Anglo-Norman baronage, whilst the use of 'locative' to refer to names has been criticized by linguists and anthroponymists.[3] Toponymic has been considered to comprehend names derived from both placenames and features in the landscape.[4] In this study, toponymic denotes exclusively names originating from placenames. For names referring to features in the landscape, the term conventionally used by the ESS, topographical, is retained. Toponymic thus comprehends such names as *[de] Leycestre*, whilst topographical is reserved for those like *[atten] Ok*.

Occupational names are self-explanatory, but include those implying status or office. Nicknames are those which impute characteristics, sometimes used ironically.[5] Bynames and surnames derived from personal names comprise those evolving out of 'forenames' or first names, such as Scolace, found at Kibworth Harcourt, which represents the forename Scholastica or Scolasse. Within this category, however, are important subsets. In this study, patronyms and metronyms are unelided forms whether in the

1

vernaculars (Middle English or French) or Latin, and thus comprise such bynames or surnames as Johnson (vernacular Middle English with the suffix -son), *filius Johannis*, and *fitzJohn*. Nevertheless, the Latin form is particularly problematic, since its rendition into the Middle English vernacular might not consist of a form in -son. An alternative translation into the Middle English vernacular might be elided patronyms and metronyms, in the form William — that is, for example, John William. Moreover, the translation into Middle English vernacular could also consist of the elided patronym or metronym with the genitival -s, as in John Williams. Finally, elided patronyms and metronyms have also been designated appositional patronyms and metronyms.[6] The terms usually employed in this study are: patronyms and metronyms for -son bynames and surnames and also, ambiguously, for Latin forms; appositional patronyms and metronyms for William forms; and genitival patronyms and metronyms for Williams forms.

The term personal name, however, is itself ambivalent, for, in onomastics, it might embrace all forms of personal names, including bynames and surnames, by comparison with placenames. In the convention of the ESS, personal names have been taken to be equivalent to what are colloquially designated firstnames, forenames or Christian names, but those terms are inaccurate in onomastic and historical considerations. Christian names should, *stricto sensu*, be applied only to Saints' and Biblical names and that strict usage is the one respected here. Until the thirteenth and even the early fourteenth century in our two counties (and elsewhere) a small number of the peasantry continued to be identified by only a single name without a byname or surname. Consequently, the terms firstname or forename are infelicitous. Fontname has been suggested as an alternative term, but that too lacks authenticity if, before 1215, names were conferred before baptism or not at baptism, and that consideration excludes baptismal name.[7] The most tenable term has been promoted by French anthroponymists, who prefer the Latin noun *nomen*, but, although that term should certainly be adopted in anthroponymic discussions, it is perhaps inappropriate here.[8] This study therefore retains the term personal name for this restricted sense.

Similarly, whilst there is considerable justification for the adoption of the term *cognomen*, which is also advanced by the French anthroponymists, not least because of its contemporary usage in the records, the term employed here, consistent with previous usage by the ESS and, indeed, in onomastic studies in the English language more widely, is byname — a second, qualifying name, additional to the personal name or *nomen*, which is yet unstable and may apply only to an individual and has not yet been transformed into an hereditary surname or family name.

The etymology of some personal names is particularly difficult to ascertain, although the vast proportion is fairly determinable. Confusion may arise for some names from the directions of their introduction into England. The corpus of West Germanic names and name forms directly introduced into England by the Anglo-Saxons comprises Old English (OE) names. The Scandinavian invasions, however, introduced some similar West Germanic name forms which had been diverted through Scandinavian countries and thus, although cognate, are different from the OE forms. The disparity exists in both the lexis of some names (that is, some names were introduced which did not exist in OE forms in England), in the phonemic variation (that is, some names which did exist in OE guise are, in their Scandinavian form, changed orthographically) and in syncopation.[9] By and large, the different forms (OE and Scandinavian) can be differentiated. In some cases, however, there is some ambiguity; one example is Cole, which might derive from OE Cola or OSc Kolr or Kolí (discounting for the moment the possibility that it originates as a French-influenced hypocoristic or pet form of Nicholas).[10] This overall corpus of pre-Conquest names and name forms — both OE and Scandinavian (the latter henceforth Scand and Anglo-Scand) — is designated insular Germanic. The term insular without qualification is taken more widely to comprehend not only OE and Scand but also PCeltic and Godoilic (Old Irish: OIr) forms.

The corpus of names and name forms introduced after the Conquest was composed of a number of strands: Continental-Germanic (C-G) or West Frankish (and Flemish); Norman Scandinavian; PCeltic or Brettonic; and Christian. Preponderantly the C-G forms were different from the pre-Conquest names and name forms, but there remain problems at the margins of these name items. One technique of differentiating ambiguous forms is through phonemic changes between West Germanic and C-G forms.[11] The degree to which that is completely satisfactory and conclusive is, however, uncertain; a particular example is Orger from Leicestershire.[12] Even more problematic are the Norman Scand forms of name introduced after the Conquest. Their dissimilarity from Scand forms introduced into the insular corpus at an earlier term can only be established problematically. Lexical differences can be assessed by reference to Fellows-Jensen's corpus of Scand names in Lincolnshire and Yorkshire, less firmly (because of regional difference) to Insley's for Norfolk, and then to the Norman corpus collected by Adigard des Gautries.[13] Where the same names existed in both corpora — insular and Norman Scand — the phonemic differences may be determined by reference to des Gautries.

In the case of PCeltic and Brettonic forms, it is almost necessary to adopt a rule of faith. Some forms must unambiguously be Brettonic — for example, Joel (Middle Brettonic Judhael), although this is not prominent in Leicestershire and Rutland. Other names, such as Brian and Alan, must be assumed to be Brettonic re-importations rather than, for example, Brian being a Godoilic form. One of the most extensive PCeltic forms in the two counties, both as personal name and byname, was Davy, whose precise origins must remain speculative.

Christian names are, by comparison, relatively straightforward. The conundrum with these names concerns the nature of their acceptance as personal name forms. Although the names of Saints of western Christendom had been received and were familiar in pre-Conquest liturgy and veneration, yet these names were not adopted as personal names until after the Conquest, and, indeed, not until the late twelfth century in any popular or extensive manner.[14]

Finally, a few other onomastic and related terms require explanation. Where the same personal name is adopted by two different people, sometimes close kin, the term homonymous is used here.[15] When referring to a dominant or pervasive culture (perhaps of naming), the descriptive term used here is homologous. Where an occupational byname or surname seems still to correspond with the real occupation of its bearer or where a bearer of a toponymic byname still seems to be resident at the placename, that byname is described here as eponymous. Finally, when there seems to be articulated in a byname a term symbolizing the trade or occupation of its bearer, the byname is here described as metonymic.

Methodology and sources

One of the principal difficulties for comprehending medieval naming patterns and processes is the official and formal nature of the record sources. In very few instances are insights given into colloquial naming patterns — the records only exceptionally illustrate informal speech communities. The language of the records presents another dilemma. In some records, particularly centrally-produced records, some forms of byname were rendered in what can only be described as 'low' Latin. Nevertheless, some of these Latin forms persisted as English surnames (for example, Sutor or Suter and Faber), but it is not clear if these names in the formal records actually represented the names used by the speech community or whether the vernacular term was colloquially employed. Latin forms are particularly problematic in the case of patronyms and metronyms, for their vernacular equivalent is significant but ambivalent — did it consist of a patronym or metronym in -son, an elided patronym (William) or a genitival form (Williams)? That question is critical for this transitional region between 'north' and 'south' and Scandinavian and West Saxon influence.[16] For at least some of the English middle ages, both French and ME constituted vernacular languages, but where bynames and surnames were constructed in French in the formal (and even informal records), it is not at all certain that these forms were anything more or less than the language of the clerk rather than the speech community.[17]

The records available for the study of naming patterns and processes were more or less formal, but always there was some degree of formality. That level of formality was related to some extent to the place of their production: whether localized or not. In particular, lay subsidy records were redactions or copies produced in the Exchequer, even the particular assessments which included the nominal evidence of individual taxpayers. There are, consequently, problems inherent in using their contents for assessing naming patterns. Apart from the obvious problem of contemporary clerical errors of transcription, which can sometimes be reconstructed without too much effort, lay subsidies may distort dialectal and lexical material. Since they were not localized or locally-produced documents, it has been suggested that lay subsidies cannot be used for dialectal material in names.[18] Again, this complication ensued from the relationship between speech community and clerk — how the clerk interpreted what the jurors imparted. The true nature of this interface is by no means clear.

The criticism, however, is important for the work conducted by the ESS which has established as its primary sources lay subsidies. In this study, the following Exchequer-based records are adduced for their evidence: the lay subsidy of Rutland of 1296; the lay subsidy of

Leicestershire in 1327; the Poll tax returns for most of Rutland in 1377; the Poll Tax returns for the Hundred of Gartree in 1381; and the lay subsidies of the two historic counties in 1524–5 (in the case of Rutland, enhanced by the military survey or musters roll of 1522).[19] Such evidence provides synchronic assessments of naming patterns at specific points.

Excluding the linguistic and lexical problem, two other difficulties inhere in these records. The first concerns their geographical coverage. Particular assessments, with nominal evidence, for the Poll Tax for Leicestershire are extant only for 1381 and only for Gartree Hundred in the east and south-east of the county. Comparable Poll Tax data are available for most of, but not all, Rutland in 1377. Whilst the early sixteenth-century taxation material is complete for the whole of Rutland, the Leicestershire data is defective since it excludes some parts of the south-west of the county, in particular in Sparkenhoe Hundred. This lacuna cannot be easily rectified, since the next available subsidy is illegible for precisely this area.[20] In any case, that subsidy, in view of the decline in the reliability of Tudor subsidies, is unlikely to have been an adequate substitute.

Perhaps more intractable still is the matter of the 'population' comprehended by the different subsidies. The subsidies of the late thirteenth and early fourteenth centuries were especially wealth-specific; a large proportion of the real population was omitted since it fell below the taxable threshold. The mean level of omission may have been as high as 60%. At best, these taxation returns reveal the names of the middling and higher peasantry upwards.

Complications arise naturally when these records are used for any attempt at diachronic analysis, such as comparing the proportions of different forms of byname and surname in 1296/1327 and 1524–5, regardless of any changes in the heritability of surnames in the intervening period. The sample populations embraced by the records of the earlier and later periods are dissimilar. These taxable populations are tabulated below:

Leicestershire

1327	4128	(whole county)
1381	2476	(Gartree Hundred only)
1524	2683	(most of the county)
1525	3924	(most of the county)

Rutland

1296	1868
1377	917
1522	1661
1524	1401

In general, the real population in 1296/1327 was probably considerably higher than in 1524–5, so that it is fairly conclusive that the taxation of 1524–5 captured a larger proportion of the population than those of the earlier period. If names were associated in any way with social group or wealth at an earlier time, then the reliability of the earlier subsidies as static representations and also by comparison with the later subsidies, will be suspect.[21]

To compensate for the problems of Exchequer records, a wide variety of 'locally-produced' documents has been introduced into the analysis. Rural Leicestershire, however, is not well-endowed with medieval documentation, nor its small towns. Two principal series of manorial court rolls have been examined in detail: Kibworth Harcourt and Barkby.[22] Whilst both were manors of Merton College, Oxford, the extent of the properties diverged. Merton's manor of Kibworth comprised a larger part of the township than the College's manor in Barkby. Both series of court rolls allow an analysis of the extent of the localized persistence of bynames and surnames over the later middle ages, although there is a break in the Kibworth rolls between 1298 and 1320. Other, short or broken series of court rolls have also been introduced to enhance the character of the data: Kibworth Beauchamp; Owston Abbey properties; Hallaton; and Breedon on the Hill.[23] Additionally, manorial surveys complement the material in court rolls, but, whilst series of court rolls provide a diachronic analysis, the surveys and rentals of Leicestershire estates allow, by and large, only a static, localized view. The surveys include the custumal of the soke of Rothley which can be assigned to *c.*1245, the survey of the manors of the Bishop of Lincoln of perhaps 1225x1258, the properties of Owston Abbey in east Leicestershire, the rentals of the estates of Leicester Abbey in 1341 and 1477 and the sequence of rentals for the Merton College manors.[24] Finally, a wide range of charters and cartularies has been used for supplementary material, including the Garendon and Brokesby cartularies.[25]

Nevertheless, these sources too present their problems. First, the geographical coverage is skewed towards east Leicestershire, particularly the manorial records, although the charter material does include considerable evidence for the Forest area in the Hastings MSS.[26] In a sense, that geography reflects the population density of different 'regions' of the county. The second problem is how localized these 'locally-produced' records actually were. Where the record related to a property in the county held by a lord resident outside the shire and region, then the evidence is equally as open to criticism for dialect and lexical evidence as lay subsidies. For example, it can be demonstrated that the dialect evidence in some charters may have reflected more that a religious house at some distance used a scribe local to the house rather than the property. The extent to which beneficiaries or religious houses were responsible for the drafting of charters rather than clerks local to the property should not, however, be over-emphasized. It is possible too that rentals and court rolls for the manors of Merton College or other non-resident lords might have been produced by 'foreign' clerks who accompanied the estate steward. Here again, the clarity of the relationship between information imparted by local speech community and 'foreign' redactor is opaque.

The secular trend of bynames and surnames in Leicestershire and Rutland over the later middle ages

As a framework for what follows throughout this discussion of the bynames and surnames of the two counties, long-term developments are presented in Table 1.1, which, however, needs to be contextualized.

Table 1.1

Long-term changes in the taxonomy of bynames and surnames in Leicestershire and Rutland, 1296–1665

Form of byname or surname	% 1296/1327	% 1377/1381	% 1522	% 1524	% 1525
RUTLAND					
toponymic	18.9	23.3	23.6	21.3	22.9
topographical	12.9	7.0	9.4	10.1	10.4
occupational	17.4	32.3	21.3	19.7	20.2
pat/metronymic	15.7	5.5	5.2	6.4	6.4
personal	11.6	13.8	15.3	14.4	14.1
nickname	17.4	18.1	16.5	21.4	18.2

Form of byname or surname	% 1296/1327	% 1377/1381	% 1522	% 1524	% 1525
LEICESTERSHIRE					
toponymic	25.0	23.8		21.7	22.3
topographical	7.0	6.6		8.7	7.5
occupational	16.0	29.4		19.5	18.1
pat/metronymic	11.0	5.6		6.2	4.8
personal	18.0	20.3		15.7	17.5
nickname	17.0	14.4		22.1	20.1

First, some description of the sources is necessary, to relate the proportions of different forms of bynames and surnames to the complexities of the sources. The percentages represent the proportion of taxpayers and, in 1522, those liable to musters service, not different bynames or surnames. In general, the sources consist of taxation lists with varying levels of inclusion and exclusion and a military survey. The different levels of comprehension of the population in the sources complicates interpretation of the proportions of different forms of bynames and surnames, since the 'populations' encompassed are inconsistent.

Accounting for a lower proportion of the global population, the tax lists of 1296 and 1327 belonged to the series of direct taxations levied on the laity between 1275 and 1332. The assessment was levied on personal estate at various levels in different years (but most frequently a tenth and fifteenth for respectively urban and rural 'communities'), but with exemption for those whose chattels not required for subsistence were valued below a minimum level (quite often 10s.). Whilst the lists record individuals, nevertheless the proportion of the total population included in the taxable population is estimated to have been quite small.[27] The extent to which the tax lists contain only heads of households is a further complexity. Certainly, however, the enumeration is almost exclusively males allowing little reflection of the naming processes of women.

On the other hand, the attribute of the tax lists is their geographical coverage, for the whole of the two counties is contained. Unfortunately, the next taxation lists which incorporate nominal data do not share that property. Although the Poll Tax for Rutland in 1377 comprehends most of the county, the comparable listing for Leicestershire in 1381 survives only for Gartree Hundred, in the east of the county. That geographical bias imports also some tendentious complications for naming processes, since the east of the county had received a heavier Scandinavian influence. Demographically, however, the taxable population is more inclusive, comprehending in 1377 all persons over the age of 14 and in 1381 those over the age of 15, but thus occasioning some difference between these two cohorts resulting from the slight difference in age qualification.[28] In compiling nominal data from the Poll Taxes, the principle observed has been attribution of an independent byname or surname. The cohorts involved thus consist largely of heads of household — male or female — and servants who were accorded an independent byname or surname. Figures cited in the table thus pertain to this net population rather than the taxable population in the listings.

By comparison with the Poll Tax, the muster roll of 1522 for Rutland comprehended males only, able-bodied and between the ages of 16 and 60.[29] The total corpus of surnames within Rutland may thus be consequently under-represented on the assumption that the continuity of some families may have depended on females. Nevertheless, the muster approaches a full complement of names by comparison with the deficiencies of the thirteenth- and early fourteenth-century sources. More equivocal is the degree of inclusion of the lay subsidies of 1524–5. Levied at the inconsiderable minimum level of 20*s*. on wages, goods or land, their comprehensiveness has been confirmed.[30]

Consequently, the segment of society captured by the taxations of 1296 and 1327 incorporated a wealthier section than the wider populations comprehended in 1377–1525. From that inconsistency may have arisen disparities in the proportionate use of forms of bynames and surnames, particularly if some forms of bynames were associated with social cachet at the earlier period when the bynames were sufficiently flexible to allow variation, variability and change in names.

Transpiring further from flexibility, some forms of byname did not achieve their final form until the middle of the fourteenth century. Patronymic and metronymic bynames particularly lacked final definition; Latin forms (*filius* or *filia Johannis*) in the two counties might subsequently be transformed into either patronyms and metronyms with the element -son or into elided or appositional patronyms and metronyms such as William or, inflected, Williams. That transition explains the higher frequency of patronyms and metronyms in 1296 and 1327, for Latin forms have been classified within that category although their final evolution is unclear.[31] The consistency of the proportion of patronyms and metronyms from 1377 to 1525 suggests that the actual frequency was about 5 to 6%.

Inherent in the classification of bynames and surnames, however, is a certain margin of error, because of ambiguities and uncertainties of etymology. For example, there remains a difficulty in differentiating some compounded bynames and surnames in -man into either occupational or topographical bynames.[32] Similarly, some bynames or surnames cannot be clearly distinguished as nickname or occupational (status) or pageant names — King, Bishop, Monk and cognates. This last dilemma was not, however, in the two counties one of considerable proportions, for the bynames King, Bishop and Abbott, for example, occurred collectively only 19 times in the lists of taxpayers in 1524 and 1525, encompassing only 0.7 and 0.5% of the taxable population in the respective years. The taxonomy of bynames and surnames is, nevertheless, necessarily imprecise.

With these qualifications, some general observations can be adduced from the figures in the table. Over the late middle ages, there was a constancy in the proportion of toponymic bynames and surnames within the taxable populations, regardless of the composition of the listings, contributing 19 to 24% of the population in Rutland and 22 to 25% in Leicestershire. Considerably below equivalent levels in those counties with a greater incidence of dispersed settlement, toponymic bynames and surnames in these two counties reflected and derived from the higher density of nucleation of settlement. Here, toponymic bynames originated in actual migration rather than the identification of people within a dispersed settlement pattern with multiple hamlets within a single parish. Some limited dispersal of settlement certainly existed in these counties, illustrated by the hamlets of Barkby Thorpe, Hamilton and part of Thurmaston within the parish of Barkby with its principal vill of Barkby, but the extent of dispersal was restricted. Characteristically, Leicestershire and Rutland conformed to the nucleated settlement associated with the commonfield and champion *pays* or 'countries' which were some (although only some) of the constituent features.

Comparatively low proportions of the population bore topographical bynames in these two counties. In Leicestershire merely 7 to 9% of the taxable populations were identified by reference to topography and in Rutland from 7 to 13%. Some explanation may reside partially in relatively low polyfocal settlement in many parts of the counties, but not exclusively all.

Less consistency was exhibited by the volume of the assessed population identified by occupational bynames and surnames, although the anomaly is the discrepancy of the Poll Taxes of 1377 and 1381 in which occupational names appear to be over-represented by comparison with the consistent levels of other sources. Excluding the Poll Taxes, the levels conform with those predominantly found in some other counties, between 16 and 21% of taxpayers.

Comparative with these other forms of byname and surname, patronyms and metronyms were insignificant, at levels of 5 to 6% of taxpayers. By comparison with counties in the south and south-west, where these forms of byname were almost non-existent for most of the later middle ages, the quotient was relatively high, but considerably inferior to the incidence in the north of England. Precisely in this respect was the significance of the general situation of the two counties most manifest, for the incidence of patronyms and metronyms in the two counties was directly associated with the intermediate position between 'North' and 'South' and Scandinavian and West Saxon influence.

These characteristics of personal naming in the two counties are discussed in more detail below, with more attention to particular and specific aspects of the different forms of personal name and predominant names and name forms. The purpose here has been simply to establish the secular development of naming patterns in the formative later middle ages when bynames developed in use, were confirmed as heredity surnames and then configured by demographic vicissitudes.

Leicestershire and Rutland

Geographically, these two counties are located in central England, in the belt sometimes described as the Midland Plain, within the Lowland Zone. The geomorphology and topography of the counties are, however, complex and diverse. The eastern half of Leicestershire and most of Rutland are dominated by uplands rising to over 400 feet, principally escarpments of Jurassic limestone and ironstone overlaid by Boulder Clay, comprising the Wolds and High Leicestershire.[33] Dissected by the dendritic drainage pattern of the tributaries of the rivers Soar and Wreake, by the Wreake itself, and by the Eye

FIG 1 THE REGIONS OF LEICESTERSHIRE

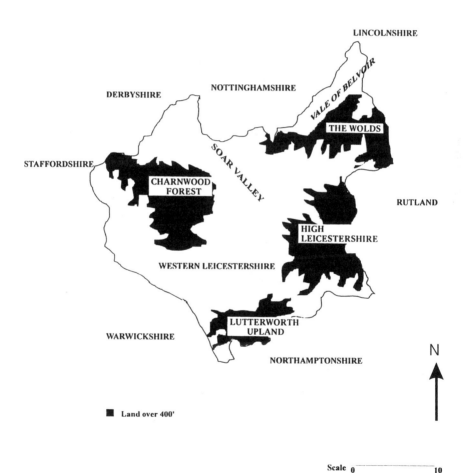

LINCOLNSHIRE

VALE OF BELVOIR

NOTTINGHAMSHIRE

DERBYSHIRE

THE WOLDS

STAFFORDSHIRE

SOAR VALLEY

CHARNWOOD FOREST

RUTLAND

HIGH LEICESTERSHIRE

WESTERN LEICESTERSHIRE

LUTTERWORTH UPLAND

WARWICKSHIRE

NORTHAMPTONSHIRE

N

■ Land over 400'

Scale 0 _____ 10

Brook and (Vale of) Catmose in Rutland, the dip slopes were settled late and inconclusively. To the north of the Wolds in Leicestershire is a clay vale extending from the scarp foot, the Vale of Belvoir. In contrast, the western half of Leicestershire contains reduced woodlands of two residual forests, Charnwood in the north-west and Leicester Forest directly east of the City. Rising to over 800 feet, Charnwood is composed of pre-Cambrian rock overlaid by Triassic Clay, the superimposed drainage thus creating in miniature, deep gorges, such as that of the River Lin in Bradgate Park. To the north of Charnwood lies another area of undulating Wolds, around Ashby, leading to the flood plain of the River Trent in south Derbyshire and Staffordshire. Below Leicester Forest is a pastoral *pays* in the south-west of the shire. The county of Leicester is bisected by the valley of the River Soar, which, above Leicester, has produced a wide flood plain and meadows, towards its confluence with the River Trent in south Nottinghamshire.

Consideration of the historical development of Leicestershire has thus understandably tended to contrast east and west, with the perception that the western half only developed later as woodland was reduced. Comparisons have been made between the mainly agrarian occupational structure of eastern Leicestershire and Rutland and the wood-pasture character of the western half, with the later development of by-employment or industries in the country-side or, in the terminology of some, 'proto-industrialization'.[34] By-employments did, indeed, progress during the later middle ages, but more particularly from the sixteenth century, in the west and especially on the periphery of Charnwood, but the contrast on a single criterion between east and west is too stark since both east and west encompassed a number of *pays*.

Both Leicestershire and Rutland are enveloped within the area of the Five Boroughs (Derby, Nottingham, Lincoln, Stamford and Leicester) of Scandinavian settlement and influence. Place-names, particularly in east and north-east Leicestershire, predominantly exhibit Scandinavian generic elements, -by and -thorp, with a scattering of Grimston hybrids (Scandinavian specific elements combined with Old English generic ones) and Scandinavian forms of Old English placenames, such as Carlton. From the distribution of these placenames and specifically the significance.of -thorp, it has been suggested that the Scandinavian settlement of the East Midlands was extensive and, moreover, that the south-western boundary of

Leicestershire, demarcated now by the A5, divided Danish from English Mercia.[35] Several onomastic issues are raised by this prospect: to what extent did Scandinavian forms of personal name survive in Middle English personal naming?; how far were Scandinavian graphemic forms represented in Middle English personal naming?; and how far did the line of the modern A5 constitute a 'dialect boundary', where bundles of isoglosses coalesced?[36]

Such questions may be considered in the context of the general linguistic location of the two counties. The traditional division of Middle English into dialect regions placed the two shires in the middle but towards the north of East Midlands ME dialect, Watling Street forming the divide with West Midlands ME.[37] More recent and more sophisticated investigation of dialect has tended to dissolve dialect regions in favour of a dialect continuum, in which each area 'is, in respect of some of its features, a border-area'.[38] It might then be expected that there was at least some dialectal overlap between these two counties and adjacent shires, but that there may have been some discrete and different dialect usages. As much is indeed suggested by the study of vernacular texts within Leicestershire, which seem to identify north-eastern, north-western and south-western internal traits.[39] Moreover, the dialect of north-east Leicestershire, Rutland, north Northamptonshire and north Huntingdonshire exhibited analogical development with at least one 'northern' ME syntactical rule.[40]

The influence of northern dialects may have been introduced into north-east Leicestershire through Lincolnshire, which, to some extent, represented a south-easterly extension of northern dialects.[41] Indeed the county was in many respects a melting pot of dialect elements and items, with influences from northern and West Midland dialects, which can be illustrated by a few examples. The phoneme she- was represented principally as stressed sche- in much of Leicestershire, but with unstressed she- in the south of the shire; in Rutland, she- was prevalent; but in Warwickshire, stressed and unstressed forms appeared equally. Whilst the grapheme eche/ich was widely distributed throughout Leicestershire, ylke appeared in the north-east of the county, as also in Rutland, associated with the prominence of ilk in Lincolnshire. By contrast, iche/eche was prevalent in Warwickshire and Northamptonshire.

Whilst the vocalic interchange o/a has been traditionally considered as producing an isogloss between East and West Midlands dialect regions, the item mony occurred in south-west Leicestershire, an extension of its dominance in Warwickshire, but in most of Leicestershire the graphemic representation was many; this pattern was replicated in ony/any. In literary texts, palatal c[h]/k produced a clearer distinction, for /k/ occurred mainly in the east of Leicestershire. On the other hand, hundred was the norm throughout the county, as in Warwickshire, Northamptonshire and Derbyshire, by comparison with hundreth (with the influence of Scandinavian ð) in Lincolnshire.

Whereas mykel was characteristic of north and north-east Leicestershire, moch/myche appeared in texts from the centre and south-west of the shire, associated with moche/muche in Warwickshire and Northamptonshire (muche transposing OE reflex /y/ as /u/). Rutland was divided by moche and mekyll, the latter conforming to the pre-eminence of mekyll in Lincolnshire. In terms of other lexis, the item are was employed in north-east Leicestershire in association with the same lexical item in Lincolnshire, but in the north-west and south-west of Leicestershire ben was in use, as in Derbyshire, Warwickshire and Northamptonshire.[42]

Emphasis, however, should be directed to the fact that these data are acquired from literary texts, which, although localized, will not necessarily reflect the dialect pronunciation or lexis of the speech community, for reasons both of social group as well as regional origins. It may then be possible that name items may help elucidate aspects of dialect, provided that sufficient attention is given to the nature of the production of the records in which they are represented. Even with ostensibly localized record sources, the relationship between written representation and speech community is ambivalent.

The valuable recent research into dialect items does, however, allow a framework from which to start, assisting in the location of Leicestershire and Rutland within a wider picture. What is quite evident is that Leicestershire in particular constituted an assemblage and intermixing of various dialect influences, from the north through Lincolnshire, and from the south and west of the county. One further method of situating the two counties within a wider linguistic framework is to select a single, but very distinctive, onomastic item, patronyms and metronyms.

Patronyms and metronyms: the wider context

Although the precise influences on the formation of patronyms

FIG 2 PATRONYMS/METRONYMS LAY SUBSIDIES 1296-1332

- ■ A (3)
- ■ B (5)
- ▨ C (2)
- ▨ D (3)
- □ E (5)
- □ F (9)
- □ G (15)

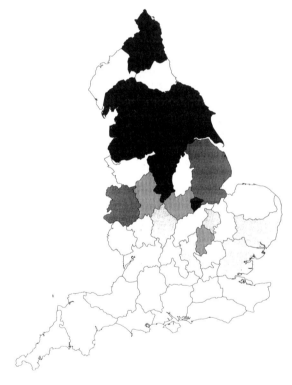

A= >25% C= 11-15% E= 1-5% G= no data

B= 16-20% D=6-10% F= <1%

and metronyms are still debatable, there is no doubting the actual distribution of this lexical item in naming, which is represented in Figure 2.[43]

Exhibited in this map is the gradation from north to south of patronymic and metronymic forms of byname in the late thirteenth and early fourteenth century, although the data contain Latin (*filius/ filia*) as well as vernacular forms (-son/-doghter).[44] Whilst some of the Latin forms theoretically might not have stabilized as vernacular patronyms and metronyms with the suffix -son, yet there is something of an association between areas with a high incidence of both Latin and vernacular forms of patronym and metronym, which is illustrated in Table 1.2.

Table 1.2

Patronyms and metronyms by county in lay subsidies 1296–1332

County/date	*filius/ filia*	-son/ -doghter	total taxpayers [legible]
Cumberland/1332	876	125	3833
Lancashire/1327	633	30	3219
Northumberland/1296	1314	4	3767
Yorks E.R./1297	294	2	2290
Yorks W.R.	213	0	1093
Derbyshire/1327	225	10	1506
Staffordshire/1327	396	27	4353
Lincolnshire/1332	2875	115	19690
Lindsey	1886	86	11817
Kesteven	622	15	5453
Holland	367	14	2420
Leicestershire/1327	426	12	3871
Rutland/1296	291	3	1868
Huntingdonshire/1327	174	7	2345
Warwickshire/1332	100	20	3385
Worcestershire/1327	11	11	
Shropshire/1327	602	30	4895
Gloucestershire/1327	17	10	9000+
Bedfordshire(part)/1297	56	3	987
Buckinghamshire/1332	53	6	
Suffolk/1327	198	20	10000+
Essex/1327	75	8	8326

County/date	*filius/* *filia*	-son/ -doghter	total taxpayers [legible]
Wiltshire/1332	0	4	2778
Somerset/1327	10	18	
Devon/1332	4	4	10614
Kent/1334	78	7	11016
Surrey/1327	11	7	4951
Sussex/1327	9	3	

Nevertheless, the data in the Table should be refined, as it is fairly evident that until the early fourteenth century, Latin forms predominated in lay subsidies, replaced by vernacular forms only during the early fourteenth century.[45]

Whatever the causes of the formation of patronyms and metronyms, there is a clear distribution, with higher proportions in the north by comparison with the south, and a greater density in areas of Scandinavian influence by contrast with West Saxon dominance, by the early fourteenth century. Exceptionally, Shropshire had a higher incidence of patronyms and metronyms, perhaps associated with the Welsh patronymic system. Significantly, Leicestershire resides at the junction of the these broad belts, whilst Rutland had some affinity with the more northerly structure of names.

Conclusion

That theme, consequently, of the location of the two counties at the junction and fusion of several different onomastic influences, forms a predominant and recurring background to this discussion of naming patterns and processes in the two counties. Beyond patronyms and metronyms, the influence of this location informed dialect items in naming, the extent of survival of Anglo-Scandinavian name forms in bynames and surnames, and the lexis of topographical forms of bynames and surnames. In view of the importance of this geographical position, an attempt has been made throughout the discussion to make comparisons with onomastic features in adjacent counties, particularly Derbyshire, Warwickshire, Staffordshire and Lincolnshire. None the less, there was no absolute and clear boundary between these different influences, but rather they were in competition and were mediated so that different onomastic and lexical items achieved different distributions and extents of influence. As those processes of mediation and competition were important, the next chapter addresses the issues of dialect and local usage.

References

1 M Bourin, ed., *Genèse Médiévale de l'Anthroponymie Moderne* (Tours, 1990); M Bourin and P Chareille, eds., *Genèse Médiévale de l'Anthroponymie Moderne Tome II Persistances du Nom Unique,* (Tours, 2 vol., 1992); Bourin and Chareille, eds., *Genèse Médiévale de l'Anthroponymie Moderne Tome III Enquêtes Généalogiques et Données Prosopographiques,* (2 volumes, Tours, 1995); R Bartlett, *The Making of Europe. Conquest, Colonization and Cultural Change 950-1350,* (Harmondsworth, 1994), 270-80; M Bourin, ed., *Genèse Médiévale de l'Anthroponymie Moderne: l'Espace Italien Chronique,* (Rome, 1994); D Herlihy, 'Tuscan Names, 1200-1530' in *idem,* ed., *Women, Family and Society in Medieval Europe. Historical Essays 1978-1991,* (Oxford, 1995), 330-52; M Mitterauer, *Ahnen und Heilige Namengebung in der Europäischen Geschichte,* (Munich, 1993).

2 G Fellows-Jensen, 'Some problems of a maverick anthroponymist' in H Voitl, ed., *The Study of the Personal Names of the British Isles,* (Erlangen, 1976), 43-62; C Clark, 'Anthroponymy' in N Blake, ed., *The Cambridge History of the English Language Volume II 1066-1476,* (Cambridge, 1992), 551-87.

3 J C Holt, *What's in a Name? Family Nomenclature and the Norman Conquest,* (Stenton Lecture, Reading, 1981); Clark, 'Anthroponymy', 572; personal communication from Professor W Nicolaison

4 Clark, 'Anthroponymy', 572.

5 P McClure, 'The interpretation of Middle English nicknames', *Nomina,* 5, (1981), 95-104.

6 Clark, 'Anthroponymy', 568.

7 See the criticism of G Fellows-Jensen, 'Some problems of a maverick anthroponymist'.

8 For example in Bourin, ed., *Genèse Médiévale de l'Anthroponymie Moderne* as n.1 above.

9 See now J Insley, *Scandinavian Personal Names in Norfolk. A Survey Based on Medieval Records and Place-Names*, (Acta Academiae Regiae Gustavi Adolphi LXII, Uppsala, 1994), xxxvi-xxxix and *passim.*

10 *Ibid.,* 275-7, rehearses the problem.

11 C Clark, 'English personal names *c.*650-1300: some prosopographical reflections', *Medieval Prosopography,* 8, (1987), 31-60.

12 See below, 309-10.

13 Insley, *Scandinavian Personal Names in Norfolk,* as n.9; J Adigard des Gautries, *Les Noms de Personne Scandinaves en Normandie de 911 à 1066,* (Nomina Germanica 11, Lund, 1954); G Fellows-Jensen,

Scandinavian Personal Names in Lincolnshire and Yorkshire, (Navnestudier udgivet af Institut for Navneforskning 7, Copenhagen, 1968).

[14] V Ortenberg, *The English Church and the Continent in the Tenth and Eleventh Centuries: Cultural, Spiritual and Artistic Changes*, (Oxford, 1992).

[15] In preference, for example, to the term homogeneous used by Bartlett, *The Making of Europe*, as n.1; for homonymous, see, for example, M J Bennett, 'Spiritual kinship and the baptismal name in traditional European society' in L O Frappell, ed., *Principalities, Power and Estates*, (Adelaide, 1979), 1–13.

[16] See below, 16–19.

[17] For a résumé of the use of French as a spoken language, R A Lodge, 'Language attitudes and linguistic norms in France and England in the thirteenth century' in P R Coss and S D Lloyd, *Thirteenth Century England IV Proceedings of the Newcastle upon Tyne Conference 1991*, (Woodbridge, 1992), 73–84; M D Legge, 'Anglo-Norman as a spoken language', in R A Brown, ed., *Proceedings of the Battle Conference on Anglo-Norman Studies II 1979*, (Woodbridge, 1980), 108–17; M T Clanchy, *From Memory to Written Record England 1066-1307*, (Oxford, 2nd edn., 1993), 197–220.

[18] P McClure, 'Lay subsidy rolls and dialect phonology' in F Sandgren, ed., *Otium et Negotium Studies in Onomatology and Library Science presented to Olof von Feilitzen*, (Acta Bibliothecae Regiae Stockholmiensis 16, 1973), 188–94; but see also G Kristensson, 'Lay subsidy rolls and dialect geography', *English Studies*, 57 (1976), 51–9.

[19] *AASR*, (1888–9); PRO E179/165/1 (Rutland); PRO E179/165/21 (1377); PRO E179/133/35 (1381); PRO E179/133/104–124 (Leics, 1524–5); *Tudor Rutland* (1522 and 1524–5). For comments on the Poll Taxes as a source, C Fenwick, 'The English poll taxes of 1377, 1379 and 1381', unpublished PhD, University of London, 1983, esp. 445–60.

[20] PRO E179/133/133 (1544–5).

[21] R Smith, 'Human resources' in G Astill and A Grant, eds., *The Countryside of Medieval England*, (Oxford, 1988), 189–91; B M S Campbell, 'The population of early Tudor England: a reinterpretation of the 1522 muster returns and 1525 lay subsidies', *Journal of Historical Geography*, 7 (1981), 145–54.

[22] MM 6367–6405 and 6563–6575.

[23] PRO SC2/183/51–52; PRO SC2/183/76–77; PRO SC2/183/87–90; PRO DL30/80/1102.

[24] Rothley dated by comparison with PRO C260/86; Queen's College, Oxford, MS 366, fos. 16r–19r: Bodl. MS Laud Misc 625; *AASR*, 23 (1895-6), 413–17; and above, n.22. For the Leicester and Owston Abbey estates, R H Hilton, *The Economic Development of Some Leicestershire Estates in the XIVth and XVth Centuries*, (Oxford, 1947).

[25] B L Lansdowne MS 415; Bodl. MS Wood empt 7.

[26] *Hastings MSS.*

[27] See now C Dyer, 'Taxation and communities in late medieval England', in R Britnell and J Hatcher, eds., *Progress and Problems in Medieval England Essays in Honour of Edward Miller*, (Cambridge, 1996), 168–90, esp. 171; the *locus classicus* is J F Willard, *Parliamentary Taxes on Personal Property 1290 to 1334. A Study in Mediaeval English Financial Administration*, (Cambridge, Massachusetts, 1934), 87–92, but see also J R Maddicott, 'The English peasantry and the demands of the Crown 1294-1341', in T H Aston, ed., *Landlords, Peasants and Politics in Medieval England*, (Cambridge, 1987), 294; for an extreme example of omission, A Jones, 'Caddington, Kensworth and Dunstable in 1297', *Economic History Review*, 2nd ser., 32 (1979), 316, 319–22, 324 and A T Gaydon, *The Taxation of 1297*, (Bedfordshire Historical Records Society, 39, 1959 for 1958), xxxiii.

[28] Fenwick, 'The English Poll Taxes', 24–5, 167.

[29] *Tudor Rutland*, 11; J C Cornwall, *Wealth and Society in Early Sixteenth Century England*, (London, 1988), 1–2.

[30] B M S Campbell, 'The population of early Tudor England: a re-evaluation of the 1522 Muster Returns and the 1524 and 1525 Lay Subsidies', *Journal of Historical Geography*, 7 (1981), 145–54; and, more generally, Cornwall, *Wealth and Society*, esp. 3–4.

[31] See further below, 16–19.

[32] G Fransson, *Middle English Surnames of Occupation 1100–1350*, (Lund Studies in English, Lund, 1935).

[33] For the historical significance of the Wolds, H S A Fox, 'The people of the Wolds in English settlement history', in M Aston, D Austin and C Dyer, eds., *The Rural Settlements of Medieval England*, (Oxford, 1989), 77–101.

[34] For the most recent statement of this contrast by a medieval historian, E Acheson, *A Gentry Community Leicestershire in the Fifteenth Century c.1422-c.1485*, (Cambridge, 1992), 8–18, which encapsulates all the previous comment on the medieval distribution

of wealth and settlement in the county. For the most recent discussion of 'proto-industrialization' as concept and empirical development, M Zell, *Industry in the Countryside Wealden Society in the Sixteenth Century*, (Cambridge, 1994), 1-9, but specifically for the later progress of framework knitting in north-west Leicestershire, D Levine, *Family Formation in an Age of Nascent Capitalism*, (London, 1977) (Shepshed).

[35] K Cameron, 'Scandinavian settlement in the territory of the Five Boroughs: the place-name evidence' in *idem*, ed., *Place-Name Evidence for the Anglo-Saxon Invasion and Scandinavian Settlement*, (Nottingham, 1977), 115-71, esp. 115-16, 121.

[36] M Wakelin, *English Dialects*, (London, 1977), 10; I Hjertstedt, *Middle English Nicknames in the Lay Subsidy Rolls for Warwickshire*, (Acta Universitatis Upsaliensis, Studia Anglistica Upsaliensia, 63, Upsala 1987), 26-7; G Kistensson, *A Survey of Middle English Dialects 1290-1350: the West Midland Counties*, (Publications of the New Society of Letters at Lund, 78, Lund 1987). But see the comments further below, 34-6.

[37] Summarized in A C Baugh and T Cable, *A History of the English Language*, (3rd ed., London, 1987), 190 and B M H Strang, *A History of English*, (London, 1986), 224 *et seqq*.

[38] A M McIntosh, M L Samuels and M Benskin, *A Linguistic Atlas of Late Mediaeval English*, (4 vols., 1986), I, 4, 12; but note the caveat at page 6 that the authors recognize that their examination concerns only the relationship between phonology and orthography and not necessarily that between phonemes and graphemes and also that the necessary concentration (at that stage) on literary texts may reflect local scribal habits rather than speech.

[39] *Ibid.*, 209-10 The source texts for Leicestershire are listed at pages 97-8, 208-10, principally versions of Mirk's *Festial*

[40] *Ibid.*, 27; A M McIntosh, 'Present indicative plural forms in the later Middle English of the North Midlands' in D Gray and E G Stanley, eds., *Middle English Studies Presented to Norman Davis*, (Woodbridge, 1983), 235-44.

[41] This judgement is posited on the dotmaps in A M McIntosh, M L Samuels and M Benskin, *Linguistic Atlas*, 314 (maps 39-40), 317 (maps 51-2), 325 (maps 82-4), 331 (maps 105-6, 108), 335 (maps 121, 124), 337 (maps 131-2), 340-1 (maps 144, 145, 148), 346-7 (maps 168, 170), 377 (maps 290-1), 383 (maps 309, 314-15), 391 (maps 345-6). For the assumption of this relationship: G Kristensson,

A Survey of Middle English Dialects 1290-1350. The Six Northern Counties and Lincolnshire, (Lund Studies in English, 35, Lund, 1967) and *Studies on the Early Fourteenth Century Population of Lindsey*, (Royal Society of Letters, Scripta Minora, Lund, 1976-7).

42 These items are based on A M McIntosh, M L Samuels and M Benskin, *Linguistic Atlas*, vol. 2, 10-11, 16-17, 22-3, 28-9, 40-1, 46-7, 52-3, 58-9, 64-5, 70-1, 76-7, 82-3, 238-9, 250-1, 292-3.

43 For different explorations of the influences, P H Reaney, *The Origins of English Surnames*, (London, repr. 1987), 86-90, followed by C D Rogers, *The Surname Detective. Investigating Surname Distribution in England, 1086-Present Day*, (Manchester, 1995), 221-3, and, in contrast, J K Sørensen, *Patronymics in Denmark and England*, (Dorothea Coke Memorial Lecture, 1982, London, 1983).

44 The sources for the data are: J P Steel, ed., *Cumberland Lay Subsidy . . . 6th Edward III*, (Kendal, 1912); C M Fraser, ed., *The Northumberland Lay Subsidy Roll of 1296*, (Society of Antiquaries of Newcastle upon Tyne, Record Series 1, 1968); W Brown, ed., *Yorkshire Lay Subsidy . . . 25 Edward I (1297)*, (Yorkshire Archaeological Society Record Series, 16, 1894); J P Rylands, ed., 'The Exchequer lay subsidy roll of Robert de Shireburn and John de Radcliffe, taxers and collectors in the county of Lancashire', *Miscellanies Relating to Lancashire and Cheshire*, vol. ii, (Lancashire and Cheshire Record Society, 31, 1896); J C Cox, 'Derbyshire in 1327: being a lay subsidy roll', *Journal of the Derbyshire Archaeological and Natural History Society*, 30 (1908), 23-96; G Wrottesley, 'The Exchequer lay subsidy of A.D 1327', *Collections for a History of Staffordshire*, [William Salt Archaeological Society], 7 (1886); PRO E179/135/14-16 (Lincolnshire); *AASR*, (1888-9); PRO E179/165/1 (Rutland); J A Raftis and M P Hogan, eds., *Early Huntingdonshire Lay Subsidy Rolls*, (Pontifical Institute of Mediaeval Studies, Subsidia Mediaevalia, 8, 1976); W F Carter, ed., *The Lay Subsidy Roll of Warwickshire of 1332*, (Dugdale Society, 6, 1926); F J Field, ed., *Lay Subsidy for the County of Worcester 1 Edward I (sic)*, (Worcestershire Historical Society, 9, 1895, but actually 1 Edward III); W G D Fletcher, 'The Shropshire lay subsidy of 1 Edward I', (Shropshire Archaeological Society, 1907); P Franklin, *The Taxpayers of Medieval Gloucestershire An Analysis of the 1327 Lay Subsidy Roll with a New Edition of its Text*, (Stroud, 1993) [for the numbers of legible taxpayers, P Franklin, 'Gloucestershire medieval taxpayers', *Local Population Studies*, 54 (1995), 17]; A T Gaydon, ed., *The Taxation of 1297*, (Bedfordshire Historical Record

Society, 39, 1959 for 1958) [but only part of the county]; A C Chibnall, ed., *Early Taxation Returns* (Buckinghamshire Record Society, 1966); E Powell, ed., *Suffolk in 1327 being a Subsidy Return*, (Suffolk Green Books, IX, vol. 11, Woodbridge, 1906); J C Ward, ed., *The Medieval Essex Community. The Lay Subsidy of 1327*, (Essex Record Office, Essex Historical Documents, 1, 1983); D Crowley, ed., *The Wiltshire Tax List of 1332*, (Wiltshire Record Society, 45, 1989); A D Mills, *The Dorset Lay Subsidy of 1332*, (Dorset Record Society, 4, 1971); F H Dickinson, ed., *Kirkby's Quest for Somerset*, (Somerset Record Society, 3, 1889); E M Erskine, ed., *The Devonshire Lay Subsidy of 1332*, (Devon and Cornwall Record Society, n.s 14, 1969); H A Hanley and C W Chalklin, 'The Kent lay subsidy of 1334/5' in F R H DuBoulay, ed., *Medieval Kentish Society*, (Kent Records, 18, 1964); *Surrey Taxation Returns*, (Surrey Record Society, 33, 1932); W Hudson, ed., *Three Earliest Lay Subsidies for the County of Sussex in the Years 1296, 1327, 1332*, (Sussex Record Society, 10, 1910).

[45] Regression analysis on the data of 1327–32, regressing *filius/filia* against the predictor -son/-doghter, produces $R^2=52.9\%$ with $p=0.000$.

CHAPTER 2

DIALECT AND LOCAL USAGES

Dialect lexis: Walker

Commonly it is recognized that the lexis of beating wool contained dialectal contrasts, since Walker was more northern, Fuller eastern and Tucker southern and western.[1] Consequently, Leicestershire and Rutland were at the juncture of at least two competing dialects in this regard — northern Walker and eastern Fuller. The earliest references to the occupational name in the two counties are ambivalent because the Latin disguises any vernacular content. Thus the Pipe Roll of 1190 referred to Hugh *Fullo* at one of the Peatlings.[2] Amfrid *filius Alwini fullonis* was mentioned in a charter relating to Burton on the Wolds.[3] Enumerated in the survey of the Bishop of Lincoln's manor at Lyddington was another *Fullo*, Hugh, one of the Bishop's tenants in 1225×1258, who held a toft.[4] Significantly, however, whereas Hugh *Fullo* was listed amongst the tenantry of the soke of Oakham at Thorpe with Twyford in 1305, in the same survey for Oakham itself is listed Robert le Fuller.[5] Subsequently the Poll tax for Rutland in 1377 included John and William Fullersman at Tolthorpe.[6] Moreover, Hugh Fuller was listed and assessed at Ryhall in 1522 and 1524.[7] With two exceptions, when Fuller occurred it did so in the easternmost area, in Rutland, the exceptions comprising Robert Fuller at Loughborough in an account roll of 1474 and Robert le Fulur at Bitteswell in the later middle ages, both possibly resulting from later immigration.[8] The eastern Fuller was thus confined to the easternmost edge of the two counties, whilst the northern Walker exerted a greater presence throughout the area.

In the borough of Leicester, walker remained the exclusive term and occupational byname. For example, the assessment for the *Nonarum Inquisitiones* of 1340-2 in the borough included John le Walker, Robert le Walker, Roger le Walker, Michael le Walker, and Power le Walker.[9] Michael had entered the freedom in 1335 and was assessed in the borough's tallage of 1336, whilst Power (*alias* Poger) had been admitted as a freeman slightly earlier, in 1330 and contributed more highly, at 2*s.*, to the same tallage.[10] Although Thomas Fulle attested a charter in 1266, it is probable that this denomination was a rendition of the Latin form of his name.[11] Subsequently, Annes [Agnes] Walker was assessed in the subsidy of 1505, concurrently with John Walker; two years previously Thomas Walker had attained the freedom and in 1525 Henry Walker was included in the lay subsidy of 1525.[12]

Walker, nonetheless, was more evident in rural places in the later middle ages and, indeed, not visible at all before the late fourteenth century, perhaps obscured by Latin terms. Alongside the two Fullersmen in the Poll Tax of 1377 for Rutland were two Walkers, complemented by three in Gartree Hundred in the Poll Tax of four years later. By 1522, Rutland males eligible for the musters included eight Walkers.[13]

The surname had become established in the late middle ages at several places, particularly lesser urban settlements with their indigenous cloth industries. In the small town of Loughborough in the north of Leicestershire, John Walker and Richard Walker were tenants in the rental of *c.*1370. Subsequently, the court rolls between 1397 and 1412 contain numerous entries relating to both John jnr. and John snr. Walker, and again in 1429 to a John Walker. Those same court rolls alluded to Roger Walker between 1402 and 1412 and Thomas Walker between 1398 and 1412, whilst William Walker was fleetingly mentioned in 1403. By the early fifteenth century, the town contained so many John Walkers that it was necessary to differentiate them in the court rolls by the use of affixes: John Walker *frater Rogeri Walker* in 1412; John Walker *in le Byggyng* (a street) in 1430–1; and John Walker *in le Kirkgate* in 1430. Furthermore, Walkers had become established in the adjacent suburban parish of Cotes, close by Loughborough, as cases of trespass in Loughborough involved Nicholas Walker of Cotes, Roger Walker of Cotes and Thomas Walker of Cotes, the last of whom, Thomas, was also chief pledge for Cotes. On the opposite side of the small town, there was resident another Walker, Roger Walker of Garendon, party to a plea of debt in Loughborough in 1412.[14] Another small town in north Leicestershire, Castle Donington, was also inhabited by Walkers, the court rolls referring to Ralph in 1512–15, John in 1516, Agnes in 1517, and Ralph in 1564.[15] At an earlier time, Walkers (John and William) had been mentioned in charters relating to lands in Melton Mowbray, a market town in the north-east of the county.[16]

Walkers featured also in rural 'communities', however, represented by Henry Walkar at Stoughton, Robert Walker at Shepshed, Thomas Walker at Thurmaston, and William Walker at Quorn, all tenants of Leicester Abbey in its survey of 1477.[17] Exceptionally, but in isolation, two Walkers appeared in the court rolls of Kibworth Harcourt in 1346, Hugh and Richard.[18]

Subsequently, alternative lexis did intrude into Rutland, but without jeopardising the dominance of Walker. In the Hearth Tax of 1665 for the county, 16 of the 2920 heads of household were Walkers. By contrast, only two were designated Tucker, John and Thomas Tucker at Whitwell; significantly, both were not chargeable and thus possibly poor immigrants.[19] Fuller did not feature at all amongst the taxpayers in 1665, but by 1851 a household in Ashwell contained Fullers, the head born outside the county, in Hampshire.[20] Of the Tuckers in four households in the census, in Exton and Whitwell (where the name had persisted), most had been born within the county. Nevertheless, 44 rural households included Walkers, located in 18 parishes in the county, with a concentration of 11 in Edith Weston and five in Langham. Fully 82% of these Walkers were natives of the county. In the two market towns, Oakham and Uppingham, no Tuckers or Fullers were resident, in contrast to the 12 households containing Walkers, almost exclusively indigenous to the county.[21]

The northern dialect term Walker was thus ascendant, displacing the eastern lexis, Fuller. The development of the occupational surname reflects once again the position of the two counties at the junction of different dialectal influences, from which evolved a lexical and phonemic intermingling.

Reve(s)/Greve(s)

During the late middle ages, the surname Grevis/Greve(s)/Grevys was introduced into the two counties. In 1429–30, John and Richard Greve appeared in the court rolls of the small town of Loughborough, although they were not necessarily resident there.[22] Both the military survey of 1522 and the lay subsidy of 1524 enumerated John Grevis or Grevys at Morcott in Rutland, whilst the lay subsidy for Leicester-shire of 1524 recorded John Greves at Waltham, William Greves at Abbeygate just outside the borough of Leicester, Thomas Grevis at Sileby, Anthony Grevys at Ullesthorpe, and John Grevys at Great Dalby.[23] With the exception of Ullesthorpe and Abbeygate, these places were located in the east and north-east of the counties, which suggests an origin for their intrusion.

The prevalent form of vernacular Old English *gerefa* and Latin *prepositus* in the two counties was almost certainly reeve. Although the lay subsidy of 1296 for Rutland contains only *prepositus* (30 instances), that for Leicestershire in 1327 has both the Latin noun (16) and vernacular ME le Reue (23). In the Poll Tax for Gartree Hundred in 1381, Reue occurred 10 times and Reues once, although the same assessment for Rutland (in 1377) has only one Reue.[24] Confirmation of this form is contained within court rolls, which referred to one or more tenants called John Reue/Reve of Owston in 1418–20, 1440 and 1465–68, Ralph Reue at Hallaton in 1383–84, William Reue at Kirkby Mallory in 1477, W. Reueson at Hallaton in 1363 and Martin Reve at Twyford in 1467.[25] The form of the byname and surname in the two counties thus represented the loss of initial ge-.

By contrast, in Lincolnshire the form of the byname in 1332 retained OE ge- as Greyue. Thus, in the parts of Lincolnshire adjacent to the two counties, in Holland and Kesteven, were recorded Greyueson at Frampton and Marton, Greiueson at Little Paunton, Greyue at Kirton, Butterwick, Freiston, Ingoldsby and Broughton, Graue at Leake, and Fengreyue at Swineshead.[26] The filtration of Grevis/Grevys into Leicestershire and Rutland in the later middle ages may have owed something to this origin and reflects again the location of the two counties at the juncture of several dialect regions and open to their competing influences. In 1665 in Rutland, although there were no Graves or Greaves households, six contained Reeve; in the same county in 1851, four consisted of Graves, Greaves or Grieves, but nine of Reeve.[27]

The suffix -ster

As a suffix to bynames and surnames of occupation, the suffix -ster could imply either regional and dialectal variation or difference of gender. In some regions of England, particularly the south-west, the early construction of this form was often associated with female naming, so that the earliest instances of occupational bynames of this type, before the middle of the fourteenth century, were usually borne by women.[28] On the other hand, in eastern England, and in East Anglia in particular, the suffix had no implications of gender, was frequent, and had more dialectal significance.[29] To some extent, Leicestershire and Rutland are at the conjunction of these two customs of naming, and, although the data are not extensive, they may have a wider importance.

The tax lists of the thirteenth and fourteenth centuries contain taxpayers with occupational bynames and different occupational bynames as described in Table 2.1.

Table 2.1

Occupational bynames and taxpayers with occupational bynames in taxation lists, 1296–1381[30]

Date	Area	N of taxpayers with occupational bynames	N of different occupational bynames*
1296	Rutland	319	70+
1327	Leicestershire	660	120+
1377	Rutland	281	80+
1381	Gartree	627	130+

* Approximate figure, since it is difficult to distinguish some bynames and because of the complication of Latin and ME forms of some bynames.

Notwithstanding these large numbers of taxpayers with occupational bynames and the number of different occupational bynames, the element -ster could not be applied to all occupational names. In fact, its range of association was fairly limited. In the two counties, its application was restricted, in general, to four particular occupational bynames and surnames: Baxter (and variants); Breuster (and variants); Dexter; and Webster (and variants). In comparing the comparative use of -ster and other forms, therefore, it is appropriate only to consider the forms of occupational byname and surname to which -ster might have been attached. In the lay subsidy for Rutland in 1296, only one taxpayer with an occupational byname with the appendage -ster was assessed, Robert le Webistere at Uppingham, but there are no variant forms of occupational bynames without the suffix (for example, Baker).[31] Slightly later, in the lay subsidy for Leicestershire in 1327, 11 taxpayers were attributed an occupational byname with -ster — seven Baxters, three Breusters (and variants), one Conestere, and a solitary Webbestere. Alternative forms did occur, however, with a Bakar at each of Market Bosworth and Broughton Astley, a Webbe at Normanton le Heath, and a le Webbe at Twycross.[32] These aberrant forms without -ster were significantly located in the west of the county.[33]

By 1377, the element -ster was more conspicuous in the Poll Tax for Rutland which contained Elizabeth Lister at Ketton, Edith and Joan Seustere at Belmesthorpe and Caldecott (but these two may exhibit the influence of gender), and Websters at Ryhall, Barrowden, Thorpe, Morcott and Seaton. By comparison, however, there was a Baker at Ketton and a Brewer and a Bruer at Lyddington.[34] Four years later, the Poll Tax for Gartree Hundred revealed a greater concentration of -ster forms, although that distribution is partly predictable since the area covered was situated in the east of Leicestershire. Baxters (and variants) were assessed in Lubbenham and Great Bowden, Breusters in Owston, Shangton, Noseley and Saddington, a single Dexter in Hallaton, a Seuster also in that vill, and Websters much more widespreadly in Hallaton, Wistow, Great Bowden, Knossington, Market Harborough, Ingarsby, Ilston, Baggrave, Easton and Billesdon. The only exceptions to this pattern consisted of one Baker at Husbands Bosworth and two at Market Harborough.[35] Amongst the tenantry of Leicester Abbey, dispersed throughout much of the county, in 1341, -ster forms were exclusive, comprehending Ba(u)xters at Thurmaston, Lockington and Thornton, without any Bakers.[36] Baker, however, was recorded in the court rolls of Breedon on the Hill in 1362 and in the rental of Loughborough in 1370, perhaps through an influence from north of the county.[37]

Until the late fourteenth century, therefore, where -ster forms might be added to occupational bynames, they usually were. Exceptionally, some forms deviated from this pattern in the early fourteenth century, but were confined to the west of the county, whilst Baker was a more persistent difference. By the later middle ages, Baker had become even more intrusive, perhaps through immigration. In Rutland, in the early sixteenth century (1522–25), Bakers appeared in Uppingham, Caldecott, Braunston, Morcott, Burley, Cottesmore, Whissendine, and Ridlington, whilst simultaneously (1524–5) they occurred in Leicestershire at Croxton Kerrial, Knighton, Sewstern, Ab Kettleby, Loughborough, Bringhurst, Plungar, Wymondham, and Great Bowden.[38]

Brewer(n), rather than Brewster, identified taxpayers in Burton Lazars, Kirby Bellars, Beeby and Belgrave, and was reflected also in a Bruyer at Thurmaston.[39] More significant perhaps was the intrusion of variants of Weaver as an equivalent of Webster, represented in Wever at Morcott (*bis*) and Bridge Casterton in Rutland in 1522, three Weyvars at Cosby in 1525 and one at Carlton Curlieu at the same time.[40] Moreover, the surname Weyver had become established in Castle Donington between 1458 and 1490.[41]

By comparison, there were 11 Baxters in six vills in Rutland in the early sixteenth century, although only one in a single township (Waltham) in Leicestershire.[42] Brewsters existed in five vills, each with one taxpayer of this designation, but two at Great Bowden.[43] In complete contrast, Websters, despite the introduction of variants of Weaver, were extensively recorded in the early sixteenth century: 14 in 11 parishes distributed throughout Leicestershire and seven in six vills in Rutland.[44]

Further context is provided by the development of some dynastic kinships or dominant individuals in the evidence of court rolls, such as in the profusion of references to Baxters in Loughborough (1397–1412), the Breusters at Owston (1371–1465), the Dexters also in the small town of Loughborough (1370–1431) and the Websters in Hallaton (1363–85).[45] Leicestershire and Rutland thus exhibited in this respect characteristics of the margin or fringe of the East Anglian onomastic tradition of the suffix -ster.

Correspondingly, the addition of -ster was not generally associated with any significance of gender, but was employed equally by men and women, it seems. For example, in the lay subsidy of 1327 for Leicestershire, 10 men bore bynames with the suffix, but only one female; even the byname Breuster, perhaps more frequently associated in some regional lexica with female brewers, was held by Roger le Breustre at Loddington and John le Brewstere in Abbeygate, and only by one female taxpayer, Cecily la Broustere at Waltham, although female taxpayers under-represented the female population.[46] Only a single employment of the byname has strong gendered associations, the enumeration of John *filius Edithe le* (sic) *Coyffester* in the survey of Oakham and its appurtenances in 1305.[47] In the late fourteenth century, some bynames with -ster had some association with gender, for Edith Seustere and Joan Seuster were included in the Poll Tax of 1377 at Belmesthorpe and Caldecott and such bynames had elsewhere connotations of informal and less rewarding female occupations, particularly in urban centres.[48] Even so, perhaps because these names were becoming hereditary despite their very specific imputations, Richard Seuster was assessed in the Poll Tax of 1381 at Hallaton and John Seuster was mentioned in the court rolls of Loughborough in 1430.[49] More certain, however, is the case of Isabel Kem(p)ster, repeatedly mentioned in the court rolls of Loughborough in 1403–29, whose byname probably ensued from her engagement in this modest trade associated with women in the context of the small town.[50] With the exception of a few bynames with imputations of gender, which occurred very infrequently, occupational bynames with the suffix -ster were not associated with women, and certainly not influenced by gender in their origin.

The suffix -man

The distinguishing characteristic of the suffix -man in the two counties was its relative paucity. For example, in 1327 only 1.3% of taxpayers in Leicestershire bore a byname compounded with this element, whilst a similar proportion (1.3%) occurred in the lay subsidy for Rutland in 1296.[51] The lay subsidies, however, were wealth-specific. If more comprehensive taxation lists are considered, the proportion of taxpayers with bynames and surnames of this type is slightly higher. For example, of the 2,476 taxpayers with independent bynames and surnames in the Poll Tax of 1381 for the Hundred of Gartree in Leicestershire, 2.6% had such names with the element -man, whilst in the Poll Tax of 1377 for much of Rutland the rate was 3.4%.[52] In the lay subsidy for most of Leicestershire in 1524 and 1525 the proportion was 2.4 and 1.8% respectively.[53] In the Rutland lay subsidies of comparable date, the percentage had diminished to 1.4%, whilst in the military survey of 1522, the level was 1.2%.[54]

Table 2.2

Proportions of taxpayers bearing bynames and surnames compounded with -man, 1296–1525

Date	N	%	Population*
Leicestershire			
1327	53	1.3	4128
1381	64	2.6	2476
1524	63	2.4	2683
1525	71	1.8	3924
Rutland			
1296	25	1.3	1868
1377	27	3.4	806
1522	20	1.2	1661
1524	19	1.4	1400
1525	3	1.0	297

* The different significances of the population of each tax listing is described above under *Methodological questions*.

Bynames and surnames formed with element -man were preponderantly occupational bynames, with only a few topographical and nickname forms. Aggregating the tax lists for Leicestershire (1327, 1381 and 1524–5), some seventy-four different bynames and surnames with -man existed in the county over the later middle ages, whilst in Rutland (in lists of 1296, 1377, 1522 and 1524–5) the number was merely twenty-seven. With the exception of Chapman and Freman and, to a lesser extent S(c)herman or Sharman, no bynames or surnames of this type existed in any number rather than as isolated examples, whilst Pakeman was associated — although not exclusively — with a family which achieved gentle status during the later middle ages.

The dialect form of this element has been considered to have been diagnostic between 'East Midlands' (-man) and 'West Midlands' (-mon) dialect 'regions'. The isogloss of the two forms is presumed to have followed the county boundary between Leicestershire and Warwickshire (and Staffordshire and Derbyshire).[55] It appears that this lexical element predominantly conformed to the 'East Midland' form of -man with little or no infiltration of the 'West Midland' form -mon. In the lay subsidy of 1327, the form -mon occurred in John Blakemon at Hallaton and Henry Dermon at Fleckney (both probably from OE personal names) (although the printed transcription has not been checked against the original manuscript).[56] The record, however, has inherent problems in this respect: it was an Exchequer redaction and the locality of the clerk of each part is not known. In the lay subsidy for Leicestershire in 1524–5, a larger number of 'West Midlands' forms insinuated into the Leicestershire record. In 1524, -mon forms occurred in Chapmon and Hardymon in Claybrooke, Colmon (OIr or Germanic personal name) at North Kilworth, and Hardymon at Bitteswell.[57] In 1525, the dialectal variant is represented in Chapmon at Ashby Magna, Claybrooke and Dunton Basset, Dormon at Arnsby, Fremon at Aylestone, Hardymon at Claybrooke and Bitteswell, Mon at Ullesthorpe, Normon at Swinford, and Wonemon at Claybrooke.[58] Indeed, in 1525, the grapheme -man did not occur in the south-west at all, replaced by the form -mon. Nevertheless, the problem remains that the origin of the compiler of the record is not known and these intrusions across the boundary between Warwickshire and Leicestershire and between presumed 'West Midlands' and 'East Midlands' dialects may simply have resulted from the locality of origin of the writer. Independent evidence occurred in a more localized document of the possible intrusion of the form -mon across the county boundary (from Staffordshire in this case), for a charter of 1292 relating to Appleby Magna included the byname le Fremon of Norton, but it is still possible that the clerk had origins across the boundary.[59]

In a few instances, the element represented the status of employee or servant (in the wide medieval sense of servant), as in Walterman at Branston in 1327 and, later in 1524–5, William Thoriman at Bottesford (1524) and Richard Hykman in an unidentified place in Gartree Hundred.[60] In the Rutland Poll Tax of 1377, this relationship is represented in Parsonman at Great Casterton and Fullersman at Tolthorpe.[61] In the Poll Tax for Gartree Hundred in 1381, the compound occurred in Richardmay at Fleckney and East Langton, Parsonman at Houghton on the Hill, Symmesman at Marefield, and Parsonesman at Carlton Curlieu.[62] This particular form was also included in Richard Duceman in the custumal of Rothley *c*.1245 and possibly Howeman on the manor of Stoughton in the rental of Leicester Abbey's lands of 1341.[63] The incidences of this syntactical meaning were, however, few, with the exception of the local usage of the element -man in the town of Loughborough in the later middle ages.

In virtually all the occurrences of names with the suffix -man in the town, the prototheme is a byname or surname, although not a personal name (forename). This local usage is quite distinctive. In Lancashire, for example, compounds of -man with this significance were not extensive in the middle ages.[64] Reaney maintained that bynames and surnames compounded of -man and a personal name (forename) were more common.[65] In Loughborough, the first element was, however, a byname or surname.

The particular nature of these name forms is indicated in Gloureman *v.* Gloure in the court rolls of the manor of Loughborough in 1397–8, in which Gloureman compromised his two actions against Gloure, but the defendant, Gloure, acted as the plaintiff's pledge.[66] The implication here is that Gloureman was or had been in the service of Gloure. Unfortunately, the records reveal nothing of John Gloure, although Robert Gloure held a messuage in the rental of *c*.1370, and a Thomas was a chief pledge in 1411. A similar case occurred in the view of frankpledge in 1403, when Thomas Smythesman, presented for battery, found as his pledge John Smyth, with, again, the imputation that Smyth was Smythesman's master or employer.[67] John Smyth appeared in court on many occasions between 1397 and 1429, in personal actions, but was also presented as a brewer in 1397, 1398 and 1429 (assuming that these were the same person). In 1397, John Bretonman compromised his action of debt against Ralph Irnemongere; he was also involved in a plea of detinue with Edith Cutte in 1398, and another of debt in 1404, reflecting that the form of name continued with an individual over a number of years.[68] John Breton held a shop, three messuages, a *placea*, a virgate and three acres, a grange, two selds, a stall, and two crofts in the rental of *c*.1370 and attested a charter in 1386.[69] Robert Breton appeared in court in personal actions many times between 1397 and 1411, although Ralph and Richard appeared in only 1405 and 1411. Simon Breton, perhaps of the same kinship group, appeared in many personal actions there in 1397–1412 and in 1430.[70]

In 1403, Robert Spencereman was presented for battery against Richard de Wysowe, but little is known of John Spencer except that he was presented as a brewer in 1404 and fined the significant amount of 16*d*.[71] Richard Pegman was placed in mercy in the previous year for non-suit of his action of debt against John Sclatere.[72] The Pegge kinship was a local dynastic family, later of gentle status. In the rental of *c*.1370, Hugh Pegge held a messuage and 5a.3r., William Pegge two cottages, Robert Pegge a messuage and 13½a., Roger Pegge a bovate, and the heirs of Roger, who must have died recently, a messuage and a croft.[73] In the lay subsidy of 1327, Robert Pegge had been taxed at 6*s*.[74] A successor, Thomas Pegge, was parker in the manorial account of 1376 and appeared in court in many personal actions between 1376 and 1412 and in 1430–31 (if these were the same person).[75]

In 1402 also, William Galmyntonman concluded his action of debt with John Skynnere by compromise and he was impleaded by John Castr' for debt in 1403.[76] His putative employer was Roger de Galmynton, who pursued or was involved in many personal actions in the court between 1397 and 1403.[77] In 1403 also William Slyngesbyman brought an action of debt against John Duffeld, the details of which intimate that Slyngesbyman had formerly been in the employ of Duffeld, since the claim was for 10*s*. owed as his wage for a long time with damages claimed at 1*s*. and which Duffeld acknowledged or admitted.[78] The case confirms Slyngesbyman's status as a servant or labourer. John Slyngesby was involved in many cases in the manorial court between 1398 and 1412, mainly personal actions such as debt, trespass and covenant.[79] In the case of John Roberteman, in court in 1404, nothing can be ascertained about the surname Roberte; it is possible that in this one case the prototheme derived from a forename, although William Robert was involved in a case of trepass in the manorial court in 1431.[80]

A more conclusive context can be established for John Maltonman who held a messuage and bovate in the rental of *c*.1370. That situation is unusual because there is no evidence that any of the other bearers of bynames or surnames with the element -man were tenants, although the nature of the records may partially account for this problem. Two possible interpretations may be placed on Maltonman: either John had been a servant or employee who had made good or the -man element was tautologous so that Maltonman was equivalent to Malton. The latter suggestion seems less plausible since in the same rental were listed Alice de Malton who held a messuage, a cottage and two bovates, and Robert de Malton who held a messuage and 5a.1r. Perhaps as significant, however, are the messuage once (*quondam*) held by Richard de Malton and the cottage once (*quondam*) held by Robert de Malton, the parker (*parcarius*).[81] Whilst Agnes de Malton occurred in a case of trespass in 1398, the situation is confounded by Alice Malton Mayden who appeared in court in 1404.[82]

Nevertheless, there seems to be sufficient evidence to conclude that the vernacular suffix -man, almost exclusively compounded with a byname or surname in Loughborough, represented there the status of a servant or employee.

Elliptical by/bi

The preposition by was used in most regions in the formation of some topographyical bynames in the middle ages, although the numbers were usually very small. There appear not to be more than a few instances of this type of byname in the lay subsidy of 1327 for Leicestershire.[83] Other records reveal a few other occurrences. In the court rolls of Kibworth Harcourt was mentioned Richard bi le Brok in 1295 and the rental of Leicester Abbey's lands in 1341 enumerated Amery bythe Water at Thurmaston.[84] The syndetic form persisted at Lougborough in 1403 (in the court rolls) in Alice Bydebroke.[85] Such forms were, however, very sparse in Leicestershire and did not survive into the later middle ages.

By contrast, the preposition by/bi was integrated into topographical bynames much more frequently in the Rutland lay subsidy of 1296 and in a distinctive manner. At Morcott were enumerated Henry BiWestoun, William ByWestoun and Robert *filius Radulphi ByWestoun* and these bynames are representative of a construction based in Rutland on by/bi, a point of the compass and toun (township), indicative of the position of the taxpayer's habitation within the township.[86] This form of topographical byname is encountered in the 1296 lay subsidy at Glaston (ByWestoun), Stretton (Henry and John Byestoun), Greetham (John and Simon Byestoun), Martinsthorpe (John and Roger Byestoun), Normanton (Matilda and Roger Byestoun), Glaston (Byestoun), Langham (Byestoun), Pickworth (Byestoun), North Luffenham (Byestoun), Teigh (Byestoun), Caldecote (Bynorthetoun), and Kilpisham (Bywestoun).[87] At Kilpisham, a more elaborate form occurred in the lay subsidy: Byestecross and Bywestekirk(e) (*bis*).[88] The elliptical use of by- did not persist into the later middle ages and nor did these particular bynames.

These forms of name with the elliptical by- may be analogous with another use of the elliptical -by in the lay subsidies of 1327 and 1332 for Lincolnshire, which assumed a construction such as Southiby, Northiby and Estiby.[89] The variant form in Rutland may be a southerly extension from Lincolnshire, perhaps indicative of Scandinavian influence.

Other records throw some further reflection on this form of byname. The 'Oakham survey' of 1305 included William Byeston at Langham and the syndetic form of this type of name survived at Morcott in the Poll Tax of 1377 with John Byweston.[90] Finally, this type of name existed at Barkby in Leicestershire in isolation in the form bi/by Westo(u)n. Robert bi/by Westoun appeared in the court rolls of the manor of Merton College at Barkby between 1279 and 1282 and William By Westo(u)n in 1289 (*bis*) and 1300.[91] Barkby is, however, some 12 miles from the boundary with Rutland and it is difficult to explain the occurrence of this type of byname there.

Palatal Sc-

Throughout the later middle ages, initial sh- reflected the different dialectal influences bearing on the two counties. Basically in the east of the county, stressed palatal sch- persisted into the sixteenth century. Most of the instances of the stressed palatal (sch-), as opposed to the unstressed sh-, occurred in the east and in Rutland. In particular, two bynames or surnames incorporated this difference, variants of Shepherd and Sherman.

Table 2.3

Stressed and unstressed palatals in two bynames or surnames in late medieval Leicestershire and Rutland[92]

County/date	stressed (sch-) N	unstressed (sh-) N
Variants of Shepherd		
Rutland 1296 (no data)*		
Leicestershire 1327	7	2
Rutland 1377	15	5
Gartree Hundred 1381	22	22
Leicestershire 1524	6	8
Variants of Sherman		
Rutland 1296 (no data)		
Leicestershire 1327	1	1
Leicestershire 1524	1	2

* Latin form only.

Additionally, Nicholas Schyphurd was recorded in the court rolls of Kibworth Beauchamp in 1348.[93] The stressed palatal affected other bynames and surnames through the middle ages, not least Sharp. In the Poll Tax of Gartree Hundred, in the east of Leicestershire, in 1381, Scharps were recorded at Houghton (two) and Pickwell, whilst others had been assessed to the lay subsidy in 1327 at Melton Mowbray and Rearsby.[94] William Scharp, recorded in the taxation at Melton, appeared in a charter in the same guise in 1324.[95] Other William Scharps appeared in the court rolls of Owston in 1386 and 1420–21 and Agnes Scharp at Hallaton in 1380.[96] In 1524–5 Scharpes were assessed in South Luffenham, Cottesmore and Coston, whilst Richard Scherpe was enumerated in Oakham in the military survey of 1522.[97] The stressed palatal was incorporated in John and William Schyrlok(e) in the court rolls of Barkby in 1434–37 and in Schakeloke at Kirby Bellars in 1341.[98] Other examples could be recited to illustrate that the stressed form persisted through the later middle ages in both central fiscal and localized manorial records, predominantly in the eastern parts. That distribution accords well with the dominance of this form in Lincolnshire in the lay subsidy of 1332, where Scheperd and variants occurred consistently with the stressed palatal, as did Scherman.[99] Illustrative of this tendency are Scherman and Scheperd at Stamford in 1332.[100] Equally, the tax list for Lincolnshire included a Bischop, Schillyng, Scherlok, Schyrreues, Scharps, and a Schypman.[101] Ultimately, however, the palatal became universally unstressed during the early modern period, but the stressed syllable continued into the sixteenth century. Alongside it the unstressed palatal was evident by the fourteenth century, reflecting the diversity of dialect coalescing in the county.

Palatal k/c

Although there were dialect differences in late ME in palatal consonants, evidence of the alternative use of /c/ and voiceless stop /k/ is not abundant. Principally, in this respect, the competition between more northern and more southern dialects was expressed through Church/Kirk(e)-Kyrk(e), but some other occasional material can also be adduced. Nevertheless, ambiguity arises from the nature of the production of the record sources, whether local or 'central'. Corroborative matter is thus presented from 'localized' records wherever possible.

In the lay subsidy of 1327 for Leicestershire, all nine taxpayers with topographical bynames referring to the parish church were identified as atte Kirk or atte Kyrke with additionally Geoffrey atte Kirkestile, the grapheme ch- entirely absent.[102] With the exception of William atte Kyrke of Stoke Golding, these taxpayers were, however, located in the east of the county, leaving uncertainty whether the west came under different influence. The sources of the early sixteenth century present the same inherent problem, since their evidence in this regard is also predominantly from the east. Confirmation of the exclusiveness of Kyrk(e) is represented in those liable to militia service and as taxpayers in Rutland in Uppingham (Bartholomew Kyrk, 1522), Cottesmore (Thomas, 1524), Morcott (John, 1522), Ayston (John jnr. and snr. in 1522, John in 1524, Robert in 1524 and Thomas in both years), Pisbrook (John, 1524), Caldecote (Richard, 1522), Pilton (Thomas Akyrk, 1522), Whissendine (John Kyrkeale,

1522) and Burley (William Kyrkman, 1522 and 1524).[103] Similarly, the homonymous taxpayers in Leicestershire were concentrated in the east, in Garthorpe (Sampson Kyrke *alias* Kerke, 1524-5), Galby (William, 1525), Thurcaston (Richard, 1524-5) and King's Norton (William, 1525), but exceptionally Thomas Kyrke in Lutterworth in 1524.[104]

Such formations can be substantiated from local sources in the later middle ages, where Kirk is exclusive. In particular, the court rolls of the manors of Owston Abbey referred continuously to John (atte) Kirk(e) or Kyrk in 1418-66.[105] Charters relating to lands in Gaddesby in 1412 and 1436 mentioned Henry and Robert atte Kyrke, whilst Felice and William atte Kyrke were grantors of land there in those same years, and Thomas atte Kyrke acquired land in the same vill in 1406. Another charter referring to land in Wartnaby in 1399 was attested by John Kyrke, and Robert atte Kyrke subsequently, in 1418, alienated land there.[106] In 1379-83, John Kirkewrith appeared in the manorial court at Hallaton.[107]

The exceptions to this predominance were only Thomas Chirch at Ryhall in 1524, Richard Churche at Cossington in the following year, John A Chirche in Melton in 1524, and, much earlier, William attechyrche at Great Stretton in 1290.[108] Problematically, however, all the material derives from eastern Leicestershire and Rutland, with no confirmatory evidence from west Leicestershire. Moreover, the quantity of data is slight. If any area of the two counties might be expected to succumb to a more northerly influence, the east was the most susceptible, whilst the west might have experienced a different influence.

Incidental material on other bynames and surnames suffers from the same geographical deficiency, as well as problems of the size of the sample. In these cases, /k/ occurred where /c/ might have been expected, as in Ralph Karectarius and Robert le Kupere in the court rolls of Kibworth Harcourt in 1291.[109] Similarly, Adam Kartere was a tenant of the Abbey of Leicester in Lockington in 1341 and Robert le Kartere a taxpayer at Weston in Rutland in 1296.[110] In that lay subsidy of 1296, Alice Kade was assessed at Oakham.[111]

Other forms of byname and surname are more ambivalent, but may reflect on the conjuncture of different dialectal influences. In charters relating to Melton Mowbray throughout the fourteenth century (1319-84), Philip and Richard Cut(t) were described in that form 34 times, but Richard twice as Kut.[112] In west Leicestershire in the lay subsidy of 1524–5 were assessed Nicholas Kotton at Lutterworth and Thomas Kotton at Misterton, but here are encountered two problems: the intractable question of whether the tax list reflected local orthography and the possibility of immigration introducing by this later time variant forms of surnames. Variants of (le) Coc are equally ambiguous, ranging from (le) Koc in the lay subsidies of 1296 and 1327, some in west Leicestershire, and through the later middle ages, to three taxpayers called Kok in 1296, and Kockes and Kocson at Castle Donington in respectively 1457 and 1515 and Shearsby in 1524.[113]

Over the long term, however, the influence was not enormous, for even the surname Kirk declined in significance. For example, in Rutland only three taxpayers called Kirk(e) were enumerated in the Hearth Tax of 1665, all exempted (not chargeable), in Egleton, Uppingham and Lindon.[114] The surname was represented in the census of 1851 only at Greetham, Morcott, Oakham and Uppingham, and, paradoxically, all its bearers had been born outside Rutland, at Breaston, Derby and Gresley (Derbyshire), Castle Donington and Melton (Leicestershire) and Birmingham (Warwickshire).[115] Although no Church was included in 1665, Allen Church, a shepherd, was enumerated at Burley in 1851, although he had been born in Northamptonshire.[116]

The consonantal change had thus no substantial effect on surnames after the late middle ages, but reflected the confluence of two different dialectal influences at that time. It was principally expressed through the predominance of the surname Kirk rather than Church, but the failure of Kirk to persist in quantity after the late middle ages, at least in Rutland, weakened the potential effect of dialect reception. Indeed, some inconsistencies were also apparent. Whereas, in 1665, the Hearth Tax conformed to dialect in listing Richard Kosterton [*sic*] at Greetham, conversely Elizabeth Cue, listed at Wing, may reflect a different influence.[117] Presumably Cue entailed a consonantal change from /k/ in the etymon Keu, the OFr equivalent of occupational cok, although the form Kew was predominant in the county (six Kew households at Market Overton in 1851, eight at Thistleton, and others at Greetham, Exton and Empingham).[118] The clerk of the lay subsidy of 1524 for Leicestershire, moreover, exhibited a different influence in describing John Cheytyll (Scand Ketel) at Leire.[119]

Devoiced t in some toponymic surnames

In Rutland in 1851, the surnames Musson and Crowson were distributed throughout several parishes. For example, Musson existed in three households in Stretton, two in Whissendine and one each in Greetham, Langham and Oakham, whilst Crowson had a similar degree of disposition in four households in each of Caldecott and Oakham, two in Empingham, and one each in Whissendine, Ayston and Bisbrooke. Complementing this form of surname was Beeson, in three households in Stretton one in Greetham, whilst Branson and Ilson had less frequent incidence.[120] Although superficially appearing to be patronymic or metronymic, these surnames derived from toponymic names from local placenames — Muston, Croxton (South Croxton or Croxton Kerrial), and Ilston on the Hill, all in Leicestershire, Braunston(e) in Rutland, Leicestershire, or Northamptonshire and Beeston (probably the settlement in Nottinghamshire, but not certainly). In these instances, the /t/ had become devoiced, probably in the early modern period, if not later.

At an earlier time, in the Hearth Tax of 1665, Mr Thomas Musson had been assessed for 2s. at Hambledon, Widow Crosan at Bisbrooke, Widow Crosen at Oakham and William Crosen at Whitwell.[121] The /t/ had already become devoiced in both surnames by the middle of the seventeenth century, although Crosen had still to develope into its later variant, Crowson.

Furthermore, Musson had stabilized in this form in Nottingham. In St Mary's parish, Rebecka Musson, daughter of John and Rebecka, was baptised on 24 November 1661, and additional Musson baptisms were celebrated in the parish in 1672, 1675, 1676 and later.[122] Musson had become established in that form in All Saints parish, Nottingham, with the first Musson burial, that of Josiah, in 1708 and subsequently 11 other Musson burials before 1810.[123] In Northamptonshire, John Muson, weaver, was enumerated in the militia list of 1777 at Clay Coton.[124]

Nevertheless, the ME form of the placename and, indeed, the byname and surname, had continued to voice the /t/. In the early thirteenth century, charters for the area neighbouring Muston had been attested by or involved Laurence de Muston, Andrew de Muston, Warner de Mustun, Thomas de Muston and Walter de Muston.[125] In 1327, Simon de Muston contributed to the lay subsidy at Croxton Kerrial.[126] By the late fourteenth century, a Muston kinship had been established at Owston, where William, John and Robert Muston were assessed to the Poll Tax in 1381, William also being presented in the manorial court for a nuisance.[127] Even in the early sixteenth century, the consistent form of the surname remained Muston, reflected in the taxpayers in the lay subsidy of 1524–5 at Rotherby (Hugh Muston), Asfordby (Robert Muston), Cossington (Thomas Muston), Wigston Parva (William Muston) and Aylestone (William Muston).[128]

In a similar manner, the /t/ in Croxton was voiced through the late middle ages and into the early sixteenth century. Albert de Croxton contributed tax at Branstone in 1327 and in 1323 Robert de Croxston *manens in Melton'* alienated a shop in Melton.[129] Slightly earlier, in 1298, Robert de Croxston fleetingly appeared in the court rolls of Kibworth Harcourt, representing Nicholas Polle in an essoin.[130] In the Poll Tax of Gartree Hundred in 1381, Roger de Croxton and Emma Crouxton, a servant, both contributed at Goadby.[131] On the other Merton College manor in the county, John Croxton *alias* de Croxston acquired and relinquished land in 1413–20.[132] Subsequently, a Croxton kinship became established at Owston and appurtenant Twyford, where William de Croxton and Thomas Croxton appeared in the court of the Abbot of Owston between 1465 and 1468.[133] By the early sixteenth century, the surname had proliferated, but in variant forms, through the county, in the taxpayers John Croceton at South Croxton, Ralph Croceton at Twyford and John Croxton at Cold Overton.[134] More importantly, however, the /t/ had become voiceless in the surnames of some others assessed to the lay subsidy of 1524–5, in particular John Croceson at Hungarton, William Crokeson at Ashby Folville, John Croson at South Croxton, William Croson at Kibworth Beauchamp and Richard Croson at Stoughton, most of whom contributed at the lowest level of assessment.[135]

Whilst taking into account the paucity of the information, it appears that the ME forms of the bynames and surnames constantly voiced the medial /t/, which is consistent with the orthography and voicing of the place-names.[136] During the early modern period, the /t/ became devoiced, resulting in the dissemination, both locally and further afield (such as in Nottingham), of surnames in which the /t/ remained devoiced. In this manner, toponymic surnames came confusingly to resemble patronymic forms of surname.

From syndetic to asyndetic forms of byname and surname

The movement from syndetic forms of byname and surname to asyndetic forms involved the loss of prepositional prefixes and articles, such as le, atte and de in respectively nickname and occupational forms of byname, topographical forms and toponymic types. The significance of this transformation was the change from lexical phrases — descriptive words — to surnames which had no lexical content. On the other hand, the transition was not synonymous with the development of hereditary surnames from unstable bynames, since syndetic forms had been inherited. Conversely, some bynames, particularly occupational ones, evolved into an asyndetic form (without the article le) but were nonetheless still eponymous, unstable bynames into the later middle ages (see below). Moreover, in some cases, particularly in some topographical forms, the syndetic form persisted so late into the middle ages (for example, Atwell) that a hereditary surname developed in an elided syndetic form. The transformation from syndetic to asyndetic forms was not, however, a uniform process. Change happened at different times in different parts of the country. Moreover, there was a difference in timing between toponymic names, nickname forms, occupational forms and topographical types. Furthermore, within each category of surname the surnames of some individuals might continue in syndetic form for a longer period of time because, in their case, lexical content persisted; in particular, the toponymic names of some people persisted in syndetic form into the later middle ages with the implication, perhaps, that these people may have been recent migrants, whilst most bore asyndetic forms of toponymic surname. These problems are explored below, but it should be remembered that the issue may be complicated because some of the record sources (taxation records) were not necessarily localized and might have been Exchequer copies.

In the lay subsidy of Rutland in 1296, only 5.9% of toponymic bynames occurred in asyndetic form. Amongst occupational bynames in the vernacular languages, ME and French (thus excluding Latin forms), 40% were syndetic in form and 60% asyndetic. Topographical forms in these vernaculars were most likely still to be syndetic and only 12 had become asyndetic.[137] In the lay subsidy of 1327 for Leicestershire, topographical and toponymic forms were predominantly syndetic, but 75% of occupational names were syndetic and only 25% asyndetic.[138]

In the Poll Tax for Rutland of 1377, 43% of toponymic bynames remained syndetic, 71% of topographical, but only 2% of occupational.[139] The comparative proportions in the Poll Tax for

Gartree Hundred in adjacent Leicestershire in 1381 were 21.7% of toponymic, 65.5% of topographical, and a mere 1.9% of occupational.[140] The differential rate of change by form of byname and surname is thus evident, with occupational forms moving more precociously to asyndetic forms (as also did nickname forms), whilst topographical forms remained predominantly syndetic.

Locally-produced records, however, may be more reliable in assessing this development. Taking an intermediate point of Geryn's rental of the Leicester Abbey estates in 1341, toponymic forms were syndetic, as were topographical bynames, but amongst vernacular forms of occupational bynames (in French or ME) 37.6% of names had progressed to asyndetic form, whilst 62.4% retained their syndetic content.[141] The court rolls of the manor of Breedon on the Hill provide only cursory evidence, but at a critical juncture, in 1342 and in 1362-63.[142] In these rolls, toponymic names were consistently syndetic in form in 1342, whilst occupational (and nickname) forms were predominantly, but not exclusively, syndetic. About a third of these latter names were asyndetic, whilst one, John (le) S(o)uter of Tong occurred in both modes. By 1362-63, although toponymic forms were predominantly asyndetic (with only two of 19 in the syndetic), toponymic remained comprehensively syndetic. At Kibworth Beauchamp, according to the court rolls, this transition in the written form of occupational and nickname names was precipitated in *c.*1346-48.[143] In 1346, most of these names were recorded in asyndetic form, but a substantial number still with syndetic character. Those in syndetic mode were transformed into asyndetic form in 1348: Robert le Yonge to Robert Yonge, Joan la Smyth to Joan Smyth and Thomas le Cartere to Thomas Carter, for example. Subsequently, these forms became the norm for occupational and nickname names, whereas toponymic names largely still persisted in syndetic form.

In the court rolls and rentals of Hallaton between 1363 and 1385, counting instances of the appearance of bynames and surnames rather than different ones, in 57.6% of cases toponymic bynames and surnames were still entered on the rolls in syndetic form (total of incidences = 139; syndetic incidences = 80).[144] By contrast, only one occurrence of an occupational byname was constructed in syndetic form (William le Webster in 1384) (total N = 277 incidences). Correspondingly, all 74 written entries of nickname bynames or surnames were construed in asyndetic form.

The court rolls of Owston Abbey lands, also in east Leicestershire, because of the smaller number of tenants, allow only an impressionistic perception of change, although the chronology is longer, if a broken sequence. In 1365, five toponymic names occurred in syndetic form and only two in asyndetic, whilst all 12 occupational forms had already been conceived in asyndetic mode. Toponymic bynames and surnames appeared in the rolls concurrently in syndetic and asyndetic forms through to 1386 (courts of 1370, 1371, 1372, 1374 and 1386) — for example, John Sywoldeby in 1372 and 1374, John de Sywoldeby in 1386, and John Sywoldeby in 1387. From 1388, however, the consistent usage for toponymic bynames and surnames was the asyndetic form (courts of 1387, 1388, 1418–21 and 1440).[145]

Considering a more substantial source, the rentals of the estates of Leicester Abbey in 1477, only eight of 120 toponymic surnames were constructed in syndetic manner, eight of 28 topographical forms, and none of the 111 occupational names.[146] By the lay subsidies of the early sixteenth century, to return to records produced for the Exchequer, the movement to asyndetic forms had been completed. In the Leicestershire lay subsidy of 1524–5, only 14 toponymic and 21 topographical names were inscribed in the syndetic form, now with the particular preposition A (Aglenne, Agrene) (see further below), whilst in Rutland in 1524–5 only one toponymic and two topographical forms occurred in syndetic manner, although in the military survey of 1522 eight toponymic and five topographical had been listed.[147]

Evidently the transition to asyndetic forms began to occur in the late 1340s for occupational and nickname bynames. That change was consolidated in the next two decades. Toponymic and topographical bynames and surnames, however, persisted in syndetic form for a longer period, as illustrated further by toponymic names in the small town of Loughborough in the later middle ages.

In the rental of *c*.1370 for Loughborough, 37 toponymic bynames had the syndetic form, whilst only four (Caldwell, Quynton, Roudeland and Thurnbu) had transmuted into asyndetic. Five occurred in both syndetic and asyndetic form (Chesterschyr', Folkyngham, Kylburne, Lewes and Whychenor).[148] Whilst some asyndetic forms did appear in the court and account rolls of the late fourteenth century, the preponderant number was still syndetic. Asyndetic forms occurred in Annesley (1376, account roll), Brokstowe *alias* Broxtowe (1376 acount roll), Burbach (1397–1412 court rolls), Chesterschyr' (1370–1405 rental and court rolls), Claybroke

(1397 court roll), Halom (1376–1430 court rolls), Keworthe (1398 court roll), Okouere (1396 court roll), Roudeland (1397–1431 court rolls), Slyngesby (1376–1430 rental and court rolls), Stretton (1391 court roll), Tekill (1376 account roll), Tyken(h)ale (1397–98 court roll), and Warwik (1398 court roll). More usual, however, were forms which were either consistently syndetic or occurred in both syndetic and asyndetic forms into the early fifteenth century and only changed permanently to asyndetic form in the fifteenth century. For example, de Barowe occurred in 1398 and 1404, but had become asyndetic in 1429–30. Similarly de Barton (1411–12) assumed asyndetic form (Barton) by 1411–12.[149] The following listing provides more detail about this transition:

syndetic form	asyndetic form
de Bodeworthe 1398–1403	1403–05
de Bowdon 1398–1405	1397–1404
de Burton 1370–1412 (68 instances)	1376–1430 (52)
de Bytham 1403–04	1411–30
de Croft 1370–1405	1403
de Derby 1370–1404	1376, 1397–1430
de Duffeld 1370, 1403	1398–1412
de Ecton 1398, 1412	1397–1412
de Gedlyng 1402, 1411	1397–1430
de Hedon 1397	1398
de Kilburne 1370, 1402–12	1397–1405
de Kirkeby 1398	1398
de Lughtteburgh 1405	1411–12
de Luddelowe 1403–05, 1411, 1428	1376, 1403–30
de Melburn 1370	1403–04
de Ramsey 1370	1403–05
de Scaresdall' 1370, 1412	1376–1429
de Shakeston 1403–05	1405
de Stowe 1397–1412 (25 instances)	1397–1411 (8)
de Sta(u)nton 1397–1411	1411–30
de Suddebery 1403	1403
de Thornton 1370–1412	1376, 1398
de Tokeby 1402	1403–04
de Welton 1411	1412
de Whatton 1398–1412	1376, 1411, 1430
de Whychenor 1370	1404
de Wysowe 1370–1412 (46 instances)	1403–30 (12)

Some forms occurred only in their syndetic form, disappearing before the transition to asyndetic: de Baddesley (1411); de Bredon (1397–1405); de Dalby (1412); de Galmynton (1397–1404); de Gerondon (1404–05, 1412); de Leyke (1398, 1404); de Lewes (1370, 1402–04); de Lokynton (1398, 1404); de London (1370, 1398); de Naylston (1411); de Pakynton (1403); de Sheyle (1404); de Thorp (1370, 1398); and de Wakefeld (1405). Many names which occurred for the first time in the early fifteenth century, however, did so only in the asyndetic form: Appulby (1411); Belgraue (1430); Bitham (1429–31); Blakfordby (1402–11); Kendale (1403–05); Langtoft (1429–30); Lichfeld (1430); Marnham (1429–31); Paunton (1430); Rempston (1411, 1430); Rothley (1429–30); Saxilby (1429–31); Scaldeford (1403); Stepyngley (1429–31); Tannesley (1402); Trowell (1430); Walton (1430); and Whytyngton (1430–31). An irreversible change to asyndetic forms of toponymic name did not occur until *c*.1430; into the late fourteenth century, syndetic forms were customary and the early fifteenth century constituted a period of transition. The nature of the transitional period, however, is obscured by the gaps in the court rolls between 1412 and 1429. The evidence is ambiguous because of a further problem: litigants in the court rolls were not necessarily resident in Loughborough. On the other hand, the court rolls state so frequently the places of residence of litigants from outside Loughborough that it would seem that where no place of residence is specified, the litigant was an inhabitant of the manor.[150]

A similar situation obtained in and around another small town in north Leicestershire, Melton Mowbray, according to charters transcribed into the Brokesby Cartulary.[151] Although the cartulary was compiled in the fifteenth century, it is probably reliable in its representation of these forms of names. Charters relating to Melton recorded most toponymic surnames in syndetic form: de Frisby (1398); de Houby (1393); de Manton (1397); de Norton (1398); de Rethurby (1396–98); de Sutton (1394); and de Wytham (1398). The transition probably happened in the 1390s, for the cartulary then recorded Edmund Waltham (1391, 1394) as well as Edmund de Waltham (1384, 1397), Roger Waltham (1385–98) and Roger de Waltham (1394–5), and, simultaneously in 1393, John de Sixtenby and John Sixtenby.

Some more precise information about the transition may be reflected in the court rolls of the manor of Barkby. In 1367, John de Lynburgh' married Isabel, the widow of Adam Wright and came into court to be accepted as a tenant of Merton College.[152] By 1370, however, he was consistently recorded as John Lymbury for default of suit, for a licence to compromise actions, and when placed in mercy for contempt of court.[153] In 1389, nevertheless, when he died, Richard de Braylesforde was still so recorded, in the syndetic form of his name.[154] Once each in 1409, 1415 and 1417, Stephen de Bockyngham was thus described in the court rolls, but on 46 other occasions between 1409 and 1439 as Stephen Bokyngham or Stephen Bu(c)kyngham, whereas the surname of the Holbec(h) or Holbek family, introduced into the manor in 1434, was never recorded in syndetic form, nor was the Braundeston *alias* Braunston *alias* Brawnston name (1395–1544).[155] One possibility which ensues, although it does not account for de Braylesforde and Braunston, is the inconsistent norm that when new toponymic names entered the manor, they were accorded their syndetic form, reflecting recent introduction of the name, even in the late fourteenth and fifteenth centuries, but once the name was established, it was adopted in its asyndetic form.

Toponymic surnames thus became stabilized in asyndetic form much later than occupational or nickname types of name, perhaps only comprehensively transformed in the early fifteenth century. Some topographical forms of surname, because they persisted so long in that manner, became fossilized asyndetically. This contrast is illustrated in the court rolls of the decaying small borough of Castle Donington in N.W. Leicestershire.[156] All other forms of surname had developed into their asyndetic form by the commencement of the extant court rolls in 1457, even toponymic forms: John Dalby sold meat; Robert Tapton cut branches; William Langton poorly ploughed the demesne as well as withdrawing his suit of court, as did Thomas Burton.[157] Henry attWell, however, was presented by the 'Inquisicio liberorum' for cutting branches, as also in 1458 and he may have been the same Henry Attewell who surrendered a toft and croft and bovate *ad opus et usum Willelmi Taylour* in 1477.[158] By contrast, Thomas Atwelle was selected as one of the members of the 'Inquisicio liberorum' in 1465.[159] In 1464, Edward Atwell was a member of the 'Inquisicio Natiuorum'; in 1885, Edward Attwell was one of the 12 jurors on the 'Inquisicio' (and again as Attewelle in 1477 and Attwell in 1482) and was appointed an affeeror; and in 1486, he was again one of the 12 and also elected a chief pledge, as again in 1478 and 1480.[160] From 1467, Edward AttWell had held a

messuage and virgate.[161] Also selected to the 'Inquisicio' was
William Attewelle, in 1476.[162] In the succeeding generation, Thomas
Atwell was selected to the 'Inquisicio magna' of 12 jurors in 1516,
remaining on the list through to 1522.[163] In that year too, Robert
Atwell, son and heir of William Atwell, took a messuage and one
virgate lately held by Thomas, William's father.[164] When the extant
court rolls resume in 1532, Robert Atwell was presented for cutting
branches.[165] By 1543, Robert Atwell had emulated his predecessors
and been selected for the 'Inquisicio'.[166] Atwell was the solitary
surname to become consolidated and preserved in Castle Donington
in syndetic form; all other surnames, of whatever type, had
developed asyndetically. The family was evidently an important
kinship group within the borough and a syndetic topographical
surname was not considered inappropriate to its position.

The prepositional form A-

Some toponymic and topographical forms of surname assumed a
different prepositional form in the later middle ages, with A replacing
de or atte. An example was A Sybsdon in Loughborough, in the
court roll of 1403.[167] The Poll Tax of Gartree Hundred in 1381
included John A Leke in West Langton, whilst the rental of Leicester
Abbey lands of 1477 enumerated Margaret A Barow at Lockington
and John A Lye at Thurmaston.[168] This form of syndetic surname
was most widely represented in the lay subsidy rolls of 1524-5, which
included 14 taxpayers with toponymic examples in Leicestershire
(mainly Aglene or A Glen and A Dalby) and 21 with topographical
names (mainly Agrene or A Grene).[169] In Rutland, although eight
taxpayers with toponymic and five with topographical names
occurred in the military survey of 1522, only three with this preposition
appeared in the taxation of 1524-5.[170]

Aliases

The introduction of aliases reflected upon the stability and
heritability of family surnames. Before the general inheritance of
surnames, aliases were not necessary as bynames were inherently
unstable and naming was more flexible. Aliases thus evolved during
the later middle ages. In Leicestershire and Rutland, however, their
use was ostensibly less frequent than in some other areas of
England.

In the 'Liber Gersumarum' of Ramsey Abbey, for example, aliases were often associated with customary holdings, so that new tenants assumed an alias which was the surname previously associated with the tenement.[171] Only one specific example of this use of an alias has been discovered for Leicestershire and Rutland. At Kibworth Harcourt Adam Valentyne, who held a virgate in customary tenure, surrendered it in the early fifteenth century *ad opus Henrici Valentyne alias dicti Henrici Norman*.[172] Perhaps an implicit instance of the same phenomenon occurred amongst the enumeration of the free tenants of Leicester Abbey at Laughton in 1477, which included John Bocher *alias vocatus Wynnall*, who held a messuage and virgate *quondam* W. Fleshewer — although the synonyms Bocher and Fleshewer may not be conclusive in this case.[173]

A different implication behind aliases is that the bearer had migrated and was known by another surname in the new community. For example, in 1397, John *filius Thome filii Nigelli Orger* of Melton Mowbray alienated all the lands in Melton which he had inherited from his father, Thomas, to Henry Wright of Melton Mowbray. In 1414, he transferred to Wright a residual messuage in the town, but then his style in the charter was John Tailour of Twyford *alias vocatus Johannes filius Thome filii Nigelli·Orger*.[174] Some other aliases may have developed under the same influence. When he was presented for having left the lordship of Barkby in (?)1439, Thomas Pykard was presented as Thomas Dey *alias* Pykard, perhaps suggesting that he had different surnames in his old and new communities.[175] Similarly, Henry Bonde *alias vocatus Henricus Nicholson* was another villein *fugitivus* from Barkby living in [Smeeton] Westerby in the late fourteenth century.[176]

In the two counties, aliases resulted from other influences too. Agnes atte Crosse, the surname from her first marriage, married secondly Nicholas Thorth, and was subsequently, on at least one occasion, described as Agnes atte Crosse *alias vocata Agnes Thorthe*.[177] In the case of the Burgeys family, the epithet (de) Melton may have arisen from its dominant position in Melton, especially by the early fifteenth century.[178] It was possible too for an alias to derive from a maternal name. Thus John Lymour was also known by the surname Denys, his mother's name.[179] In other cases, however, the reason behind the alias is not clear.[180]

The frequency of aliases, however, was sporadic. Two possibly occurred in the rental of the estates of Leicester Abbey in 1341, although the feature may equally have resulted from the instability of bynames.[181] A very small number subsequently occurred in the rental of the Abbey's lands in 1477.[182] Only a single alias occurred in the lay subsidy of 1524.[183] Several appeared occasionally in the court rolls of some Leicestershire manors in the fifteenth century.[184]

The largest profusion, however, is manifest in the rentals and court rolls of the small town of Loughborough in the middle of the sixteenth century.[185] Aliases did not exist in the court rolls of Loughborough before the sixteenth century and only one alias appeared in the rental of 1526, Ralph Ward *aliter* Plummer. In the rental of 1559, however, aliases were more abundant — almost a dozen tenants with an alias. Their sudden proliferation is mysterious, however, for there are two rentals of very similar date, although one is slightly earlier, and only in the later one did the aliases appear.

One rental has a date and regnal year clearly assigning it to 1559, whilst the other is undated, but contains a heading which associated the manor with the estates of the late Duke of Suffolk. Since the last Duke of Suffolk was executed in 1554, one terminus of the rental is firmly established.[186] This rental must be earlier than that of 1559 from comparison of some of the tenants. The undated rental includes Thomas Digbe gent, whilst that of 1559 refers to the heirs of Thomas Digbye. The undated rental lists John Sutton *alias* Bell as the tenant of three shops opposite the market cross, whilst in 1559 are enumerated the heirs of John Sutton *alias* Bell for the Crosse Keyes in the market place at a rent of £1 per annum. It is reasonably established then that the undated rental can be assigned after 1554 but before 1559, but is very close in date to the rental explicitly dated 1559.

All but one alias, however, did not occur in the earlier rental. The earlier, undated rental is almost devoid of aliases, but the second, of 1559, contains a considerable number. Both rentals, because of their proximity, however, enumerate substantially the same tenants. Some of those with aliases in 1559 can be cross-referred to the earlier rental. In 1559, Margery Wheateleye *alias* Clowdeslee held a tenement in Hallgate for 8s. annual rent; in the earlier rental Nicholas Clowderlsey held this property at the same rent. Joan Rigmaiden *alias* Eglott was the tenant of a tenement in Kirkgate and 1½a. at a rent of 5s.2½d. per annum, which were held precisely for the same rent in the earlier rental by Joan Eglett as a cottage and garden in Kirkgate and 1½a. Whilst in 1559 a cottage in Kirkgate was held by Elizabeth Arsar *alias* Banckes for an annual rent of 4*s*.2½*d*., the same rent was required for the same property in the earlier rental from Elizabeth Banckes. Equally as conclusively, Alice Kettyll *alias* Barton was listed in 1559 with extensive holdings: a tenement, garden, orchard and toft in Hallgate; a tenement, garden and toft in Woodgate; three shops on the corner of Baxtergate; a messuage, garden and orchard in Woodgate; another messuage, garden, houses and a bovate; and a cottage, garden, and orchard in Leicester Lane. These properties were attributed in the earlier rental to simply Alice Kettell. Similarly, the rental of 1559 included John Andrew *alias* Raper who can be associated with John Andrewe in the earlier rental.

The rental of 1559 thus has many aliases: Bell *alias* Sutton; Warde *alias* Farmer; Hughsinson *alias* Jallycock; Pighte *alias* Barbour; Wheateley *alias* Clowdeslee; Rigmaiden *alias* Eglott; Halle *alias* Smyth; Arsar *alias* Banckes; Andrew *alias* Raper; Smyth *alias* Ells; and Torr *alias* Wollande. The earlier rental has only one tenant with an alias. Many of the tenants with aliases in the later rental were common to both lists, but, although there are only a few years between the rentals, were not attributed the aliases in the earlier rental.

In only two cases is there direct evidence of an explanation of the aliases. In 1559, Agnes Pighte *alias* Barbour held a messuage, barn and garden *nuper in tenura Johannis Barbour*, so that her alias was related to the surname previously associated with the property. Also in 1559, Margery Wheateleye *alias* Clowdeslee held a tenement in Hallgate which was held in the earlier rental by Nicholas Clowdersley, exhibiting the same phenomenon. In the other cases, however, ambiguity prevails, for the same tenant held the property in the earlier rental and in 1559, but was described by the alias only in 1559.

About this time, too, aliases occurred more frequently in the court rolls of the manor of Loughborough, adding to the corpus of aliases. In the court roll of 1559 appeared Elizabeth Sareson *alias* Ormestone and John Laurence *alias* Mourfyn, as well as Joan Tarre *alias* Wollande who also existed in the rental. John Sutton *alias* Bell, who was enumerated in the earlier rental and whose heirs were listed in 1559, was succeeded in the court rolls in 1559–64 by George Bell *alias* Sutton and Geoffrey Bell *alias* Sutton, transmitting an alias over two generations, it seems.

Despite this profusion of aliases in this small town in the middle of the sixteenth century, aliases had not featured largely in the onomastic practices of rural Leicestershire and Rutland during the later middle ages. Although some resulted from association of surnames with tenements, their number was minimal by comparison with the number of transactions in land recorded in manorial court rolls, such as for Barkby, Kibworth Harcourt, Owston and Hallaton, in the later middle ages.

Aliens and their names

By comparison with some other counties, aliens existed in Leicestershire in very small numbers.[187] Merely 20 aliens were itemized in the aliens subsidy for the county in 1452.[188] All were accorded English forenames or their forenames were Anglicized to Peter, John, Anthony, James, Nicholas, Thomas, Martin, Alexander, Margaret, Elizabeth and Alice. At least 10 were attributed surnames which were recognisably of English stock, including one or two toponymic ones such as Byngham (etymon Bingham, Nottinghamshire). Occupational surnames included Shepherd, Skynner, Preest, Taylour and Dryver. Foreign surnames comprised only Janyn and Duncan, the former borne by an alien from 'Francia' and the latter from Scotland. A further five were described by generic toponymic bynames or surnames reflective of their nationality: four Scot(te)s from Scotland and a Braban from Brabant.

These assessed aliens consisted of 11 *tenentes hospicium* and nine *non tenentes hospicium*, the latter consequently all servants. Only three, all servants, were female. The taxed aliens were mainly distributed singly throughout the county, but with three aliens in Loughborough, and two in each of Leicester and Saltby. Less than half inhabited towns, including small towns such as Hallaton and Waltham on the Wolds.[189] Many were thus located in rural villages, including Anthony Shepherd, from 'Francia', at Cold Newton, which was becoming a depopulated deserted village in a region becoming dominated by sheep farming.[190] By nationality, 11 were Scottish, of whom nine were servants (comprehending all the servants, therefore), whilst two heralded from Brabant, three from 'Francia' and four from Flanders.

The extent and distribution of taxed aliens in Leicestershire was thus quite different from the larger numbers in coastal counties like

Devon, with its concentrations of aliens in ports and trading places. The onomastic effect, however, was the same, that aliens were attributed indigenous names in the the records and probably in the local speech community.

Conclusion

Consideration of dialect and local usage — lexical and phonemic/ graphemic — reflects on the mélange of influences which had their confluence in the two counties. The lexical item Walker illustrates the strength of one element in the competition between dialect forms, in this case the ascendancy of a more northern influence. By contrast, the contest between Reve and Greve was less unequivocal. Although the elliptical by- achieved some degree of reception in medieval Rutland, perhaps reflecting an influence active also in Lincolnshire, it was not extensive in contemporary Leicestershire, it seems. The assimilation of palatal and stressed phonemes remained ambiguous in ME bynames and surnames. Such items illuminate how the two counties were located at the confluence of several different and competing dialect influences.

Other items inform a broader regional variety within England, represented, for example, by the varying pace of the transition from syndetic to asyndetic forms of byname and surname or the different levels of use of aliases. Similarly, the relative employment of the suffixes -ster and -man reflect on that regional dimension at the macro-level.

Furthermore, at both levels of difference and transition, a principal, exogenous infuence might have been the extent of migration, particularly immigration into the two counties. The volume and distance of that migration in combination remained a potential for onomastic change. In the event, migration of people was so localized and contained that external influences were mitigated and lexical and phonemic change was slight and protracted, as indeed reflected in the competition between Walker, Fuller and Tucker, examined above.

References

1 G Fransson, *Middle English Surnames of Occupation 1100–1350*, (Lund Studies in English, 3, Lund, 1935), 100–1.

2 *Great Roll of the Pipe for the 2nd Year of Richard I*, (PRS, n.s 1, 1925), 40.

3 BL, Lansdowne 415, fo. 18r.

4 The Queen's College, Oxford, MS 366, fo. 16v.

5 *Oakham Survey*, 21–2, 45.

6 PRO E179/165/21, m.15.

7 *Tudor Rutland*, 43, 97.

8 HAM Box 58b; Bodl MS Laud Misc 625, fo. 26v.

9 BR III/4/70–73.

10 *RBL*, I, 134, 254, 247, 357; II, 4, 6, 36, 51, 56, 158, 203, 373–4, 417, 466.

11 Bodl. MS Ch. Leicestershire A1, no. 15.

12 *RBL*, II, 373–4, 466.

13 Above, n.6; PRO E179/165/21, m.3, E179/165/21, m.3; *Tudor Rutland*, 21, 34, 39, 54, 58, 61–2, 68, 70, 95, 99, 101, 104, 106, 112.

14 HAM Box 20, Flders 2, 4, 5–9; Box 21, flders 1–3.

15 PRO DL30/80/1093–1094.

16 Bodl. MS Wood empt 7, fo.25r (before 1340).

17 Bodl. MS Laud Misc 625, fos. 119v,124r, 130v, 141r

18 MM 6406.

19 *Rutland Hearth Tax*, 14, 18, 28, 30, 31, 32, 33, 35, 39, 42.

20 PRO HO 107/2092 (household 11 at Ashwell).

21 PRO HO 107/2092 (Exton: households 72, 92b, 157; Whitwell: household 4; Edith Weston: households 26, 34, 38, 40, 43, 51, 56; Langham: households 72, 81, 91); for Oakham and Uppingham, PRO HO 107/2093 (for example, Oakham: Lord's Hold, first section, households 22, 179, 182, Lord's Hold, second section, households 50, 102, Dean's Hold, household 10; Uppingham; households 21, 69).

22 HAM Box 21, flder 3.

23 *Tudor Rutland*, 50, 90; PRO E179/133/108, m.6 (Waltham); PRO E179/133/110, m.2d (Great Dalby), m.5 (Abbeygate); PRO E179/133/116, m.7d (Sileby); PRO E179/133/122, m.3d (Ullesthorpe); perhaps two cases, however, suffer from metathesis, confusing Gervys and Grevys. For the limited subsidy of 1603–4, encompassing Robert Greaves at Great Dalby and Richard Reave

at Twyford, H Hartopp, 'Leicestershire lay subsidy roll, 1603-4', *AASR*, 24 (1897-8), 607, 608.

24 PRO E179/133/1, 35; *AASR*, (1888-9).

25 PRO SC2/183/88, 90; PRO DL 30/80/1102; Bodl. MS Laud Misc 625, fo. 75v.

26 PRO E179/135/14, mm.1, 4, 18-19; E179/135/15, mm.15, 20, 27.

27 *Rutland Hearth Tax*; PRO HO 107/2092-2093.

28 R McKinley, *The Surnames of Oxfordshire*, (English Surnames Series III, London, 1977), 137-40; Fransson, *Middle English Surnames of Occupation*, 42-4.

29 Fransson, *Middle English Surnames of Occupation*, 41-5.

30 PRO E179/165/1, 21; *AASR*, (1888-9); PRO E179/133/35.

31 PRO E179/165/1, m.4.

32 *AASR*, (1888-9), 264, 279, 300.

33 *AASR*, (1888-9), 264, 279, 300.

34 PRO E179/165/21, mm.3, 8, 12, 17, 18, 22; E179/165/21, mm.3, 13.

35 PRO E179/133/35.

36 Bodl. MS Laud Misc 625, fos. 198r-v, 203r-204v, 207v

37 PRO SC2/183/52; HAM Box 20, flder 4.

38 *Tudor Rutland*, 18, 19, 50, 54, 64, 71, 91, 105, 111, 113, 115; PRO E179/133/108, mm.5, 7, 9d; E179/133/109, m.12; E179/133/112, m.10; E179/133/115, m.2; E179/133/116, m.2d; E179/133/121, m.15.

39 PRO E179/133/104, m.4d, 5d, 6; E179/133/108, m.3, 8d

40 *Tudor Rutland*, 40, 50; PRO E179/133/109, m.8; E179/133/121, m.9.

41 PRO DL 30/80/1090-1092; HAM Box 8.

42 *Tudor Rutland*, 22, 37, 38, 44, 47, 74, 89, 90, 94, 96, 106; PRO E179/133/108, m.6.

43 PRO E179/133/109, m.12.

44 *Tudor Rutland*, 11, 29, 53, 64, 75, 85, 92, 103, 111, 116.

45 PRO DL 30/80/1102; HAM Box 20, flders 2-9; Box 21, flders 1-3.

46 *AASR*, (1888-9), esp. 211; J M Bennett, *Ale, Beer, and Brewsters in England Women's Work in a Changing World, 1300-1600*, (Oxford, 1996), 3.

47 *Oakham Survey*, 31; this infrequent byname occurred in Oxfordshire contemporaneously: McKinley, *Oxfordshire*, 138, but is evidently not recorded by Fransson.

48 PRO E179/165/21, mm.22, 36; M Kowaleski, 'Women and work in a market town: Exeter in the late fourteenth century' in B Hanawalt, ed., *Women and Work in Pre-Industrial Europe*, (Bloomington, Indiana, 1986), 145–64

49 PRO E179/133/35; HAM Box 21, flder 3.

50 HAM Box 20, flders 6–9; Box 21, flders 1–3; Kowaleski, 'Women's work'.

51 *AASR*, (1888–9); PRO E179/165/1.

52 PRO E179/133/35; PRO E179/165/21.

53 PRO E179/133/104, 108–10, 112–18, 121–22, 124.

54 *Tudor Rutland*.

55 I Hjertstedt, *Middle English Nicknames in the Lay Subsidy Rolls for Warwickshire*, (Acta Universitatis Upsaliensis, Studia Anglistica Upsaliensia, 63, Uppsala, 1987), 27, 242; M F Wakelin, *English Dialects An Introduction*, (revised edn, reprinted 1981), 96.

56 *AASR*, (1888–9), 236, 244.

57 PRO E179/137/122, mm.3, 6, 8.

58 PRO E179/133/121 mm.4d, 11, 13d, 14, 14d. Corroborative forms may be Bloxsom (from the placename Bloxham) in Bruntingthorpe in 1524 and 1525: PRO E179/137/122, m.7d; E179/137/121 m.13.

59 *Hastings MSS*, 48.

60 *AASR*, (1888–9), 227; PRO E179/133/108, m.6.

61 PRO E179/165/21, mm.9, 15.

62 PRO E179/133/35.

63 Rothley, 101; Bodl. MS Laud Misc 625, fo. 191v.

64 R A McKinley, *The Surnames of Lancashire*, (English Surnames Series IV, London, 1981), 152.

65 P R Reaney, *The Origins of English Surnames*, (London, repr. 1987), 192, 194–5, 196.

66 'Johannes Glouereman ponit se in misericordia pro licencia concordandi cum Johanne Glouere seniore in .ij. placitis per plegium eiusdem Johannis Glouere.' HAM Box 20, flder 2.

67 HAM Box 20, flders 4–5; Box 21, flder 1.

68 'Johannes Bretonman ponit se in misericordia pro licencia concordandi cum Radulpho Irnemongere in placito debiti', [1397]. HAM Box 20, flders 2–3, 6; Box 21, flder 3.

69 HAM Box 20, flder 4; *Hastings MSS*, 80.

70 HAM Box 20, flders 2–3, 5–9; Box 21, flders 1, 3.

71 HAM Box 20, flder 6.

[72] HAM Box 20, flder 6.
[73] HAM Box 20, flder 4.
[74] *AASR*, (1888–9), 152.
[75] HAM Box 20, flder 1; Box 21, flders 1, 3.
[76] HAM Box 20, flders 5–6.
[77] HAM Box 20, flders 2, 5–6.
[78] 'pro stipendio suo detento per longum tempus ad dampna .xij.d.' HAM Box 20, flders 5–6.
[79] HAM Box 20, flders 3, 5–9; Box 21, flder 1.
[80] HAM Box 20, flders 6–7; Box 21, flder 3.
[81] HAM Box 20, flder 4.
[82] HAM Box 20, flders 3, 6–7.
[83] *AASR*, (1888–9).
[84] MM 6390; Bodl. MS Laud Misc 625, fo. 203r.
[85] HAM Box 20, flders 5–6.
[86] PRO E179/165/1, m.9.
[87] PRO E179/165/1, mm.3, 5, 6, 7, 8, 9, 10, 11.
[88] PRO E179/165/1, m.6.
[89] K Cameron, 'Bynames of location in Lincolnshire subsidy rolls', *Nottingham Medieval Studies*, 32 (1988), 156–64.
[90] *Oakham Survey*, 30; PRO E179/165/21, m.12.
[91] MM 6563–6567.
[92] PRO E179/133/35; PRO E179/165/1, 21; *AASR*, (1888–9); PRO E179/133/104–10, 112–18, 121–22, 124
[93] PRO SC2/183/76.
[94] PRO E179/133/35; *AASR*, (1888–9), 231.
[95] Bodl. MS Wood empt 7, fo. 52r.
[96] PRO SC2/183/87–88; PRO DL 30/80/1102.
[97] *Tudor Rutland*, 79, 89, 112.
[98] MM 6601–6602; Bodl. MS Laud Misc 625, fo. 210r (but at fo. 210v Alice Shakelok).
[99] PRO E179/135/14, mm.1, 2, 17, 18; E179/35/15, mm.2, 15, 20, 21, 22, 28, 29.
[100] PRO E179/35/15, m.2.
[101] PRO E179/135/14, m.18; E179/35/15, mm.3, 5, 14, 19, 26.
[102] *AASR*, (1888–9), 154, 228, 250, 252, 254, 256, 288.
[103] *Tudor Rutland*, 18, 45, 51, 54, 63, 71, 94, 97, 106, 107, 112.
[104] PRO E179/133/108, m.4; E179/133/110, m.7; E179/133/115, m.4; E179/133/121, m.2.
[105] PRO SC2/183/88–90.

106 Bodl. MS Wood empt 7, fos. 128v–129v, 131v.
107 PRO DL30/80/1102.
108 PRO E179/133/108, m.1; E179/133/116, m.9; *Tudor Rutland*, 97; Bodl. MS Ch. Leicestershire A1, no. 25.
109 MM 6388.
110 Bodl. MS Laud Misc 625, fo. 208v; PRO E179/165/1, m.5.
111 PRO E179/165/1, m.3.
112 Bodl. MS Wood empt 7, fos. 18r *et seqq.*
113 PRO E179/165/1, mm.5, 10 ((le) Koc at Weston and Bisbrooke); *AASR*, (1888–9), 266, 267, 279 ((le) Koc, but also Cokes, at Nailstone, Barwell and Market Bosworth, all in west Leicestershire); PRO DL30/80/1090, 1093; PRO E179/133/121, mm.2d, 6d (but both as Cotton at E179/133/122, mm.6, 9d); *AASR*; Ham Box 8; PRO DL30/1090–1101 (Castle Donington); PRO E179/133/122, m.1 (Shearsby).
114 *Rutland Hearth Tax*, 23, 40, 42.
115 PRO HO107/2092–2093.
116 PRO HO107/2092 (Burley: household 40).
117 *Rutland Hearth Tax*, 31, 44.
118 Fransson, *Middle English Surnames of Occupation*, 64; PRO HO107/2092.
119 PRO E179/133/121, m.15 (possibly influenced at an earlier time by Anglo-Norman phonemic change).
120 PRO HO 107/2092, *passim*. My interpretation of Musson is thus different from P H Reaney and R M Wilson, *The Oxford Dictionary of English Surnames*, (revised edn, Oxford, 1997), 318 (added by R M Wilson).
121 *Rutland Hearth Tax*, 18, 22, 32, 38.
122 Nottinghamshire Archives Office St Mary's, Nottingham, parish registers: from the transcription on the Genuki site at Manchester University Computer Centre (URL: http://sentinel.mcc.ac.uk/genuki/bcg/eng/NTT/Nottingham/St Mary): in the register of 1782–94 occurred two Musson baptisms (1784 and 1787).
123 Nottinghamshire Archives Office All Saints parish registers, burial registers from 1579: from the transcription at the Genuki site on the World Wide Web (URL http://sentinel.mcc.ac.uk/genuki/bcg/eng/NTT/Nottingham/All Saints) For the distribution of this surname in the rest of Nottinghamshire in 1664–74, see below 160.

[124] W A Hartley, ed., *Northamptonshire Militia List 1777*, (Northamptonshire Record Society 25, 1973), 62.

[125] *Rutland MSS*, 12, 142.

[126] *AASR*, (1888–9), 228.

[127] PRO E179/133/35, SC2/183/90.

[128] PRO E179/133/116, mm.7, 9; 179/133/117, m.4d; 179/133/121, mm.4, 6.

[129] *AASR*, (1888–9), 227; Bodl. MS Wood empt 7, fos. 19v–20r.

[130] MM 6392.

[131] PRO E179/133/35.

[132] MM 6592.

[133] PRO SC2/183/90.

[134] PRO E179/133/110, mm.2d, 4; 179/133/108, m.8; E179/133/112, m.9.

[135] PRO E179/133/104, m.4; E179/133/110, m.4d; E179/133/104, m.4; E179/133/109, mm.3, 14. Compare also in 1603–4, Thomas Croson of Humberstone, William Croson of Frisby near Galby and John Musson of Rotherby: H Hartopp, 'Leicestershire lay subsidy roll, 1603–4', *AASR*, 24 (1897–8), 604, 605, 625.

[136] B Cox, 'The Place-Names of Leicestershire and Rutland', unpublished PhD, University of Nottingham 1971, 146–7, 158–9, 160–1, 232–3, 227, 228, 256, 486–7.

[137] PRO E179/165/1.

[138] *AASR*, (1888–9).

[139] PRO E179/165/21.

[140] PRO E179/133/35.

[141] Bodl. MS Laud Misc 625, fos. 191r–211r.

[142] PRO SC2/183/51–52.

[143] PRO SC2/183/76–77.

[144] PRO SC2 30/80/1102. For example, Alice de Blaston 'venit et fecit fidelitatem et tenet de Domino ad voluntatem .xij. acras terre'.

[145] PRO SC2/183/87–89. For example, for syndetic forms, in 1370: 'Johannes de Empyngham taylloure venit in curia et cepit de domino unum croftum quod Galfridus de Welleham quondam tenuit.'

[146] Bodl. MS Laud Misc 625, fos. 12v–82r, 101r–141v.

[147] PRO E179/133/104–10, 112–18, 121–2, 124; *Tudor Rutland*.

[148] HAM Box 20, flder 4.

149 HAM Box 20, flders 1–9, Box 21, flders 1–3.
150 HAM Box 20, flders 1–9, Box 21, flders 1–3.
151 Bodl. MS Wood empt 7.
152 MM 6577: 'Johannes de Lynburgh' quia desponsauit Isabellam relictam Ade Wright venit in Curia . . .'
153 MM 6577.
154 MM 6584: 'Ricardus de Braylesforde qui tenuit de domino unum mesuagium unam bouatam terre cum suis pertinenciis per seruicium .ix.s. .viij.d. diem clausit extremum.'
155 MM 6588–6629.
156 PRO DL30/80/1090–1101; HAM Box 8. Overall 1457–1564.
157 PRO DL30/80/1090.
158 *Ibid.*; HAM Box 8.
159 HAM Box 8.
160 PRO DL30/80/1092; HAM Box 8.
161 HAM Box 8.
162 HAM Box 8.
163 PRO DL30/80/1094–1095
164 *Ibid.*
165 PRO DL30/80/1096.
166 PRO DL30/80/1098.
167 HAM Box 20, flders 5–6.
168 PRO E179/133/35; Bodl. MS Laud Misc 625, fos. 104r, 141r.
169 PRO E179/133/104–10, 112–18, 121–2, 124.
170 *Tudor Rutland.*
171 E B DeWindt, ed., *The Liber Gersumarum of Ramsey Abbey*, (Toronto, 1976).
172 MM 6419.
173 Bodl. MS Laud Misc 625, fos. 82r and 174r.
174 Bodl. MS Wood empt 7, fos. 44r–v.
175 MM 6598: 'Et quod Thomas Dey alias Pykard qui de dominis tenuit .j. mesuagium . . . recessit extra hoc dominium et dimisit tenementa predicta ruinosa.'
176 MM 6589.
177 MM 6419.
178 Bodl. MS Wood empt 7, fos. 65r (1427), and 93r (1445): 'que quondam fuerunt Johannis Burgeys alias dicti Johannis de Melton' '; William Burgeys *alias dictus Melton'* disposing of hereditaments in Melton and Thorpe Arnold 'que nuper fuerunt Johannis Burgeys alias dicti Melton' patris mei'.

179 Bodl. MS Laud Misc 625, fo. 76v: 'Memorandum quod Johannes Lymour cognominatus Denys a nomine matris sue . . .'

180 MM 6616 (Barkby, 1472): 'De Johanne Randall alias dicto Johanne Tayllour et Johanna uxore eius de fine ad ingressum in uno mesuagio eis dimisso ad terminum annorum .viij.d.'; Bodl. MS Laud Misc 625, fo. 80r (1477): 'Parcelle terre Ricardi Hotoft ibidem nuper Radulphi Humburston' alias Brasiar.'

181 Bodl. MS Laud Misc 625, fos. 193r, 204r (both 'qui alio nomine vocatur').

182 *Ibid.*

183 John Wormell *alias* Hine at Melton Mowbray: PRO E179/133/108, m.1.

184 See above.

185 HAM Box 24, flders 2, 4, 6, 7.

186 E B Fryde, D E Greenway, S Porter and I Roy, *Handbook of British Chronology*, (Royal Historical Society Guides and Handbooks, 2, 3rd edn., London, 1986), 484. The heading runs: 'Rentale manerii de Loughborough percella possessionum nuper Ducis Suffolk'.

187 S Thrupp, 'A survey of the alien population of England in 1440', *Speculum*, 32 (1957), 262–73.

188 PRO E179/235/53.

189 The criterion for a small town in the county is listing in P Clark and J Hosking, *Population Estimates of English Small Towns 1550–1851. Revised Edition*, (Centre for Urban History, University of Leicester, Working Paper No 5, 1993), 91–5.

190 H S A Fox, 'The people of the Wolds in English settlement history', in M Aston, D Austin and C Dyer, eds., *The Rural Settlements of Medieval England*, (Oxford, 1989), 77–101.

CHAPTER 3

MIGRATION AND MOBILITY

The localization or movement of bynames and surnames depended ultimately on the movement of people. It is therefore useful to reconstruct patterns of mobility and migration as a control for the movement of surnames. The movement of surnames, however, might ultimately result not from the single migration of an individual but from continuous and stepwise migration by several individuals or kinship members — in a cumulative way. Several patterns of historical migration have been identified: betterment; subsistence; and cyclical.[1] More particularly for the middle ages, geographical patterns of migration have been conceived as very localized, although where the movement was rural-urban it has been considered how far distances of migration were related to the status of the town or borough within the urban hierarchy.[2] Historical localized patterns of migration produced 'countries' or social regions which were distinctive, such as the tightly circumscribed area around Spalding defined by the movement of farm servants over a long period of time.[3] Social neighbourhoods have also been detected in which kinship groups have extended into adjacent parishes.[4] Data about historical migration, however, allow little discernment of the variables conceived by geographers, such as changes in intervening opportunities and intervening obstacles.[5] It has, none the less, been posited that the change of opportunities caused by the demographic changes of the mid fourteenth century allowed shorter distances of migration in the late middle ages, although some evidence from the manors of Spalding Priory in the fifteenth century is more ambiguous.[6] The detection of 'cultural provinces' throughout England over a broad chronology may also have both influenced and resulted from patterns of migration.[7]   In this respect, it has been suggested that Lindsey was effectively separated from the other Parts of Lincolnshire and was associated more with the West Riding of Yorkshire, a proposition based upon the evidence of toponymic bynames in the lay subsidy for Lindsey in the early fourteenth century.[8] Most specific to the middle ages, however, was the impact of lordship, both as a push and pull force for mobility and migration. It is interesting in this respect that a 'regional dimension' of the medieval peasantry has been predicated on the evidence of bynames in an axis of manors in Huntingdonshire, which, in fact, comprised less a 'region' than a lordship — some manors of Ramsey Abbey.[9] Some of these influences may help to explain the distributions of bynames and surnames; consequently some idea of actual patterns of migration of people is a helpful balance.

Unfortunately, data reflecting patterns of migration in late medieval Leicestershire and Rutland are fragmentary. The material accumulated here is aggregated from a number of different events. The experience of lordship involves two major types of evidence: justiciability — the service of attending (suit of) courts; and licit and illicit migration or flight from manors.[10] That evidence in manorial court rolls is complemented by other material from the same source, relating to informal trading. Finally, the commission of crimes furnishes evidence of the movement of people, whether victims or perpetrators.[11]

Since Leicester Abbey held the view of frankpledge in some of its manors but not in others and since some of its properties were rather meagre, its tenants were required to attend the view of frankpledge at some central locations. Their movements are illustrated in Figure 3. Tenants from [South] Croxton were required to attend the view at Thurmaston, a distance of four miles, whilst those from Mowsley visited nearby Langton. From [Long] Whatton tenants travelled the three miles to the view at Shepshed. At Stoughton, a principal manor, assembled tenants from Hungarton (four miles), Baggrave (six), Ingarsby (three), Humberstone (two), Burton [Overy] (three), Kilby (five), Knighton (three), Thurnby (two) and Fleckney (six). The view for tenants of Theddingworth was held at Cosby, about six miles away, whilst the tenants of Thornton attended the court at the Abbey (some seven miles). The tenants from South Croxton encountered at the view at Thurmaston tenants from Hose (15 miles distant from Thurmaston), Kirby Bellars (eight), Gaddesby (five), Queniborough three), Barkby Thorpe and Barkby (one) and Cossington (four).[12] In fact, the evidence of toponymic bynames in the rental of the Abbey's lands in 1341 suggests that tenants were migrating within the estate.[13]

In the later middle ages, however, occurred considerable leakage from the manors by *fugitivi*, customary tenants leaving without

FIG 3 PATTERNS OF MIGRATION AND MOVEMENT IN LEICESTERSHIRE IN THE LATER MIDDLE AGES [LATE THIRTEENTH TO LATE FIFTEENTH CENTURIES]

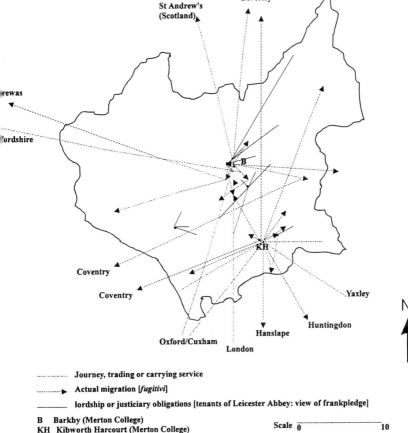

St Andrew's (Scotland)

Beverley

rewas

ordshire

B

Coventry

Coventry

KH

Yaxley

Huntingdon

Hanslape

Oxford/Cuxham

London

N

.... Journey, trading or carrying service

.........▶ Actual migration [*fugitivi*]

_____ lordship or justiciary obligations [tenants of Leicester Abbey: view of frankpledge]

B   Barkby (Merton College)
KH Kibworth Harcourt (Merton College)

Scale $\overline{010}$

licence.[14] The details of the *fugitivi* were collected in the rental from the court rolls.[15] Catherine de Lotryngton had fled the 15 or so miles to Lubbenham, whilst Henry Porter had migrated from Ingarsby into Northamptonshire at Kettering. John Porter had moved a smaller distance from Ingarsby to either one of the Frisbys or to one of the Wigstons.[16] In all, 18 *fugitivi* were recorded. Three had disappeared from the Abbey's lands outside Leicester into the borough; another four moved less than 10 miles, whilst three moved between 10 and 15 miles. Some, however, like Catherine de Lotryngton, embarked on longer journeys, some perhaps to escape recovery, others to attractive urban centres. Despite its decline, Coventry received Thomas Harry from Wibtoft and Agnes Margery from Tilton.[17] William Amison escaped from Leicester to Alderwas in Staffordshire, a small town, whilst the destination of William Amyson from Thurnby was simply described as Staffordshire, but perhaps there was a kinship link in this migration.[18]

Evidence from other manors contains ambiguities, not least in that the new place of residence is rarely stated.[19] There appears also to be a difference in seignorial interest before and after 1348; in the earlier period, lords — at least Merton College — seem to have been more concerned about immigrants into its lordship, but its attention turned to illicit emigrants after the plague. Lords placed fewer restrictions on female migrants and were less concerned with their movement.[20]

Before 1348, Merton College recorded only five *fugitivi* from its manor of Kibworth Harcourt: Robert and Hugh sons of Robert Chep who had sallied as afar as Huntingdon in 1279, Roger Parson who had made the shorter journey to [Market] Harborough, the nearest small town in 1280 and two in the early fourteenth century whose location was apparently unknown.[21] From *c.*1354, however, the College maintained a careful record in the court rolls of traceable *fugitivi*.[22] Many of these illicit migrants had ventured only short distances to neighbouring villages — Shangton, Wistow, Carlton, Saddington, Fleckney, Stoughton, Kibworth Beauchamp, Mowsley, Ilston, Tur Langton and Smeeton Westerby — or slightly further to Gilmorton in the south-west of the county and Waltham on the Wolds (via Wymeswold) in the north, but two entered Coventry, one journeyed to Hamslope in Bedfordshire southwards, one to Beverley in East Yorkshire northwards, and one not quite so far northerly to Grantham. The surnames of many of these *fugitivi*, nevertheless, like those from the Man(ne) kinship, remained in Kibworth, perpetuated by their *consanguinei*, but a small number of surnames disappeared as a result of these flights.[23]

This pattern of the College's interest and the recording of unlicensed migration by its customary tenants is replicated for the manor of Barkby. Less interest was exhibited in recording the exact movement of unmarried daughters.[24] An exception to this norm was Matilda Carpenter, who migrated the enormous distance to St Andrew's in Fife by stages about 1290. At issue here, however, seems to have been a general principle of custom: the method of assessing merchet paid by women of some means, in this case an *ad valorem* assessment of her wealth.[25] The few unlicensed migrations after 1348 were directed to very local rural villages: Robert Heryng to Queniborough;[26] John Fraunceys to the Abbot of Leicester's lordship in Barkby;[27] Amice, widow of John Hicson who remarried in Bushby;[28] William Souter in another lordship in Thurmaston;[29] and William Bate at Scraptoft.[30] Only one migration was long-distance, that of John Lynbury, who relinquished his ruined tenement to move to Beverley; John had been a recent immigrant into Barkby.[31]

Most migration from manors in Leicestershire was, with a few exceptions, thus extremely localized, mainly to other nearby rural manors. Whilst the surname was disseminated with this permanent movement, in most cases it did not disappear from the place of the migrant's origin. In most, but not all, cases, close kin remained in that vill to perpetuate the surname, at least for some time. Although subtraction from the manor did cause the loss of some surnames, the number was relatively small. In the case of female migrants, bynames and surnames were not deducted because of the instability of female names. The process of migration of one individual, as recorded in court rolls, by and large caused bynames and surnames to be distributed over only short distances within the same locality.

The movement of individuals can be further elucidated from the court rolls, in the sense of movements rather than permanent migrations, but illustrating, perhaps, the patterns of potential migration. Lordship and trading were important considerations. The reeve and other tenants from Barkby, for example, were required to travel to Oxford and Cuxham (Oxfordshire), another of the College's manors, where the College held its chapters.[32] One of the customary tenants, Henry Bonde, journeyed there to pay an entry fine to inherit land in the late thirteenth century.[33] Another tenant travelled to Oxford to be admitted to the land formerly of Thomas *molendinarius*, about the same time.[34] To petition to be admitted to half a virgate of demesne land in Kibworth, Robert, son of John Thorth made the journey to Oxford.[35] The reeve was compelled to make numerous trips to Oxford, but also visited Belvoir and Tilton, and the county court at Leicester, on the lords' business.[36] The customary services at least theoretically required from the College's tenants at Kibworth Harcourt included carrying grain to the market at Leicester and elsewhere within the county.[37]

Debt litigation in the manorial courts allows a further perspective on linkages. William le Chapman was bound to another tenant at Kibworth Harcourt in 4s 11¾d. which he had lost at Yaxley, with the imputation that Chapman was actually a petty trader purchasing on behalf of villagers at the market at Yaxley.[38] About the same time, John Walter and his brother were bound to William le Chapman of Kibworth Harcourt in 4d. which he had dispensed on their behalf at Medbourne, a market vill in south-east Leicestershire.[39] Whilst Medbourne was only seven miles from Kibworth, Yaxley was about 31. Heyne v. Boton in the manorial court of Kibworth concerned a horse which Adam had sold through an agent (*per attornatum suum*), William Fauconer, in the market at Lutterworth, for 10s.[40] Whilst most litigation about debt and detinue involved inhabitants of the manor, one of the parties, usually the plaintiff, was an outsider. Almost exclusively, these outsiders were from neighbouring villages, suggesting private trading at a very local level. The residence of outside debt litigants in the manorial court of Loughborough extended over a wider area, but was still localized — excluding Leicester, within a radius of seven miles.[41] During the late middle ages, villagers may have increasingly resorted to courts other than the manorial court and outside their vill. John Hichebon, a tenant of Merton College's manor of Barkby, initiated a case in London in 1445 — and was fined 3s. 4d. by the College for this irregularity.[42] In 1447, and reiterated in 1448, the College had to pronounce a general injunction against using courts other than the manorial court at Barkby, perhaps indicating a quite extensive problem.[43]

In a few cases, linkages are demonstrated by marriage to outsiders. Walter Gretham of Shangton married Agnes, daughter of John Man of Kibworth Harcourt, a *nativa*, but paid 2s. to Merton College for licence to live outside the manor.[44] As a consequence of marrying another *nativa* of the College in Kibworth, Alice, daughter of William Polle, William Prechour of Wistow was summoned into court at Kibworth to perform fealty.[45] At adjacent Kibworth Beauchamp, John Asteyn the younger fined for permission to marry Agnes Smyth at Kibworth Harcourt; since he also promised to pay chevage of 2*d.* each year, he presumably intended to reside in Harcourt.[46] The marriage horizon for these three fourteenth-century unions was less than three miles.

Finally, the evidence of criminal proceedings illuminates personal movement in the later middle ages, although the criminals may not be a representative sample.[47] For example, in 1339 William de Kylby was accused of the murder of Richard Astel at Newton Harcourt, both resident in Wigston.[48] John le Milnere, son of John le Ladycnave of Foxton was killed in Market Harborough by John Prat of East Carlton in 1351.[49] Movements (both of victim and perpetrator) at the time of the event are represented in Figure 4. Out of 21 movements, 15 did not exceed five miles, whilst two others extended to between six and 10 and a further two 11 to 15; only five might be considered to be long distance. The mean distance of movement at point of contact was about 12 miles (including the two long-distance movements), but, adopting the trimmed mean to exclude those two unusual values, 5.05 miles.[50] Amongst the longer-distance movements in the early fourteenth century, Alexander Pulewere and his wife, Alice, from Brackley (Northants) were taken on appeal by an approver for the death of a man and woman at Thurmaston, although acquitted, and Roger *mercator* of Leicester was killed in a wood at Carlton (Northants).[51] In the late fourteenth century, John Bakere of Oakham stole seven old veils and a towel worth 20*d.* from the church of Thornton next to Horncastle in Lincolnshire.[52] In the reverse direction, Robert Fraunkhome of Colsterworth (Lincolnshire) stole 50 sheep at Dalby and 30 sheep at Burton Lazars, both in north-east Leicestershire, which he sold in several places in Lincolnshire on his return there.[53]

More difficult to establish is the extent of migration and mobility in Leicestershire and Rutland during the early modern period. For one market town, Ashby de la Zouch, there is interesting information for part of the seventeenth century. Ashby was a small town in north-west Leicestershire, dominated by the Hastings family.[54] Communicants in the *Liber Cleri* numbered 700, indicating a total population of

FIG 4 MOVEMENT OF SOME CRIMINALS AND THEIR VICTIMS
FOURTEENTH AND FIFTEENTH CENTURIES

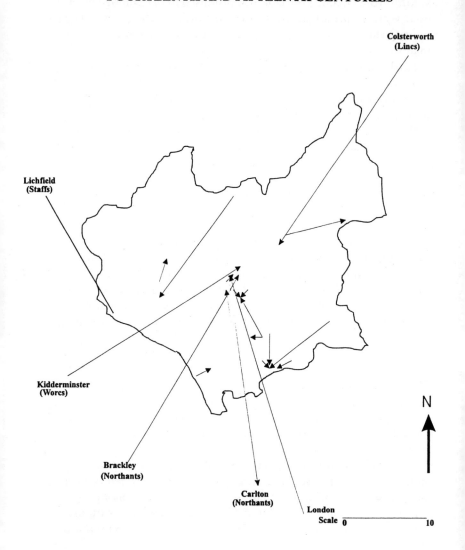

about 1,200. In the Compton Census of 1676 were enumerated 700 communicants, reflecting a total population of some 1,350.[55] The population may have increased by 50% between c.1570 and c.1603, from the evidence of parish register estimates.[56] By 1640, the population had attained about 1,500, representing about 300 adult male householders.[57] Parish register data of the early seventeenth century allow observation of stability of population in and migration into a small town in the two counties at this time through the place of residence of marriage partners at the time of their union. Residing within the parish were 1,766 partners, with only 322 partners residing outside the parish. 61% of these 322 outsiders had a place of residence within 10 miles of Ashby; 86% originated from within 20 miles. Of 313 whose precise place of residence can be identified, 158 (50.5%) inhabited a place within five miles of Ashby, whilst another 89 (28.5%) between five and 10 miles. A further 10% (31) originated between 11 and 15 miles away. A high degree of stability of population thus characterized this small market town, which had a marriage horizon basically within 10 miles or two parishes from its centre.[58]

With only a small number of longer distances, personal movement and migration in Leicestershire, since there is little evidence for Rutland, was intensely localized, largely confined within the villager's rural 'country'. During the later middle ages, it was the extent of that personal migration which determined the migration of bynames and surnames, although, even during this period, incremental migration by successive members of the same kinship group disseminated names further afield. That step-migration by later generations, however, was more active after the middle ages.

More information is available about patterns of migration in the nineteenth century from the census enumerators' books for the population censuses. The extent to which surnames became more distributed in the nineteenth century may have increased as communications improved, rural societies experienced a relative decline, and industrial societies developed. On the other hand, it is possible that some rural societies remained largely endogamous into the late nineteenth century, and consequently the composition of their surnames too. The following discussion attempts to assess the nature of migration within and into Rutland in the middle of the nineteenth century as a control for the composition of surnames.

In the exposition of the plot of *The Mayor of Casterbridge*, set about a generation before the 1851 census, Michael Henchard, his wife Susan and their child Elizabeth-Jane, tramped to Weydon Fair, into a local society obviously unknown to them, since Henchard was required to ask questions about the area, work and housing. The reasons why the hay-trusser and his family needed to move are not explicit, but implicitly seem to revolve around finding work and new opportunities. When his later life in Casterbridge went awry, Henchard tramped again, for personal reasons, resuming his working life as a hay-trusser, moving 50 miles from Casterbridge (revealed as three days tramping), but along a major thorough-fare so that the personal news which he was expecting from Casterbridge should not be denied him. Henchard, however, seems singular in this rural society, which is otherwise rather stable and enduring, except that, in another section, Hardy alluded to the mobility of farm servants, when two lovers (both servants in husbandry) were on the point of being separated by new employment contracts by a distance of 35 miles, but their plight was alleviated by Donald Farfrae, partly at the instance of Lucetta Templeman, hiring the male servant and his father in Casterbridge. The implication is that rural society was both stable and enduring, but also for some rural labourers disrupted by short- or longer-term migration in search of short- or longer-term employment.[59]

Hardy's representation of a rural life-cycle tramping culture resonates only partly with historical reconstruction, at least for those areas other than 'Wessex' where considerable research has been possible. Mobility of farm servants can be perceived through the records of earlier statutes or hiring-fairs, in particular that for the hundred of Elloe in Lincolnshire, centred at Spalding.[60] Between 1767 and 1785, servants hired there moved median distances of 12 km (males) and 10 km (females), but more importantly were indeed frequent and inured movers, racking up high cumulative mileage over the years. Hiring at statutes, however, catered essentially for more distant farmers, creating abnormally long journeys for servants. More representative then might be the distances involved in settlement examinations, which, Kussmaul found, tended to be very much shorter. In both cases, moreover, the distances were circumscribed within customary and localized societies.[61]

Advanced here is the suggestion that patterns of rural migration in the nineteenth century were, *ceteris paribus*, still intensely localized and circumscribed, reflecting established and customary local societies, which, although not completely timeless and perduring, persisted over several generations into the middle of the nineteenth century. This degree of localized mobility existed alongside high levels of social stability and endogamy and, indeed, the two were complementary. Whereas a high proportion of local populations had the opportunity to remain settled in their native rural parish, others, for life-cycle or other reasons, were forced to move to find employment, but their migratory patterns were so localized as to reinforce customary regional identities. The area selected for examination is the registration county of Rutland in 1851, before the decline of rural fertility and exodus from the countryside in the late nineteenth century. The area and its demographic development and structure are described in more detail below.

Recent studies of nineteenth-century patterns and processes of migration in England and Wales have tended towards analyses of urban and industrializing communities. Use of the census data in 1851 for Preston, an industrializing urban community, remarked upon the large element of social endogamy even within such newly developing types of community. There, 48% of the population had been born in the town, whilst in-migration was largely short-distance, 42% from within 10 miles and only 30% from further than 30 miles.[62] The perception that migrants exceeded indigenous inhabitants even in large towns in 1851 was thus qualified, if not fully contradicted, by detailed examination of Preston.[63] Nevertheless, the deficiencies of census data for a complete picture of patterns of migration has also been conceded: movement from place of birth to place of residence in (for example) 1851 did not represent the full extent of step-wise migration, nor fully the frequency of movement at different life-cycle stages. To some extent that problem could be reconciled by tracing movements by the place of birth of children, but that method still did not represent movements through the entire life-cycle of individuals.[64]

In recognition of these problems with the census, the study of migration has turned to other sources, most recently the records of occupational friendly societies, which reflect in great detail how individuals and their families 'moved frequently and routinely'.[65] The tramping culture of artisans has thus been re-established and refined. How far that particular form of mobility, however, reflected non-artisanal culture and movement merits further reflection. For,

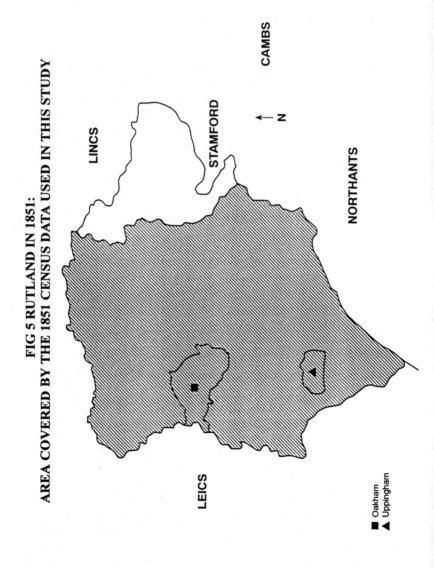

FIG 5 RUTLAND IN 1851:
AREA COVERED BY THE 1851 CENSUS DATA USED IN THIS STUDY

firstly, the migration patterns of rural labourers might not have been effected and affected by the same causes of distress which dislocated the lives of artisans in industrializing contexts; secondly, the pattern of availability of rural employment was likely to differ from artisanal provisions; and finally, there may have been differences in their respective information fields.

Considerations of rural mobility in the nineteenth century have been perhaps less well explored. One effective use of census data has involved the consideration of aggregate, intercensal (decadal) population change at the level of registration county.[66] Some local studies of rural migration have been conducted using census data, but further studies may help expand and refine our knowledge of that phenomenon.[67] Following a re-examination of the appropriateness of using census data, consideration is given to the character of Rutland; and discussed next are demographic data exploring levels of recent social endogamy in and patterns of migration into the rural communities of the county as well as in its two 'urban' centres, Oakham and Uppingham.

At the heart of any discussion of rural migration and endogamy lies the question of whether rural communities had yet reached the point of relative decline. Recent opinion suggests that notions of rural depopulation before 1861 are premature.[68] Between 1811 and 1851, the rural population of England increased vigorously, for, whilst agricultural employment rose only modestly, increased agricultural output *per capita* encouraged the rural development of service crafts.[69] Examination of migration and endogamy in rural societies is thus likely to be reasonably representative of some other English regional societies in the mid-nineteenth century.

The example used here to illustrate the extent of that social endogamy and localization is Rutland, or more correctly the registration county of Rutland in the 1851 census. Counties are artifical units of administration, but are convenient spatial measures. Registration counties are less easy to justify, except for the obvious convenience of data collection and analysis. Nevertheless, there is a rationale here, for the two registration districts in question (in common with most such units) consisted of the hinterlands of the principal market towns, in these cases Oakham and Uppingham, neither of which had great urban pretensions and so can be presumed to have been closely related to their rural environs. The registration county comprehended by these two registration districts omits the far east of the county, adjacent to Lincolnshire, and more particularly influenced by Stamford. Included in the analysis, then, are 45 parishes in the county, but 12 are excluded (Figure 5).[70]

Rutland was almost untouched by industrial development, since even staymaking at Caldecott was uniformly rural employment. The single exception, which affected migration patterns at the margins, was the development of the railway through the county. The rail industry attracted longer-distance migrants; 98 male lodgers in rural parishes were employed by the railway, for example, of whom only 10 were born within the county. The most evident longer-distance migration, from Ireland, was closely related to agricultural employment. Rutland is ranked fourth in terms of the proportion of families occupied in agriculture in 1851, at 61.2%, compared with the joint first counties — Bedfordshire, Herefordshire and Huntingdonshire — at 61.9%.[71] By comparison in the adjacent counties of Leicestershire, Northamptonshire, Lincolnshire and Cambridgeshire agriculture provided employment for 35.4, 53.4, 59.4 and 60.7% respectively.[72] In the registration county in 1851, 412 farms required labour, 314 did not; 677 heads of household were farmers and/or graziers, whilst a further 102 were gardeners and nurserymen.[73] Only 26.3% of families were, by contrast, engaged in trade, manufacture of handicraft.[74] Farm servants (living-in agricultural workers on annual contracts) continued at a moderate level in the county; in Rutland they comprised 15–19% of all farm hands, compared with 20–29% in Leicestershire and Lincolnshire, but only 4–9% in Northamptonshire.[75] The predominantly rural, agrarian character of the county is thus evident, reflected also in the composition of the workforce in 1841, for 2,612 of the 7,184 persons whose occupational data were registered were agricultural labourers, almost exclusively male (for only 40 females were thus registered).[76]

In common with several other predominantly agrarian counties in the early nineteenth century, the population of Rutland was increasing, but at a relatively slower rate than in counties with urbanizing and industrializing trends. Subject to opinions as to the accuracy of the census enumerations and calculations of 1801–31, the registration county experienced a demographic increase of 32.55% between 1801 and 1851, by comparison with the faster rate in Leicestershire (75.36%) and Lincolnshire (94.65%).[77] In global terms, the population thus increased from just over 18,000 in 1801–11 to in excess of 24,000 in 1851, in a county which, in 1841, comprised a total area of 97,500 acres or 149 square miles.[78]

In the census of 1851 for Rutland, frequent life-cycle migration is little in evidence. William Towell, registered at Langham (household 97) in 1851, had been born in Oakham, his wife, Alice, in Ayston (although their residences at time of marriage should be determined from the marriage registers); one of their daughters was born in Oakham and one in Somerby (Leicestershire). Joseph Baines, a farmer at Ayston in 1851 (household 82), had been born in Thorpe (Rutland), married Sarah (born in Welham, Lincolnshire), and of their children, two daughters were born in Uppingham, another in Gretton (Northamptonshire) and another and their only son in Preston (Rutland). Such examples of repeated migration, are, however, difficult to elicit; more usual is the case of John Sewell of Langham, linen weaver (household 141), who married Frances, also born in Langham, and whose daughter and five sons were all born there too, or that of George Pick, a labourer in Whissendine in 1851 (household 51), born there, who married Ann, also born there, and whose nine children were also born in the same parish. What these examples qualitatively reflect is that a high proportion of the population of Rutland in 1851 was endogamous, having been born in the place of residence, and that mobility was intensively localized and not often repetitive. Endogamy encouraged stability and extremely localized migration reinforced it.[79] The purpose of the quantitative data presented below is to confirm and nuance these suggestions, with the caveat that they are influenced or biased in the direction of exogamy and longer-distance migration since they comprehend the entire population of the registration county, including landowners, gentry, incumbents of livings and non-beneficed clergy, and professional people.

Over half the male heads of household in the 1851 census for rural parishes in Rutland (excluding Oakham and Uppingham) had been born endogamously, that is they were born in their parish of residence in 1851. Furthermore, over half of those who were exogamous had been born in another parish within the county (Table 3.1). In fine, only 22.3% of male heads of household had not been born within this very compact county. Other social categories (particularly females) tended to be more exogamous in that a higher proportion were not born in their parish of residence in 1851, but even in those cases they were predominantly born within the county, for only 29.6% of female heads and 39.7% of wives of heads had been born outside Rutland.

Table 3.1

Social endogamy and exogamy in rural Rutland in 1851

Endogamous		Exogamous				Exogamous Origins					
				Rutland		Lincs.		Northants.		Leics.	
N	%	N	%	N	%	N	%	N	%	N	%
Male heads (N=2487)											
1295	52.1	1186	47.7	623	52.5	100	8.4	163	13.7	157	13.2
Female heads (N=375)											
122	32.5	251	66.9	140	55.8	22	8.8	36	14.3	31	12.3
Wives of heads (N=2171)											
514	23.6	1646	75.8	784	47.6	169	10.3	213	12.9	287	17.4
Lodgers (male) (N=322)											
73	22.7	239	74.2	55	23.0	22	9.2	27	11.3	38	15.8

Notes: Here and elsewhere 'rural' signifies that Oakham and Uppingham are excluded. Percentages do not always add up to 100% as place of birth of some actors was not specified. In the columns for exogamous origins, percentages refer to the proportion of exogamous actors, not all actors. Here and elsewhere, endogamous signifies birth in the parish of residence, exogamous birth elsewhere, and Rutland birth in another parish in Rutland.

Servants, by their nature, tended too to be less endogamous in these terms, but even so only 28.5% of male servants and 37.4% of female servants had origins outside the small county, whilst 80% of servants in husbandry or living-in farm servants were born within the county (Table 3.2). Since the households of gentry and parochial and nonconformist clergy are included in the analysis, the exogamy of household servants is perhaps slightly exaggerated, since those households recruited servants from other parts of the country and migration of their servants was determined partly by the movement of their employers.

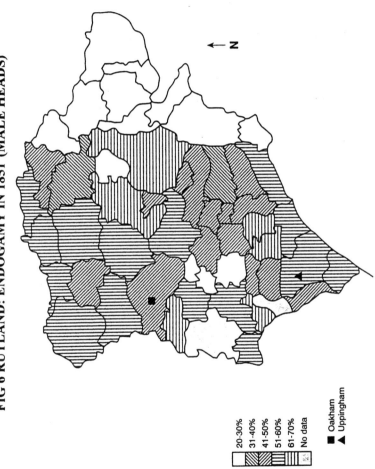

FIG 6 RUTLAND: ENDOGAMY IN 1851 (MALE HEADS)

20-30%
31-40%
41-50%
51-60%
61-70%
No data

■ Oakham
▲ Uppingham

Table 3.2

Endogamy and exogamy of servants in rural Rutland in 1851.

Endogamous		Exogamous		Exogamous Origins							
				Rutland		Lincs.		Northants.		Leics.	
N	%	N	%	N	%	N	%	N	%	N	%
All male (N=568)											
147	25.9	415	73.1	253	61.0	39	9.4	47	11.3	41	9.9
All female (N=643)											
120	18.7	521	81.0	281	54.0	52	10.0	60	11.5	57	10.9
Husbandry (N=246)											
79	32.2	166	67.5	116	69.9	Numbers insignificant						
General (N=755)											
147	19.5	603	79.9	346	57.4	60	10.0	77	12.8	70	11.6

Notes: All represents all categories of servant. Husbandry embraces those described as servant as their status and any of the following as their occupation: agricultural labourer, farm servant or farm labourer. General relates to those simply described as servant, assumed to be household servant, but without a specific description (e.g. butler, groom, housekeeper). Husbandry comprises exclusively males, but general includes both sexes. Servants also include journeymen and apprentices when described as servants in the enumerators' books.

The direction of movement of male heads was predominantly within the county at a localized level. Similar localized patterns were exhibited by those migrants who had origins in Leicestershire and Northamptonshire. Of 609 male heads who migrated internally within the county, 224 (36.8%) were located in 1851 in the parish or village next to their place of birth. Those from Northamptonshire included 22 (14.4%) who moved from a village in Northamptonshire to the next village in Rutland, just across the county boundary. A further 84 (54.9%) moved from a village in Northamptonshire on the county boundary to another village in Rutland and another 21 (13.7%) moved into Rutland from a parish of birth in Northamptonshire within eight miles of the county boundary. The movement from Northamptonshire was thus intensely localized and shallow; it pre-eminently involved movement within the Welland valley and did not extend up into the Northamptonshire Wolds. Some 101 migrants

(66%) from Northamptonshire settled in a parish in Rutland close to the parish boundary: 23 at Barrowden; 12 at Morcott; 12 at Caldecott; 13 at North and 11 at South Luffenham; nine each at Seaton and Lyddington; and seven at Glaston. A considerable proportion had natal origins in a few boundary parishes in Northamptonshire on the Welland's terraces: 31 from Harringworth, 18 from Wakerley and 10 from Gretton. In similar vein, migration from Leicestershire into Rutland mainly derived from contiguous parts of east Leicestershire, an extension of the upland Wolds. Indeed, 41 were born in settlements on the county boundary and another 12 in parishes one settlement removed from that boundary.

Table 3.3

Migration into rural Rutland in 1851 (male heads): descriptive statistics

Direction	mean	trmean	standdev	median	Q1	Q3	min	max	N
From Leics.	8.7	8.1	6.400	7	4	11	1	38	153
From Lincs.	15.5	13.9	13.090	11	6	20	1	58	91
From Northants.	7.5	7.1	5.740	5	3	12	1	30	153
Internal	3.8	3.6	2.307	3	2	5	1	13	609

Notes: Decimals to one place only, except standard deviation.
trmean=trimmed mean (using Minitab, which topslices 5% of the values);
Q1 and Q3=first and third quartiles. Distances are in miles.

Table 3.4

Distances of migrations into rural Rutland in 1851 (male heads).

Miles	From Leics.		From Lincs.		From Northants.		Internal	
	N	%	N	%	N	%	N	%
1–5	66	43.1	15	16.5	77	50.3	498	81.8
6–10	43	28.1	29	31.9	31	20.3	102	16.8
11–15	22	14.4	14	15.4	31	20.3	9	1.5
16–20	12	7.8	12	13.2	11	7.2		
21–25	8	5.2	5	5.5	2	1.3		
26–50	2	1.3	13	14.3	1	0.7		
50+			3	3.3				

Note: Percentages are to one decimal point, so do not add up precisely to 100%.

By contrast, the drift of migration from Lincolnshire was of a different order, for only five exogamous male heads (5.5%) derived from adjacent parishes, although 45 came from parishes close to the county boundary. Nevertheless, migration from Lincolnshire tended to be longer-distance and from deeper within Lincolnshire, which might reflect not only labour and economic opportunities but a developing cultural relationship between Rutland and Lincolnshire.[80] Whilst migration from Lincolnshire was penetrative, that from the two other adjacent counties was essentially shallow and circumscribed.

Immigration into rural parishes was overwhelmingly from other rural communities, reflecting the nature of economic opportunities. Only 11.6% of male migrants into rural parishes had been born in 'urban' communities: 43 in Oakham; 21 in Stamford; 31 in Uppingham; and 22 in other urban places. Preponderantly, they ultimately derived from small market or statute towns, such as Grantham, Melton and Bourne additionally to those listed above, whilst only seven derived from a conurbation (all from Leicester).

The migrational patterns of servants in husbandry (exclusively male) was even more circumscribed than that of male heads of household, excluding that small number which came from Ireland. Internal movement within the county accounted for 121 servants, whilst only 10, 12 and 19 derived respectively from Lincolnshire, Leicestershire and Northamptonshire. A considerable number (51) had moved from their natal parish only to the next parish, although distances from Lincolnshire tended again to be greater (including, for example, journeys of 10, 11, 14, 24, and 26 miles). Mean distance of their movement from parish of birth to that of residence in 1851, however, was only 4.6 miles.[81]

Migration into small towns has been largely neglected, but some comparative date is available for two such towns in adjacent Leicestershire. One, Melton Mowbray, had a similar character to the two small towns in Rutland, Oakham and Uppingham. In Melton in 1851, in-migrants comprised 50.97% of the population, whose mean distance of 'migration' (from place of birth to Melton) was 46.83 kilometres (about 29 miles). Melton is some 11 miles north-west of Oakham in a not dissimilar topographical position. By contrast, in the industrialized small town of Hinckley, in south-west Leicestershire, where hosiery provided considerable employment, in-migrants accounted for only 29.79% of the 'urban' population, mean distance of migration being 42.48 km (26.55 miles).[82]

Table 3.5

Social endogamy and exogamy in two small towns in 1851

				Exogamous Origins							
Endogamous		Exogamous		Rutland		Lincs.		Leics.		Northants.	
N	%	N	%	N	%	N	%	N	%	N	%
Oakham											
Male heads (N=467)											
192	41.1	272	58.2	117	43.0	30	11.0	44	16.2	24	8.8
Female heads (N=101)											
43	42.6	57	56.4	26	45.6	4	7.0	8	14.0	3	15.3
Wives of heads (N=408)											
111	27.2	293	71.8	124	42.3	25	8.5	58	19.8	20	6.8
Male servants (N=79)											
18	22.8	61	77.2	8	45.9	6	9.8	14	23.0	5	8.2
Female servants (N=164)											
37	22.6	127	77.4	83	65.4	8	6.3	9	7.1	11	8.7
Uppingham											
Male heads (N=350)											
178	50.9	172	49.1	52	30.2	22	13.0	24	14.0	38	22.1
Female heads (N=61)											
29	47.5	32	52.5	11	34.4	4	12.5	5	15.6	9	28.1
Wives of heads (N=287)											
90	31.4	197	68.6	66	33.5	24	12.2	26	13.2	37	18.8
Male servants (N=63)											
21	33.3	41	65.1	17	41.5	3	7.3	10	24.4	5	12.2
Female servants (N=119)											
27	22.7	92	77.3	47	51.0	2	2.2	12	13.0	20	21.2

Note: As Table 3.1.

Levels of endogamy in Oakham and Uppingham are closely comparable with those in Melton, with which they shared similar characteristics as small market towns with a high service element for rural hinterlands, although Oakham was additionally a small county town. Social endogamy was greater in Uppingham, the smaller of the two towns, than in Oakham, the county town, which still, however, maintained a high level of endogamy. Of migrants (male heads) into Oakham, 43% derived from within the county, although migrants from within Rutland accounted for only 30% of the social exogamy in Uppingham, perhaps understandably given Oakham's more central position in the county and Uppingham's proximity to the boundary with Northamptonshire. Excluding immigrants born in Ireland (two), Scotland (one) and Africa (one), the mean distance from birthplace of male heads to Oakham was 19.98 miles, whilst into Uppingham it was 23.4 miles.[83] Male and female servants immigrated from slightly shorter distances, respectively means of 13.0 and 16.4 miles to Oakham and 15.3 and 13.8 miles into Uppingham.[84]

Migration from other 'urban' communities was minor, since only 22 male heads originated in cities or large towns and 44 from other small market towns. In fact, as many male heads (69) had origins in parishes within a radius of three miles of Oakham, including 11 from each of Langham and Hambleton; 10 from each of Burley and Braunston; eight from Egleton; and six from each of Ashwell, Barleythorpe and Manton. In terms of distance from birthplace, 40.9% of male heads came from within five miles of Oakham, 56% from within 10 miles, 67% from within 15 miles and 75.8% from within 20 miles, a pattern slightly divergent at Uppingham, where 31.9% derived from within five miles, 48.2% from within 10, and 60.8% from within 15 miles.[85] Whilst Uppingham was characterized by a higher level of social endogamy, yet a larger number of its in-migrants derived from further afield, except for female servants who were predominantly local in origin.[86]

Conclusion

Proposed here then is the notion that, into the middle of the nineteenth century, rural society in Rutland continued to be a 'local social system',[87] not wholly contained within the county boundaries, since all networks spill out, but that the predominant social character of the county was rural social endogamy which was confirmed, rather than dissipated, by intensely localized migration. Identity of interest was engendered by physical attachment to place and locality, but this attachment is considered here not from the positive, idealistic notion of the 'imagined commmmunity', but rather from the more neutral, perhaps even negative, consideration of a 'community by inertia'.[88] The importance of locality and place was enforced by endogamy at the level of both parish and county, whether through immobility or highly circumscribed migration. Further confirmation of local identity ensued from occupational culture, an element of extreme social homogeneity, since livelihoods in the county depended on agriculture. Endogamy, migration and occupational cultures converged and were integral: amongst male farmers and/or graziers, 49.6% were born in their parish of residence in 1851, whilst a further 29.2% had origins in another parish in the county, so that fully 78.8% were born within the county. Amongst female farmers, the respective proportions were 41.7% (parochial endogamy), 30% (born in another parish in the county) and 71.7% (overall endogamy at the level of the county). Of agricultural labourers (exclusively male), 62.1% resided in 1851 in the parish of their birth, 24.4% had another native parish within the county, so that 86.5% had been born within the county. Taking further those employed in Wrigley's 10 occupations which expanded in the countryside in the early nineteenth century, 44.8% had been born in the same parish as their residence in 1851, whilst 24.6% had been born elsewhere in the county, and fully 69.4% thus derived from within the county.[89] Local identity was thus reinforced by both social endogamy and an 'occupational commmunity'.[90] The small towns of Oakham and Uppingham functioned and were situated entirely within that rural social location, sharing its endogamy and migrational patterns.

Some variables not mentioned here probably contributed to the consolidation of local social identity. Nothing has been suggested about the pattern of 'open' and 'closed' parishes, an ambiguous concept in itself.[91] Movement for both subsistence and betterment migration may have depended too on the nature of 'information fields', which might have involved ability to read or at least have access to the news in local newspapers and how the regional nature of those newspapers coincided with and moulded local societies, but with two caveats: how far newspapers provided news of opportunities at this level and how far information passed through other means.[92] Those other means may have included ties of kinship and acquaintance. Those influences seem, however, to be only subsidiary aspects of the general social and occupational endogamy of a rural society which, although it spilled over into adjacent counties, was substantially a social location of its own.

Although some of the boundaries of Leicestershire were more open and traversible, less well defined, migration into the early modern period was circumscribed and also largely internal. This long-term delimited geographical horizon of migration of people controlled also the diffusion of bynames and surnames, which might stand as an ambiguous surrogate indicator of the localization of societies and populations.

Appendix

Endogamy of male heads: parish-level data: rural Rutland, 1851.

Parish	No. of households	No. of male heads	Endogamous male heads	
			N	%
Market Overton	99	83	47	56.6
Thistleton	30	25	13	52.0
Stretton	44	35	16	45.7
Greetham	140	120	46	38.3
Cottesmore	111	92	48	52.2
Barrow	27	25	13	52.0
Teigh	33	28	14	50.0
Burley	43	34	18	52.9
Ashwell	51	46	23	50.0
Exton	165	145	101	69.7
Tickencote/Horn	26	23	5	21.7
Empingham	182	151	106	70.2
Whitwell	30	24	11	45.8
Edith Weston	80	67	32	47.8
Lyndon	23	19	4	21.1
Manton	63	53	23	43.4
Brooke	20	17	9	52.9
Martinsthorpe	1	1	0	—
Gunthorpe	2	2	0	—
Egleton	33	27	15	55.6
Hambleton	62	52	28	53.9
Barleythorpe	43	35	14	40.0
Langham	151	128	73	57.0
Whissendine	176	145	77	53.1
Braunston	102	79	50	63.3

Parish	No. of households	No. of male heads	Endogamous male heads	
			N	%
Ridlington	61	53	31	58.5
Leigh	5	5	4	—
Belton	92	81	42	51.9
Wardley	13	12	8	66.7
Preston	74	58	28	48.3
Ayston	21	19	5	26.3
Bisbrooke	53	43	27	62.8
Lyddington	132	100	53	53.0
Stoke Dry	12	10	5	50.0
Beaumont Chase	3	3	0	—
Caldecott	73	61	34	55.7
Seaton	75	61	32	52.5
Thorpe by Water	20	19	9	47.3
Barrowden	145	124	67	54.0
Morcott	123	94	42	44.7
Glaston	57	53	21	39.6
Wing	92	65	30	46.2
Pilton	6	4	0	—
S. Luffenham	*	75	33	44.0
N. Luffenham	*	89	36	40.5

Note: Endogamy is by parish, that is, the place of birth is the parish of residence.

* The enumeration of households in these two villages was taken together by the enumerators, comprising 192 households in the two villages. The percentage of endogamous male heads is as a proportion of all male heads.

References

[1] P Clark and D Souden, eds., *Migration and Society in Early Modern England*, (London, 1987), ('Introduction') 11–48.

[2] P McClure, 'Patterns of migration in the late middle ages: the evidence of English place-name surnames', *Economic History Review*, 2nd ser., 32 (1979), 167–82; M Kowaleski, *Local Markets and Regional Trade in Medieval Exeter*, (Cambridge, 1995), 84–6; S A C Penn, 'The origins of Bristol migrants in the early fourteenth century:

the surname evidence', *Transactions of the Bristol and Gloucestershire Archaeological Society*, 101 (1983), 123–30; S H Rigby, *Medieval Grimsby. Growth and Decline*, (Hull, 1993), 20–3.

3 A Kussmaul, 'The ambiguous mobility of farm servants', *Economic History Review*, 2nd ser., 34 (1981), 222–35; R M Smith, 'Hypothèses sur la nuptialité en Angleterre aux xiiie–xive siècles', *Annales ESC*, 38 (1983), 128–9.

4 A Mitson, 'The significance of kinship networks in the seventeenth century: south-west Nottinghamshire' in C Phythian-Adams, ed., *Societies, Cultures and Kinship, 1580–1850. Cultural Provinces and English Local History*, (London, 1993), 24–76.

5 H Jones, *Population Geography*, (2nd edn., London, 1990), 178–228.

6 Ex inf. Dr R M Smith; E D Jones, 'Villein mobility in the later middle ages: the case of Spalding Priory', *Nottingham Medieval Studies*, 36 (1992), 149–66; see also, R K Field, 'Migration in the later middle ages: the case of the Hampton Lovett villeins', *Midland History*, 8 (1983), 29–48.

7 C Phythian-Adams, 'Introduction: an agenda for English Local History' in *Societies, Cultures and Kinship*, 1–23.

8 G Kristensson, *Studies on the Early Fourteenth Century Population of Lindsey*, (Royal Society of Letters, Scripta Minora, Lund, 1976–7).

9 A DeWindt, 'Redefining the peasant community in medieval England: the regional perspective', *Journal of British Studies*, 26 (1987), 163–207.

10 J A Raftis, *Tenure and Mobility. Studies in the Social History of the Mediaeval English Village*, (Toronto, 1964).

11 B A Hanawalt, *Crime and Conflict in English Communities 1300–1348*, (London, 1979).

12 Bodl. MS Laud Misc 625, fos. 54r, 56r, 81r, 82r, 124r, 131r, 133r, 134r, 138r, 141v, 180v, 211r. For example, [Thurmaston] 'Habemus ibidem visum franciplegii de omnibus tenentibus nostris cum omnibus libertatibus ad eum pertinentibus ad quem venient omnes nostri tenentes de Thurmaston de Hows de Kyrkby Bellers Gadsby Croxton Quenyboro Barkby Thorp Cosington Barkby' (fo. 141r.); [Hose] 'Iidem ij tenentes venient cum dicto Roberto ad visum nostrum de Thurmodeston' (fo. 211r).

13 See below.

14 Bodl. MS Laud Misc 625, fo. 215r.

15 'Hec sunt ville in quibus infra breue natiuos habuimus sicut patet in Rotulis nostris curialibus in quibus curiis presentatum fuit ubi tunc manserunt diuersi natiui nostri.'

16 'morans apud Frysby uel Wyginston'.

17 C Phythian-Adams, *Desolation of a City: Coventry and the Urban Crisis of the Late Middle Ages*, (Cambridge, 1979).

18 For Alderwas, at an earlier time, H Graham, 'A social and economic study of the late medieval peasantry: Alrewas, Staffordshire, in the fourteenth century', unpublished PhD thesis, University of Birmingham, 1994.

19 For example, PRO SC2/183/52 (Breedon on the Hill): 'Johannes filius Roberti Watteson Henricus frater eius Thomas frater [eius] natiui manent extra dominium'. Owston Abbey knew only that six named 'natiui et fugitiui domini manent extra dominium sine licencia' (PRO SC2/183/87).

20 PRO SC2/183/77 (Kibworth Beauchamp): 'Auicia et Alicia filie Roberti Balle habent licenciam comorandi extra dominium ubicunque voluerint', for which they paid 8*d*, 'et non plus quia pauperes'.

21 MM 6384.

22 MM 6404-6410; C Howell, *Land, Family and Inheritance in Transition: Kibworth Harcourt 1280-1700*, (Cambridge, 1983), 44-7.

23 MM 6420: 'Preceptum est proximo consanguineo videlicet Johanni Gud ʒ er reducere [Robertum God ʒ er] infra hoc dominium citra proximam'; MM 6422: 'ideo Willelmus Herry frater dicti Johannis Herry in misericordia domini quia non reducit ipsum infra dominium'; MM 6421: 'Ideo preceptum est Johanni Carter patri eorum [of John and Thomas Carter] eos reducere sub pena.' But compare MM 6420: William Harry: 'natiuus domini se elongat extra hoc dominium et moram trahit apud Tyrlington sine licencia domini Et nullum habet consanguineum infra hoc dominium qui eum reducere potest.'

24 MM 6570 (1287): ' "Matill" et Agnes filie Hugonis Fraunceys venerunt in curia et habent licenciam se maritandi ubicunque voluerunt. Et dant domino pro licencia habenda .ij.s.' Compare MM 6565: 'Quia Willelmus filius Roggeri de Syston' non venit in libertatem dominorum quorum custumarius ipse est set se subtraxit de dominis suis et est in seruicio extra libertatem ideo preceptum est facere ipsum venire cognossendi dominos suorum (*sic*) et capiendi ab eis licenciam seruiendi ubi voluerit' (similar date).

25 MM 6570: William Carpenter 'invenit plegios . . . quod veniet ad proximam Curiam satisfaciendo dominis pro Matillde sorore sua desponsata apud Warrum sine licencia'; 'Inquisicio facta de Catallis et bonis que Matill' Carpentar' habuit die quo perexit

apud sanctum andream in Scocia quia maritatur dudum extra
libertatem dominorum sine licencia . . .' R Faith, 'Seignorial control
of women's marriage', *Past & Present*, 99 (1983), 133–48.

26 MM 6576–6579. Heryng's surname remained in Barkby: 'Ideo
preceptum est Roberto Heryng Auunculo quod ipsum reducat
citra proximam sub pena . . . set est dubium utrum est (*sic*) natiuus
necne et ideo pena non posuit in certum' — thus his legal and
personal status was unclear. Seven years after Heryng's migration
to Queniborough, he had disappeared: 'ut dicitur manet extra
dominium ubi nescitur' (MM 6579).

27 MM 6570.

28 MM 6577.

29 MM 6580.

30 MM 6584.

31 MM 6588.

32 P D A Harvey, *A Medieval Oxfordshire Village. Cuxham 1240 to 1400*,
(Oxford, 1965), 48, 87.

33 MM 6563: 'fecit finem apud Couxham pro terra patris sui pro
ingressu habendo .vj.s. viij.d.'

34 MM 6563: Richard *prepositus* required to find pledges '. . . eo quod
uxor sua culpauit quemdam hominem quia iuit apud Oxonias
[*sic*] pro terra empta quondam Thome molendinarii.'

35 MM 6404.

36 For example, William de Hamelton's, reeve's, account MM 6572,
which includes the journeys mentioned above; seven visits were
made to Oxford.

37 MM 6370: 'Extencio manerii': [virgaters] 'et cariabunt cum j equo
proprio bladum domini ad forum Leyc' et non ulterius nisi infra
Comitatum' — perhaps the implication was that they should
carry within the county no further than the distance to Leicester,
that is within the south of the county.

38 MM 6404.

39 MM 6404.

40 MM 6407: 'in foro de Lutterworth'.

41 D Postles, 'An English small town in the later middle ages:
Loughborough', *Urban History*, 20 (1993), 21.

42 MM 6603: 'Ideo incurrat penam de .xl.d.'

43 MM 6605: 'Item Ordinatum est in plena Curia per Avisamentum
Senescalli quod si Aliquis Tenens infra dominium predictum
prosecutus fuerit Aliquem visinorum suorum nisi in ista predicta

Curia quod soluet seu supportabit dominis istius dominii tociens quociens sic[ut?] prosecutus fuerit .vj.s.viij.d.'

44 MM 6408: 'et non plus quia pauper.'

45 MM 6407.

46 PRO SC2/183/77: 'Johannes filius Johannis Asteyn Natiuus domini habet licenciam desponsandi Agnetem Smyth apud Kybworth Harcort Et dat domino de chiuagio per Annum .ij.d.'

47 *Chancery Miscellanea Part IV*, (List and Index Society, 38, 1968); references are to file numbers given in this volume.

48 *Ibid.*, file 2/34.

49 *Ibid.*, file 3/78.

50 The trimmed mean in this case, using Minitab, omits the top and bottom 5% of values.

51 M Gollancz, ed., *Rolls of the Northamptonshire Sessions of the Peace*, (Northamptonshire Record Society 11, 1940), 56, 83.

52 R Sillein, ed., *Some Sessions of the Peace in Lincolnshire 1360–1375*, (Lincoln Record Society 30, 1937), 90–1.

53 *Ibid.*, 169.

54 For what follows, C J M Moxon, 'Ashby-de-la-Zouche: a social and economic survey of a market town, 1570–1720', unpublished D.Phil, Oxford, 1971. The Hastings family's influence declined in the late seventeenth century: *ibid.*, 37.

55 *Ibid.*, 25–6, 38.

56 *Ibid.*, 26, 37–8.

57 *Ibid.*, 68.

58 *Ibid.*, 60–6.

59 T Hardy, *The Mayor of Casterbridge*, (Harmondsworth, 1994), 1–19, 183–5, 367–71; the evidence of the hiring fair at Casterbridge has also been used to make different points by M Roberts, ' "Waiting upon chance": English hiring fairs and their meanings from the 14th to the 20th century', *Journal of Historical Sociology*, 1 (1988), 121–3, who also alludes to the tramping of Gabriel Oakes (in *Far from the Madding Crowd*) after his misfortunes as an independent shepherd.

60 A Kussmaul, 'The ambiguous mobility of farm servants'.

61 Compare also E J Buckatszch, 'Places of origin of a group of immigrants into Sheffield, 1624–1799', *Economic History Review*, 2nd ser., 2 (1949–50), 303–6, where two-thirds of immigrants derived from within a radius of 21 miles of this developing market

town, and, for some general comments, D B Grigg, 'E. G. Ravenstein and the "Laws of Migration" ', repr. in M Drake, ed., *Time, Family and Community. Perspectives on Family and Community History*, (Oxford, 1994), 147-64.

[62] M Anderson, *Family Structure in Nineteenth Century Lancashire*, (Cambridge, 1971), 37.

[63] *Ibid.*, 34, but a phenomenon also noted, perhaps, by J Langton, 'The industrial revolution and the regional geography of England', *Transactions of the Institute of British Geographers*, n.s., 9 (1984), 145-67, and summarized by R A Butlin in R A Dodgshon and R A Butlin, eds.; *An Historical Geography of England and Wales*, (2nd edn, London, 1990), 243-6.

[64] M Anderson, 'Indications of population change and stability in nineteenth-century cities: some sceptical comments' in J H Johnson and C G Pooley, eds., *The Structure of Nineteenth-Century Cities*, (London, 1982), 283-98; P N Jones, *Mines, Migrants and Residence in the South Wales Steamcoal Valleys: The Ogmore and Garw Valleys in 1881*, (Occasional Papers in Geography, 25, University of Hull, 1987). See also, however, the preliminary results of migration patterns from the National Sample of the 1851 census reported by M Anderson, 'The social implications of demographic change' in F M L Thompson, ed., *The Cambridge Social History of Britain 1750-1950: volume 2: People and their Environment*, (Cambridge, 1990), 11-12.

[65] H R Southall, 'The tramping artisan revisits: labour mobility and economic distress in early Victorian England', *Economic History Review*, 2nd ser., 44 (1991), 273.

[66] D Friedlander and R J Roshier, 'A study of internal migration in England and Wales, part I', *Population Studies*, 19 (1966), 239-79; and D Bains, *Migration in a Mature Economy. Emigration and Internal Migration in England and Wales, 1861-1900*, (Cambridge, 1985), especially ch. 8, but which again concentrates mainly on rural-urban migration at the time of rural depopulation.

[67] S A Royle, 'Aspects of nineteenth-century small town society: a comparative study from Leicestershire', *Midland History*, 5 (1979-80), provides very helpful comparative material for this present study, which involves the small towns of Oakham and Uppingham, and since one of Royle's towns (Melton Mowbray) was very much within a rural context; C S Hallas, 'Migration in nineteenth-century Wensleydale and Swaledale', *Northern History*, 27 (1991),

139-61, concerns rural communities whose relative decline was already evident, because of the demise of the leadmining industry.

68 E A Wrigley, 'Men on the land and men in the countryside: employment in agriculture in early nineteenth-century England' in L Bonfield, R Smith and K Wrightson, eds., *The World We Have Gained. Histories of Population and Social Structure*, (Oxford, 1986), 295-336; R Samuel, 'Village labour', repr. in P Thane and A Sutcliffe, eds., *Essays in Social History*, vol. 2, (Oxford, 1986), 79, 84-5.

69 Wrigley, 'Men on the land', 300-1, esp. Table 11.2; see also the comments of R Lawton in Dodgshon and Butlin, eds., *An Historical Geography*, 302-5.

70 PRO HO107/2092-2093. Omitted from the analysis are then Clipsham, Pickworth, Essendine, Great Casterton, Little Casterton, Tinwell, Ketton, Ryhall and Belmesthorpe. Parts of Stamford were in Lincolnshire, Northamptonshire and Rutland. Whilst some of the census data abstracted in British Parliamentary Papers have been used, much of the analysis is reworking the original data in dBase III+, since the surname data had in any case to be entered and some further refinement could also be achieved. In analyzing the data, the main concern has been to investigate in great detail the movements of the population at risk to *decide* to migrate; in that sense, child dependants of families have not been included — such as through migration and age distribution — since their migration was determined by the movement of their parents. The statistics have largely been produced using Minitab, which will explain, for example, the nature of the trimmed mean where cited.

71 Wrigley, 'Men on the land', 326, Table 11.9.

72 *Ibid*.

73 *Ibid.*, 310-11, Table 11.5.

74 *Ibid.*, 326, Table 11.9.

75 A Kussmaul, *Servants in Husbandry in Early Modern England*, (Cambridge, 1981), 20, Fig. 2.3.

76 *Parliamentary Papers*, 1841, 148.

77 *Parliamentary Papers*, 18 (1831), Tables V, VII and IX; for recent deliberations on the accuracy of the 1801 abstracts, E A Wrigley and R S Schofield, *The Population History of England 1541-1871. A Reconstruction*, (Cambridge, pb edition, 1989), 122-6.

78 Demographic decline occurred after the peak of 1851, the

population falling to just under 22,000 in 1861 and then falling through the rest of the late nineteenth century to below 20,000 in 1901.

[79] A rather exotic comparison is G Bouchard, 'Mobile populations, stable communities: Saguenay, 1840–1911', *Continuity and Change*, 6 (1991), 59–86; closer to home, M R Bouquet, *Family, Servants and Visitors*, (Norwich, 1985), found very similar conditions in mid-nineteenth-century Hartland, Devon.

[80] C V Phythian-Adams, 'Introduction' in *Societies, Cultures and Kinship*.

[81] Trimmed mean 4.0 miles, standard deviation 4.131, median 2 miles.

[82] Royle, 'Aspects of nineteenth-century small town society'.

[83] Oakham: standard deviation 30.53, but the trimmed mean was 15.5 miles and the median distance only 9 miles. Uppingham: standard deviation 32.11 and trimmed mean 19.3 miles. The respective values for female heads were: (Oakham) mean 23.5 miles, trimmed mean 16.7 miles, standard deviation 42.07, median 8 miles; (Uppingham) mean 16.03 miles, trimmed mean 11.3 miles, standard deviation 24.12, median 7 miles. Values are omitted for one male head and two male servants at Uppingham whose place of birth was entered as simply 'Scotland'.

[84] Oakham: (males) trimmed mean 9.9 miles, standard deviation 19.73, median 6 miles and (females) trimmed mean 11.5 miles, standard deviation 29.62, median 6 miles; Uppingham (males) trimmed mean 11.3 miles, standard deviation 23.90, median 7 miles and (females) trimmed mean 9.5 miles, standard deviation 25.27, median 4 miles.

[85] For other social categories, the values are as follows:

	within 5 miles	within 10 miles	Within 15 miles
Oakham			
female heads	40.0	56.4	65.5
male servants	49.2	71.2	78.0
female servants	47.2	74.0	81.1
Uppingham			
female heads	43.3	60.0	73.3
male servants	48.7	64.1	74.4
female servants	64.1	79.4	82.6

[86] See figures in previous note.

[87] G Crow and G Allan, *Community Life. An Introduction to Local Social Relations*, (London, 1994), 193, for this phrase, which is less emotive than 'community'. For how that social organisation might have been influenced by the earlier origins of Rutland as a distinct territory, C Phythian-Adams, 'Rutland reconsidered' in A Dornier, ed., *Mercian Studies*, (Leicester, 1977), 63–84.

[88] Z Bauman, *Intimations of Postmodernism*, (London, 1992), xix.

[89] For the list of occupations (masons, tailors, bricklayers, butchers *et al.*), Wrigley, 'Men on the land'. The calculation here is slightly problematic, since a small number of heads pursued 'dual occupations', usually as farmer and a by-employment (for example, farmer and publican in some cases). For the purpose here, I have omitted from the figures dual occupations and only counted single occupations given in the census, although they may not represent the full truth of occupational status.

[90] Again, no emotive nuance is placed on the term 'community'. For the phrase 'occupational community', see, for example, Crow and Allan, *Community Life*, 78.

[91] See most recently S J Banks, 'Nineteenth-century scandal or twentieth-century model? A new look at "open" and "close" parishes', *Economic History Review*, 2nd ser., 41 (1988), 51–71.

[92] For some general comments on migration patterns and motives, see the editors' introduction to Clark and Souden, *Migration and Society*, 11–48. The distinction between subsistence and betterment in the context of nineteenth-century migration within a rural society is perhaps ambivalent. For the influence of newspapers, see the résumé by L Brown, *Victorian News and Newspapers*, (Oxford, 1985).

CHAPTER 4

THE DEVELOPMENT
OF HEREDITARY SURNAMES

Although the development of hereditary surnames involved a process of diffusion down through social groups, the rate of change was also regionally varied. Moreover, within social groups, some kinship groups were attributed hereditary surnames before others; the transition was not uniform within social groups and even within social groups the pace of change was variable.[1] In general the important process concerned the change of emphasis from the personal name (*nomen*) — in the case of pre-Conquest nomenclature often the single name — to include the byname (*cognomen*) and finally the hereditary surname.[2] Although the byname allowed a second qualifying name additional to the *nomen* or personal name, the byname retained the character of an idionym, in that it was not necessarily hereditary and, indeed, an individual might be known in different circumstances (and records) by different bynames. The byname remained inherently unstable, whereas the surname represented the kinship and family rather than just the individual.

The nobility

In 1066, a few English thegns had been attributed a byname, *cognomen* or patronymic description according to the Leicestershire sections of *Domesday Book*. Alwin Pbochestan held Birstall, Edwin Alferd held at Kibworth Beauchamp, Leofric *filius Leuuini* at Stathern and in the soke of Melton, and Alric *filius Meriet* at Husbands Bosworth.[3] Those thegns, however, who continued to hold as mesne tenants in 1086, were identified in *Domesday Book* simply by an insular personal name without a byname, such as Æthelelm at Hoby, Ælmar at Fenny Drayton and Alfsi at Swinford.[4] Altogether, more than 30 mesne tenants in 1086 were known in *Domesday Book* by an insular personal name without a byname. English comital tenants were identified by their title and personal name, as Countess Alveva (1066), Countess Godiva (1086), Earl Morcar (1066), Earl Waltheof

(1086) and even Harold Godwinsone, described as Earl Harold (1086). This pattern is replicated in *Domesday Book* for Rutland, in which the 19 principal tenants of 1066 were accorded only a personal name or *nomen*, without a byname, although three were dignified by a title.[5]

Although the new Anglo-Norman tenants in chief were attributed bynames, even hereditary surnames, in *Domesday Book*, that form of address did not extend to all levels of the new nobility. In its description of Anglo-Norman mesne tenants, those of knightly status, *Domesday Book* emphatically referred to the *nomen*, the real name. It is possible, however, that this form of identification of substantial knights and mesne tenants was determined by the nature of the record and the tenurial relationships inherent in it, so that *cognomina* were unnecessary, even if they existed at that social level at that time. By the tenurial relationship in Domesday, mesne tenants were sufficiently identified by their real name and their relationship to superior lords. More detailed information was unnecessary for the purposes of this record. Nevertheless, the emphasis was firmly directed to the personal name.

Even in the case of some tenants in chief, no further identification was imperative, had it existed, since title or status and real name sufficed. Thus Earl Aubrey (de Vere) held at Knaptoft *et alibi* and Earl Hugh (of Chester) the soke of Barrow on Soar, recently acquired from William, formerly the estate of Earl Harold. Comital status thus dispensed with a *cognomen* in this record at this time.

Most other tenants in chief were, however, attributed a byname in *Domesday Book*, such as Geoffrey Alselin, Drogo de Beurere (de la Beuvrière), Mainer and Oger Brito, and, despite comital status, Earl Hugh de Graintesmesnil. Of 27 tenants in chief, consequently, 25 received some form of *cognomen*, 14 of whom had acquired toponymic *cognomina* derived from their continental fees. Similarly in Rutland, nine of 11 tenants in chief were identified with bynames, the other two being identified by their comital status.

Inferentially, therefore, these toponymic bynames referring back to continental fees were already becoming hereditary in the late eleventh century, if not before.[6] Only two tenants in chief in Leicestershire assumed toponymic titles from their English holdings (Stafford and Chester). Reflecting the continental toponyms was Graintesmesnil, from Le Grand-Mesnil, the *caput* of the Norman honour in Calvados (arrondissement Lisieux, canton St Pierre-sur-Dives), although this particular name was not longevious in Leicestershire or, indeed, England. Similarly fleeting was de Todeni, from Tosny (Eure, arr. Louviers, cant. Gaillon), for the honour of Belvoir in the late eleventh century.[7] In contrast, only a small number of these bynames represented office: *camerarius, dispensator, hostiarius*, and the metonymic nickname *buenvalet*, whilst the residue consisted of nicknames, such as Pev(e)rel, or appositional patronyms, although these last were a minority.

The record sources, however, do not fully reflect the *cognomina* of the Anglo-Norman aristocracy, particularly in the case of the two principal comital families, the earls of Chester from the late eleventh century and the earls of Leicester from the early twelfth. The *cognomina* associated with the earls of Chester were not recorded in Domesday or in many other records, such as the earls' charters, since their comital style was sufficient. Earl Hugh of Avranches (c.1071–1101) was the hereditary *viscomte* of the Avranchin (dépt Manche), as was the second earl, Richard (1101–20), but, in the circumstances of the formation of the earl of Chester, the English title was ascendant. Both Ranulf I (1120–29) and II (1129–53) were accorded bynames, respectively *le Meschin* and *de Gernons*, although again comital style was sufficient in formal records.[8]

Meanwhile, the Graintemesnil fees were transferred to Robert, count of Meulan, then to one of his sons, another Robert, and afterwards to his son, a further Robert. These new earls of Leicester, the first three Roberts, were designated in the records not by the family name of Beaumont, but rather by their style, as earl Robert and earls of Leicester, even in their own *acta*, although it is known that contemporary commentators also knew them informally by nickname *cognomina*. These *cognomina* are repeated, for example, in the sections of commentary in the rentals of Leicester Abbey, founded by Robert II. The thirteenth-century compiler, Pyn, referred back to the founder as Robert [le] Bossu and to Robert III as Robert *filius Petronille*. More pertinently, Geryn's rental of 1341 enumerated all the nicknames of the successive earls: Robert le Boczeu, founder of the Abbey, succeeded by his son, Robert *as Blanchesmeyns*, who married Petronilla, whose issue comprised three sons and two daughters, of whom the eldest son was nicknamed Robert *filius Petronille* to distinguish him from the previous Roberts.[9]

Ipse [sic] quoque Roberto defuncto successit ei Robertus le Boczeu
filius et heres eiusdem et de consilio domini Alexandri tunc Episcopi
Lync' et aliorum discretorum fundauit Abbatiam istam de pratis
Leyc' transferens possessiones et prebendas dicte Ecclesie sancte
Marie de Castro cum omnibus aliis Redditibus et possessionibus
suis in usum canonicorum istius Abbathie Qui quidem Robertus de
consensu Amicie uxoris sue sumpsit in Abbathia ista habitum
nostre religionis uiuens iuste et sancte quindecim Annis et
amplius ... Isto Roberto fundatore nostro defuncto successit ei in
hereditatem Robertus filius eius et vocabatur Robertus as Blanches
meyns qui Robertus accepit in uxorem Petronillam filiam Hugonis
de Grantmeynil cum honore de Hynkelee et aliis possessionibus
ipsius Hugonis quas habuit in Anglia et extunc Primo Honor de
Hynkelee coniunctus Comitatui Leycestr' Et ex dicta Petronilla
genuit tres filios et duas filias scilicet Robertum qui vocabatur
Robertus filius Petronille ad differenciam predictorum ...[10]

Mesne tenants and knights

In 1086, at least 42 mesne tenants in Leicestershire were described simply by their 'forename' and their tenurial relationship to a superior lord, whilst 18 were attributed some further description or *cognomen*. Of these 18, however, six constituted tenants in chief holding other fees as mesne tenants. The remaining 12 mesne tenants bore either patronymic *cognomina* (six) or appositional patronyms (four), although one received a toponymic byname. So also in Rutland, only four of 14 mesne tenants were attributed bynames.[11]

The territorial organization of the 'Leicesterhshire Survey' of *c.*1130 required more definite identification than the tenurial arrangement of *Domesday Book*.[12] Virtually all mesne tenants, as well as tenants in chief, were accorded a byname in the Survey, so that 34 mesne tenants had bynames whereas only five others were simply identified by a 'forename': Ansketil at Husbands Bosworth and Kibworth Harcourt (the *antecessor* of the Harcourt family);[13] Eustace at Thorpe Langton; Thomas at Hoby and Thrussington; Walkelin at Donisthorpe; and William at Slawston. By 1166, in the *Carte Baronum* returning knights' fees in Leicestershire and Rutland, all 33 tenants of fees were accorded bynames, as also were the many more tenants of full fees or parts of fees enumerated in the returns of 1235–36 (there being no extant returns for the two counties in 1212).[14]

The preponderance of bynames of these mesne tenants in the twelfth century, as well as of tenants in chief, was toponymic, predominantly relating back to fees of origin in Normandy. Such bynames were mainly hereditary, amongst tenants in chief *ab initio* in the two counties, and amongst mesne tenants by the early twelfth century. Nevertheless, patronymic *cognomina* remained unstable until the middle of the twelfth century, examples including the *antecessores* of the Harcourt and Foxton families.

In about 1130, Ansketil (or Anschetil with its Norman influence) held fees in Husbands Bosworth and Kibworth Harcourt; he was one of the eight sons of Robert *filius Ansketilli* (decd. 1118) and succeeded to the English lands of the patrimony. His brother, William, was mentioned in the Pipe Roll of 1130 as William *filius Roberti filii Anschetili* and Ansketil was singularly known in that record as Anschetill de Herolcurt. On Ansketil's death, without issue, his brother, Ivo de Harcourt acceded to the English lands, assuming the surname given as an affix to the Leicestershire manor, and that name became henceforth the hereditary family surname associated with this lordship and honorial baronage of the earldom of Leicester.[15] By 1148/9, the style de Haruecurt was employed in the charters of Ivo and his brother, William, particularly in two charters to Garendon Abbey.[16]

Also of knightly status, the lordship of Foxton (actually described as a *baronia* in charters of the early thirteenth century) had a similar instability of associated byname through the early twelfth century.[17] Charters relating to the advowson of five churches in Leicestershire and Rutland granted to Daventry Priory allow a reconstruction of the naming of the family. Robert *filius Vitalis alias filius Violi* had issue two sons, Simon *filius Roberti* (*c*.1148–66) and Jordan *filius Roberti filii Violi*; Simon was the progenitor of Richard *filius Simonis de Foxtona* (*c*.1160–89), who produced a son Richard *filius Ricardi de Foxton'* (*c*.1210). The patronymic *cognomen* thus continued to be unstable throughout the first half of the twelfth century.[18]

Perhaps in contrast the nickname-surname Putrel seems to have become hereditary during the early twelfth century, if not before. The deficiencies of *Domesday Book* may be illustrated, since mesne tenants were there identified merely by a 'forename' and their tenurial relationship to a tenant in chief, as in the case of the Earl of Chester's subinfeudated tenants in north Leicestershire, who included Robert Putrel.[19] A confirmation charter of the Earl, however, presumed to have been issued 1071x1081, affirmed grants by the Earl's honorial baronage to the abbey of St Evroul, including tithes in Leicestershire endowed by Robert Pultrel by that description.[20] Unfortunately, the authenticity of the charter cannot be established, although the events recorded almost certainly occurred. Since, however, the charter survives in a form transcribed into the history written by Orderic Vitalis, the byname or surname was in common currency by the middle of the twelfth century. Furthermore, its common acceptance in the north of the shire is established in the late twelfth century by a grant in Hoton and Prestwold attested by Robert Putrel of Cotes, who additionally witnessed two other charters, of *c*.1200, relating to Cotes and Hoton.[21] The establishment of the surname in the north of the county is confirmed by numerous references in the cartulary of Garendon Abbey to attestations and grants by Putrels in the late twelfth century.[22] Moreover, a charter of 1184 concerning rents in Diseworth was attested by Henry Putrel.[23] Some forms of byname, therefore, allowed earlier heritability than others, even amongst the mesne tenantry and knightly families.

The peasantry

Although it seems evident that hereditary surnames developed amongst the free peasantry before the unfree, the sources, even manorial surveys, for the two counties are insufficiently precise about legal status to allow a clear differentiation of the evolution of hereditary surnames by status. Nevertheless, some documents, such as charters, were by implication legally reserved to the free and, although we cannot be conclusively sure that they were so restricted in practice, these documents provide some distinction by legal status. Moreover some, by no means all, manorial surveys did designate the customary tenantry.

In the early twelfth century, bynames had not been absorbed into the culture of naming of the peasantry, regardless of status, in Leicestershire. Two of the earliest extant manorial surveys, those of the Burton Abbey estates (Surveys A and B, *c*.1114x26) included one manor in north-west Leicestershire, on the county boundary at Appleby Magna.[24] The earlier of the two surveys enumerated 25 tenants and an indeterminate number of *filii Alurici*, of whom eight tenants were *censarii*, 14 villeins and three cotsets. Twelve held the standard holding, a virgate. Of all these tenants, only Godwin *prepositus*, the tenant of two and a half virgates and a *censarius*, was attributed a description other than a 'forename'. The second survey provides less information, but it is significant that one of the two Richards was differentiated from the other simply by the adjective *alter* (*alter Ricardus*), which suggests that, at least in written manorial records, bynames had not been assimilated into the naming processes of the peasantry.

Comprehending lands in the two counties, the Templars Inquest of 1185 constitutes the next point of reference. Incorporating disparate properties, the estate of the Templars included tenants at Tickencote (one tenant), Empingham (11), Greetham (three), Wymondham (one), and Sewstern (four), located in north-east Leicestershire and Rutland; most of these tenants held a standard holding of one bovate, which, although their status is not revealed, would suggest that they might have been unfree.[25] Of the total of 20 peasants, only three bore *cognomina*, in each case descriptive of exceptional status, and so possibly all three were free: Ascelin *sacerdos* at Tickencote; Odo *diaconus* at Empingham; and Richard de Sewsterne at Sewstern. Even in 1185, then, bynames were unusual amongst the peasantry in record sources.

By 1212, that situation may have altered radically, for the description of some tenants in Worthington and Newbold in north-west Leicestershire presents a different pattern.[26] All 11 tenants were attributed bynames, although their status is not defined. Subsequent confirmation of this change derives from the lay subsidy for the vill of Stathern in the north-east of Leicestershire, in which all 26 contributors, including, it must be presumed, peasant taxpayers, received bynames in the list.[27]

The difficulty of the last source resides in its imposition and collection by central authority, which might have influenced the method of identification. Taken, however, with the list of the tenantry of Newbold and Worthington, it does provide incontrovertible evidence of the use of bynames in the identification of the peasantry in written sources by the early thirteenth century. Manorial surveys during the thirteenth century expand upon that customary practice.

Compiled between 1225 and 1258, the survey of the Bishop of Lincoln's estate included some large manors in Leicestershire and Rutland. At Lyddington were listed 49 tenants with an additional two at Caldecott; although their status is not clearly described, 14 appear to have been customary tenants, five free, and 30 specifically enumerated as cottars. Of the 14 assumed to be customary tenants, merely two did not receive a byname, presumably because their forenames were less usual in the local context (Norman and Alexander). All five freemen were identified by a byname and only one of the cottars, perhaps because of his insular personal name (Alured), was without a byname.

Just to the north of Leicester, in Thurmaston, all 26 tenants of the Bishop were accorded bynames, with the exception of the idiosyncratically named Langefer and Ailnoht. To the north-east, in the Wreake Valley at Asfordby near Melton Mowbray, 49 tenants, of undefined status, held land from the Bishop, and of whom 34 might have constituted customary tenants since they held standard holdings of half a virgate. Only six appeared without a byname, again some perhaps because their forenames were less frequent on the manor (Humfrey, Gamel, Thengo, Silvester, and Colmus [*sic*], although hardly the Roger). With the exception of Roger, the pattern is confirmed of normative use of bynames unless the forename was distinctive in the local context.[28]

Almost contemporaneously (compiled *c*.1245), the custumal of the soke of Rothley generally confirms the patterns exhibited in the Bishop's survey, but naming processes were more complex in the Rothley custumal because of the more complicated territorial and social organization. Out of 559 tenants, 465 were identified by a recognizable form of byname, but the description of the other 94 was complicated by the custom of partible inheritance, resulting in their relationship as joint tenants of holdings. This small proportion was thus identified by this relationship of joint tenure rather than bynames.[29] Excluding these joint tenants, the residue identified solely by a forename is reduced to fewer than 20 tenants, often with less usual forenames in the local context, such as Ivo who held two virgates at Rothley, Alexander who held half a toft, Matthew, the tenant of a half bovate at Barsby, and Jere, Malbe and Bate, each holding a half bovate in the same vill.

Until the early thirteenth century, the peasantry, of whichever legal status, was identified in manorial records without reference to bynames, but by the early thirteenth century bynames started to become a normative process in peasant naming. Nevertheless, peasant tenants with forenames which were less frequent in the local 'community' might still be described solely by that forename without a byname. Thus, even in the lay subsidy of 1296 for Rutland, 10 contributors were listed without a byname: Alexander, Hamund, and Ingred at Oakham; Alwin at Langham; Aubrey at Ketton; Bartholomew at Whitwell; Gervase at Wardley; Lucy at Lindon; Remund at Greetham; and Wolewin at Essendine. In the survey of Oakham, some nine years later (1305), five tenants, consisting of one villein, three cottars, and a female tenant, were not accorded bynames, including the Hamund from the tax list above, who held a virgate. That taxation of 1296, however, comprised 1,630 taxpayers and, furthermore, each of the 3,871 legible taxpayers in the lay subsidy for Leicestershire in 1327 was accorded a byname.[30]

The free tenantry

By the middle of the thirteenth century, it was becoming increasingly common for free kinship groups to acquire hereditary surnames. The process cannot be quantified, but can be illustrated by the evidence of charters. Early in the thirteenth century, Mael de Kerebi attested a charter, as also one in which Mael *filius Ambrosii* received a virgate, whilst slightly later William *filius Mael'* attested another. Five charters of the late thirteenth century, two of which are dated 1283 and 1299, were witnessed by Simon Mael and that of 1283 also attested by Mr Robert Mael. In 1303, Lucy *relicta Simonis Mael* conveyed land in Kirby Muxloe. Since all these charters related to Kirby Muxloe, just to the west of Leicester, the development of a hereditary surname of a particular kinship is visible, with the transition from unstable patronymic naming to hereditary appositional surname.[31]

Simultaneously at Kirby Muxloe, the byname (le) Levere *alias* Lepor(e) became hereditary. Early in the thirteenth century, Warin *filius Iuonis le Levere* was a witness to charters, whilst his father, Ivo Lepore, held a half virgate there and acquired another virgate. Warin later occurred in eight other charters as Warin (once Warner) le Levere, one of which was dated 1253, another no later than 1262 and a further of 1283. In six he attested, but in the other two acted as grantor. Also witness to some of these charters was Simon *filius Warini le Levere*, but witnessing that of 1253 as Simon le Levere. In the late thirteenth century, Simon additionally attested four charters in the style Simon le Levere and was mentioned in two later ones as Simon *filius Warini le Levere*. Warin, moreover, had a brother Richard, who held a virgate and was referred to in a mid-thirteenth-century charter as Richard le Levere *frater Warini le Levere*. Warin had died by 1297, when his widow, Agnes, alienated land. Two charters of the mid-thirteenth century were attested by Ralph le Levere, whilst those of 1300 involved William le Levere as donor and witness and beneficiary of two and a half virgates of land, whilst a contemporary charter was attested by Walter le Levere. Furthermore, William le Levere was a grantor in 1303 and witness in 1316. Later, John le Levere was grantor and beneficiary in charters of 1339–54, after whose death, his son, William, was a grantor in 1361. This byname appears then to have developed into an hereditary family surname in Kirby Muxloe from around the middle of the thirteenth century, a pattern seemingly replicated there by the byname le Venur (*Venator*) contemporaneously, especially in charters of 1253 to 1292.[32]

The most conclusive evidence of the development of an hereditary surname amongst a free kinship group, that of the Pakeman family, also derives from Kirby Muxloe, but is complicated by the elevation of the family from freemen to gentry status through service in the honour of Leicester.[33] In the early thirteenth century, Simon Pakeman *alias* Simon *filius Simonis Pakeman* was a grantor and recipient of two virgates and grantor of another. His daughter, Maud, designated as *filia Simonis Pakeman*, alienated another one and a half virgates in mid century. Comtemporaneously, Gilbert Pakeman attested a charter and was mentioned as formerly holding three acres. Simon had a son, called variously Richard *filius Simonis Pakeman* and Richard Pakeman, whilst Robert Pakeman, who attested charters and acquired land, was described once as Robert *filius Roberti Pakeman*, but in 11 other cases in the later thirteenth century simply as Robert Pakeman (1277–1300 and undated). His father, as Robert Pakeman, had witnessed a charter of the early thirteenth century. Another Simon, son of the younger Robert, was grantor and beneficiary in numerous charters after 1277 relating to lands in Kirby Muxloe and was described as Simon Pakeman *filius Roberti Pakeman* in distinction from his contemporary, Simon, son of Simon Pakeman, the latter being designated as Simon *filius Simonis Pakeman* and Simon Pakeman *filius Simonis Pakeman*.[34]

An interesting aspect of the genesis of hereditary surnames is the transition from unstable patronyms to appositional patronyms or surnames from personal names. In Melton Mowbray, Robert *filius Herberti* was simultaneously (1272) designated Robert Herbert in half a dozen charters.[35] A proliferation of names of this kind happened in Gaddesby during the thirteenth century.[36] Thirty-nine charters involved the acquisitive Henry *filius Jordani*, who was purchasing piecemeal lands in selions and roods, although in some (undated and 1275), his description was elided to Henry Jordan. His daughter, also acquiring property, was referred to as Edith *filia Henrici Jordan*, dependent on her relationship to her father, whilst his son, Ralph, was styled (undated and 1275) Ralph *filius Henrici Jordan*, Ralph Jordan *filius Henrici Jordan* and simply Ralph Jordan. There too Ralph *filius Willelmi de Kayham* was also known as Ralph de Kayam (*manens in Gaddesby*). Also in Gaddesby, Roger *filius Palke* became elided to Roger Palk *de Gaddesby*, as Ralph *filius Roberti de Rerisby* occurred regularly in other charters as Ralph de Rerisby, although his father had been consistently designated Ralph de Rerisby. Although only documented over two generations, these elided patronyms reflect an incipient heritability of surnames; indeed, the surname Jordan persisted in charters relating to lands in Gaddesby into the fifteenth century. Nevertheless, a *caveat* should be introduced in that the patronymic description might have been employed in some instances to reflect or confirm the hereditary descent or succession to land, with the consequence that hereditary surnames might have been developing at an even earlier time.

The converse of these developments is the persistent instability of some bynames, but the examples in the thirteenth century are so minimal as to confirm the general trend towards heritability. The specific case of Henry *capellanus filius Johannis Geroud* at Gaddesby is explicable by the probable nature of a real vocation, although Thomas *de aula filius Thome de Disewrth*, grantor of four selions at Diseworth from about 1241 to 1255, is one of the few examples of genuine instability.[37] By the middle of the thirteenth century, therefore, stable family names appear to have been evolving amongst the free tenantry of Leicestershire.

The unfree peasantry

The processes of change amongst the unfree peasantry are illuminated by a series of court rolls for manors in Leicestershire from the late thirteenth century. Although the inherent difficulty is that the condition of naming is invisible before those rolls began, there is sufficient evidence in the first court rolls to suggest strongly that hereditary surnames were novel at that time and that any surnames developed initially only amongst a core of influential families in the manors. Even without earlier material, therefore, it can be proposed that incipient hereditary surnames evolved first amongst core kinship groups from the 1270s and 1280s, but the wider dissemination of this process was not achieved until about 1300, and that even then some kinships and individuals retained unstable bynames.[38]

That instability pertained particularly to incomers; thus when William de Pek responded in 1288 in the manorial court of Kibworth Harcourt about his entrance into land in the manor, it was evident that, at least in the written record, he was known by an unstable byname (which, however, later became hereditary in the vill):

> *Willelmus de Pek scilicet filius Stephani de Rolland venit in plena Curia et promulgauit In qua continetur quia feoffatus est de toto tenemento quod Johannes de Chauesby habuit vel habere [potuerit]* . . .[39]

Nevertheless, the established families were moving towards hereditary surnames. In view of the difficulties of estimating populations and of comprehensively reconstructing kinship groups from broken series of manorial court rolls, the material here is impressionistic rather than quantitative.[40] It is substantially derived from the rolls of the two manors of Merton College in Leicestershire, Barkby and Kibworth Harcourt.[41]

The extent to which the peasantry on these two manors had adopted bynames is revealed in the manorial rentals in the late thirteenth and early fourteenth century. In that for Barkby in 1311, all 27 unfree male customary tenants assumed bynames, whilst in 1312 all 29 were so designated, except for Hakeman who held the mill. Similarly, the rental of 1315 recorded all 28 tenants with bynames. At Kibworth in two rentals of about 1300, 26 customary tenants and eight cottars in the first and 29 customary tenants and five cottars in the second were attributed bynames, the only exception in both lists being the widow *Scolacia alias Scholac' vidua*.[42]

Exceptional to these general trends were the 'marginals', women and relative 'outsiders', as well as the persistent instability of patronymic and metronymic descriptions. This fluidity of naming at the social margins is well illustrated in the Kibworth court rolls, where considerable volatility of population was evident. Some outsiders who gained a tenuous foothold in the 'community' were accorded a lesser, if sufficient, form of identification, epitomized by Luke (*Lucas*). Appearing first in the court rolls in 1283, when he found pledges for fealty on entering the lordship, Luke was still on the manor in 1291, during which time he was continuously known only by his 'forename'.[43] Although this name was distinguishing and not common in the local context, the refusal to accord him a byname seems also to owe something to his social position.

One way of establishing the tendency to hereditary surnames amongst core kinship groups is to take the most intractable examples, in particular surnames derived from the names of widows. The Sibile kinship group at Kibworth was one such important illustration. It is certain that this kinship group belonged to the most influential unfree peasant families, both in terms of tenure of land and office-holding. The widow, Sybil, antedated the earliest surviving court rolls, but she is represented in the earliest rental and memoranda of fines in the metronymic bynames Ivo *filius Sybille*, who, a *nativus*, held half a virgate. In the court roll of 1280 Nicholas Polle was presented for battery against John *filius Sibille*.[44]

Despite the repetition of forenames within the Sibile kinship, preventing an exact chronology, the accumulation of appearances in the court rolls confirms the hereditary nature of the surname. The same Ivo Sibile recurred in the rolls between 1280 and 1292, was elected one of the chief pledges of the manor in 1291, as well as one of the aletasters in 1291–92.[45] A tithing list which enumerated over 140 males over the age of 12 in the entire vill comprehended Robert Sibile, his son Roger, Ivo Sibile, William Sibile, Alexander Sibile and William *filius Roberti Sibile*.[46] Robert Sibile, reflecting the important position of the kinship, occurred frequently in the court rolls between 1279 and 1291, held a virgate in unfree tenure, and had been reeve in at least 1287 as well as affeeror.[47] Ivo Sibile had a daughter, Matilda, a constant brewer between 1281 and 1298, who was most often described as Matilda Sibile, but on three occasions as Matilda *filia Iuonis Sibile*.[48]

In the last decades of the thirteenth century, the prominence of the kinship group and the hereditary surname was represented by Robert Sibile the elder and younger. Robert senior held the significant office of one of the *custodes aule et curie* and the younger Robert acted as a chief pledge.[49]

During the early fourteenth century many incidental references establish the extent of the kinship: Constance Sibile (1333–45);

Agnes Sibile (1324–26); Henry Sibile (1334); Alexander Sibile (1334); Alice Sibile (1344); Emma Sibile (1331); William *filius Alexandri Sibile* (1326–34), who was probably identical with the William Sibile accused of hamsoken (housebreaking) in 1349 and battery in 1352; John *filius Rogeri Sibile* (1330–35) also known as John Sibile (1330–32); and Joan Sibile.[50] The most frequently mentioned member of the family was Adam Sibile (*fl.* 1320–48) who held a virgate, had been a chief pledge in at least 1320, 1324–25, 1329, 1331 and 1333–34, and aletaster in at least 1320, 1324–26, 1331–32 and 1333–34, epitomizing not only the consolidation of the hereditary surname but also the influential position of this unfree kinship in the vill and manor.[51]

The approximate genealogy of the Sibile family thus reveals significant developments in the naming processes of the unfree peasantry. First the visible trend towards hereditary surnames in the late thirteenth century affected even the most difficult forms of bynames, those derived from widows' forenames. Second, the earliest developments of hereditary naming occurred amongst the core or most influential unfree families in the 'community'.

The same direction is evident with another problematical surname at Kibworth, Scolas, intrinsically difficult because again derived from a widow's forename. In this case, the forebear Scolas is visible in the records, variously described simply as Scolasse or, occasionally, *Scolacia vidua*, who, in the undated rental of the late thirteenth century, was designated a *nativa*. In her widowhood, she was identified simply by her 'forename', unusual within the 'community', and her status as a widow, without a byname or reference to her husband.

Her son, John, occurred in the court rolls during her lifetime as John *filius Scolace* and John Scolace. When, in 1299, he offered an entry fine of 16*s.* 8*d.* for the land previously held by his mother, he was recorded as John *filius Scolac'* with reference to his claim on the familial holding, but even on his own death a heriot was claimed in respect of John *filius Scolastice*. Her other son, Hugh, was most usually known in the rolls by the metronymic form, Hugh *filius Scolasse* or *filius Scolast'*.[52] Subsequently, the surname was established in its elided form in the early fourteenth century, especially through Robert Scola(s)ce who was a chief pledge in 1334–35, as well as his brother, John Scolace, executor of Robert's will in 1349.[53]

In similar vein, the bynames of other core kinship groups in Kibworth simultaneously tended towards hereditary surnames, including the principal unfree tenant families of the Harcourts (unfree despite the surname), Godwynes, Heyns and the *filius Alexandri* or *Alisaundre* or, as it ultimately became established, Saunder family. At the College's other manor, Barkby, the same process was in operation at the same time. Again, the progress to hereditary surnames amongst the unfree peasantry may be best illustrated by taking an intractable example, that of the family whose *antecessor* was the tenant known simply as Sampson for most of his appearances in the court rolls. Identified simply as Sampson in the rental of about 1300, he held in customary tenure a messuage and bovate with an additional four acres and half a rood. References to him in the first extant court roll, for 1279, reflect his idiosyncratic position, for, whilst all the other suitors to the court had bynames, Sampson was identified without one. In two unusual instances, he was accorded a byname in the record, but different bynames on the two occasions. When Ralph Franceys found two pledges, one was Sampson *filius Ricardi*, and when Sampson impleaded Hugh *faber*, the plaintiff was described as Sampson de Bark' (1296–97).[54]

Sampson's son, Henry, was initially described by a patronym, as Henry *filius Sampsonis*, but that description quickly became elided to Henry Sampson, certainly by 1294, during Sampson's lifetime. Rentals of 1311 and 1312 included Henry Sampson as tenant of his father's land, then slightly augmented, whilst that of 1315 recorded Amice *uxor Henrici Samsoun* as the tenant. Subsequently, from 1346, Robert Sampson was repeatedly involved in cases of debt, detinue and trespass, usually as defendant. Continuously holding the familial land *in bondagio*, he was, however, presented for leasing parcels without licence. His successor, Richard Sampson, sporadically appeared in the court rolls in 1363–65.[55] Other bynames in Barkby stabilized more precociously as hereditary surnames, particularly amongst the principal customary tenantry, such as Ernald or Arnold, Holand, Fraunceys, Playtur and (de) Dalby.

Burgesses in the borough of Leicester

Amongst a core group of burgess families, inheritance of surnames occurred earlier than amongst rural peasant populations, but later than amongst knightly families, in the early thirteenth century. This intermediate naming process is complicated by the nature of the evidence, since none is available before the inception of the gild merchant rolls in 1196. Specifically, no series of charters enables reconstruction of naming processes at an earlier time.

Entries to the gild merchant are one potential indicator of heritability of bynames over two generations, from father to son, where the son entered under his forename and byname with the qualifying identification of father by forename and surname. This description quite often, but not exclusively, occurred when the basis for entry to the freedom was patrimony (*habet sedem patris*). The usual form entailed: *Willelmus de Crouden filius Walteri de Crouden intrauit*. Unknown, however, is the proportion of inhabitants of the borough and its suburbs who were admitted to the freedom. Comparative figures from other boroughs, such as York and Exeter, suggest that only a minority of inhabitants achieved this status. Consequently, these entries probably represent inheritance of bynames over two generations only amongst a burghal élite.[56]

Between 1196 and 1273, 1,296 males entered the gild and were admitted to the freedom.[57] In 32 cases the entrant was designated by forename and byname and father's forename and byname, comprising the following bynames: de Crouden, Patric, le Mercant, de Luteboru, Iring, Cruke, de Carleton, le Chat, *cum barba, faber, sub muro*, le Paumer, *rotarius*, Folebarbe, de Blaby, de Blanke, Parser, *Blundus*, le parcheminer, Drueri, Curlevache, Ouirnon, Pite and *Caritas* (the latter *bis*), le dextere/*tinctor*, Glide (*bis*), de Sileby, Trunchun, de Rolea, and le Paumer.[58]

Some of these bynames may have continued in the second generation purely as unstable bynames, if, for example, a son was involved in the same occupation as his father (*faber, rotarius*, for example) or continued to inhabit the same area of the borough (*sub muro*). By contrast, the continuance of bynames from nicknames, toponymic bynames and bynames from personal names (elided or appositional patronyms) implies incipient heritability. Nevertheless, many of these inherited bynames were transient in the recorded *corpus* of burghal bynames and surnames, not surviving in the records beyond the mid or late thirteenth century, although a small proportion did continue as the bynames of core burghal families.

Equally, instability of bynames is represented in the naming formulae for other entrants to the gild, for, in 13 instances where fathers' forenames and bynames are also specified, the bynames differed, as Geoffrey Spik *filius Ricardi furnarii* or John Amice *filius Walteri de Cropston*.[59] Possibly, in some cases, the formula indicated instability of byname of the father only, since it is conceivable that

Richard *furnarius* was known not only by his occupation but also by the byname Spik, but that his son, Geoffrey, was consistently designated Spik. This hypothesis may receive confirmation from the simultaneous admission of William Spik *filius Ricardi furnarii*.[60] Most instability seemingly ensued from immigration, as in the cases of Walter *Niger filius Rogeri de Stocton*, admitted in 1220, John Amice *filius Walteri de Cropston* (1258), Robert le Paumer *filius Roberti de Merkingfeld* (1261), Henry *de marisco filius Reginaldi de Caludon* (1263) and Roger le Taylur *filius Willelmi de Tamwurth*, who entered in 1264.[61] Some, however, represented unstable occupational and other bynames such as Hugh Cupere *frater Willelmi Damisele* (a sibling relationship), Robert Duce *filius Willelmi Wintrican*, Richard Curteys *filius Roberti le parcheminer*, and Robert le roer *filius Rogeri molendinarii*.[62]

Such entries on the gild merchant rolls thus reflect the incipience of heritability of bynames, over two generations only, amongst the burghal élite during the mid and later thirteenth century, whilst, nevertheless, there was still some continued instability of bynames. The development of more complete inheritance is revealed in only one admission which refers to a stable surname over three generations, when Thomas de Blanke *filius Petri de Blanke filii Ricardi de Blanke* entered in 1258.[63] The development of heritability of surnames amongst a core burghal élite can, however, be demonstrated through the collation of a wider range of sources. Some of the genealogies can be only supposititious, but others have a more concrete foundation, and, in any case, the evidence is drawn exclusively from those apparently unusual bynames which are unlikely to be greatly polyphyletic within the community.[64]

One of the pledges for admissions in the morningspeech of the gild merchant in 1196 was Abraham (with no byname), whilst in 1225 Geoffrey Abram was admitted. This byname recurred [including the hypercorrected Habraham] with Peter in the tallage of 1271, Roger in that of 1307 (assessed at 36*d*.) and Robert who was admitted to the freedom in 1311 for the customary fine of 36*d*. paid by denizens of the borough. Although no connections can be made, the byname is sufficiently unusual to suggest some kinship relationships. The only other known bearer of this forename, Abraham de Euenton, occurred later in the tallages of 1307–18.

The byname Ace had similar origins in the forename Aco, which was borne by Aco *filius Simonis de Petra* and Aco *filius Ricardi de Vuncha*, who were both admitted to the freedom in 1196, and by Aco *cum barba*, who entered the gild in 1258. The proceedings of the morning-speech referred to Robert *filius Aconis* in 1225 and he may be the same contributor in the tallages of 1270 and 1271. In those tallages, William Ace was also assessed and Alice Ace paid 24*d*. in that of 1286. Subsequent references to Aces included: Richard in the tallages of 1307 (24*d*.) and 1311 and mentioned in the gild merchant rolls of 1310 and 1314; William, who entered the gild in 1314, in the tallages of 1311, 1318 and 1336 (18*d*.); Matilda similarly in 1318; and Ralph, who was admitted to the freedom in 1344 and listed in the tallage of 1354 (6*d*.). Despite the slightly polyphyletic origins of this byname, the inference can be drawn that it had become hereditary by the later thirteenth century.

The byname Aldith first occurred in the loan of 1253, in which Roger was assessed at 60*d*. and he re-entered the gild merchant in 1259 at a fine of £1, having been expelled in 1254. He was impleaded for another trespass in the morningspeech in 1263 and contributed to the tallage of 1271. William Aldith also paid to that tallage and he may have been the William *filius Walteri Aldith* who entered the gild in 1253, significantly for the fine of 36*d*. reserved to inhabitants of the borough. The tallage of 1276 included Thomas Aldith (12*d*.), whilst Walter Aldith entered the gild in 1299. In the fourteenth century, references to Aldiths comprised: another Walter in a charter of 1314 and who had entered the gild in 1310; William who contributed to the lay subsidy of 1327, the tallage of 1336, was mentioned in a charter of 1339 and held two tenements and a *placea* in the rental of Leicester Abbey in 1341; his son, Walter, who entered the gild in 1341; Henry (admitted to the freedom in 1334 and mentioned in a charter of 1343); Margaret, mentioned in the morningspeech in 1336; Henry, tallaged in 1336 and an auditor in 1346; and Geoffrey, who contributed 3*d*. to the tallage of 1354.

Having a similar etymology, the byname Alsi (Alsy) became closely associated with the burghal élite in the early fourteenth century, for John Alsi was treasurer in 1303, receiver in 1304, and mayor in 1310, 1312–13, 1315, 1317, 1327–8, 1336 and 1338, having entered the gild in 1299 for the significant fine of 36*d*., contributed 10*s*. to the lay subsidy of 1327 and 12*s*. to the tallage of 1336. He may have been the son of that John Alsi mentioned in the gild records from 1260 and who paid 6*d*. in the tallage of 1286. The *antecessor* may have been Henry Alsi, involved in a plea of debt in the morningspeech in 1239, who was probably the Henry *filius Henrici Alsi* who had been admitted to the freedom in 1225. Alexander *filius Willelmi Alsi*, who entered the gild in 1242 by patrimony, was tallaged in 1271, in which tallage was also assessed Alice Alsi. Another William Alsi entered the gild in 1268.

The Curlevache kinship group established a much earlier pre-eminence in the borough, in the person of Simon Curlevache. Robert Curlewache was admitted to the freedom in 1199 and attested charters and Alan *filius Simonis Curleuache* admitted to the freedom in 1214, but the later Simon, who entered the gild in 1225, held the office of alderman in 1225, 1234, 1239 and 1242. Simon was mentioned in the gild records through to 1242. Henry Curlewache was admitted in 1242, as was Geoffrey Curlewache, and Henry's son, Henry (Henry Curlevache *filius Henrici Curlevache*) gained the freedom in 1260. Henry senior had been assessed at 5s. for the loan of 1253, whilst Geoffrey had contributed 6s. 8d. The tallage of 1271 comprehended both Henry junior and Matilda Curlevach, whilst there was a passing reference in the accounts to Edusa Curlevach in 1270. Geoffrey died of accidental death in 1298, but may have been that Geoffrey who had formerly (*quondam*) held a tenement of Leicester Abbey, according to the rental of 1341. Another Simon Curlyvache had been admitted to the freedom in 1319, who was assessed at 6d. in the tallage of 1336. Subsequently, in 1345, Thomas Curlevach entered the gild, whilst Margaret Curlevach held a house in a rental of c.1380. Such an unusual Anglo-Norman byname associated with a distinguished family seems certain to have been monophyletic within the borough and to have related to one kinship group.[65]

Allusion has been made above to the clear heritability of the byname de Blanke by 1258, since it had seemingly passed through three generations. Earlier antecedents of this byname occur in the gild merchant rolls, as Peter *filius Ricardi de Blanke* and Richard *filius Rogeri de Blanke* were both admitted in 1214 and Richard *filius Geruasii de Blanke* in 1220. Thomas, who entered the gild in 1258, was son of Peter de Blanke son of Richard de Blanke, and was assessed in the tallage of 1271. Other de Blankes included Matthew, who entered the gild merchant in 1247, William, mentioned in a plea of debt in the morningspeech in 1233 (not necessarily resident in the borough), and Adam, who became free in 1315 and was listed in the tallage of 1318.

Since the nickname-byname Blund(us) is a common one, it is difficult to establish its heritability. Simply taking entrants to the gild produces a long list of bearers of this byname, who were admitted in 1196, 1199, 1206, 1211 (two), 1214, 1222, 1225, 1227, 1250, 1252, and 1258. Nevertheless, it is possible to confirm some relationships. Robert Blunds were admitted in 1196 and 1211 and William *filius Roberti Blund* in 1214, who may have been the William le Blund tallaged in 1271. More conclusively, Geoffrey *filius Roberti Blund* entered in 1227, succeeded in 1250 by Simon *filius Galfridi Blund*, who was mentioned further as S. Blund in the morningspeech in 1252. Although the byname was probably polyphyletic, it can be established that it passed over three generations in one kinship group during the early thirteenth century.

A more unusual byname was Cag(g)(e) which first occurred in the person of Richard son of Gervase Cagge, who entered the gild merchant in 1211. Martin Cagge was involved in litigation before the morningspeech in 1225 and 1239 and contributed 10*d*. to the loan of 1253, and whose son, Peter *filius Martini Cagge*, was admitted in 1250 for the significant fine of 36*d*., and who appeared before the morningspeech in 1260 as Peter Cagge. Subsequent Cagges in the borough included Matilda, a vintner, who was assessed in the tallages of 1271 and 1276, Philip assessed at 12*d*. in that of 1286, John (appearing in the records from 1274 to 1314, mayor in 1308), Richard (between 1297 and 1327), Peter and William who entered the gild in respectively 1315 and 1319, and John who was a former tenant of a tenement listed in the rental of Leicester Abbey in 1341.

The byname Caritas (Charite) was strongly associated with the borough and Leicester Abbey, appearing first when William Caritas and Robert Karitas entered the gild in respectively 1226 and 1236. The former's sons, John Caritas *filius Willelmi Caritas* (*sic*) and Simon Caritas *filius Willelmi Caritas* (*sic*) were both admitted in 1265, John paying the concessionary fine of 36*d*. Simon was entered in the tallage of 1271, but John in those of 1286, 1307 (18*d*.), 1311 and 1318. The tallages comprehended others with this byname: Roger in 1286 (12*d*.), Richard in 1286 (3*d*.), and Nicholas in 1307, 1311 and 1318. Nicholas had entered the gild in 1293, at the significant fine of 36*d*., and a William Caritas in 1327 also for a fine of 36*d*., denoting their status as deriving from a resident burgess family. The family attained its apogee of influence in the fifteenth century, especially through the person of Thomas, who was mayor in 1442 and 1454,

M.P. in 1432 and steward of the fair in 1451 and 1454. Both Alice and Joan Charite held tenements in a rental of 1458.

The distinctive metonymic byname Cokunbred had a more attenuated existence in the borough but earlier heritability. It was principally represented by two Ralphs, the first of whom entered the gild merchant in 1209. The second Ralph is more evident in the records, having become free in 1299, tallaged at 8*d.* in 1307 and reappearing in the taxation lists of 1311 and 1318, recurring in other records through to 1323, but whose final appearance in the records in 1327 was the Coroner's verdict of his murder. Other Cokinbreds included Adam, who entered the gild in 1265 and was listed in the tallage of 1271, Matilda, mentioned in the gild records in 1335, and Robert, a pledge in the gild in 1336. Although no genealogical connections can be established, the byname was probably unique within the urban community.

Some specific connections can be made for the byname Fode, of which there were numerous bearers between 1239 and 1384. Ralph Fode entered the gild in 1239, but the Ralph Fode who was admitted in 1269 was probably the Ralph junior *filius Mathei Fode* listed in the tallage of 1271. Matthew had earlier appeared as Matthew *filius Simonis Fode* on attaining the freedom in 1239, the same year as Ralph senior. Matthew was also later known as Matthew Fode in the loan of 1253, when he contributed 36*d.*, when mentioned in the morningspeech in 1258-59, as also in the portmoot in 1260, as a taxor in the tallage of 1270, and in accounts of 1278. This byname thus passed through three specific generations of the same kinship between 1239 and 1271. Moreover, many other bearers of this uncommon byname existed contemporaneously in the borough. The tallage of 1271 comprehended not only Matthew Fode, but also Richard (who recurred in those of 1274 and 1286, had entered the gild in 1269 and was presented as a brewer in 1293), William, and Ralph; that of 1318 included Robert and Alice Fode. Robert had entered the gild in 1310, paying the 36*d.* assessed on inhabitants of the borough, and he was later taxed in the tallages of 1336 (3*d.*) and 1354 (1*s.* 6*d.*). Another Ralph had held a tenement recorded in the rental of Leicester Abbey in 1341. John Fode was perhaps the most distinguished bearer of this byname as he represented the borough in the Commons in 1384; he had been assessed in the parish of All Saints in the tallage of 1354 at 5*s.*

Fewer connections can be effected for the Anglo-Norman nickname byname Folebarbe, but its unusualness suggests that it represented a kinship group whilst it was in evidence in the borough between 1196 and 1286. Simon Folebarbe was admitted to the freedom in 1225, followed by his son, John *filius Symonis Folebarbe* in 1257, to whom the gild rolls referred as John Folebarbe when he was involved in a case of trespass in 1258. In 1196, William *filius Geruasii Folebarbe* had been admitted to the gild and he was known subsequently in the year as William Folebarbe when he acted as a pledge for other entrants. Finally, another William Folebarbe was assessed at 6*d*. in the tallage of 1286 and 1*s*. in 1307.[66]

The byname Glide became hereditary, it seems, at a slightly later time, being first in evidence when Ralph Glide entered the gild merchant in 1233; he contributed 3*s*. to the loan of 1253 and was listed in the tallage of 1271. His son, John Glide *filius Radulphi Glide* received the same privilege in 1263, for the significant fine of 36*d*. and subsequently occurred in the tallage of 1271 as John Glide. In 1265, also for the significant fine of 36*d*., Ralph's other son, Simon Glide *filius Simonis Glide*, was admitted to the freedom and he too recurred in the tallage of 1271 as Simon Glide, as also in that of 1307, when he was assessed at 2*s*. Furthermore, Roger Glide had entered the freedom in 1239 and contributed 4*s*. in the Earl's caption of 1266. John Glide junior was assessed in the tallage of 1318, whilst subsequently Joan Glide was taxed in 1354 (3*d*.), Roger Glide held a tenement in the parish of St Leonard's in the rental of 1341 of Leicester Abbey, and William Glide was involved in a case of detinue in the portmoot in 1379.

One of the origins of the byname Griffin was from the nickname forename Griffin in the early thirteenth century. Thus Alexander *filius Griffin'* and Ealf *filius Griffini* were both admitted to the freedom in 1219. The first firm evidence of its being transmitted over two generations occurred in 1260 with a reference in the morningspeech to Henry *filius Roberti Griffyn*, who was subsequently designated Henry Griffin in the portmoot in a case of debt in 1260 and in the morningspeech in 1262. Robert Griffin had been known in an undated charter, in which he was the grantor, as Robert *filius Gryffyn'*, but in another, which he attested, as Robert Griffin.. Robert Griffins were mentioned in the morningspeech in 1258 and the tallages of 1271 and 1286, the latter also including William Griffin, taxed at 6*d*.

The most frequently recurring byname in the borough in the

thirteenth and fourteenth centuries was Keling, to which there were about 60 references between its first incidence in the form of Simon Keling in 1225 and John Keling, to whom the last reference occurred in 1357, when he was a juror in the gild merchant. The tallage of 1271 included six Kelings: Robert, Peter, Henry, two Johns and Simon. Unfortunately, no relationships are mentioned, except for John *filius Roberti Kelyng* who entered the gild as a denizen of the borough in 1319. It seems likely that this byname became hereditary during the middle and later thirteenth century.

Similarly few relationships can be established for the Middle English nickname byname Kepegest and its occurrences are far fewer, although concentrated between 1208 and 1271. Robert *filius Roberti Kepegest* and William *filius Roberti Kepegest* both entered the gild merchant in 1208, succeeded by Ralph Kepegest and another William Kepegest in 1242. Curteys Kepegest was mentioned in the morningspeech in 1264 and Simon and Walter Kepegest both listed in the tallage of 1271. Such an unusual byname was probably an hereditary family name.[67]

The byname Patri(c)(k) was equally unique within the borough, first occurring when both Philip *filius Nicholai Patric* and William Patric *filius Nicholai Patric* were admitted to the freedom in 1225. The byname recurred infrequently in records thereafter, when Jake Patric was a juror in the gild merchant in 1281, Nicholas Patrik's death was adjudged to be a murder by the coroner in 1323, and Henry Patryk entered the gild merchant in 1330.

Other unusual bynames may similarly have become hereditary during the thirteenth century, but they are largely concealed from the records. Thus, for example, Ralph Spurnecurteis entered the gild merchant in 1227 and a Hugh Spurnecurteis was listed in the tallages of 1271, 1286 (3*d*.) and 1307 (6*d*.). Geoffrey Tichin was admitted to the freedom in 1199, as was William *filius Willelmi Tichin*, and Philip *filius Roberti Tichin* in 1225. They were followed by Roger *filius Ricardi Tichine* in 1242, who, as Roger Tichin, contributed 5*s*. to the loan of 1253, and was mentioned in the morningspeech in 1257 and 1260. Finally, both Richard Tichin and Matilda Tichin were assessed in the tallage of 1271. Similar cases could be recounted for the byname Sturdi, but which may have been polyphyletic, and also Urr(i)(y).

Several bynames were thus becoming hereditary surnames amongst some core families in the borough by the mid and late thirteenth century. These families all contained members who had beem admitted to the freedom and so belonged to the burghal élite. Some of these surnames, however, did not persist in the borough, although others did continue to be associated with important families.

Conclusion

Regional differences in the development of hereditary surnames were complemented by variance by social group. By and large, hereditary surnames developed amongst the Anglo-Norman nobility first, were then attributed to knightly families, and were finally accorded to the peasantry, initially the free and then the unfree. Nevertheless, too much reliance should not be placed on cultural conflation or diffusion on a gravity-feed model, since important questions remain to be answered. Perhaps most critical is why, if the *cognomina* of the Anglo-Norman nobility were hereditary surnames in the late eleventh century, the other social groups acquired first not hereditary, family surnames but unstable bynames which attached only to the individual and varied from generation to generation. Two potential answers might be suggested: either the lower kinship groups were deemed too ignoble to receive family surnames or these social groups were acculturated only in an indirect manner. The second caveat is that within social groups, surnames were acquired unevenly, first by some influential families in the 'community', but only at a much more protracted pace by other families, whether in urban or rural contexts.[68]

References

[1] For a more detailed discussion, D Postles, 'Notions of the family, lordship and the evolution of naming processes in medieval rural society: a regional example', *Continuity and Change*, 10, (1995), 169–98.

[2] G Tengvik, *Old English Bynames*, (Nomina Germanica 4, Uppsala, 1938).

[3] A Farley ed., *Domesday Book seu Liber Censualis Willelmi Primi Regis Anglie* , (2 vols., London, 1783), ed. H Ellis (London, 1816), I, fos. 232b, 234a, 234d, 235d. For such bynames, Tengvik, *Old English Bynames*.

[4] *Domesday Book*, fos. 231a, 231c, 231d, 232c, 234b, 235d, 236a, 236c, 236d, 237b. These variants are the Latinized forms of the insular personal names in Domesday; for Æðelelm, see O von Feilitzen, *The Pre-Conquest Personal Names of Domesday Book*, (Nomina Germanica 3, Uppsala, 1937), 140.

[5] *Domesday Book*, fos. 293a–297d.

[6] J C Holt, *What's in a Name? Family Nomenclature and the Norman Conquest*, (Stenton Lecture, University of Reading, 1982).

[7] L C Loyd, *The Origins of Some Anglo-Norman Families*, (Harleian Society, 103, 1955), 47, 104; I J Sanders, *English Baronies. A Study of their Origins and Descent*, (Oxford, 1960), 12, 61.

[8] C P Lewis, 'The formation of the honour of Chester, 1066–1100' in A T Thacker, ed., *The Earldom of Chester and its Charters. A Tribute to Geoffrey Barraclough*, (*Journal of the Chester Archaeological Society*, 71, 1991), 37–68; see also the genealogical table at 8, (A Thacker, 'Introduction: the earls and their earldom').

[9] D Crouch, *The Beaumont Twins. The Roots and Branches of Power in the Twelfth Century*, (Cambridge, 1986), xii; *idem*, 'The foundation of Leicester Abbey and other problems', *Midland History*, 12, (1987), 4–5; Bodl. MS Laud Misc 625, fo. iv^r.

[10] Bodl. MS Laud Misc 625, fo. 186r.

[11] *Domesday Book*, I, fos. 223b, 230a–237b, 272d, 273b, 274b, 278a, 293a–297b.

[12] C F Slade, *The Leicestershire Survey (c.A.D. 1130)*, (Leicester University Occasional Papers in English Local History, 1st series, 7, 1956).

[13] See below 115.

[14] H Hall, ed., *The Red Book of the Exchequer*, vol. I, (Rolls Series, 1896), 328–9, 336, 506, 516–25; D E Greenway, ed., *Charters of the Honour of Mowbray 1107–1191*, (British Academy Records of the Social and Economic History of England and Wales, New Series 1, 1972), 256–7 (no. 401).

[15] Crouch, *Beaumont Twins*, 220 (Appendix II, Table II); J Hunter, ed., *Magnum Rotulum Scaccarii vel Magnum Rotulum Pipae*, (Record Commission, 1833), 87, 98; Slade, *Leicestershire Survey*.

[16] BL Lansdowne MS 415, fos. 15v–16r. 'Anno ab incarnatione domini M^{o}C^{o}xl^{o}viii^o Stephani regis Anglie [*sic*] .xij.^{mo} Domni Godefridi abbatis .iiii.^{o} Sexto id' Martii apud Geroldonia coram omni conuentu huius conuentionis tractata est causa et ad finem usque producta inter Willelmum de Haruecurt et predicte

ecclesie monachos Notum sit . . . quod ego Willelmus de Haruecurt
concessu et bona uoluntate yuonis fratris mei . . .'; 'Notum
sit . . . quod ego yuo de haruecurt . . . concedo et do et firmiter
confirmo donationem et uenditionem fratris mei Willelmi de
haruecurt . . .'

17 M J Franklin, ed., *The Cartulary of Daventry Priory*, (Northamptonshire
    Record Society, 35, 1988), 290-6 (nos. 884-96).

18 For the development of the surname of the Basset family, see Postles,
    'Notions of the family', 176-8.

19 The earl's tenants are listed in *Domesday Book*, I, fo. 237a.

20 G Barraclough, ed., *The Charters of the Anglo-Norman Earls of Chester
    c.1071-1237*, (Record Society of Lancashire and Cheshire 126,
    1988), 1 (no. 1).

21 F M Stenton, ed., *Documents Illustrative of the Economic and Social History
    of the Danelaw*, (British Academy Records of the Social and
    Economic History of England and Wales, 5, 1920), 13-14, 35-7
    (nos. 18, 53-5).

22 B L Lansdowne MS 415, fos. 9v, 18v, 23r, involving Robert,
    Henry, Richard and William Putrel, principally relating to Burton
    on the Wolds. The date of completion of the cartulary is discussed
    by D Postles, 'The Garendon cartularies in BL Lansdowne 415',
    British Library Journal, (forthcoming 1997). The byname or surname
    subsequently infiltrated the borough of Leicester, as the *Nonarum
    Inquisitiones* of 1340-2 for the borough recorded Nicholas,
    Thomas, Joan and Alice Poutrell: Leicestershire Record Office
    BRIII/4/70-73.

23 *Berkeley*, 13-14 (no. 22). Other charters attested in the late twelfth
    and early thirteenth century by Henry include: *ibid.*, 19-20 (no. 41),
    43 (no. 109), 47 (no. 124). In the early thirteenth century, Robert
    Puterel attested *ibid.*, 45 (no. 119), 48 (no. 130), 50 (no. 136, also
    witnessed by Geoffrey Puterel), 61 (no. 175), 69 (no. 200), 86 (no. 253),
    87 (no. 256), 88 (no. 259), 140 (no. 444). In addition, Richard
    Puterel of Cotes attested a charter before 1241: *ibid.*, 190 (no. 269).
    In 1236, Geoffrey Puterel leased pasture in Hose to Croxton
    Abbey: *ibid.*, 82 (no. 239). For John Putrel: ibid., 128 (no. 413). As
    these charters concern acquisitions of lands by the rising Stephen
    de Segrave, this evidence consolidates the position of the Putrels
    within the nexus of 'gentry' families in the north of the county in
    the late twelfth and early thirteenth centuries. Indeed, before
    1241, Geoffrey Putrel granted to de Segrave the manor of Hose:

ibid., 90 (no. 270). For the later development of the family as 'petty' gentry, G G Astill, 'The medieval gentry: a study in Leicestershire society, 1350–1399', unpublished PhD thesis, University of Birmingham, 1977, 359–60.

24 Burton Surveys, 244–6.

25 *Templars*, 112–13.

26 *AASR*, 34 (1917–18), 170 (no. 157).

27 E Niermeyer, 'An assessment for the fortieth of 1232', *English Historical Review*, 24 (1909), 733–5.

28 The Queen's College, Oxford, MS 366, fos. 16r–19r; see also G Fellows-Jensen, 'The surnames of the tenants of the Bishop of Lincoln in nine English counties', in T Anderson, ed., *Norna-Rapporteur*, 8 (1975), 39–60, and *eadem*, 'The names of the Lincoln-shire tenants of the Bishop of Lincoln *c*.1225', in F Sandgren, ed., *Otium et Negotium. Studies in Onomatology and Library Science Presented to Olof von Feilitzen*, (1973), 86–95.

29 Rothley, 89–130; dated by comparison with PRO C260/86.

30 PRO E179/165/1; *Oakham Survey*, esp. 23 (Hamond); *AASR*, (1888–9).

31 *Hastings MSS*, 12–19.

32 *Ibid.*, 12–15, 64.

33 Astill, 'The medieval gentry: a study in Leicestershire society, 1350–1399', 325.

34 *Hastings MSS*, 12–21.

35 Bodl. MS Wood empt 7, fos. 29v–30r.

36 Bodl. MS Wood empt 7, fos. 107v–140r.

37 Bodl. MS Wood empt 7, fos. 120r–v; *Berkeley*, 103 (no. 313).

38 J M Bennett, 'Spouses, siblings and surnames: reconstructing families from medieval village court rolls', *Journal of British Studies*, 23 (1983), 24–46.

39 MM 6376.

40 L R Poos, Z Razi, and R M Smith, 'The population history of medieval English villages: a debate on the use of manor court rolls', in Z Razi and R M Smith, eds., *Medieval Society and the Manor Court*, (Oxford, 1996), 298–368.

41 MM 6367–6405, 6563–6575; the material for Kibworth is supple-mented by the manorial accounts, MM 6196–6244; for medieval Kibworth, C Howell, *Land, Family and Inheritance in Transition. Kibworth Harcourt 1280–1700*, (Cambridge, 1983) and for early modern Barkby, S Postles, 'Barkby: the anatomy of a closed township,

1535-1780', unpublished M.A. thesis, University of Leicester, 1979.

[42] MM 6568, 6367, 6370.

[43] MM 6376–6385.

[44] MM 6367, 6376.

[45] MM 6367–6389.

[46] MM 6376.

[47] MM 6376–6389.

[48] MM 6376–6396.

[49] MM 6382 (*custos*); MM 6376–6383.

[50] MM 6395–6402.

[51] MM 6392–6400.

[52] MM 6376, 6208.

[53] MM 6401–6403.

[54] MM 6556, 6564–6565.

[55] MM 6565, 6567, 6568, 6575.

[56] *RBL*, I, 17; M Kowaleski, 'The commercial dominance of a medieval provincial oligarchy: Exeter in the late fourteenth century' in R Holt and G Rosser, eds., *The Medieval Town. A Reader in English Urban History 1200–1540*, (London, 1990), 4, n.4.

[57] *RBL*, I, 13–112.

[58] *RBL*, I, 17, 26, 31, 67, 74, 76, 88, 92, 97, 100, 103, 106–7, 112.

[59] *RBL*, I, 65, 82 for these examples and, for all discordant bynames, 24, 26–7, 65, 67, 73–4, 82, 94, 100, 103.

[60] *Ibid*., I, 65.

[61] *Ibid*., I, 24, 82, 94, 100, 103.

[62] *Ibid*., I, 26–7, 74.

[63] *Ibid*., I, 76.

[64] Hereafter, the material is derived from *RBL*, vol. I and II and can be traced through the indices to those volumes. The data are held in dBase IV file (Leibor.dbf).

[65] For the family, see further below, 321.

[66] For this name, see further below, 321.

[67] See further below, 322.

[68] For some consideration of these questions, D Postles, 'Cultures of peasant naming in twelfth-century England', *Medieval Prosopography*, (forthcoming, 1997). For regional variations in the acquisition of surnames, compare R McKinley, *The Surnames of Oxfordshire*, (ESS, III, London, 1977), 7–40 and McKinley, *The Surnames of Lancashire*, (ESS, IV, London, 1981), 9–76.

CHAPTER 5

TOPONYMIC BYNAMES AND SURNAMES

Despite the problem of ambiguous placenames, fairly conclusive statements can be ventured about the significance of toponymic bynames and surnames in Leicestershire and Rutland, in particular about the geographical pattern of migration of bynames and surnames.[1] Since the north-east and east of Leicestershire and contiguous parts of Lincolnshire were both subjected to Scandinavian influence, particularly in placename formations, some duplication of settlement names occurs in the two counties.[2] Equally, some replication exists in south-west Leicestershire and adjacent Warwickshire. Duplication existed in Leicestershire and Northamptonshire, not least in the placename Loddington. Neverthless, the general problem is not insurmountable. More problematic are especially and generally ambiguous placenames such as Thorpe, Ashby, Burton and Newton. Moreover, some placenames within the two counties had the same etymon: Braunston (Rutland) and Braunstone (Leicestershire, now in Leicester), compounded further by Branston, and Belton (Rutland and Leicestershire).[3] Less important is the relationship between topographical and toponymic bynames and surnames, since the two counties exhibited less dispersed settlement and consequently hardly any minor placenames which might be confused with topographical terms. Nevertheless, exceptions existed, less in the form of minor placenames, but in the nucleated settlements of, for example, Brooke (Rutland) and [King's] Cliffe (Northamptonshire).

More intransigent are the sources available for the analysis of toponymic bynames, particularly since the lay subsidies of 1296 and 1327 for Rutland and Leicestershire respectively are wealth-specific and thus exclude a large proportion of the population. Nevertheless, these taxations are the most comprehensive in terms of geographical coverage. To compensate for their deficiencies in social inclusion, other sources have been adduced to determine if any differences existed in the origins of toponymic bynames.[4]

Medieval Leicestershire

The origins and movement of toponymic bynames and surnames in medieval Leicestershire were, as in many other counties, extremely localized. In the lay subsidy of 1327 just about a quarter of taxpayers were identified by a toponymic byname, but, by excluding generic toponyms (such as le Northerne) and Anglo-Norman toponyms of the nobility, the proportion is reduced to just under a quarter.[5] Taking the taxpayers with toponymic bynames in 1327 with the exclusion of the gentry, the movement of toponymic bynames from the origin of the placename to the settlement where tax was assessed was predominantly within a distance of 10 miles, as illustrated in Table 5.1.[6]

Table 5.1

Distances of migration of toponymic bynames in Leicestershire in 1327

Distance of movement from placename of origin (miles)	Percent of taxpayers with toponymic bynames
0 (eponymous)	8.8
1–5	32.2
6–10	22.1
11–15	12.1
16–20	6.4
21–25	4.9
26+	13.5

Merely 8.8% of the taxpayers with this sort of byname derived their toponym from the parish or township in which they were assessed to the taxation in 1327. In contrast over 50% of toponyms of the taxpayers with toponymic bynames had origins within 10 miles of the place of assessment; extending that distance to 15 miles encompassed over two-thirds of these taxpayers with this form of byname. Whilst in Nottinghamshire, 58–61% of such migrations were within 10 miles, in Leicestershire about 56% were so circumscribed.[7]

Whilst other sources might act as a corrective to the wealth-specific lay subsidies, since these other sources comprehend a wider social spectrum, they are geographically more limited, even specific, and also quantitatively the data sizes are less significant. The custumal of Rothley, produced in the middle of the thirteenth century (*c*.1245), encompassed about a dozen manors in the north-east of the county.[8] A virtue of the custumal is that it was compiled before bynames of the peasantry generally evolved into hereditary surnames, so that actual movements of individuals are implicit in the toponymic bynames. The inferred distances of movement are tabulated in Table 5.2.

Table 5.2

Distances inferred from toponymic bynames, c.1245–1354

| | Number of bearers of toponyms | | |
| | PLACE | | |
Distance (miles)	Soke of Rothley	Kibworth Harcourt	Barkby
0	14	1	5
1–5	14	17	8
6–10	8	4	6
11–20	10	5	0
21+	10	3	3

Exceptionally high, the proportion of toponyms derived from the place of residence in the Rothley custumal is almost certainly determined by the territorial organisation integral to the record. With a centre at Rothley, the custumal comprised the dependent manors of the Templars, so that there was a tendency to identify some of the tenants on other manors by toponyms of those places of residence. Consequently there is a higher element of eponymous bynames derived from places of residence rather than movement.

In contrast with the wider geographical coverage of the custumal, the court rolls and rentals of the two manors of Merton College in the county, Barkby and Kibworth Harcourt, represent much more restricted localities.[9] These data emanate from sources belonging to a longer temporal span, 1277–1348 in the case of Kibworth and 1279–1354 for Barkby. Consequently, it should be recognized that some of the bynames were tending to become hereditary. The data for Barkby reveal an inferred distance of migration of toponymic bynames even more circumscribed than in the custumal of Rothley, for, whilst in the custumal the mean distance of migration was 9.04 miles (with the median at four miles), the equivalent measure at Barkby consisted of a mean of 5.45 miles, although the median was sustained at four miles. Since the parish of Barkby did, perhaps unusually, comprise some dispersed settlement, with hamlets at Barkby Thorpe, North Thurmaston and Hamilton, a small number of eponymous toponymic bynames came into existence. Tenants at those hamlets tended to be known in the manorial records by their hamlet of residence.

In comparison with Barkby, the mean distance of migration of toponymic bynames in Kibworth extended to 13.06 miles, although, in conformity with the other places, the median remained consistent at 4.5 miles. Significantly, the highest proportion of these bynames in Kibworth originated within five miles of the settlement (Table 5.2).

For a slightly later date, the rental of the manors of Leicester Abbey of 1341 (Geryn's rental) provides more complex data, because the general tendency towards hereditary surnames had by this time accumulated some pace and since the estate contained properties of disparate size.[10] Of the unfree tenants of the Abbey, 19% were attributed toponymic bynames, whilst 18% of the cottars were similarly identified. The mean distance of migration of the bynames was consistent with the data discussed above, in the region of 9–10 miles in the case of the bynames of the unfree.

Similar patterns can be discerned in the *Rotuli Hundredorum* of 1279–80.[11] In view of the vagaries of the document, a later transcription of the rolls for part of Leicestershire, to the south and west, the toponymic bynames of all tenants holding less than two and a half virgates, most of whom were free, have been analysed, but also including a smaller number of the unfree. Of the 261 tenants so selected, 66 bore toponymic bynames, but one was illegible (except for the syndetic element *de*), nine were generic toponymic bynames, and 10 were unreliable in the later transcription, not seeming to make sense. The remaining 46 bynames provide an inferred mean distance of migration of 4.5 miles, much lower than in the other data, with a more consistent median at three miles. Discounting four eponymous toponymic bynames, 18 of the 42 (43%) constituted movement of less than five miles.

In general, then, the extremely localized nature of migration of bynames and surnames evident in the lay subsidy of 1327 is confirmed by analysis of the data in manorial and other records, which, although more specific geographically, are more complete in encompassing a greater proportion of the male population. The preponderance of toponymic bynames and surnames in rural settlements within Leicestershire in the middle ages derived from places

FIG 7 ORIGINS OF TOPONYMIC SURNAMES ON
PROPERTIES OF OWSTON ABBEY , 1365-1465

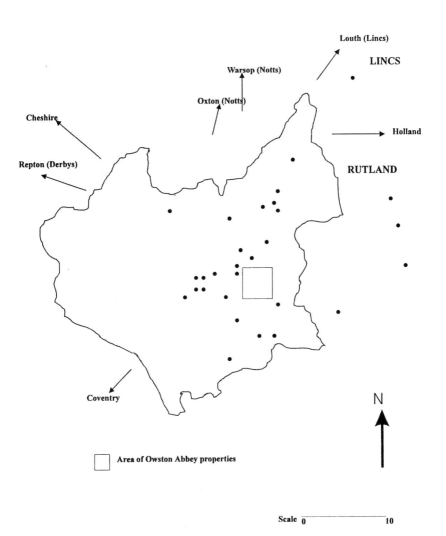

within a distance of 10 miles, with a very high proportion deriving from within five miles, that is, probably from adjacent parishes.

Rutland: the long-term, 1296–1665

Assuming some degree of, if not complete, representativeness in the toponymic bynames and surnames in the taxation returns, a longer term reconstitution of the origins of this form of names can be attempted for the county of Rutland, as reflected in Table 5.3.

Table 5.3

Distances from origin of toponymic bynames and surnames in Rutland, 1296–1665

Distance (miles)	1296	1377	1522(1)	1522(2)	1524(1)	1524(2)	1665(1)	1665(2)
1–5	53	25	10	12	12	12	11	14
6–10	19	27	17	21	15	15	12	15
11–15	7	15	14	16	18	18	9	12
16–20	6	12	7	6	7	7	9	11
21–25	4	5	7	8	7	7	6	7
26–30	2	6	5	6	11	11	7	8
31–40	3	5	10	11	11	11	9	6
41–50	4	3	5	4	5	5	9	6
50+	2	2	24	16	16	15	28	20

Note: Percentages are given as integers.[12]

In the lay subsidy of 1296, about 19% of taxpayers were identified by toponymic bynames, a figure which had increased to 23% in the Poll Tax of 1377. In the musters of 1522, the proportion had stabilized at about 24%, but declined to 21–22% in the lay subsidy of 1524–25, rising again to just over 24% in the Hearth Tax of 1665.[13] Over the long term, therefore, the proportion of taxpayers with toponymic bynames was remarkably stable, but considerable change occurred in the composition of the origins of the surnames.

In 1296, 20 bynames, 11% of the toponymic corpus, were eponymous with the place of assessment. Over 53% derived from places within five miles of the place of assessment of the taxpayer and a further 19% from within 10 miles. Almost three quarters of bynames which reflected movement thus had origins within 10 miles of the place of assessment. During the later middle ages, the relative proportions of surnames deriving locally and from more distant places altered quite considerably, marked principally by a decline in the intensely localized element. Thus, in 1377, the proportion which had origins within five miles declined to 25%, diminishing further to about 11–13% in the sixteenth and seventeenth centuries. Whilst there was a concomitant reduction in those with origins between six and 15 miles, the decline was not as precipitous; this figure increased from 26% in 1296 to 42% in 1377, but became attenuated to 20 to 35% in the sixteenth and seventeenth centuries. In contrast, there occurred a marked increase in the sixteenth and seventeenth centuries in surnames from more distant origins, over 50 miles, an increase from about 2% in 1296–1377 to 15–28%.

Nevertheless, the data for the sixteenth and seventeenth centuries are complicated by the existence of surnames with distant origins in several 'communities' in the county. Assuming that these names probably proliferated within the county rather than represented separate migrations of surnames into it, allowance has been made in Table 5.3 in constructing two columns for these data. In the first column, places of origin are included for all their separate incidences in Rutland, but in column two only one incidence, representing the shortest route and nearest entry into the county. Regardless of this complexity, the data present little difference.

Presented in another manner and taking into account the small size of the county, in 1296 the proportion of toponymic bynames in the county derived from place-names in the county attained a fairly high level — some 63% in comparison with almost 37% from placenames in other counties. By 1377, those proportions had been reversed, for only 34% of toponymic bynames were endogenous — from within the county — whereas almost 66% were exogenous. Subsequently that reversal continued, for in 1522, merely 16% were indigenous, but over 84% had migrated into the county. Those respective levels persisted not only in 1524 but also in 1665.[14] Indeed, the same general tendency is visible in the late middle ages in Leicestershire, although the figures are slightly different. In 1327, 66% of toponymic bynames were endogenous, but 34% exogenous; in 1381, in the Poll Tax surviving only for the east of the county, 54% continued to be endogenous, with 46% exogenous; and, after further decline, 45% remained endogenous in 1524, whilst the exogenous then constituted 55%.[15] Whilst, therefore, in the late thirteenth and early fourteenth centuries, migration of toponymic names was extremely localized, with the consequence that most had origins within the counties, more exogenous names of this form were introduced by the sixteenth and early seventeenth centuries. As a result of area and relative size of boundaries, the introduction of external toponymic names into Rutland was more prolific than in Leicestershire, but the tendency existed in both counties.

The intensity of the earlier localized migration is further reflected in the migration of toponymic bynames simply to the next parish or 'community'. In Rutland in 1296, over 17% of all toponymic bynames (and over 27% of those generated within the county) migrated merely to the next community within Rutland and 1% to a neighbouring 'community' in the adjacent county. In Leicestershire the proportions were slightly lower, with just over 9% moving to the next settlement in the county and 2% to the next 'community' in an adjacent county. During the later middle ages, those proportions changed as illustrated in Table 5.4.

Table 5.4

Migration of toponymic bynames and surnames to adjacent 'communities', 1296–1665

| | Rutland | | | Leicestershire | |
| | Movement to adjacent | | | Movement to adjacent | |
Date	internal	external	Date	internal	external
1296	17	1	1327	9	2
1377	10	0	1381	12	4
1522	3	0			
1524	4	0	1524	5	4
1665	2	0			

Note: Numbers, to integers, are percentages of all the toponymic bynames and surnames in the listing.

By the sixteenth century, consequently, only a very small proportion of toponymic surnames in 'communities' in the two counties still had origins in an adjacent parish or township. In Rutland, that point is further illustrated by the change in the mean and median distances of migration of bynames and surnames in the county between 1296 and 1665. Whereas in 1296 mean and median were respectively 11 and five miles, by 1524 the figures had attained 27 to 28 and 19 miles, and by 1665 30 to 38 and 27 to 35 miles.[16]

The absorption of external toponymic bynames and surnames from adjacent counties is tabulated in Table 5.5.

Table 5.5

Absorption of external toponymic bynames and surnames with origins in adjacent counties into Rutland, 1296–1665

	Leics.		Lincs.		Northants.		All	
				Percentages				
Date	1	2	1	2	1	2	1	2
1296	18	50	2	6	9	24	29	80
1377	18	27	15	23	25	38	59	89
1522	26	31	10	11	15	18	51	61
1524	22	26	21	25	16	19	59	69
1665	18	22	13	16	13	16	43	54

Notes: Percentages to integer numbers: 1 represents the proportion of all toponymic bynames or surnames; 2 symbolizes the proportion of exogenous bynames or surnames.

Again, significant changes seem to have happened over the late middle ages. Whilst in 1296 bynames from Leicestershire constituted a very high proportion of all exogenous bynames, at about 50%, that level more than halved, to about 22%, by 1665. Correspondingly, this decline was compensated by incoming toponymic names from Lincolnshire, although the complement from Northamptonshire was relatively stable. By the middle of the seventeenth century the sourcing of exogenous toponymic names was relatively equal from the three neighbouring counties.

Lordship

Although often difficult to perceive, lordship was a contributory influence on the migration of bynames and surnames, particularly within estate structures. This aspect is particularly revealed by the rental of the estates of Leicester Abbey in 1341.[17] Ten of the 23 villeins with toponymic bynames on the estate held names derived from other manors of the Abbey. Thus at Thurmaston was listed Ivetta de Stocton (Stoughton), whilst at Stoughton were enumerated

Roger de Barkeby and William de Ansty and William de Humburston held land in Lockington. The vills of Barkby, Anstey and Humberstone all included manors of the Abbey. Almost half the unfree tenantry of the Abbey with toponymic bynames may thus have migrated from one of the Abbey's manors to another. Furthermore, the names of six of the 21 cottars with toponymic bynames exhibited the same pattern, rising to about a third if generic toponymic bynames (for example, la Norrice, Norreys) are excluded. Lordship thus exerted an influence on the migration of bynames, whether for labour resources, to fill vacant tenements, or more indirectly as an information field.

Nor was the influence restricted to rural communities, for the same phenomenon can be observed amongst the tenants of the Abbey in the borough of Leicester. Amongst the Abbey's tenants in the parish of St Leonard were listed Christine de Ansty and John, Roger and Robert de Sto(u)cton and in St Peter's Henry de Barkeby.[18] Most interesting, however, were the several tenants called de Kokerham or de Cokerham in St Leonard's, where Alice de Kokerham held a tenement, Adam de Cokerham two crofts and a tenement, and William de Cokerham a tenement.[19] Their singular existence in the borough may be explained by the Abbey's tenure of the manor of Cockerham in Lancashire. Some substance might be added to this suggestion by the distribution of the surname Cockerham or Cockram later in mid-Derbyshire, at Duffield, Alderwasley, Hulland, Shottle and Smithsby, but also at Derby, in the late seventeenth century, for the Abbey had an estate in the Peak district also, where it collected extensive tithes.[20]

A small town: Melton Mowbray

Whilst the evidence for the migration of bynames and surnames into small towns in Leicestershire and Rutland is fragmentary, some material exists which allows some appreciation of the processes in Melton Mowbray in the thirteenth and fourteenth centuries. Part of Melton was included in the custumal of the soke of Rothley in *c*.1245; its taxpayers were listed in the lay subsidy of 1327; and, more importantly, several hundred charters relate to urban and rural property in the parish between *c*.1272 and 1350.[21] The custumal, however, contains very few toponymic bynames in Melton, comprising only four identifiable ones recruited from distances of about three, five, 18 and 19 miles. Similarly, the lay subsidy of 1327 comprehended only eight toponymic bynames amongst the taxpayers, which were, however, very much more localized, providing a mean distance of recruitment of 6.12 miles (with a narrow standard deviation of 5.33) and median of five miles.

Taking into account the rather selective nature of its material, the Brokesby cartulary paradoxically offers more substantial data, yielding a total of 26 different toponymic bynames in the small town. Since the material involves some attestations, which might not establish residence in Melton, the prosopography of individuals has been considered closely to confirm their residence, most particularly through the affixes *de Melton'* and *manens in Melton'*.

The mean distance of recruitment of these bynames did not exceed 13 miles (12.62 miles with standard deviation quite narrow at 13.67), whilst the median was even more circumscribed at seven miles. In particular, the mean is affected by longer-distance migration, by the two bynames de Northfolke and de Rameseye (Ramsey, Huntingdonshire). Adam de Rameseye had arrived in Melton by 1272 and married Margery Orger, the daughter of a prominent family in Melton. By her, he had two sons, the homonymous Adam, and Ralph. The elder, Adam, died by 1301. Having settled in the town by 1324, William de Northfolke was succeeded by John de Northfolk.[22] If these two remoter bynames are excluded from the analysis, the mean distance of recruitment is reduced to 9.25 miles (standard deviation 6.99). Consequently, the distance of recruitment of bynames into this small market town in the late thirteenth and early fourteenth century was hardly wider than the distances to market related by the author of 'Bracton' in the 1220s and 1230s.[23] Nevertheless, the evidence of the cartulary is highly selective and possibly incomplete and, moreover, during the later middle ages the commercial networks of the town may have become wider as its trade became more specialized in cattle and leather.[24]

A small town: Loughborough in the later middle ages

The distribution of the origins of toponymic bynames and surnames found in Loughborough also exhibits distinctive patterns. Some caution, however, is necessary in the analysis because of the nature of the evidence. Principally, there remains the question of whether bynames and surnames of litigants in the manorial court represented residents of Loughborough or whether some of the litigants with toponymic names were, particularly in cases of debt and detinue, outsiders. Since the court rolls do seem to specify outsiders by appending their place of residence to their name, it might be assumed that all other litigants were residents within the manor of Loughborough. Secondly, although the rental of *c*.1370 appears to be almost complete, it does lack some initial membranes, but it is uncertain how many. More complicated is the jurisdictional question, for the view of frankpledge extended to comprehend some tenants (in most cases a small number) in several other townships, including, importantly, Burton on the Wolds, and, less significantly, Mountsorrel, Quorndon, Barrow, Prestwold, and Cotes as well as the hamlets and smaller manors within the parish (Woodthorpe, Serlethorpe and Knighthorpe). The court rolls, moreover, are a very broken series, with significant gaps, especially between 1412 and 1429 and then through the rest of the fifteenth century. This deficiency is not compensated by the rentals, which are only extant for *c*.1370, 1526 and *c*.1550 and 1559. As always with toponymic bynames and surnames, there exists the problem of ambiguous placenames, ones which — like Burton, Walton, Sutton, Stanton, and Kirkby — were common placenames. That methodological question has been cogently addressed.[25] In the case of Loughborough, the proportion of ambivalent placenames is not excessively high and some can be determined more precisely by associated evidence. A final problem involves the lack of knowledge of the pattern of migration of these names into Leicestershire and into Loughborough because of insufficient data. For example, the byname or surname of de Ramesay (Ramseye, Ramsey) occurred in the rental of *c*.1370, in the person of Robert de Ramesay who was formerly (*quondam*) tenant of a bovate, 17a.1r. of land, pasture and the tollbooth, and appeared later in the court rolls in the guise of John in 1403–05.[26] This byname, however, had become established in Melton Mowbray by the late thirteenth century and it is possible that it migrated from there to Loughborough.[27]

Figure 8 represents the distribution of the origin of toponymic bynames and surnames in Loughborough in the later middle ages, from the rental of *c*.1370 through to that of 1559, with the intervening data derived from the rentals of 1526 and *c*.1550, the account roll of 1376, and the court rolls of the late fourteenth and early fifteenth centuries. Chronological variation is not indicated in the figure, except for toponymic bynames and surnames which existed in the rental of *c*.1370. Overall, the distribution exhibits four marked

FIG 8 THE ORIGINS OF TOPONYMIC BYNAMES AND SURNAMES IN LOUGHBOROUGH c.1370-1559

- **Places of origin from the late fourteenth century to 1559 from court rolls, lay subsidy and rentals.**
- **Places of origin in the rental of c.1370**

features. First, there is a very localized concentration from other places in Leicestershire, fairly evenly distributed through the county. Second, there is a concentration of origins of names in three counties of the north Midlands: Derbyshire; Nottinghamshire; and Lincolnshire. Third, there is a scattering of origins in the northern counties of England, and fourth, by contrast, very few origins of toponymic bynames and surnames were located in counties south of Leicestershire.

Localized origins from other placenames in the county might be expected. The even distribution throughout the whole county, however, may reflect the development of Loughborough through the later middle ages, with an enhancement of its position and importance. To some extent, the distribution of origins in the counties immediately to the north of Leicestershire conforms to the Trent Valley, although the origins extend into northern Derbyshire. This northward extension through Derbyshire may, however, owe something to the Derwent Valley, which runs south to its confluence with the Trent. Two places of origin in Staffordshire, Wichnor and Yoxall (both in the rental of c.1370), also lie within the Trent Valley. The further northward extension of the origins into northern England is an interesting phenomenon, which may reflect the apparent northerly characteristics of naming in Loughborough more widely.

Taking the rental of c.1370, the mean distance of place of origin of toponymic bynames and surnames was 30.61 miles, although the trimmed mean was 25.34 miles, with a standard deviation of 35.88.[28] The median distance was 19 miles with first and third quartiles of nine and 33 miles. Even at this time, therefore, the distance of origin was quite wide. By the rental of 1526, the number of toponymic surnames had declined and the composition altered, but the distances of origin were comparable with c.1370 overall: a mean of 31.52 miles, trimmed mean of 24.9 miles, with standard deviation at 40.89, with a median of 22 miles and interquartile range of 10 and 38 miles. The rental of 1559 includes too few toponymic surnames (14) for any significant analysis to be made.

The composition over this timespan changed quite radically, in line with the general turnover of surnames in the town during the later middle ages. Only four toponymic bynames from the rental of c.1370 (less than 4%) recurred in the rental of 1526 and only five (about 20%) from the rental of 1526 into that of 1559. The total numbers of toponymic bynames and surnames declined from 42 in c.1370, to

24 in 1526, and subsequently to only 14 in 1559. All this analysis excludes the small number of complex names, including generic toponymic names (Irelonde, Breton) and French toponymic names (Bretuill'). The problem is, however, compounded by toponymic names of some local families which assumed gentle status in the later middle ages (Digby). Finally, the most complex problem, which cannot really be addressed, is the seignorial and territorial geography of Loughborough. Loughborough comprised an urban nucleus within a very large parish, the parish itself divided into several lordships. It is always possible that bynames and surnames migrated backwards and forwards between town and rural parish and between lordships. It is not possible to take account of that issue.

The medieval borough of Leicester

Although McClure has analysed the pattern of migration into the borough in the late thirteenth and early fourteenth centuries, it is worth expanding on his examination. In using the tallages of 1269-71, 1286, 1311 and 1318, he may have been using a highly selective sample, if the liability to taxation was confined to burgesses of more substance.[29] As a control on those data, a rather different taxation, the *Nonarum Inquisitiones* of 1340-42, has been employed here, since, in its four instalments, it comprehended more than 700 townspeople, a much greater number than any of the tallages.[30] The purpose of the taxation and the extensive number of taxpayers captured by it suggest that it was more regressive than the other tallages. Indeed, the vast majority of the contributors who featured only in one or two instalments contrasts quite prominently with those wealthier townspeople who were embraced by all four instalments and seem to be typical of the more restricted number of taxpayers in the tallages.

In his analysis of the tallages, McClure discovered that the catchment area for immigrants into Leicester was quite restricted by comparison with many other boroughs, even Nottingham, with its primary catchment area — defined by the distance of migration of at least 50% of the migrants — within 10 miles.[31] Taking unambiguous toponymic bynames, 16% derived from within five miles, just over 27% between five and 10 miles, almost a further 22% from 11 to 15 miles, almost 14% from 16 to 20 miles, and over 21% from more than 20 miles.[32]

The *Nonarum Inquisitiones* contain over 130 unambiguous different toponymic bynames, the origins of which can be described as follows:

1–5 miles	16.8%
6–10 miles	27.0%
11–15 miles	13.9%
16–20 miles	16.1%
21+ miles	26.2%

Almost three-quarters of these toponymic bynames thus originated from within 20 miles of the borough, 57.7% within 15 miles, and 43.8% within 10 miles. Despite the different composition of the taxation, the data confirm the patterns suggested by McClure. In terms of its attraction to migrants, Leicester ranked amongst the county towns, not as influential as Nottingham, nor in the same level of the urban hierarchy as the regional capitals which acquired a significant number of their immigrants from more than 25 miles distant.[33]

Moreover, about 54% of the toponymic bynames in the borough in 1340–42 had their origins within the two counties, Leicestershire and Rutland. Whilst merely 3.6% accrued from Rutland, over 50% originated within Leicestershire.

Beever and variants (Belvoir)

Distributed in its phonetic rather than its lexicographical form, variants of Beever (from Belvoir in north-east Leicestershire) exhibit interesting distributions, the first, like many toponymic bynames and surnames, intensely localized and clustered not too distant from the place of origin, the second remote from the place of origin and probably transferred through the influence of lordship.

Around the castle and priory of Belvoir briefly developed a settlement with ambiguous urban characteristics, at the lowest level of burghality, represented by reference to a burgage.[34] A foot of fine of 1203 relating to Redmile, hard by Belvoir, referred to William de Beuver.[35] In the late thirteenth century, some inhabitants of Belvoir were known eponymously, such as Philip de Beuver, father of Richard *clericus* who alienated a toft and croft there.[36] Another charter of the thirteenth century in favour of Belvoir Priory was attested by William de Bever.[37] In 1309, the lord of Belvoir, William de Roos, granted a messuage in Belvoir and a selion in Redmile to William de Belver, clerk, although William was alternatively designated in a charter some 20 years later as William *clericus de Belver*.[38] Just below Belvoir lies Woolsthorpe and a charter of the thirteenth century concerning land there was attested by William de Beuver and Odinel de Beuver, although the latter was also described as Otinel de Aubeni, a byname formerly associated with the lordship of Belvoir.[39]

In the lay subsidy of 1327 for Leicestershire, Robert de Beauuer was assessed at nearby Muston, between three and four miles from Belvoir.[40] In 1332, Richard de Beuuer and Robert de Beuuer were taxed in Grantham in Lincolnshire, a market town about seven miles from Belvoir, and thus within customary peasant marketing.[41] There, the byname persisted at least into the fourteenth century, as, in 1351–54, Robert de Beauuer brewed and was also a juror and Thomas de Beauoire was his contemporary in the market town.[42] By the later middle ages, the surname had become established on the estate of Owston Abbey in east Leicestershire, about 17 miles south of Belvoir. Consistently presented for brewing at Owston in 1466–68 was Isabel Bever, a common brewer.[43] Nevertheless, the byname seems also in isolated cases to have extended more widely, into south Derbyshire, in Repton Hundred, where a de Beauuer was assessed in 1327. [44]

As a consequence of this localization, the surname Beaver expanded throughout Rutland. In the Hearth Tax of 1665, 11 Beavers were assessed, in nine different settlements — Oakham, Langham, Cottesmore, Burley, Empingham, Tickencote, Tinwell, Uppingham and Manton.[45] By 1851, however, the pattern of that distribution had altered quite considerably, for, whereas there remained only four households with Beavers in rural settlements, comprising two each in Braunston and Market Overton, there was an extraordinary concentration in the county town, Oakham. Over 20 households there contained a Beaver, the majority of whom had been born in Rutland.[46] At nearby Glapthorn in Northamptonshire, the surname had also become established in the census returns of 1841–71.[47] Not surprisingly, the surname had expanded from Rutland and Leicestershire into Northamptonshire by the seventeenth century, just across the border at Duddington, in John Beaver, servant, and at Islip, also not distant from the boundary, in the person of John Bever, miller.[48] By the seventeenth century, a wider distribution had happened, but characterized by isolated incidences, as, for example, in Widow Bever at Metfield, the only Bever in Suffolk, and John Bever of

Bermondsey, the sole bearer of the surname in increasingly cosmopolitan Surrey.[49]

In 1402, however, a deposition had been made in the York consistory court by John Bever of the parish of All Saints in Fishergate, York, in Wylson v. Fox.[50] The transference of the surname over this distance might be explained, tenuously perhaps, by earlier seignorial history. Since Ekwall lists only one placename Belvoir, it seems clear that Belvoir in Leicestershire is the only significant settlement of this name.[51] Although the surname might still have derived from minor placenames, a seignorial relationship existed between Belvoir in Leicestershire and Yorkshire which might explain the earlier migration of the byname.

In the late twelfth century, the stewards of the Mowbray honour included Ralph de Bevver, who held that position between 1169 and 1182. Although evidently originating in the Mowbray fees in the honour centred on Belvoir, Ralph assumed stewardship of the Yorkshire estates in the Mowbray honour.[52] Before receiving the office, he attested a charter relating to Burton Lazars, as Ralph de Belverico, in 1162.[53]

Significantly, the relationship of the byname and surname to lordship might have influenced its later dissemination, for the current distribution exhibits a strong concentration in Yorkshire. For this exercise, the entire series of telephone directories has been examined for England, with the results revealed in Table 5.6. Simply, the analysis relates only to the numerical preponderance of the surname without reference to the distribution of population, so it remains at best an ambiguous representation, since areas of higher population density might inherently have contained higher numbers of the surname. Nevertheless, the patterns are significant. Although electoral registers might have provided a more reliable source, since these records certainly comprehend a higher proportion, if not the total, population of adults, telephone directories were not only more accessible but also normally count by household rather than adult electors. Only the data in residential telephones were accepted, encompassing the surnames Beaver(s), Beever(s), Beevor(s) and Bever. Finally, the areas of analysis in Table 5.6 are compiled arbitrarily into 'regions', a not inconsiderable task given the districts covered by individual telephone directories.

Table 5.6

The current distribution of surnames putatively derived from Belvoir

Region	N	Region	N
East Midlands[54]	204	South Midlands[55]	93
East Anglia[56]	142	Kent[57]	28
North-West[58]	226	W. Midlands[59]	135
Southern England[60]	130	Yorkshire[61]	693
North-East[62]	56	South-West[63]	92

In the immediate vicinity, the East Midlands, the surname was widely dispersed with no intense concentrations, except for 36 in Leicestershire and Rutland. Nevertheless, the level was not comparatively much higher than in many other parts of England. In East Anglia, despite low numbers distributed throughout the area, concentrations existed in Norwich (42) and south Norfolk with Lowestoft (36). The figure for the North-West is relatively high as a result of a dense concentration in Manchester (119) and a lesser frequency in Blackpool (44). In the West Midlands, the number is elevated considerably by 46 in Gloucestershire.

Most interestingly, however, the densest concentration of the surname was located in Yorkshire, particularly in the West Riding, comprising 63 in the directory for Leeds, 34 in Bradford, 31 in Halifax, 107 in Huddersfield, 77 in Sheffield, 58 in Rotherham, 169 in Barnsley and 52 in Doncaster. Although the West Riding is now metropolitan, with extensive conurbation, these directories also comprehended the rural parts of the county. In the aggregate, these entries for the West Riding composed 591 of the 693 in Yorkshire, complemented by 62 in York. Consequently, the most remarkable concentration of the surname in the late twentieth century occurs in the former West Riding, predominantly in the form Beever(s).

Although toponymic bynames and surnames normally continued to be located around the place of their origin, reflecting circumscribed migration of people and names, the influence of medieval lordship could induce a much wider dissemination of some bynames and surnames. Amongst these dispersed bynames, Beever was characteristically from Leicestershire, deriving from Belvoir in the north-east of the county. Although the toponymic byname initially clustered in adjacent Rutland and south Lincolnshire, the later conformation was completely different and very particular, concentrated in Yorkshire, assuming that the etymon of this Beever(s) was the placename Belvoir in Leicestershire.

Outmigration of toponymic bynames and surnames

Only an impression can be given of the distribution of bynames and surnames from Leicestershire and Rutland, for a number of reasons. First, analysis is necessarily based on toponymic bynames and surnames only, excluding other forms of name which it is impossible to track. Second, this process of analysis of toponymic names is inherently complex because of the large proportion of 'ambiguous' placenames throughout England.[64] That problem is compounded for Leicestershire and Rutland since there is a considerable number of ambiguous placenames at the edges of the county. The eastern, particularly north-eastern, periphery contains many placenames duplicated in adjacent Lincolnshire, both highly influenced by Scandinavian placename elements. The western and south-western margin shares a number of placenames in common with adjacent Warwickshire, mainly of OE construction. The following discussion attempts to take into consideration these complexities and is confined to the dissemination of these names during the middle ages, particularly before 1350.

For medieval migration of these bynames and surnames, two datasets have been employed: lay subsidies and other, miscellaneous records. Lay subsidies for most counties have been examined, consisting mainly of those in print, but additionally some (especially Lincolnshire) which are unpublished. The principal lacunae are Nottinghamshire and Northamptonshire. Lay subsidies, however, because they are exclusive by wealth, probably represent only successful migrants (through toponymic bynames). To compensate for this problem and also for the geographical coverage in adjacent counties, a wide range of other sources has been consulted, although with a concentration on charters, which may still, however, be reflective of only limited social groups, in the case of charters by legal status (the free).

One final complexity is the precise meaning of *de legr'*, *de leyc'* or *de leycestre* in areas distant from Leicestershire. It might have been that migrants from minor places in the county, that is rural vills, were designated by their county of origin rather than specific placename, or even by the county town.

FIG 9 TOPONYMIC BYNAMES FROM PLACES IN LEICS AND RUTLAND IN OTHER COUNTIES FROM SOME LAY SUBSIDY ROLLS, 1280-1332 AND (KENT) 1334

nd   no data for these counties

⌐⌐ Stamford (several bynames)
∟∟

x   Toponymic name from a rural place or market
    vill in Leics or Rutland

▪   de leyc' or de leycestre in urban context

■   de leyc' or de leycestre in rural context

●   de ocham or variant in rural context

◆   de roteland or variant in rural context

Figure 9 illustrates the distribution of taxpayers with bynames or surnames from places in Leicestershire and Rutland in the lay subsidies of other counties between 1280 and 1332, but including the 1334 lay subsidy for Kent which is a particular assessment with nominal evidence. The clustering is largely in adjacent counties, especially for names in rural vills in other counties or from rural vills in Leicestershire and Rutland. In the urban context, the name exclusively represented derives from the county town, Leicester. The exception is Stamford, which includes a large number of toponymic bynames which have origins in rural vills in Rutland, at very short distances. Longer-distance movement is also represented by *de roteland* in Cumberland and Northumberland and *de ocham* in Sussex and north Lincolnshire.[65]

To some extent, the other sources confirm the distributions in the lay subsidies, particularly in the urban context of the byname from Leicester, although the distribution is shown to be much wider from the other sources, extending to Shrewsbury, Winchester, Canterbury, Oxford, London, Derby and King's Lynn. By 1350, therefore, the byname from Leicester existed in many of the principal boroughs south of the Humber and east of the Cotswolds. Toponymic bynames from rural vills were, as in the subsidies, concentrated in adjacent areas of neighbouring counties, but the concentration in south Nottinghamshire is revealed. A further, more distant example of *de roteland* is represented in Worcestershire.

These miscellaneous sources, however, divulge some other patterns, in particular the concentration of toponymic bynames in Coventry and Westminster. Moreover, the lay subsidies provide only a fairly static pattern at a later time, whilst the other sources, although less comprehensive and incidental, do allow some idea of the diachronic development of these distributions.

The urban distribution of the byname from Leicester seems to have been established first in an easterly direction, consonant with the trading linkages developed by the woollen cloth trade. John and William de Leycestr' appeared in the gild rolls of early [King's] Lynn to which Leicester merchants were trading in woollens from before 1200. Much later, in 1322-23, Hugh de Leycestre was listed as a wool trader in Lynn.[66] The presence of the byname was established in many other larger boroughs in central England during the thirteenth and early fourteenth century. Admissions to the freedom of

FIG 10 TOPONYMIC BYNAMES FROM PLACES IN LEICS AND RUTLAND IN OTHER COUNTIES BEFORE 1350 (FROM SOURCES OTHER THAN LAY SUBSIDY ROLLS)

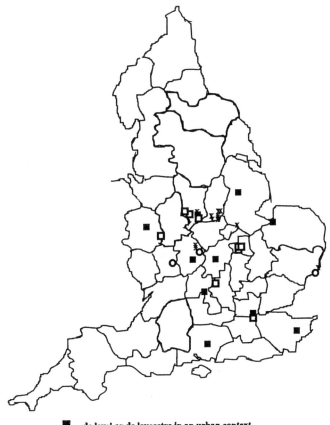

■   de leyc' or de leycestre in an urban context

□   de leyc' or de leycestre in a rural context

O   de roteland or variant

O   Coventry: toponymic bynames from 14 places in Leics

□   Westminster: toponymic bynames from 9 places in Leics and Rutland

x   toponymic bynames from rural places

Shrewsbury did not apparently include any freemen with a byname from Leicestershire before Robert de Leycestre in 1318, although it was a major wool town.[67] The byname was established in Oxford by 1279–80, for Matilda widow of Philip de Leycestr' and Walter de Leycestre each held a messuage there and John de Leycestr' also inhabited the borough at that time. Matilda's husband, Philip, had been active in the urban land market in Oxford at an earlier time.[68] In the eyre of 1285, Matilda widow of Philip de Leycestria initiated a plea of debt against Adam Londyne for a debt of 14 marks which had accumulated as outstanding annual rent of two marks from property in the suburb outside the North Gate of Oxford.[69] In 1292–93, William de Leyc' acted as pledge in the Oxford portmoot.[70] Further south, the Winchester survey of c.1110 has no evidence of the name, but it was subsequently represented there by Richard de Leycestre who died before 1261, although he was not a property holder there.[71] John de Leisetre was admitted to the freedom of Canterbury in 1311–12; since he was entitled to enter by patrimony, it seems that the name might have existed there earlier, and, indeed, R. de Leycester sponsored the admission of John Wolnoth in 1302–03.[72] When the borough of Stratford upon Avon was developed about 1252, burgesses bearing the byname from Leicester had already arrived: Ralph and Henry de Leycestre each held parts of burgages in the *burgus*.[73] In Ipswich, the byname de Rodland was established by the early fourteenth century, perhaps a variant of Rutland. Robert, the main bearer, was involved in wills and charters relating to burgage property in the borough in 1318–26 and was a juror on an assize in 1327.[74]

In London, bynames from the two counties appeared by the late thirteenth century. The will of Hugh de Clothale in 1273/4 left a bequest of a house in tail to William de Leycestre, cordwainer. In 1287, the will of Alexander de Leycestre was proved in the London hustings court, including houses which he owned. Thomas de Okham's will was proved in the same court in 1304. More ambiguously, wills of several testators with the byname de Leyre received probate in the hustings in 1322/3, 1328, 1330, 1336 and 1349. The will of Robert de Walcote, goldsmith, left bequests to John de Leycestre, when it was proved in 1361, whilst further wills of de Leyrcestres (John, merchant, and Walter) were examined in the hustings in 1391 and 1393/4.[75] Neighbouring Westminster was equally as attractive as the city, since residents there before 1350 bore bynames from Aylestone, Belgrave, Frolesworth, Hoby, Hinckley, Leicester, Oakham, Segrave, and Theddingworth, at distances of 78 to 95 miles.[76]

These bynames entered neighbouring boroughs too, but sometimes the evidence is less complete. Robert junior de Leic' attested a charter relating to two houses in Northampton before 1215.[77] Ralph de Lokinton was included amongst the burgesses of Nottingham who took a lease of the tolls of Retford in 1315/16.[78] John de Leicestre became a member of the Mayor's Council at Lincoln by 1314 and John de Leir' (an ambiguous name) had been bailiff there in the late thirteenth century.[79] The presence of the byname from Leicester was established in Derby by the thirteenth century, for a charter records that Henry de Leycestre, chaplain, assigned a rent of 6*d*. from a toft there once held by his father, Henry de Leyrcestre, and Adam de Leycestr' was a parishioner of St Peter's, Derby, in 1338.[80] Moreover, John de Bredon held a toft in the New Land of Derby in 1248x1261 and that name was replicated in 1352 when another John de Bredon was defendant in a case of nuisance.[81] More material exists for Coventry, which attracted inhabitants with bynames from adjacent south and south-west Leicestershire — Hinckley, Cotesbach, Burbage, Polesworth, Claybrooke, Sheepy, Shilton, Braunstone, Croft, Bowden, Lutterworth — as well as Leicester, many of whom attested charters relating to burgage property in Coventry, acquired property there or were listed as burgesses and burgage tenants in the Hundred Rolls of Coventry.[82]

Bynames and surnames in rural vills in other counties predominantly originated just across the border in Leicestershire or Rutland — the migration of the names was short-distance and clustered. Representative of this clustering is the concentration of bynames in south Nottinghamshire villages. Richard de Bottelesford gave land in Wiverton to Thurgarton Priory in 1253x1258, whilst the byname from Bottesford occurred in relationship to a toft in Hawksworth.[83] Robert, son of Ivo de Kegeworth gave to the same Priory in 1280 a toft and bovate in Cropwell Butler.[84] Consequently, in the survey of the Priory's lands in 1328/9, Mabilia de Holewell held a toft and croft in Hickling and Henry de Bottelesford two selions and meadow in Sibthorpe.[85] Such clustering just across the county boundary from places of origin was preponderant. In Northamptonshire, jurors for two adjacent hundreds included Roger de Medburn' and Robert de Barkeston', whilst Thomas de Leycestr' acted in the same capacity in the borough of Northampton.[86] On the other side of the law, William de Foxton of Rothwell was accused of stealing a horse in Rothwell.[87]

To the north-east, Thomas de Thurmaston was arraigned for burglary and rape in Lincoln in 1351, at which time Thomas de Okeham was a member of the jury of presentment in that City.[88] About a decade later, John de Redmyld was reported to have been a servant of John West of Carlton in Lindsey in the north of Lincolnshire.[89] The jury at Corby in Kesteven included John de Okam.[90] Much closer, but still in the same county, at Stamford in the 1360s and 1370s, Thomas de Haloughton', servant, John de Stauern, another servant, and Agnes de Castel donyngton' were accused of theft, but John Empyngham acted as a pledge.[91] In the mid-1370s, John de Barkeston' was presented for battery, whilst Hugh de Barkeston' was a juror in Grantham.[92] Further south, in Kirkton in Holland, Richard de Leycestre was a juror in the late fourteenth century.[93] As early as 1203x1225, William de Blaston had attested a charter relating to Great Carlton in Lindsey, which represents some of the longer distances of migration of bynames and surnames into deeper parts of medieval Lincolnshire.[94]

Nevertheless, even before 1350, scattered, but isolated, more distant incidences were evident in rural vills. Charters relating to lands in Kniveton (south-west Derbyshire) were attested by Henry de Leycestr' *c*.1200 and Aco de Leyc' *c*.1220, whilst Roger de Leyc' held in nearby Parwich part of a bovate before 1240x1250.[95] Very much more distant was William de Leycestr' in Clayhanger in Herefordshire in 1290.[96] At a similar distance was another William de Leicestr' who attested a charter relating to land in Stoke Hammond in Buckinghamshire before 1219.[97] A small assemblage of the byname from Leicester materialized in thirteenth-century Cambridgeshire. Milicent de Leycestr' *alias* Milicent *relicta Willelmi de Leycestr'* was a free tenant in Threvesham, a *hundredarius* (*sic*) holding by suit to the hundred and county courts.[98] In Gamlingay, William de Leycestr' had held half a fee which he had alienated to Merton College.[99] A William de Leycestre was also a tenant of Barnwell Priory in Madingley in 1295.[100] Another distant example is Robert Roteland at Henbury in Marsh (Worcestershire) in 1299, holding five acres.[101] In the city of Worcester, the surnames of Hynkeleye and Leycestr' were present in the late fourteenth century.[102]

The fairly circumscribed distribution of toponymic bynames and surnames from Leicestershire and Rutland remained a pattern which persisted into the seventeenth and even the eighteenth century, perhaps even the nineteenth. Again, however, it is important to emphasize the selective nature of the sources considered, which may influence the ostensible pattern. Nevertheless, a fairly systematic effort has been made to consult a source which has a fairly comprehensive coverage — the Hearth Tax for the late seventeenth century. That source has been complemented by miscellanous other material which allows some perception of localized distributions of surnames.

Despite its proximity to Leicestershire, Derbyshire contained only a scattering of toponymic surnames from that county in 1662–70. The analysis is not without difficulty because of ambiguous surnames, but it seems most probable that the quite prolific Rolleston or Rolston derived from Rolleston in Staffordshire or Nottinghamshire, rather than from the eponymous place in East Leicestershire.[103] Perhaps equally ambiguous is Mos(s)(e)ley, although its origin in Leicestershire might be suggested by Benjamin Mowsley at Lullington, Thomas and Edward Mowsley at Croxall and Mrs Mowsley at Dronfield.[104] The distribution of this surname also extended to Measham, Chesterfield, and Brassington.[105] Equally uncertain, because of Haughton in Nottinghamshire, is Houghton, which was listed at Derby, Horsley, and Chesterfield.[106] Hambleton too escapes certainty of origin, but was distributed at Bradley, Bowden Chapel, and Thorpe with Mapleton.[107] More concretely, Francis and Ralph Osbiston contributed tax at Hulland, Thomas Tongue in Derby, Henry Bosworth at Sawley, Joseph Shilton at Stanton, Abraham Shilton at Appleby, William Whatton at Bretby, Michael Watton at Chesterfield, Thomas Saxbey at Newbould, and (perhaps less convincingly) Thomas Worthington at Killamarsh.[108] At Melbourne, the taxpayers included Priscilla Brookesby, Thomas and Richard Sheepey and William Bosworth.[109] Accepting only the surnames more certainly from Leicestershire and Rutland, and allowing for a slight scattering in the north of the county, the preponderance of these surnames clusters in the south of Derbyshire, as reflected in the nexus in Melbourne. The distance of dissemination was still tightly defined.

Northwards into Nottinghamshire, migration might have been less closely circumscribed, as the Trent Valley provided a conduit. Analysis is, however, compounded by the complexity of some ambiguous toponymic surnames, principal of which is Hooton or Houghton. Adding to the intricacy of the problem is the wide dissemination through Nottinghamshire of this surname, in at least 18 settlements in the Hearth Tax for the county in 1664 and 1674.[110] Whilst a considerable part of the distribution probably derived from the Nottinghamshire placename Haughton — which developed in ME with a vocalic interchange as Houghton — some must have been influenced, particularly in the southern extremities of the county, by Houghton in Leicestershire.[111] For the purposes of this examination, however, this surname has been completely excluded.

Neither was that the only contentious surname. Some obviously inextricable toponymic surnames such as Broughton have equally been omitted.[112] Rolleston or Rolston was comparable with Houghton, for much of the distribution in the county must be explained by the parish of Rolleston between Southwell and Newark in Nottinghamshire rather than its eponymous equivalent in east Leicestershire.[113]

Even more complex is the distribution of surnames which might have originated from minor placenames in Nottinghamshire, comprising, for example, Horsepool, Tong(u)(e) and Thornton. Although Horsepool was a settlement in Thurgarton parish which was deserted at an early time, the concentration of the surname in Averham (multiple taxpayers in 1664 and 1674), Elton, Upton and Bleasby, in the vicinity of Thurgarton, suggests that this toponymic surname probably derived from the minor settlement in Nottinghamshire rather than from the eponymous place in Leicestershire.[114] Consequently, Horsepool has been discarded from the assessment.

Still more complex is the distribution of the surname Tong(u)(e), which was concentrated in two clusters, in mid-Nottinghamshire and in the extreme north of the county. The latter grouping — with incidence in 1664 and 1674 in Misterton, West Stockwith, Gringley, Everton and Wakeringham — was almost certainly related to the minor placename Tong's Wood, which existed in the medieval parish of Beckingham, just to the south of this cluster of parishes.[115] Moreover, the same explanation may lie behind the distribution slightly further south and in the middle of the county, in East Retford, Laneham, Tuxford, Kneesall, and Norwell.[116] Whether, however, the same sort of influence explains the incidences in the south of the county at Newark, Balderton, Lowdham, Car Colston, and Bleasby, cannot be resolved nor whether the source emanated from a different direction, from Tong in north-west Leicestershire.

FIG 11 DISTRIBUTION IN NOTTINGHAMSHIRE
OF TOPONYMIC SURNAMES FROM LEICESTERSHIRE
AND RUTLAND IN 1664 AND 1674

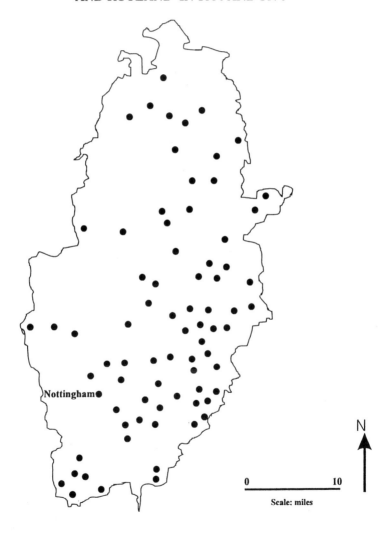

FIG 12 DISTRIBUTION IN NOTTINGHAMSHIRE OF MUSSON AND BREEDON IN 1664 AND 1674

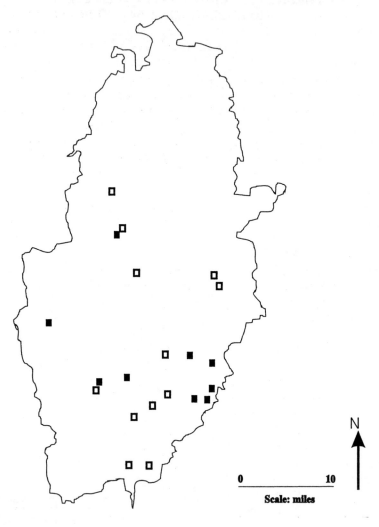

■ Musson

□ Breedon

Other superficially ambiguous surnames were perhaps less complex, in particular Musson or Mussen and Thornton. It seems fairly certain that the etymological content of Musson was Muston in Leicestershire rather than Misson in the extreme north of Nottinghamshire.[117] By a different explanation, Thornton Holt is excluded as the etymology of the surname, since the minor placename is late, allowing the more pertinent origin of Thornton in Leicestershire.[118] To some extent, the surname Musson persists in the area around its placename of origins today.[119]

With these allowances, the distribution in Nottinghamshire in 1664–74 of toponymic surnames with potential origins in Leicestershire and Rutland placenames is displayed in Figure 11. With but slight exception, the strongest concentration is in the east of the county, influenced by the Trent Valley. Opportunities may have been greater in this more fertile area, densely settled at an earlier time, on the predominant Keuper Marl. Here too parishes were smaller, so that the concentration of settlements with these surnames is intrinsically denser, by comparison with the larger parishes in the west of the county, particularly on the Coal Measures Sandstones and Bunter Sandstones. Nevertheless, those differences in parochial structure simply reflected disparities in demography and opportunity in a still preponderantly agrarian society and economy. Further explanation might inhere in the contribution of 'drainage systems' to the formation of cultural provinces, in this case the unity of the Trent Valley.[120]

By comparison with the extent of distribution of such surnames in Derbyshire, the dispersal through so many parishes in Nottinghamshire is astonishing, confirming perhaps the influence of the lower reaches of the Trent Valley on the direction of migration of surnames. Potentially, more than 60 villages in Nottinghamshire contained a surname derived from a Leicestershire or Rutland placename, with the distinct clustering of well over 60% of the settlements where these surnames occurred in a corridor within 10 miles of the river.

The contrast is emphasized by the number of different toponymic surnames in the Nottinghamshire corpus, derived from more than 50 different settlements in Leicestershire and Rutland. Dividing Leicestershire into four arbitrary quadrants about a centre at Leicester, 26 (49%) of the surnames derived from placenames in the north-east of the county, whilst another nine (17%) originated from settlement names in the north-west, with the result that 66% emanated from the north of Leicestershire. An additional 21% (N=11) represented placenames in Rutland. Consequently, merely seven (13%) denoted placenames from south Leicestershire, almost equally from south-west and south-east.

Other sources permit a close analysis of the development in Nottingham of toponymic surnames from Leicestershire and Rutland, particularly parish registers, comprising here the parishes of All Saints and St Mary. Although the registers of All Saints were searched from 1579 (and St Mary from 1653), these surnames did not exist, it seems, in any profusion in Nottingham before the late sixteenth century, but many of them persisted over a long period in the borough thereafter, although some appear to have been more transient. The duration of the 31 surnames is represented below.

Barkston	1655	Thornton	1655–1809
Musson	1661–1787	Siston	1664
Burrough(s), Burrowes	1664–76	Woodhouse	1783–98
		Ragsdale	1784
Barwell	1783	Belton	1791
Skevington	1784–1806	Worthington	1784–92
Dalby	1790	Burley	1786–93
Saxby	1786–1801	Smeaton	1787–94
Breedon	1695–1794	Langham	1789–1812
Bosworth	1788	Hors(e)pool	1793– 5
Osgathorpe	1781–1812	Bebe	1625
Segrave	1776–1805	Donnington (ambiguously)	1772
Wardley	1741–1811		
Barwell	1776–1802	Hambleton	1792–1801
Seale	1794	Burly	1795
Leicester	1808	Hinkley	1797–1802[121]

Over half of these surnames, 17 out of the 31, had origins in the northern part of Leicestershire, defined as north of Leicester, although the distribution of origins extended throughout the whole of Leicestershire and Rutland.

Although it has not been possible to consider the Hearth Tax for the adjacent county of Northamptonshire, the dissemination of surnames from Leicestershire and Rutland can be expansively considered for a century later, from the militia lists of 1777.[122] Since there is some replication of placenames, a small number of toponymic surnames has been discounted from the analysis, principally forms of

FIG 13 DISTRIBUTION IN NORTHAMPTONSHIRE OF TOPONYMIC SURNAMES FROM LEICESTERSHIRE AND RUTLAND IN 1777

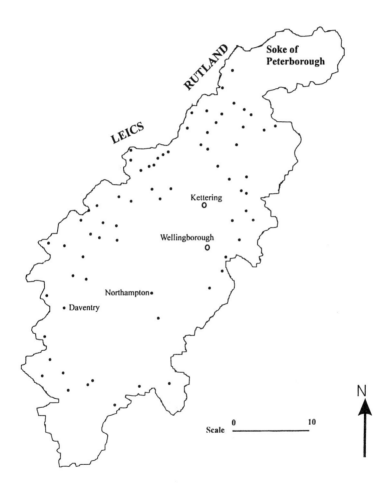

• Location of surnames

o Other principal places

The soke of Peterborough was omitted from the source

Brans(t)on and Brawnson, since this placename existed in Leicester-shire, Rutland and Northamptonshire, Houghton *alias* Hooton, Hoaten and Hoten, since this placename existed in Northamptonshire as well as Leicestershire, Broughton, Braughton or Brauton, since this placename featured in the same two counties, and Tongue may have originated from Tongue End in Northamptonshire rather than Tongue in Leicestershire.[123] Despite some remaining ambiguity for some of the surnames, the corpus of 43 toponymic surnames with origins in Leicestershire and Rutland provides some interesting illumination of the progress of distribution through Northamptonshire by the late eighteenth century.

Held by 178 males eligible for the militia, the surnames were disseminated through 81 parishes in Northamptonshire, but with a distinct clustering in the north of the county, heavily concentrated close to the boundaries with Leicestershire and Rutland and, indeed, a large proportion of these vills composed a belt within 10 miles of the county boundaries, as illustrated by Figure 13. The lack of impact on the interior of Northamptonshire may be explained by the economy of the Wolds in the early modern period and later, where employment prospects were lower than in other *pays* of Northamptonshire. The distribution of the surnames in the county might thus reflect the relative attractiveness of the economy of some areas as well as proximity to the county boundaries, such as the river valleys of the Welland and Nene and the woodland economy of north-east Northamptonshire. The composition of the surnames is tabulated below.

Table 5.7

Composition of toponymic surnames in Northamptonshire in 1777

Surname	No. of males
Burbidge	13
Crowson and variants	12
Bosworth and variants, Thornton, each	11
Manton/Munton, Beebee and variants, each	10
Barwell	8
Seaton, Daulby, Fleckno(e)(w), Knighton, each	6
Busby, Freesbee/Freesby, Arnsbee, each	5
Smeeton	4

Surname	No. of males
Liddington, Quemby (*sic*), Willabee, each	3
Shearsby, Horspool, Gadsbee/Gadsby, Blaby, Be(a)ver, Lester, Killworth, Lockington, Worthington, each	2
Saddington, Bilson, Ratlif, Stretton, Belton, Kettleby, Langton, Ridington (*sic*), Grooby, Redmile, Glenn, Laughton, Langham, Ilson, Seal, Langley, each	1

Admittedly, a small number of these surnames, because of their generic nature, are ambiguous, for example Ratlif and Worthington. Others are replicated in other counties, but it is unlikely, for example, that Burbidge derives from Burbage in Wiltshire rather than the eponymous settlement in Leicestershire. With some exceptions, these surnames related back to placenames in the southern half of Leicestershire (below Leicester) — almost half of the surnames — with an additional five from Rutland. An incidental aspect is the devoicing of /t/, as in Ilson, Bilson, and Branson.

Even by the late eighteenth century, although a considerable number of toponymic surnames from Leicestershire and Rutland had migrated into Northamptonshire, the penetration into that county was restricted largely to the north and north-east, inside a corridor extending only 10 miles from the boundary with the two counties of origin with some concentration in the Welland and Nene valleys. Furthermore, the majority of the surnames derived from the southern half of Leicestershire and from Rutland.

Extending south and east from Northamptonshire, Bedfordshire has accessible Hearth Tax returns for 1671, in which potentially 12 surnames derived from Leicestershire and Rutland.[124] Some ambiguous surnames, which occurred in Northamptonshire and for which there are eponymous placenames in that county, have been excluded, such as Houghton *alias* Hooton and Broughton, as well as the equally ambivalent Langley.[125] Distributed throughout 27 parishes in Bedfordshire, the more certain surnames comprised Stoughton (four taxpayers), Seaton (one), Burley (one), Endersby (five, but with some equivocation), Bowden (one, but also equivocally), Bushby (four), Bosworth (four), Harborough (one), Dalby (one), Skevington (three), Manton (four) and Knighton (one, but ambivalently).[126] Rather than clustered, the locations of these surnames were dispersed throughout Bedfordshire, without concentration near the Northamptonshire boundary. Although some were located near that boundary, others were situated south of Bedford and others on the boundary with Cambridgeshire and Huntingdonshire.

Considering a more distant, but not remote, county, Oxfordshire, the Hearth Tax of 1665 contains perhaps only one less ambivalent surname, that borne by Thomas Crowson who was interestingly discharged for poverty at Woodstock.[127] Hambledon, assessed at two places, and Busby, in four, appear equivocal.[128] Similarly, the Hearth Tax for Worcester in 1678–80 contained no toponymic surnames from Leicestershire and Rutland, except for the ambiguous name of Humphrey Houghton.[129] Extending further afield, the Hampshire Hearth Tax is no more productive, revealing only surnames of ambiguous derivation which might relate back to Leicestershire. Burbidge, held by Edward at Old Lymington, more probably related to Burbage in Wiltshire, whilst the etymon of Burley, held by those assessed in Portsmouth, Itchen Abbas, Gosport, Swanthorpe, Long Sutton and Aldershot, might have been Burley in Ringwood in Hampshire. The surname of Andrew, John and John Lester at Provost, Bure and Christ Church, is of uncertain etymology — improbably from the de Lestre family or a variant of occupational litster, unusual in southern England — but possibly represents Leicester.[130] Perhaps less equivocally was Mr Harby, assessed at Hambledon.[131]

Similar difficulties are entailed in analysis of the toponymic surnames in another more distant county, Suffolk, because of ambiguous surnames. Excluded from the interpretation, therefore, are Howton, Langham (a placename in Suffolk), Langly *alias* Lungly, Melton, Belton, and Mosley.[132] Discounted also must be Lister *alias* Lester, for it is inextricable whether this item derives from a toponym or from the occupational etymon litster.[133]

After those exclusions remain 14 surnames the etymology of which might reside in Leicestershire and Rutland, comprehending some 37 contributors to the Hearth Tax: Beeby (one), Belgrave (three), Bever (one), Burly (two), Croxon (two, but possibly from Lincolnshire), Dalby *alias* Dolby (five), Enderby (one, but possibly from Lincolnshire), Harbarowe (three), Kettleby (one), Manton (one), Mussen (one), Reresby (one), Rutland *alias* Rudland (nine) and Seagrave (two).[134] These 37 taxpayers were, however, dispersed through more than 30 places, with small clusters only in Ipswich (four) and Bury St Edmunds (three). The distribution of the surname

Rutland *alias* Rudland exemplifies the distribution, for it was dispersed in Shotley, Ringshall, Cavendish, Chelsworth (two), Claydon, Homersfield, Tuddenham, Ipswich, Ofton, Bures, Cockfield, Bury St Edmunds, Bramford, Chelmondiston and Hadleigh.[135]

Finally, a more cosmoplitan, but distant, county is represented by Surrey, from the Hearth Tax of 1664.[136] Here, it seems necessary to exclude as ambiguous Hambledon *alias* Hambleton, Langley, Broughton, Thornton and Presson (devoiced) *alias* Preston.[137] Additionally, Heather *alias* Hether might represent a topographical surname with -er suffix, particularly in this part of the country. After this separation, there remain only Mr Breedon at Kew, six taxpayers called Burle *alias* Burley in six different places, two called Dalbie in Reigate, John Bever at Bermondsey, Thomas Beby at Newington, three taxpayers called Saxby in three different locations, George Seaton at Rotherhithe, and two Stoughtons at two locales.[138] Considering the increasingly cosmopolitan development of parts of Surrey at this time, this accumulation of surnames is rather minimal.

Conclusion

Although a small number of toponymic surnames from Leicestershire and Rutland acquired a wider distribution, the persistent feature remained a tightly circumscribed disposition within the two counties and in the adjacent parts of bordering counties, even into the seventeenth century. Equally, the immigration of exogenous toponymic surnames was limited, perhaps even into the nineteenth century. In some of those cases which involved the migration of surnames over long distances — both in- and out-migration — a determining influence was lordship in the middle ages. To some extent, the local dissemination of surnames was configured by local social organization, the relationships of local societies, which was particularly evident in the distribution of surnames from the two counties in Nottinghamshire and Northamptonshire in the seventeenth century. Nevertheless, toponymic surnames are simply an indicator of the overall migration of surnames, since they constitute those most easily identified, despite the ambiguity of some placenames. Other surnames undoubtedly migrated, but their movement is less visible.

References

[1] P McClure, 'Patterns of migration in the late middle ages: the evidence of English place-name surnames', *Economic History Review*, 2nd ser., 32 (1979), 167–82.

[2] K Cameron, 'Scandinavian settlement in the territory of the Five Boroughs: the place-name evidence', in *idem*, ed., *Place-Name Evidence for the Anglo-Saxon Invasion and Scandinavian Settlements. Eight Studies Collected by Kenneth Cameron*, (English Place-Name Society, Nottingham, 1977), 115–71.

[3] Differentiations have been established as far as possible by reference to B Cox, 'The Place-Names of Leicestershire and Rutland', unpublished PhD. thesis, University of Nottingham, 1971.

[4] For the more precise methodology and comments on sources, D Postles, 'The pattern of rural migration in a Midlands county: Leicestershire, *c*.1270–1350', *Continuity and Change*, 7, (1992), 139–62.

[5] *AASR*, (1888–9).

[6] Potential names of gentry families are derived from G Astill, 'The medieval gentry: a study in Leicestershire society, 1350–1399', unpublished PhD. thesis, University of Birmingham 1977, *passim*.

[7] McClure, 'Patterns of migration', 175–6.

[8] Rothley, 89–130; dated by comparison with PRO C260/86.

[9] MM 6376–6406, 6556–6573.

[10] Bodl. MS Laud Misc 625, fos. 191r–211v.

[11] Bodl. MS Rawl 350, 1–51.

[12] For more specific percentages, D Postles, 'Surnames and the composition of local populations: Rutland, 13th to 17th centuries', *East Midland Geographer*, 16, (1993), 33.

[13] PRO E179/165/1, 21; *Tudor Rutland*; *Rutland Hearth Tax*.

[14] The full details are provided in Postles, 'Surnames and the composition of local populations', 31.

[15] *AASR*, (1888–9); PRO E179/133/35, E179/133/104, 108–10, 112, 114–18, 121–22.

[16] Ranges of figures take into account the methodological problem of counting surnames in different communities once or for each incidence.

[17] Bodl. MS Laud Misc 625, fos. 191r–211r.

[18] *Ibid.*, fos. 186v, 188r.

[19] *Ibid.*, fos. 188r–v.

20 D G Edwards, ed., *Derbyshire Hearth Tax Assessments 1662-1670*, (Derbyshire Record Society, 7, 1982), 3, 5, 22, 32, 89, 123.

21 Rothley; *AASR*, (1888-9), 230-1; Bodl. MS Wood empt 7, fos. 4v-91r.

22 Bodl. MS Wood empt 7, fos. 12r, 13r-14v, 17r-v, 20v, 29v-30r, 73r-v, 80v-84r.

23 S E Thorne, ed. and trans., *Bracton on the Laws and Customs of England*, vol. III, (Cambridge, Mass., 1977), 198-9.

24 Ex inf. Jane Laughton who has researched in the court rolls for Melton in the fifteenth century at Melbourne Hall, Derbyshire.

25 McClure, 'Patterns of migration'.

26 HAM Box 20, flder 4. This section relies on: HAM Box 20, flders 1-9, Box 21, flders 1-3, Box 24, flders 2, 4, 6-7.

27 D Postles, 'The pattern of rural migration in a Midlands county: Leicestershire, *c.*1270-1350', *Continuity and Change*, 7, (1992), 157, 161, nn. 38-9.

28 The trimmed mean used is the standard one in Minitab, slicing the highest and lowest 5% of values.

29 McClure, 'Patterns of migration', 174.

30 Leicestershire County Record Office, BRIII/4/70-73.

31 McClure, 'Patterns of migration', 177-8.

32 *Ibid.*, 177.

33 Compare M Kowaleski, *Local Markets and Regional Trade in Medieval Exeter*, (Cambridge, 1995), 84-6; S H Rigby, *Medieval Grimsby. Growth and Decline*, (Hull, 1993), 20-2; S Penn, 'The origins of Bristol migrants in the early fourteenth century: the surname evidence', *Transactions of the Bristol and Gloucestershire Archaeological Society*, 101 (1983), 123-30.

34 *Rutland MSS*, 19.

35 *AASR*, 34.

36 *Ibid.*, 20.

37 *Ibid.*, 119.

38 *Ibid.*, 120.

39 *Ibid.*, 168-9.

40 *AASR*, (1888-9), 212.

41 PRO E179/135/15, m.16.

42 E G Kimball, *Sessions of the Peace in the City of Lincoln 1351-1354*, (Lincoln Record Society 65, 1971), 159, 161, 176.

43 PRO SC2/183/90.

44 J C Cox, 'Derbyshire in 1327: being a lay subsidy roll', *Journal of the Derbyshire Archaeological and Natural History Society*, 30 (1908), 50.

Cox has transcribed the entry as le (*sic*) Beauuer; the MS was partly illegible at this point, explaining the lack of precise vill.

45 *Rutland Hearth Tax*, 21, 25, 28, 30, 34, 36, 37, 43.

46 PRO H.O. 107/2092–2093.

47 Genuki site on the World Wide Web at this URL: http://sentinel.mcc.ac.uk/genuki/bcg/eng/NTH/Glapthorn/surnames.html.

48 W A Hartley, ed., *Northamptonshire Militia Lists 1777*, (Northampton-shire Record Society 25, 1973), 106, 200.

49 *Suffolk in 1674. Being the Hearth Tax Returns*, (Suffolk Green Books, 11, 1905), 207; C A F Meekings, ed., *Surrey Hearth Tax 1664*, (Surrey Record Society, 41–42, 1940), 16.

50 R H Helmholz, *Marriage Litigation in Medieval England*, (Cambridge, 1974), 229.

51 E Ekwall, *The Concise Oxford Dictionary of English Placenames*, (Oxford, 4th edn., 1960), 35.

52 D Greenway, ed., *Charters of the Honour of Mowbray 1107–1191*, (British Academy Records of the Social and Economic History of England and Wales, ns. 1, 1973), xxxix, xli, lxii–lv.

53 *Ibid.*, 22–3 (no. 23).

54 Comprising the directories for North Lincolnshire, Northampton, Chesterfield/Worksop/North Derbyshire, Nottingham, Derby, Mansfield/Newark, South Lincolnshire, Leicestershire (including Rutland), Peterborough/Huntingdon, Kettering, and Mid Lincolnshire.

55 Consisting of the directories for Reading, Slough, High Wycumbe, Aylesbury, Banbury, Bedford, Hemel Hempstead, Hitchin, Luton, Milton Keynes, Bishop's Stortford, and three directories for Berkshire — otherwise, then, the northern Home Counties.

56 Comprehending the directories for Norwich, Bury St Edmunds, Ipswich, King's Lynn, Southend on Sea, Chelmsford, North Norfolk, South Norfolk/Lowestoft, Colchester and Cambridge.

57 Consisting of the directories for Medway, Tunbridge Wells, Hastings/Weald and Canterbury.

58 Composed of the directories for Blackburn, Cumbria/North Lancashire, Manchester, Chester, six directories covering South Lancashire, Blackpool, Central Lancashire, Wigan, Southport and South Cheshire.

59 Directories for Coventry, Stoke on Trent, Wolverhampton, Worcester, Burton on Trent, Birmingham, Walsall/Lichfield, Coventry/Nuneaton/Rugby, Warwick/Stratford, Shropshire,

Hereford, six directories for Gloucestershire and three for Staffordshire.

60 Directories for Guildford, Portsmouth, Southampton, Bournemouth, Mid Dorset, North-East Hampshire, West Surrey and four directories for Sussex.

61 Directories for Leeds, Bradford, Halifax, Huddersfield, Sheffield, Rotherham, Barnsley, and Doncaster for the West Riding, Hull for the East Riding, and York, Scarborough and Harrogate.

62 Directories for Northumberland, Tyneside, Durham, Darlington and Cleveland.

63 Directories for Plymouth/South-West, Taunton, Cornwall, Salisbury, North Wiltshire, and three directories for Devon.

64 McClure, 'Patterns of migration'.

65 The following have been consulted: J Ward, *The Medieval Essex Community. The Lay Subsidy of 1327*, (Essex Historical Documents 1, Essex Record Office Publication 88, Chelmsford, 1983); A M Erskine, ed., *The Devonshire Lay Subsidy of 1332*, (Devon and Cornwall Record Society, n.s. 14, 1969); D A Crowley, ed., *The Wiltshire Tax List of 1332*, (Wiltshire Record Society, 45, 1989); J P Steel, ed., *Cumberland Lay Subsidy . . . 6 Edward III*, (Kendal, 1912) (30 Rotheland at Brampton); C M Fraser, *The Northumberland Lay Subsidy Roll of 1296*, (Society of Antiquaries of Newcastle upon Tyne, Record Series 1, 1968); W Brown, ed., *Yorkshire Lay Subsidy . . . 25 Edward I (1297)*, (Yorkshire Archaeological Society, Record Series, 16, 1894); J C Cox, 'Derbyshire in 1327'; G Wrottesley, 'The Exchequer lay subsidy of A.D. 1327', *Collections for a History of Staffordshire*, (William Salt Archaeological Society), 7 (1886); PRO E179/135/14–16 (Lincolnshire, 1332); J A Raftis and M P Hogan, *Early Huntingdonshire Lay Subsidy Rolls*, (Pontifical Institute of Mediaeval Studies, Subsidia Mediaevalia, 8, 1976); W F Carter, ed., *The Lay Subsidy Roll for Warwickshire of 1332*, (Dugdale Society, 6, 1926); F J Field, ed., *Lay Subsidy for the County of Worcester 1 Edward I*, (*sic* — recte III, 1327), (Worcestershire Historical Society, 9, 1895); W G D Fletcher, 'The Shropshire lay subsidy of 1 Edward III', (Shropshire Archaeological Society, 1907); P Franklin, *The Taxpayers of Medieval Gloucestershire. An Analysis of the 1327 Lay Subsidy Roll with a New Edition of its Text*, (Stroud, 1993); A T Gaydon, *The Taxation of 1297*, (Bedfordshire Historical Record Society, 39, 1959); A C Chibnall, *Early Taxation Returns*, (Buckinghamshire Record Society, 1966); E Powell, ed., *Suffolk in 1327 being a Subsidy Return*,

(Suffolk Green Books, IX, vol. 11, Woodbridge, 1906); H A Hanley and C W Chalkin, 'The Kent lay subsidy of 1334/5' in F R H DuBoulay, ed., *Documents Illustrative of Medieval Kentish Society,* (Kent Records, 18, 1964); *Surrey Taxation Returns,* (Surrey Record Society, 33, 1932); W Hudson, ed., *The Three Earliest Lay Subsidies for the County of Sussex in the Years 1296, 1327, 1332,* (Sussex Record Society, 10, 1910); F H Dickinson, ed., *Kirkby's Quest for Somerset,* (Somerset Record Society, 3, 1889); J P Rylands, 'The Exchequer lay subsidy roll of Robert de Shireburn and John de Radcliffe, taxers and collectors in the county of Lancashire', *Miscellanies relating to Lancashire and Cheshire,* vol. ii, (Lancashire and Cheshire Record Society, 31, 1896). For Warwickshire, the bynames were located as follows (references are to pages in *Lay Subsidy Roll for Warwickshire*): 2 (de Leycestr' at Henley in Arden), 3 (same at Warwick), 24 (de Lowesby at Upton), 28–9 (de Blaby at Ladbrooke and Scrapetoft at Southam), 29 (de Enderby at Napton), 33 (de Shepeye at Arley), 35 (de Lobenham at Stretton), 36 (de Euynton at Clifton), 38 (de Leycestre at Stivichall), 53 (de Barkeby at Chilton), 58 (de Boseworth at Polesworth), 60 (de Burbache at Fillingley), 66 (de Barkeby at Kinsbury), 70 (de Hynkeley at Birmingham), 81 (de Haloughton at Ecclesall). For Derbyshire ('Derbyshire in 1327'), the locations were Bakewell (61, de Leycestre), Mackworth (75, de Kegworth) and Shirland (85, de Dalby).

[66] D M Owen, ed., *The Making of King's Lynn,* (British Academy Records of Social and Economic History, n.s. 9, 1984), 41, 49, 302, 313, 339.

[67] C H Drinkwater, ed., 'The merchant gild of Shrewsbury: seven rolls of the thirteenth century', *Transactions of the Shropshire Archaeological and Natural History Society,* 2nd ser., 12 (1900), 229–82 (1232–68) and 'Some Shrewsbury gild merchant rolls of the fourteenth century', *ibid,* 3rd ser., 3 (1903), 47–98 (1318–97), 60 (1318).

[68] *Rotuli Hundredorum,* (Record Commission, 2 vols., 1812–18), ii, 792, 794, 796, 807.

[69] J E Thorold Rogers, ed., *Oxford City Documents 1268–1665,* (Oxford Historical Society, 18, 1891), 229 (no. 117).

[70] Oxford City Archives D17/1b: 'Christoforus (*sic*) filius Simonis Beneyt perplegium Willelmi de leyc' et Johannis person querens de Rogero Abbate Oseneye Thoma de Weston et fratre Roberto de villa in placito vetiti namii optulit se . . .'

71 M Biddle, ed., *Winchester in the Early Middle Ages. An Edition and Discussion of the Winton Domesday*, (Winchester Studies, I, Oxford, 1976); D Keene, ed., *Survey of Medieval Winchester*, (Winchester Studies, 2 vols., Oxford, 1985), II, ii, 1285.

72 A F Butcher, 'Canterbury's earliest rolls of freemen admissions, 1297–1363: a reconsideration' in F Hull, ed., *A Kentish Miscellany*, (Kent Records 21, 1979), 18; S Thrupp, 'The earliest Canterbury freemen's rolls, 1298–1363' in F R H DuBoulay, ed., *Documents Illustrative of Medieval Kentish Society*, (Kent Records 18, 1964), 182.

73 M Hollings, ed., *The Red Book of Worcester*, (Worcestershire Historical Society, 1934), 483–4; E M Carus-Wilson, 'The first half century of the borough of Stratford-upon-Avon' in R Holt and G. Rosser, eds., *The Medieval Town: A Reader in English Urban History*, (London, 1990), 59.

74 G H Martin, ed., *The Ipswich Recognizance Rolls 1294–1327. A Calendar*, (Suffolk Record Society, 16, 1973), 84–5, 95, 104, 129, 135.

75 R R Sharpe, ed., *A Calendar of Wills Proved and Enrolled in the Court of Husting, London*, (2 vols., London, 1889–90); i, 17, 81, 166, 275, 300, 337, 364, 414, 568, 570; ii, 24–5, 290, 307.

76 G Rosser, *Medieval Westminster*, (Oxford, 1989), Appendix VI, 350–60 (identifications of places of origin by Rosser). Hugh Okeham (fl. in Westminster 1486–1516) was constable of the vill in 1486: *ibid.*, 393.

77 G R Elvey, ed., *Luffield Priory Charters Part II*, (Northamptonshire Record Society, 26, 1975), 34–5 (no. 327).

78 W Stephenson, ed., *Records of the Borough of Nottingham*, I, (Nottingham, 1882), 85; he recurred in 1297–8 and 1316 attesting charters: *ibid.*, 368 and 379.

79 F Hill, *Medieval Lincoln*, (repr. Stamford, 1990), 382, 401.

80 R R Darlington, ed., *Darley Cartulary*, (Kendal, 2 vols., 1945), 98 (no. A51), 330 (no. 967).

81 *Ibid.*, 148 (no. C25), 216 (no. E20).

82 P R Coss, ed., *The Early Records of Medieval Coventry*, (British Academy, Records of Social and Economic History, n.s. 11, London, 1986), 101 (no. 129, William de Borbache, merchant of Coventry), 122 (no. 185, Stephen de Claybrok, weaver), 141 (no. 232, Richard de Leycestr'), 149 (no. 256, William de Schepeye, merchant of Coventry), 226 (no. 465, William *textor* son of Geoffrey de Burbache), 241 (no. 511, John de Claybroc, weaver), 252 (no.

261, Simon de Leicestr'), 320 (no. 704, Henry de Hinkele): all thirteenth–early fourteenth century. In the Hundred Rolls of 1279–80 for Coventry, edited by T John in the same volume, the following held urban property: William de Shulton, a burgage (374, perhaps as likely Earl's Shilton as Chilton); Henry de Hinkel', a curtilage (378), Peter de Cotesbach, a burgage (380), Robert de Hinkel', a burgage (380) and Thomas de Burbache, a cottage (384); in these cases, Burbache is more likely to relate to Burbage in Leicestershire than the eponymous settlement in Wiltshire. Jurors representing Coventry at the Crown Pleas included Peter de Lutrewurth in 1232 and Laurence de Shepeye in 1306: 48, 58.

[83] T Foulds, ed., *Thurgarton Cartulary*, (Stamford, 1994), 151 (no. 242), 225 (no. 387).

[84] *Ibid.*, 585 (no. 1022).

[85] *Ibid.*, 665, 676.

[86] M Gollancz, ed., *Rolls of the Northamptonshire Sessions of the Peace*, (Northamptonshire Record Society, 11, 1940), 4, 7.

[87] *Ibid.*, 60.

[88] E G Kimball, ed., *Sessions of the Peace in the City of Lincoln 1351–1354*, (Lincoln Record Society, 65, 1971), 2.

[89] *Ibid.*, 24.

[90] *Ibid.*, 167.

[91] R Sillein, ed., *Some Sessions of the Peace in Lincolnshire 1360–1375*, (Lincoln Record Society, 30, 1937), 162–3.

[92] *Ibid.*, 194–5, 200.

[93] *Ibid.*, 234.

[94] A E B Owen, ed., *The Medieval Lindsey Marsh. Select Documents*, (Lincoln Record Society, 85, 1996), 47 (no. 18).

[95] A Saltman, ed., *The Kniveton Ledger*, (Derbyshire Archaeological Society Record Series, 7, 1972–3), 119–22, 154 (nos. 230, 233, 235–6, 310).

[96] Bodl. Herefordshire Rolls 3: 'defalta. Ricardus de Clehungr' et Willelmus de Leycestr' distringantur pro defaltis secte Curie'.

[97] J G Jenkins, ed., *The Cartulary of Missenden Abbey Part III*, (Historical Manuscripts Commission, JP 1, 1962), 36–7 (no. 589).

[98] *Rotuli Hundredorum*, ii, 433–4.

[99] *Ibid.*, 532.

[100] J W Clark, ed., *Liber Memorandum Ecclesie de Bernewell*, (Cambridge, 1907), 310.

101 Hollings, *Red Book of Worcester*, 390.
102 C M Barron, 'The fourteenth century poll tax returns for Worcester', *Midland History*, 14 (1989), 19, 24.
103 Edwards, *Derbyshire Hearth Tax Assessments*, 9, 20, 79–80, 83, 85–7, 98, 103, 111, 124, 131 for this surname.
104 *Ibid.*, 119, 129, 163.
105 *Ibid.*, 127, 134, 137, 180.
106 *Ibid.*, 91, 99, 137.
107 *Ibid.*, 29, 72, 198.
108 *Ibid.*, 23, 95, 107, 130, 131, 136, 150, 151.
109 *Ibid.*, 124.
110 W F Webster, ed., *Nottinghamshire Hearth Tax 1664: 1674*, (Thoroton Society Record Series, 37, 1988), 2, 4, 9, 13, 21, 22, 27, 40, 52, 58, 62, 67, 71, 74, 76, 84, 90, 91, 95, 107, 123.
111 A Mawer and F M Stenton, *The Place-Names of Nottinghamshire*, (English Place-Name Society, 17, 1940), 81.
112 For Broughton, Webster, *Nottinghamshire Hearth Tax*, 7 (for example).
113 Webster, *Nottinghamshire Hearth Tax*, 53, 54, 65, 74, 76, 79 for some of the incidences of the surname.
114 Mawer and Stenton, *Place-Names of Nottinghamshire*, 178; Webster, *Nottinghamshire Hearth Tax*, 1, 66, 89, 101.
115 Mawer and Stenton, *Place-Names of Nottinghamshire*, 25; Webster, *Nottinghamshire Hearth Tax*, 26, 28, 30, 31.
116 Webster, *Nottinghamshire Hearth Tax*, 5, 8, 39, 40.
117 Mawer and Stenton, *Place-Names of Nottinghamshire*, 87.
118 Mawer and Stenton, *Place-Names of Nottinghamshire*, 234.
119 Telephone directories 213 (Nottingham and District) 76 entries, 241 (Leicester and District) 57, 214 (Mansfield and Newark) 36, 608 (South Lincolnshire) 40 and 246 (Mid Lincolnshire) 28. By contrast, a purposive sample of other directories reveals the lower numbers in other areas of England. The sample was selected geographically and to reflect both urban and rural areas: directory 247 (York) seven Mussons; 604 (Kettering) five; 605 (Northampton) eight; 607 (Peterborough and Huntingdon) 11; 612 (Hereford) four; 613 (Shropshire) three; 641 (North Devon) seven; 644 (Brighton) two; 316 (Tyneside) two; 643 (Horsham) three; 647 (Stafford) one; 325 (Bedford) none; 334 (Medway) one; 338 (King's Lynn) one; 337 (Cambridge) three; 347 (Leeds) three; 366 (Colchester) none; 315 (Northumberland) two; 252 (Cumbria

and North Lancashire) six; 263–66 (Manchester) eight; 267 (High Peak) one; 330 (Birmingham) six; and 539 (Norwich and Norfolk) eight. What is remarkable is the diminution of the numbers outside a radius of about 20 miles from the source.

[120] C V Phythian-Adams, 'Introduction: an agenda for English Local History', in *idem*, ed., *Societies, Cultures and Kinship, 1580–1850. Cultural Provinces and English Local History*, (London, 1993), 16 for the extent of the Trent province.

[121] From transcriptions of the registers on the World Wide Web at this URL: http://sentinel.mcc.ac.uk/genuki/bcg/eng/NTT/ Nottingham.html. For the Thornton and Burrowes families of butchers in Ant Hill, Broad Lane, Clumber Street and Meadows Platts in Nottingham in 1813–18, see the message from Rod Neep to Nottsgen (Nottsgen@rmgate.pop.indiana.edu) of Saturday 8 March 1997 (from the St Mary's registers of baptisms with the occupations of fathers).

[122] V A Gatley, ed., *Northamptonshire Militia Lists 1777*, (Northamptonshire Record Society, 25, 1973).

[123] For these surnames, *ibid.*, 2, 8, 22, 26, 27, 58, 90, 95, 102, 108, 113, 120, 149, 172, 194 (Branson and variants) (presuming here a devoiced /t/ in the surname, since most incidences are Branson); 34, 44, 52, 81, 82, 84, 89, 96, 107, 109, 150, 211 (Houghton and variants, predominantly Houghton); 83, 157, 167, 202, 204 (Broughton and variants).

[124] L M Marshall, 'Hearth Tax Return 1671', *Bedfordshire Historical Record Society*, 16 (1934), 65–198.

[125] *Ibid.*, (Houghton and Hooton) 101, 116, 132, 139, 143, 152, 153, (index) 178, (Broughton) 68, 125, (Langley) 92, 158, (index) 180.

[126] *Ibid.*, 65, 67, 72, 75, 76, 89, 93, 101, 103, 116, 118, 121, 122, 123, 126, 128, 130, 133, 135, 137, 138, 139, 143, 146, 150. 156, 157, 158.

[127] M M B Weinstock, *Hearth Tax Returns, Oxfordshire 1665*, (Oxfordshire Record Society, 21, 1940), 113.

[128] *Ibid.*, 21, 36, 71, 162, 168, 232.

[129] C A F Meekings, S Porter and I Roy, *The Hearth Tax Collectors' Book for Worcester 1678–1680*, (Worcestershire Historical Society, n.s. 11, 1983), 51, 58.

[130] For these names, E Hughes and P White, *The Hampshire Hearth Tax Assessment 1665*, (Hampshire Record Society, 11, 1992), 7, 28, 69, 77, 85, 97, 164, 224–6.

[131] *Ibid.*, 32.

[132] *Suffolk in 1674 Being the Hearth Tax Returns*, (Suffolk Green Books, 11, 1905), (Langham) 1, 15, 61-3, 94, 139, 161, 190, 209, 266, 301, 324, (Langly/Lungly) 17, 94, 105, 111, 146, 161, 184, 201, 214, 215, 232, 163, 257, 261, 266, 273, 276, 309, (Melton) 16, 128, (Belton) 88, 276, (Howton) 214, 216-17, 235, 302, 309 320, (Mosley) 141, 318.

[133] *Ibid.*, 77, 81, 129, 275, 300, 303, 317.

[134] *Ibid.*, 8, 12, 14, 32, 39, 41, 48, 50, 58, 60, 68, 72, 76, 78, 131, 150, 160, 163, 166, 169, 178, 185, 189, 192, 207, 220, 224, 240, 243-4, 248, 262, 270, 272, 274, 289, 293, 318, 326.

[135] *Ibid.*, 39, 50, 60, 68, 72, 76, 78, 131, 159, 166, 224, 240, 248.

[136] C A F Meekings, ed., *Surrey Hearth Tax 1664*, (Surrey Record Society, 41-42, 1940).

[137] *Ibid.*, 21, 24, 70, 71, 93, 123, 152.

[138] *Ibid.*, 14, 16, 22, 27, 45, 133, 134, 146.

CHAPTER 6

OCCUPATIONAL BYNAMES AND SURNAMES

Occupational bynames and surnames in rural places

Corresponding with the levels in several other counties, the proportion of bynames and surnames from occupation, status or office ranged in Leicestershire and Rutland between 16 and 20% of taxpayers in assessments for taxation, although the proportion was higher in the Poll Tax enumerations, at 32.3% of Poll Tax payers in Rutland in 1377 and 29.4% of contributors in Leicestershire in 1381.[1]

The corpus of descriptive terms used as names was much wider in Leicestershire than Rutland, although partly a function of the disparate numbers of taxable population. About half as many occupational terms were contained in the listings in Rutland as in its sister county to the west. Nevertheless, the mean of taxpayers for each occupational name was approximately similar in both counties, at particularly low levels, reflected further in a median of only one or two taxpayers for each term and a correspondingly slight third quartile.

Table 6.1

Descriptive statistics of occupational bynames and surnames in Leicestershire and Rutland, 1296–1524[2]

	N	Mean	stdev	median	min	max	Q1	Q3
		bynames/surnames						
Rutland 1296	78	4.03	6.145	1	1	30	1	4
Rutland 1377	88	3.06	3.958	2	1	22	1	3
Rutland 1522	66	3.79	4.171	2	1	22	1	5
Leics. 1327	140	4.49	6.557	2	1	39	1	5
Leics. 1381	145	4.17	7.005	2	1	46	1	4
Leics. 1524	131	6.00	9.399	2	1	67	1	7

Table 6.1 illustrates the relationship between taxable population and numbers of occupational bynames and surnames, but requires

further explanation. The number of bynames and surnames in column two represents the number of different bynames and surnames rather than occupations. To clarify, for example, Bayl(l)y and Bailiff have been considered different bynames rather than evolving from the same office, and Bedel has been further differentiated; furthermore, the various terms resulting from milling — Mouner, Moleyn, Miller, and Milner — have been counted separately; and so also Bocher and Flesshewer. Similarly, dialect elements such as -ster have been accepted as comprising a different byname, thus differentiating Baker and Bax(s)ter (Bakster). The distinctions are complicated, at least before the middle of the fourteenth century, by the use of language, the two vernaculars, Anglo-Norman and Middle English, and the higher register, Latin. The two vernaculars can be fairly unequivocally separated, so that le bercher is accepted here as a different byname from s(c)hepard and similarly ferour/feuere from smyth(e). Less directly soluble is a small number of Latin occupational nouns, *faber*, *sutor* and *pistor*. At issue is whether these Latin terms persisted as surnames in their original rather than translated form. The later evidence for Leicestershire and Rutland is fairly conclusive that, although sutor (souter, sowter) continued as a surname, *faber* and *pistor* did not. In the calculations, therefore, *faber* has been included with Smythe and *pistor* with Baxter. Most ambiguous, however, and unresolved, is *mercator*, which did not persist as a surname, but which could have been translated in the local context into either Chapman or Merchant, with preference, certainly in the rural context, for the former.

Table 6.2 then represents the aggregate of different occupational terms employed as bynames and surnames in the two counties rather than the number of different occupations (that is, stem forms). Broadly, the table reveals that a fairly wide range of occupational descriptions was used as bynames and surnames in the two counties through the late middle ages, that the quantity of these terms remained at about the same level, and that, although a proportion was borne by a considerable number of taxpayers, the majority was associated with only a few.

Behind the figures reside some general trends which will be further elaborated. First, the composition or stock of descriptive occupational terms remained fairly consistent through the later middle ages. Concomitantly, the character of the stock outside urban places was distinctive; industry in the countryside did not significantly contribute here to the occupational terms used as bynames and surnames. In particular, the composition of bynames and surnames did not receive any consequential influence from the production of woollen cloth outside urban places, by comparison with sheep husbandry and woolgrowing in the later middle ages. The rank order of occupational terms confirms the dominance of non-industrial terms outside urban settlements. Nevertheless, change in the composition was constituted by a greater representation of terms from office and status before the middle of the fourteenth century, which declined in the later middle ages.

Table 6.2

Rank order of occupational bynames and surnames during the later middle ages

Occupation*	RUTLAND				LEICESTERSHIRE		
	1296	1377	1522	1524	1327	1381	1524
Bailiff						20	16
Baker			16	11	15		
Barker/ tanner			12	8	12		10
Bond	14				18	11	
Chaplain	12				14		
Carpenter					16		
Carter	20	13	7	9	19	23	18
Chapman					15	9	
Clerk	29	8	18	15	36	12	46
Cook	9	10	7	9	23	16	27
Cooper			12	12		12	24
Falconer				11	11		12
Fowler			10	9			10
Freeman	13			7	11		13
Knight							13
Marshal					15		13
Mason							13
Miller	12	13			13	23	25
Page						11	
Porter							18
Reeve	30				39	11	
Smith	23	22	25	22	50	22	67
Shepherd	7	20		8	19	45	16

Occupation*	RUTLAND				LEICESTERSHIRE		
	1296	1377	1522	1524	1327	1381	1524
Tailor	13	17	14	8	21		22
Walker			8				16
Ward				9	19		25
Webster		7				14	12
Wright				14			49

* In this column, reference is made to the stem occupation rather than the specific byname which resulted; the figures are numbers of occurrences in the listings, not percentages; the rationale is that the table represents occupations significantly above the mean of occurrences, for which see Table 6.1 above.

From Table 6.2, several patterns can be discerned during the later middle ages. First, in the late thirteenth and early fourteenth centuries, bynames of status or office were proportionately higher, but declined during the later middle ages. These previously numerous forms which decreased, were exemplified by bynames from bond, chaplain, freeman and reeve, although clerk remained continuously at a high level.[3] A corpus of occupational names provided continuity, at high levels throughout the middle ages: Carter; Clerk; Cook; Miller; Shepherd; Smith; and Tailor. In contrast, other occupational names featured more strongly in the later middle ages, such as Cooper, Falconer, Knight, Mason, Porter, Walker, Webster and Wright. Many of these last names, including derivations from Falconer, had, however, been present from an earlier time, but simply became slightly more numerous, it seems, during the later middle ages. Nonetheless, Fowler, Walker and Webster may have been late introductions into the rural areas of the counties. The relationship between Wright and Carpenter is more problematic, since the earlier forms of *carpentarius* and *[le] carpenter* may have become transmuted into the ME vernacular as wright.

At the core, therefore, was a collection of occupational names which was hardly distinctive, but which represented common activities in late medieval and later rural 'communities'. Exceptionally, however, Shepherd (and the related Sh(e)arman) seems to have been better represented in the Poll Tax of 1381 for Gartree Hundred in Leicestershire. The potential reasons are that *bercarii* may have been under-represented in the lay subsidy of 1327 which was wealth-specific, whilst the Poll Tax was more inclusive, or attributed to the

FIG 14 BYNAMES AND SURNAMES FROM WOOL-GROWING IN GARTREE HUNDRED IN 1381

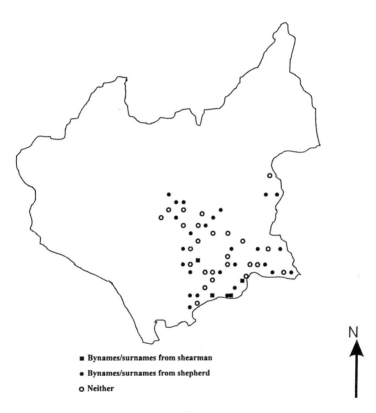

■ Bynames/surnames from shearman

● Bynames/surnames from shepherd

o Neither

Represented in this figure are data for all parishes contained in the extant Poll Tax, indicating the presence or absence of these names

Scale 0 ———————— 10

N

change in the agrarian economy of this part of Leicestershire in the later middle ages. If that economic adjustment was the cause, then its effects were already apparent in the distribution of these occupational bynames by the late fourteenth century. Demographic change in east Leicestershire, the location of Gartree Hundred, may have engendered a structural economic transformation, which encouraged the expansion of sheep husbandry.[4] There is, however, no conclusive evidence about which was the actual reason for the relative profusion of these names in the late fourteenth by comparison with the early thirteenth century.

The distribution of the occupational names Shepherd and Sherman in east Leicestershire, in Gartree Hundred, in 1381 is represented in Figure 14.[5] Although Shepherd was present in the Poll tax listings for 25 vills, in an equal number it was not represented. Sherman occurred in only three parishes. Nevertheless, the distribution of Shepherd was denser than in any other listing and, whilst Shepherd had constituted 2.9% of taxpayers with occupational bynames in the lay subsidy for the whole of Leicestershire in 1327, in the Poll Tax of 1381 for Gartree Hundred the proportion had increased to 6.2%.[6]

Whereas wool production was reflected in the occupational bynames and surnames of the county, the clothmaking processes were not as strongly represented in the names of taxpayers in rural 'communities'. Bynames and surnames did not illustrate a rural clothmaking industry.[7]

Urban occupational bynames and surnames

Whereas usually less than 20% of taxpayers in rural settlements were attributed occupational bynames and surnames during the later middle ages, with the exception of the very much higher proportion in the Poll Taxes of 1377 and 1381, the quotient in the borough of Leicester generally exceeded 20%. Depending on the inclusiveness of the source, the percentage fluctuated between 13 and 28%, but the low levels in the internal subsidies of 1307 and 1311, respectively 15 and 13%, must be attributed to the exclusiveness of these assessments, in which much smaller numbers of burgesses contributed. By comparison, the other internal subsidies of the late thirteenth and early fourteenth centuries comprehended much higher numbers of burgesses and concomitantly much higher proportions of burgesses with occupational bynames, varying from over 22 to over 27%.

Confirmation of these levels can be elicited from the *Nonarum Inquisitiones* of 1340–42 (a preparatory roll, it seems) and the rental of the tenants of Leicester Abbey in the borough in 1341. The former embraced a much wider variety of townspeople than burgesses, including, it appears, singleton females, revealing that 26.4% of townsfolk bore occupational bynames.[9] More ambiguously, the rental of the Abbey's urban tenements may have included a higher level of poorer townspeople, and accordingly only 21.7% of the tenantry were attributed occupational bynames.[10] Nevertheless, restricting the analysis to those of the status of burgess, by concentrating on admissions to the freedom (the gild merchant) between 1196 and 1350, only 14.6% of burgesses were attributed an occupational byname for the purposes of admission.

In general, however, it seems clear that a higher proportion of urban inhabitants were identified by occupational bynames in the middle ages than their rural counterparts. That urban phenomenon is ratified by the diversity of urban occupational bynames before the middle of the fourteenth century, reflecting one of the principal urban characteristics or criteria of urbanism, occupational heterogeneity.[11] Aggregating all forms of borough record — admissions to the freedom, litigation and presentments in the morning-speech and portmoot, and internal subsidies, which inherently over-represent burgesses and minimize numbers of non-burghal townspeople — some 252 different occupational bynames were represented before the middle of the fourteenth century.[12] This total comprehends forms in the two urban vernaculars, French and Middle English, but includes only those Latin forms which may have persisted, such as Pistor/Pestour or Sutor/Souter. The diversity of urban occupational bynames considerably exceeded those in the countryside in the twelfth to fourteenth centuries.

None the less, a high proportion of these occupational bynames was transient and disappeared from the borough by the later middle ages, and frequently before the middle of the fourteenth century. Indeed, a considerable number was so transitory that the names appeared only once or a few times in the records, commonly held by merely one or two townspeople. Consequently, at least 108 (42.9%) of the bynames occurring in the borough records fell into this impermanent category, represented by one or at most two urban dwellers. One explanation is that it was simply the occupational term rather than the occupation which disappeared, in that some of the earlier occupational bynames consisted of French forms, which may have been supplanted at a later time by ME vernacular.[13] For example, amongst the transient forms was le Roer, the French equivalent of wheelwright, which occurred in the borough records only in 1232 and 1286.[14] Similarly, the French byname le Corder (ropemaker) was represented only in the admission of Osbert to the gild merchant in 1227.[15] The borough's speech community may thus have been a distinctly diglossic one in the twelfth and thirteenth centuries, with a high component of French occupational bynames, but with the consequence of a considerable loss of forms during the later middle ages as ME developed into the exclusive vernacular.

Whilst it seems that French forms were more prevalent before the middle of the fourteenth century than in the later middle ages and that a proportion of losses is explicable in this way, that was not the sole explanation. For example, some ME bynames did not endure; thus ME Brasier (brassworker) was represented only in John as late as 1414–23, although Ralph appeared in the suburbs in the Poll Tax of 1381.[16] In this case, an ME form, occurring in the later middle ages, yet failed to persist. In particular, compound forms were prone to disappear, so that inherent in their creation may have been instability and the actual occupation. The transient bynames thus included Belleward, Bouwmaker, Cardemaker, Constapleman, Halleknaue, Lindraper, Maderman, Maltmongere, Melemaker, Netdryuere, Neumaister, Obleymaker, Oillemaker, Huniman, le Panne betere, Patenmaker, Spitelman, Tascheman, and Wyrdrawer. Regardless of their date of formation, whether in the thirteenth century or later middle ages, compound names were volatile.

Equally transient were occupational bynames formed in a manner mainly characteristic of the borough, although also found in association with religious houses. The byname *de Bracina* was held by Henry, Roger, Thomas and William, all assessed in the internal subsidy of 1286, William at the significant level of 4*s*.[17] In that tallage too was listed Hugh *de Pistrina* and in the earlier assessment of 1271, Simon *de Coquina* contributed as did William *de Stabulo*.[18]

Some other temporary forms of byname in fact add to the information available to Fransson, who, although he did consult the *Records of the Borough of Leicester*, missed some examples. For le Seler Fransson produced an earliest instance of 1227, but a le Seler was admitted to the gild merchant in Leicester in 1205–06.[19] Apparently omitted from Fransson, le Paneler (French) was interpreted by Bateson as a maker of pack saddles, although the *Anglo-Norman Dictionary* has a preferred explanation for panel as a horse cloth.[20] Similarly, le Flauner (French) was seemingly unknown to Fransson, but explained by Bateson as a cake- or flawn-maker; the *Anglo-Norman Dictionary* suggests that flaons or flauns were custard tarts.[21] In equal manner, Auener (1198) was not considered by Fransson, although he included ME Hauerman; presumably Auener was a French equivalent of the Latin synonym *Auenator* which occurred contemporaneously in Leicester. John Auener was admitted to the gild merchant in 1198, whilst Geoffrey and Herbert *Auenator* became freemen in 1210 and 1225. The byname le Auener recurred in the person of Gilbert (1343–47).[22] Although Fransson discovered an incidence of le Dubbere (ME, a repairer of clothes) from 1249, a freeman with this occupational byname was admitted at Leicester in 1210.[23] Equally, although Fransson has a reference to le Quareur (French, quarryman) in 1275, it is preceded by an admission in Leicester in 1252.[24] ME le Packere occurred but once in the admissions to the freedom of the borough, in 1209; its subsequent demise may have resulted from the predominant involvement of women in wool packing, unless le Packere reflected the role of the entrepreneurial organizer of the packing. Fransson's earliest reference occurred in 1275.[25] In the case of le Corder (French, ropemaker), the admission of a freeman with this byname possibly antedates Fransson's earliest instance by a few years.[26] By a similar margin — five years — the admission of a burgess called le Geliner (French, poulterer) reflects Fransson's material of 1242.[27] Finally, whilst Fransson has an earliest information of 1286 for le Cunreur or Cuureur (French, currier, tanner, preparer of leather), a burgess with this byname was admitted in Leicester in 1248, and the compounded 'Shakespeare' (or 'imperative') nickname or occupational byname Curlewache may represent an even earlier assimilation of the activity, from the late twelfth century.[28] Le Over was also not considered by Fransson, but it was presumably a French form of ME Waterman and Latin *aquarius* and *owarius*; it occurred in the admissions in 1225 and 1226.[29] Without exception, however, these early forms of bynames did not persist in the borough.

Analysis of the bynames of freemen admitted to the gild merchant before 1350 allows some reflection on the origins of occupational bynames, although a considerable number was not permanent. In this examination, Latinized forms are omitted where a vernacular form is present.

Table 6.3

Sources of occupational bynames of freemen, 1196–1350

Trade/occupation	<1250	1251–1350
leather	4	9
provisioning/services	20	21
metalworking	7	11
textiles		
woollen cloth	5	6
other textiles	5	4
building workers	1	3
hospitality	1	2
wood workers	5	5
miscellaneous	12	28

Whilst the upper categories of the table signify what might be construed as distinctively urban occupations, the lower end, in particular the bottom two classifications, include large numbers of trades which were equally rural, such as netdryuere, hayward, sheperd(e), and gardener, although others from this section had urban connotations (principally porter and hussher, hypercorrect usher). Woollen cloth contributed in only a small way to the corpus of different occupational bynames and, indeed, only a very small number of burgesses before 1350 bore bynames derived from these processes. A comparable proportion of the stock derived from leather and metal working. Overall, however, discounting the miscellaneous category, the widest range emanated from provisioning and related services, although several of these bynames were transient.

By comparison, those occupational bynames and surnames which either proliferated or persisted in the borough comprised those not necessarily urban as well as ones more usually related to towns. Although a large proportion of these bynames and surnames recurred in rural settlements, a proportion was characteristically urban and thus distinctive. Table 6.4 contains data relating to those bynames and surnames which were held by several townspeople or which persisted over a period of time.

Table 6.4
More persistent occupational bynames and surnames in the borough in the middle ages

Byname/surname	Chronology	N*	Notes†
Baker/Bakar	1266–1508	9	*de Pistrina* 1286 (1)
			Pistor/Pestour 1207–1341 (14)
			Bacstere transient see Furnur
Barber et var	1286–1505	10	
Barkere	1288–1505	16‡	see Tanur, Curreur
Burgeys et var	1199–1509	12	
Carpenter	1199–1315	7	Joynour 1377 (1) see Wryght
Cartere	1271–1379	6	le Carectar 1288 (1)
Cartewright	1354–1505	5	le Roer 1232, 1286 (2)
Combere	1211–1286	3	
Chaloner	1260–1458	13	
Chapman	1317–1455	8	le Marca(u)nt
Clerk et var	1208–1524	32	
Coc/Coke	1196–1525	24	see le Keu/Ko
Cu(n)(r)reur	1286–1375	8	see Barkere, Tanur
Cutiler	1271–1458	6	but large gap 1286–1458
Cuuer	1237–1290	7	see Cupere
Cupere et var	1225–1475	19	see Cuuer
Dexter(e)	1262–1381	12	Blacstere transient
Faber	1196–1253	18	see Smethe, Ferour
Fer(o)ur	1227–1385	8	see Smethe, Faber
			le Feure 1288 (1)
			le Feyere 1286 (1)
Fysher et var	1318–1496	13	
Fo(r)(e)ster	1232–1507	11	
Furnur	1211–	9	see Baker
Gardiner	1242–1492	10	
Glouer	1365–1505	10	le Gaunter 1286–1341 (4)
Goldesmyth	1343–1492	6	le Orfeure 1288–9 (1)
Hayward	1318–1495	4	
Keu, Cu	1199–1340	12	see Coc/Coke
Lorimer	1278–1365	4	

Byname/surname	Chronology	N*	Notes†
Marchall et var	1260–1354	9	
Mason et var	1253–1500	13	Machoun, Machyn 1318, 1477 (4)
Mercer, Merser	1199–1366	25	
Milnere	1318–1505	9	*de Molendino* 1286 (1) le munere et var 1199–1206 (2)
Mustarder	1226–1318	9	
Parcheminer	1199–1340	6	
Parmenter	1199–1341	7	see Tailur
Peyntour	1286–1354	4	
Plomer et var	1225–1505	9	Ledbetere 1286–1355 (7)
Porter	1206–1491	12	
Potter	1196–1505	4	
Ropere	1341–1362	5	le corder transient
Sadeler	1336–1452	5	see le Seler
Sawer	1332–1367	5	
S(c)(h)ereman	1205–1494	14	hiatus 1205–1286
Sclater	1271–1452	9	
Seler	1207–1343	10	le Celer 1290–3 (1) §
Skynner	1327–1508	10	le Pelter 1286 (1)
Spencer	1369–1505	6	
Spicer	1254–1376	6	Le Espicer/Lesp(e)cer 1288–93 (1)
Tailur et var	1262–1506	26	see Parmenter
Tanur	1268–1379	14	see Barkere, Currieur
Tauerner	1271–1477	10	
Turnar	1219–1477	12	
Walker	1271–1525	9	
Webster	1336–1504	10	
Whyttawere	1300–1497	3	
Wryght	1376–1507	8	see Carpenter

Notes: * N relates to the number of individual townspeople with this byname; † the column labelled Notes describes other forms of byname for this occupation, but Latin forms are omitted unless they are likely to have persisted as bynames and surnames in that register; ‡ in the *Nonarum Inquisitiones* of 1340–42, five of the assessed bore this byname (Hugh, Ivo, John, Walter, and Matilda;[30] § Laurence le Celer in 1290–93 was identical with Laurence le Seler.

Compounded occupational bynames and surnames

Within the aggregate of occupational bynames, compounded forms were never numerous in the two counties, excluding some compounds with -man. Under consideration are the suffixes -maker, -smith, -wright, -ward, -monger and -herd, and some miscellaneous forms. With the exception of -ward and -herd, these compounds were almost exclusively employed in the urban context in the later middle ages, in small towns as well as the county town, whereas -ward and -herd were self-evidently more rural in circumstance.

Compounds of -maker were both unusual and exclusively urban, confined to Leicester and the small town of Loughborough. The earliest recorded compound in the two counties concerned John le Boumaker, a juror of Leicester's gild merchant in 1281.[31] In 1307, Hugh le Oillemaker was assessed in the subsidy in the borough at 6*d*.[32] The borough tallage of 1336 comprehended Isabel Melemaker and Hawise Bouwemaker, taxed at 4*d*. and 6*d*. respectively, and Isabel was assessed at 3*d*. in the *Nonarum Inquisitiones* of 1340–41.[33] In the taxation of 1354 John Cardemaker was tallaged at 1*s*.[34] Surprisingly few further compounds were employed during the later middle ages, encompassing only William Obleymaker in 1379, William Pattenmaker in 1458 and the same or another William Patenmaker in 1495.[35] Even within the borough of Leicester -maker compounds remained at a fairly low level.

Their incidence elsewhere was largely confined to the small town of Loughborough, in the later middle ages, represented in William Cardemaker, appearing in pleas of debt and presented for nuisances in the manor court in 1404–05.[36] Also involved in litigation in that court, in debt and covenant, and presented for brewing, was John Colermaker, in 1429–31.[37] John Skepmaker made a single appearance in that court in a case of debt in 1404.[38] In a rural context, only Marger' (Margery or Margaret) Maltemaker and John Matmaker (*sic*) were seemingly recorded in Rutland, both in the Poll Tax of 1377, respectively at Great Casterton and Barrowden, although they were complemented by Isabel Westmaker at Stonton Wyville in the same taxation for Gartree Hundred in 1381.[39] The suffix -maker was relatively scarce, even in the urban context where it appeared more frequently.

Some compounds with -monger exhibit the same distribution, with a stronger concentration in towns. In 1199, Roger Maltemongere was admitted to the gild merchant of Leicester, followed by Richard Gresmongere in 1220, who, however, was a foreigner, from one of the Overtons. Taxed in the market town of Market Harborough in the Poll Tax of 1381 was Robert Garlyngmonger.[40]

Exceptionally, however, variants of Ironmonger, although still revealing a strong presence in urban places, had a much wider distribution. In the urban context, Nicholas le Irenmonger was taxed in the subsidies of 1318 and 1336 in the borough of Leicester, whilst Adam le Irnemongere was also assessed in 1318 and had been admitted to the gild merchant three years previously.[41] Irenmongeres featured strongly in the urban society of the small town of Loughborough, represented in appearances in the court rolls by Ralph (1397–1412), Robert (1397–1404), Alice (1397 and 1403), William (1405 and 1429–31) and Richard (1411).[42] It is possible, although not entirely clear, that the name was still eponymous with the trade in Loughborough, even in the late fourteenth and early fifteenth century, and a section of the market was designated *infra Irnemongeres*. Still within the urban context, although in a rather decayed borough in the north-west of Leicestershire, Castle Donington, the surname Iremonger or Irynmonger had a strong presence, in Thomas (1457–65), William (1464–86), Hugh (1464–87), another William (1510–48) and another Hugh (1532–42).[43] The byname or surname also appeared in other small towns and in market vills, in Market Harborough in the Poll Tax of 1381, in charters relating to Melton Mowbray in the fourteenth century, in the lay subsidy for the market vill of Hallaton in 1327, and in Oakham in the survey of 1305.[44]

Although predominantly located within an urban context, Ironmonger and its variants did extend into rural 'communities', particularly during the later middle ages: Ernemonger at Owston in 1372–73; the aspirated or hypercorrect Geoffrey and Agnes Hernemonger in the Poll Tax of 1377 in Lyddington as well as John Iremonger; the similar Hirnemonger in Twyford in 1387; also hypercorrect Hurmonger in Bittesby in 1327 (Peter, Richard, Roger and William in the lay subsidy); an Iremonger taxed at Kimcote and Walton in 1525; and John Yremonger of Shilton noted in records relating to Kirkby Mallory in 1477.[45]

Compounds of -smith were particularly unusual and again often more prevalent in towns than rural areas. Brounsmith seems to have become established as the name of a kinship in the small town of

Loughborough in the later middle ages, an appropriate context for a surname which reflected origins in brass foundry.[46] Robert Brounsmith, a tenant in the rental of *c*.1370, was succeeded by John (1376, 1404–12), William (1398 and 1403) and William the younger (1398), and Edward (1431), all mentioned in the court rolls.[47] Grenesmyth was also evidenced in this small town, although much later and after the disassociation of surname and occupation, through Richard (1525–26), Robert (1526) and Alice (1550) in the rentals of Loughborough.[48] Similarly, Loughborough was one of the *loca* of the compound Loksmyth, as John (1398) and William (1404–12) were involved in litigation in its manorial court.[49] In the borough of Leicester, John Loksmyth was admitted to the gild merchant in 1378, but Richard Loksmyth, who was tallaged at 7*d*. in 1354 and mentioned in 1379, was by trade a slater.[50] Although that name occurred also in the market town of Market Harborough when John Loksmyth was taxed in 1381, it extended contemporaneously to rural villages in the person of John Loksmyth of Morcott, assessed in the Rutland Poll Tax of 1377.[51]

Nicholas Showsmyth [Shoesmith] of Castle Donington (1467–82) reflected, however, how closely compounds of –smith were associated with the urban context. So also John Bondesmyth was tallaged at 3*d*. in the urban subsidy of Leicester in 1354, whilst the subsidy of 1318 for the borough had included le Arwesmyth.[52] Most especially was that urban association relevant for Goldsmith, which was necessarily in its origins very restricted in its incidence, which remained the case (omitting here the Latin [*Aurifaber*] and French [*Orfevre*] forms of the name and concentrating on the vernacular equivalent). Vernacular Goldesmyth appeared first in the borough of Leicester through Matilda Goldesmyth, mentioned in the proceedings of the morningspeech of the gild merchant in 1336, but more substantially in William (1343–54), who was probably synonymous with the William senior assessed extremely highly at 6*s*. in the subsidy of 1354. In that internal taxation, William junior can probably be identified with the William junior who contributed 6*d*., having been admitted to the freedom in the same year.[53] In the late middle ages, the persistence of the name in the borough was achieved through Henry who contributed 8*d*. to the subsidy of 1492.[54] Outside the borough, this surname was apparent only at Melton Mowbray, a small town, through John senior and junior (1414–23), and at another small town, Castle Donington, in Richard (1543).[55]

Other compounded occupational bynames and surnames were less specific to particular contexts, whether urban or rural. For example, compounds with -wright were located in both urban and rural settlements, although Cartewright was curiously more urban than rural. This surname existed in both Loughborough and Castle Donington through the late middle ages, represented by John (1370 and 1376), another John (1403–12) and John junior and senior (1428–31) and Robert (1398 and 1404) in the former small town, and by Agnes (1468) and John (1464–65) in the latter.[56] Similarly it persisted through the late middle ages in Leicester, first through Robert who was assessed to the lay subsidy of 1354 at 3*d*., John in the Poll Tax of 1381, Thomas and Henry in the rentals of Leicester Abbey tenements in the borough in 1477, and Robert in 1505.[57] By contrast, the surname appeared in a rural context only at Oadby in 1524 (Thomas) and Henry, of Sileby, who appeared in the court rolls of Loughborough in 1403.[58] The surname Kirkewrith occurred only at Hallaton, in both the Poll Tax of 1381 and the court rolls in 1379–83, in the person of John.[59] Waynewright, Wynewright or Weynewright equally occurred only in one settlement in the records consulted, at Castle Donington, in 1532 and 1540–43 (Robert), so that the surname, if not the occupation, had also become confined to the small urban sector.[60] W(h)elright was represented in Cotes in 1525 (John) and Thurmaston in 1341 (Thomas), Cotes located just a few miles north-east of Loughborough.[61] As might be expected, Glasenwright was associated with the urban context, confined to the borough of Leicester, but transiently, for it occurred only in the late fourteenth century through Andrew who was admitted to the freedom in 1354 and William, admitted in 1345.[62] Paradoxically, Ploughwright was also revealed only in the urban context, without any rural counterparts, in John Ploughwright in the borough of Leicester in 1336.[63]

-Ward and -herd compounds were almost exclusively rural and of which the most predominant was Hayward, distributed in at least 19 settlements in the late middle ages. Of the less extensive compounds, Bereward appeared in isolation at Laughton in 1381, as did Lamburhurd in Woodhouse in 1327, Ducward at Mowsley in 1525, Horsherd at Scraptoft in 1381, the hypercorrect Hoxherd at Owston in 1365 and the unaspirated Oxherd in Saddington in 1381, Gotherd at King's Norton in 1525, and Stodeherd in Loughborough in 1398.[64] Netherd, unusually, occurred more frequently, in the Poll

Tax of 1381 at Scraptoft, Pickwell, Wistow, Blaston and Fleckney, fleetingly in the court rolls of Barkby in 1367, as Neytheyrd at Prestwold in 1525, and in the form of Richard the Nethird at Tinwell in 1522.[65] Equally frequent was Swyneherd(e), located in Loughborough in 1405, and in the earlier Poll Taxes of 1377 and 1381 at Stockerston, Empingham, Market Harborough and Ryhall.[66] Although the predominant form of miller remained Milnere, le Melneward occurred at Kibworth Harcourt in 1290 and Milward at Loughborough in 1370, being possibly exogenous introductions.[67] Wodeward was distributed in five places in 1327, mostly in Charnwood or Leicester Forest, recurring at Enderby in 1477 in the Leicester Forest region, and at Glaston in 1522.[68] With the exception of the last item mostly associated with animal husbandry, these compounded surnames remained, through the late middle ages, distributed in rural settlements.

The distribution of miscellaneous compounds in the later middle ages reflected the disposition of the original occupation. For example, Sowegelder was manifest only through John Sowegelder of Houghton and William Sowegelder of Woodthorpe, both mentioned at Prestwold in 1391.[69] Meliora Kylnedryere was singularly mentioned at Stoke Dry in 1377 and Heycoper was equally distinct, represented by John at Egleton in 1524.[70] Blodlatere and Ledbetere had both urban and rural incidence, the latter distribution reflected in William and John Blodlatere at Tugby in 1327.[71] That byname, however, transpired frequently in the borough of Leicester in the thirteenth and fourteenth century, commencing with Simon and Thomas Blodlatere in the subsidy of 1271. Subsequently, William contributed to the internal taxation of 1318, followed by John who was assessed in the subsidy of 1338 at 6*d.* and in the *Nonarum Inquisitiones* at 3*d.*, by another Simon, taxed at 3*d.* in 1354, and finally by William who was admitted to the freedom in 1377.[72] Although Ledbetere was included at Market Harborough, a market town, in the Poll Tax of 1381, that name too had a greater predominance in the borough of Leicester, where plumbing and leadworking might be expected.[73] Robert Ledbetere was taxed in the borough subsidy at 3*d.* in 1286 and John at 6*d.* in 1307, whilst one Henry contributed to the subsidy of 1318 and another Henry Ledbetere to that of 1354 and entered the gild merchant in 1355. As Geoffrey Ledbetere was assessed at 3*d.* in 1354, David Ledbetere also contributed 3*d.* and was admitted to the freedom in 1355.[74]

Distinctly urban in incidence was Belyetere (bell-maker), of which occurrence involved Stephen, assessed to the lay subsidy for the suburb in 1327, whilst the others related to the urban precinct, in the persons of Roger, Stephen and Ephraim in 1307-36.[75] Similarly urbanized were Lingedraper, Lindraper or Lyndraper, represented in the borough of Leicester by Henry (1281), who contributed 6*d*. to the subsidy of 1286 and 1*s*. in 1307, and Randolph, who was assessed in 1271.[76]

Fleshewer was a predominant surname in late medieval Loughborough, where, indeed, a section of the market was named *inter carnifices*. Bearers of this surname in Loughborough, some of whom were actually engaged in the trade of butchery, included John (1370-1405), John junior (1403-12 and 1430-31), Thomas (1397-1412), but one John Flesshewer who appeared in the court rolls was an inhabitant of Kegworth, a market vill in the lower reaches of the Soar Valley, a few miles north of Loughborough, in the continuation of the meadows of the floodplain.[77] Rural Fleshewers and le Fleyshewere existed, however, in Laughton in 1477 and South Marefield in 1381 and in 1327 at Groby.[78] Nevertheless, it is possible that some of the Flecchers located in 14 places in the later middle ages might have represented Flesshewers as well as Fletchers and there is considerable evidence of the employment of the alternative (French) occupational surname in rural areas, Bocher.

In general, despite some early compositions in the borough of Leicester, compounded occupational bynames and surnames appeared only in the late middle ages in the written records. Before the middle of the fourteenth century, their existence might have been concealed by the wider employment of Latin forms of occupational bynames and surnames in the written record, so that their appearance in the sources reflects a transition to the greater use of the vernacular in the construction of names. One obvious example is the earlier use of *rotarius* for wheelwright. Nevertheless, compounded occupational bynames and surnames remained at a relatively low level, perhaps reflecting the rather limited extent of Middle English compounding in general in the fourteenth century. Compounded bynames and surnames, however, may have been associated longer with the actual trade or occupation. A further characteristic was the correlation between some compounded bynames and surnames with either urban or rural location, predominantly urban, but some specifically rural (in particular and by expectation, -herd).

Unstable occupational bynames in the later middle ages

One of the principal exceptions to the developing heritability of surnames in the late middle ages was the persistent instability of a core, if a small one, of occupational bynames. Fransson suggested that occupational names were becoming hereditary from *c*.1350 and that unstable occupational bynames were 'rare' in the later half of the foureenth century.[79] As a general rule of thumb, his statement is unexceptionable, but it is not difficult to find bearers of occupational names whose activities were eponymous with their surnames in the later middle ages.[80] What is less clear is whether, in at least some cases, the activity had been inherited as well as the name. Moreover, although in the 1360s eponymous surnames may have been more extensive in some documents (particularly central records involving prosecutions for infractions of trading), in other, especially localized, records, it is only a small nucleus of names which are descriptive and eponymous. It then becomes a question of whether there is something distinctive about any particular occupation which might be sufficient reason for this close association. In Leicestershire, one such candidate for this discussion is the surname of Milner.

Chaucer's characterization of the miller as drunken, dishonest and churlish has recently led an authority on the economic importance of mills in the English later middle ages to doubt the authenticity of the portrayal. Holt's disagreement with the picture is not only that it may be stereotypical, but that it is plainly inappropriate. Millers of the later middle ages comprised a heterogeneous group of, mainly, men, some of whom were only lessees or *firmarii* of mills who employed sub-contracted labour to perform the task of milling. Their economic status varied widely and by no means all belonged to the peasant élite. Their common attribute was the skill and ingenuity required for the job, which was incompatible with Chaucer's depiction of drunkenness and churlishness. Accordingly, Chaucer had no intimate acquaintance with millers, his characterization was speculative and not drawn from personal experience. Moreover, it is suggested, the tale was stereotypically derived from the analogue in the *Decameron*.[81]

The historical background more recently suggested by Lee Patterson is quite different, following Robert Brenner's argument of 'agrarian capitalism' in the later middle ages. Whilst acknowledging Holt's discussion about the 'profits' of milling in the later middle ages, Patterson still locates millers amongst that group of ascending agrarian artisans who were the primary agents of social change in the later middle ages. Concomitantly, the intent of the *Miller's Tale* was subversive (of the social order), evidenced in the symbolism of the miller's forename, Robin. Unlike Holt, who denies any adverse relationship between the miller and the rest of the peasant community, Patterson forebore to address this issue.[82]

Holt's speculation about the direct analogue of the *Decameron* does not ring true, since, although there may have been potential analogues in Italian, Flemish and German fabliaux, it is generally assumed that the *Decameron* is likely to be at best a 'remote source', with preference for a more direct French source. Indeed, the plot of the *Tale*, the perennial love-triangle, was common to all analogous fabliaux, including the earlier Middle English predecessor, *Dame Sirith*. Holt also criticized the scene of the *Tale*, a single house, as an extremely unlikely one, but, in fact, Chaucer's background of contemporary Oxford is, it is agreed, a very precise portrayal of place, down to quite intimate details.[83]

That kind of historical situating may help towards redressing the balance of Chaucer's portrayal of the miller, but more evidence, perhaps of a more indirect kind, can also be accumulated. Two kinds of inter-related evidence are brought to bear here: first, that from court rolls which bears closely on the relationship between miller and other peasants; and, secondly, the evidence of late eponymous bynames of occupation contemporary with the writing of the *Tale*, which is assumed here to have been constructed at the height of Chaucer's poetic powers, within the overall timespan of the whole sequence of *Tales*, begun in the 1380s and finished before his death in 1400.[84]

The evidence of late eponymous bynames may be significant because they were associated with only a small proportion of peasant society at this time, perhaps marking their distinctiveness. Bynames developed into hereditary surnames amongst the unfree peasantry, the last of the social groups to be attributed them (without being unduly culturally deterministic) at different times in different regions. Fransson, as a general rule of thumb, suggested that bynames were, by and large, an accurate indicator of the real occupations of their bearers until *c*.1350, perhaps half a century before the completion of the *Tale*.[85] In fact, bynames had become hereditary surnames well before this time in Oxfordshire, even amongst the unfree peasantry, and throughout England south of the line of the Humber/Wirral well before 1350, whilst the process evolved more slowly north of that line.[86] The way in which the bynames of some men (and, indeed, more specifically certain *femmes soles*) still related to their actual occupations is thus quite distinctive. The potential reasons for this continued association are explored further below, but quite evident amongst this group are millers.

Presentments of millers in manorial court rolls of the later middle ages reflect something more about the perception of millers within peasant society. The instances presented below are a selection of such presentments from the surviving rolls for manors in Leicestershire. A further filter criterion has been added: the data are only presented when the miller had the eponymous byname Milner (or its variants).

> Willelmus Mylner cepit tolnetum per mensuram cumulatam (Owston, 1370);

> Laurencius Mylnere cepit tolnetum excessiue Et quod idem Laurencius noluit molare grana tenentium ante grana extraneorum e patria veniencium (Castle Donington, 1464).[87]

> Et presentant unum molendinum ventriticum nuper in tenura Thome Milnere in manibus dominorum ob defectu tenentis (Barkby, 1434).[88]

At Hallaton, between 1381 and 1384, John Milner was presented for taking excess toll (multure), using a measure which was not sealed (*non sigillata*) and false measures. So also at Twyford, Ralph Mylner took multure wrongly by the heaped measure and at Hallaton, Christine Mylner, who held the windmill, took toll [excessively] breaking the assize. The millers in the small town of Loughborough also repeatedly took toll unjustly (*iniuste*) or excessively. Despite Holt's dismissal of this sort of evidence on the grounds that a miller making a small amount of illicit grain out of the other peasantry is of no great significance, the cumulative entries in the court rolls suggest a different popular perception.[89]

Table 6.5

The activities of Milneres in Kibworth Harcourt, 1362-1540.[90]

Date	Actor	Activity
1362	Simon Milnere	lessee of windmill
1363	Simon Milnere	toll *cum cumulo* (*bis*)
1366	Simon Milnere	toll *cum cumulo* (*bis*)
1366	Simon Milnere	lessee of mill
1391	William Milnere	excess toll
1394	William Milnere	excess toll
1399	Thomas Milnere	excess toll (*bis*)
1400	Thomas Milnere	excess toll (*bis*)
1403	Thomas Milnere	excess toll (*bis*)
1403	John Milner	excess toll (*bis*)
1404	John Milner	excess toll (*bis*)
1407-10	John Milner	excess toll (*bis*)
1412	John Bryslaunce Milner	took windmill and horsemill
1413	John Milnere	excess toll
1414	John Bryszelaunce	excess toll
1417-18	John Mylnere	excess toll
1419	John Bryselaunce	excess toll
1419	John Bryselaunce	surrendered cottage with common oven (upon which the whole tenentry took it)[91]
1420	John Bryslaunce	surrendered the windmill and horsemill *ad opus Ricardi Bryselaunce*
1421-22	Richard Milner	excess toll
1423	Richard Briselaunce	surrendered windmill and horsemill *ad opus Roberti Briselaunce milner*
1423	Robert Milner	excess toll
1425	Thomas Bryselaunce	took windmill and horsemill
1428-34	Thomas Mylner	excess toll
1439	Thomas Bryselaunce	excess toll
1441	Thomas Mylner	excess toll
1442	Thomas Bryselaunce	excess toll
1444	Thomas Mylner	excess toll

***

Date	Actor	Activity
1486	Thomas Milner *molendinarius*	excess toll
1506	John Milner	excess toll
1509–12	John Milner *molendinarius*	excess toll
1540	John Milner *molendinarius*	excess toll

The cumulative nature of this evidence can be best illustrated from the court rolls of the manor of Kibworth Harcourt, held by Merton College, Oxford (Table 6.5). Here too the information is only presented in those cases where the miller bore the eponymous byname. Throughout the later middle ages, the millers at Kibworth, who held the mills on customary tenures (*ad voluntatem secundum consuetudinem manerii*), were associated with the eponymous byname Milner and with constant presentment for taking excessive multure. The most pertinent reflection is the Briselaunce kinship group, which held the mills through four generations or representatives, all of whom were, on assuming the tenantry of the mills, known by the byname Milner. Unlike Holt's millers, moreover, the Briselaunces seem to have been acquisitive and monopolistic, if not necessarily successful (a trait hidden from view), for John held not only the two mills, but also the cottage in which the common oven had recently been built and which, when he relinquished it, was significantly taken by the tenantry in common.[92]

The association of eponymous byname, millers and constant infractions of multure thus tends to suggest a more nefarious picture of the miller, with the inference that the eponymous byname ensued from the notoriety of the person and occupation. The existence of late eponymous bynames, however, demands a more complex interpretation overall. Other reasons than notoriety within the 'community' may have led to the attribution of an eponymous byname. It is also necessary to establish the precise extent of eponymous bynames, the variety of trades represented, and other potential reasons for their attribution.

The extent of late eponymous occupational bynames can be estimated from analysis of the Poll Tax of 1381 for Gartree Hundred in Leicestershire, where 2,397 contributors (over the age of 14) were assessed.[93] Of these, 626 (26%) bore occupational bynames, but in only 10 instances where occupations were also denoted was the byname eponymous with the occupation: William Webster, a webster (weaver), at Easton; William Smyth, a smith there; John Taylour, tailor there; John Taylour *sissor* [*sic*], at Hallaton; there also John Scheperd *bercarius*, as at adjacent Medbourne Thomas Milner *molendinarius*, Robert Sckyner *pelliparius* and William Scheperd *bercarius*, Robert Chapman, a chapman at Market Harborough, Joan Breuster, *pandoxatrix* at Owston, and, in the suburb of Leicester, Roger Baxter *baxster* (baker) and Simon Walker, walker (fuller). The proportion of bearers of such bynames was thus distinctly small.

Several different explanations may account for these eponymous bynames, in addition to the notoriety of the trade. In 1381, John Ashbrenner (a possible metathesis here) was recorded as a maker of woodashes in the Forest of Arden in Warwickshire, presumably to be used as potash in the manufacture of glass.[94] This eponymous byname may have ensued from the distinctiveness of his craft, although it is not clear how many were engaged in this employment in woodland areas. Some occupations, such as shepherds, were common within local economies, although, even in this case, there might not have been more than one or two in each 'community'. In the case of ashburners, however, there remains the additional question of whether this craft was a by-employment, traditional in woodland economies, or (almost) a full-time occupation. Many by-employments may not have taken significantly enough time to merit eponymous bynames, for example some of the lower levels of rural cloth production.

The issue is, moreover, complicated by the possibility, at least in some instances, of the eponymous hereditary surname and occupation being coincidental. For example, Joan Breuster, who occurred in Owston in the Poll Tax of 1381, and who was fined for brewing in the court rolls (with view of frankpledge) of Owston *cum membris* (at Twyford, in fact) in 1387, may, nevertheless, have belonged to the local kinship group named Breuster. John Breuster was also assessed to the Poll Tax there; John senior brewed in 1370–71 and 1373–74 and was a chief pledge in 1373; and John junior also brewed in 1373. Amice Breuster appeared in court in 1386 and, much later, William Breuster in 1418–19 and (possibly a different William) in 1465–66.[95] Despite there thus superficially seeming to be an eponymous byname, the situation may have been more complex and ambiguous. It is, indeed, possibly even more complicated, as the surname may have originated from the kinship group being brewers to the Abbey of Owston, the lord of their manor, although this is purely speculative. Since brewing was a fairly low-cost, low-level activity, common amongst the peasantry, it is possibly unlikely that the surname would have derived from brewing purely at the peasant level of production.[96] The complexity is thus: was the eponymous byname attributed specifically as a life-cycle byname of one individual engaged in that activity?; or was it an hereditary surname the bearer of which was coincidentally involved in that occupation? Both explanations are possible in different circumstances, but it seems reasonable to assume that in some cases the former explanation obtains.

Final comment on the incidence and complexity of these bynames relates to their use as a local normative naming pattern in urban communities, pertinent to Chaucer's Oxford, but in this case in the small town of Loughborough in north Leicestershire, for which the evidence is a rental of the late fourteenth century [*c*.1370] and a broken series of court rolls between 1397 and 1431.[97] Many retail traders here consistently bore the eponymous bynames of their trades.

The instability of occupational bynames is an ambivalent indicator of the distinctiveness of Loughborough, since occupational bynames reflective of actual occupations have been shown generally to have persisted into the late fourteenth century and, indeed, some specific occupational bynames continued in Leicestershire to represent the *métier* into the later middle ages.[98] It seems, however, that these unstable occupational bynames were more widespread in Loughborough than the often single, individual unstable occupational byname in rural villages. The most significant examples in Loughborough are Baxtere and Flesshewer, but these were by no means exceptional except in the quantity of evidence relating to them.

Townspeople with this byname were persistently presented at the view of frankpledge under the assize of bread as licensed bakers. In 1398, Alice Baxtere and William Baxtere were fined 6*d*. each for baking *communiter*, as common bakers; in 1403, William Baxtere and Robert Baxtere contributed at the same level for the same practice; in 1404, Robert Baxtere [junior] paid the significantly higher rate of 18*d*. for baking *communiter*, William Baxtere 6*d*. for the same, and Robert

Baxtere senior 8*d*. for preparing horsebread (although at the second view only 6*d*.); in 1405 Robert junior again paid 18*d*. for baking *communiter* and Thomas Baxtere *et socii* 12*d*. for exactly the same privilege. Furthermore, in 1412, Robert Baxtere and William Baxtere were enumerated amongst the small number of common bakers of white bread, whilst the same list in 1412 consisted of Robert Baxtere senior and junior and William Baxtere.

The nature of their activity is further reflected in cases and actions in the manorial court rolls, as when the Abbot of Beauchief brought a plea of debt against William Baxtere in 1397 for 6*d*. 4*d*. for barley sold to him by the Abbot's proctor.[99] Similarly, in the same year, Robert Irnemongere chaplain impleaded the same William Baxtere in debt for £1 for grain sold to him, which William admitted.[100] In 1402, Robert Baxtere brought an action of trespass against John del Greene for withdrawal of suit to the common oven which Baxtere had leased from the lady of the manor and he also proceeded against Richard Derby in 1404 for the same reason.[101] In that same year, Richard Mylnere brought a case of trespass against Robert Baxtere senior for nonfeasance relating to six bushels of grain at the common oven.[102] The account for 1376–77 reveals that the common oven had been leased then to a Robert Baxtere.[103] In 1404, two Baxteres, Robert senior and junior, came into conflict over a debt incurred through Robert junior's wife, Helen, who had been directed to buy two quarters of wheat for him, whilst in the previous year Robert Baxtere senior and William Baxtere senior went to litigation about a debt of 18*d*. for baking (*pro furnagio*).[104]

A number of other pleas of debt between Baxteres and others substantiate the purchases by the Baxteres of grain and their retail sale of bread. In 1403, Robert Baxtere proceeded against John Halom for a debt of 2*s*. 2*d*. for bread sold to him (*pro pane ei vendito*) and Robert junior tried to recover a debt of 1*s*. from Richard de Derby for bread supplied (*pro pane ei vendito*).[105] In the same year, John Baxtere junior brought Margaret Syngere into court about a debt of 3*s*. 2*d*. for bread sold to her, claiming damages of 6*d*., Margaret admitting 2*s*. 6½*d*., but waging her law about the other 7½*d*.[106] Thomas Spycere also in that year acknowledged a debt of 3*d*. for bread bought from Thomas Baxtere.[107] Conversely, Thomas Clerke sued William Baxtere in 1404 for a debt of 9*s*. 8*d*. for wheat sold to Baxtere the previous year (*pro frumento ei vendito ulteriori anno*).[108] This litigation establishes that the Baxteres, whether a kinship group or individual bakers, performed the actual trade of baking and they might have congregated in the specialized street Baxtergate.

The Flesshewers were definitely located in that part of the market-place which specialized in butchery. In the rental of *c*.1370, William Flesshewer held a messuage *in le marketstede* and a shop *inter carnifices*, whilst John Flesshewer held another shop *inter carnifices*.[109] In 1402, Thomas Hutte brought five pleas of debt, totalling £9 9s. 0d., against Thomas Flesshewer for the sale of animals to Flesshewer (*pro animalibus ei venditis*).[110] John Flesshewer brought his own plea of debt in 1403 for 6s. 8d. against Richard Furnyuale for meat sold to Richard (*pro carne ei vendito*).[111] John, however, admitted a debt of 4s. 4d. to Richard del Grene for sheep which he bought from Richard in the previous year, although he asked for an inquisition about the outstanding 3s. 2d. claimed and Elias Bercolfe also impleaded him for a debt of 12s. 4d. for sheep and other animals.[112] Moreover, when Joan Crosby brought a plea of debt against John Lorde in 1404 for 5s. 3d. her claim was for meat and other victuals sold to him by William Flesshewer, her late husband.[113] In that same year, John attempted to recover 2½d. from William Shakeston for the sale of meat to him (*pro carne ei vendito*).[114] As late as 1431, John Flesshewer acknowledged a debt of 39s. 4d. to Robert Annesley for animals sold to him about the preceding All Saints.[115] Even into the early fifteenth century, therefore, the byname remained eponymous with the activity.

Some less substantial evidence suggests that a wider range of bynames may also have continued to be eponymous with the trade. In 1398, for example, John Dextere impleaded Isabella, widow and executrix of Lambert Taylour, for a debt of 18d. which Lambert owed for the dyeing of some black cloth — the clear implication being that both bynames continued to represent the activity.[116] In that year too, Henry Roper was impleaded by Agnes Burdon in a case of debt involving a stone of hemp valued at 1s., although her suit failed.[117] When in 1403 John Shepherd acknowledged a debt of 13s. 4d. to William de Stowe, the purchase involved sheep, and so also when, in 1404, William Shepherd was prosecuted for a debt by John de Burton the sale concerned sheep.[118] Shepherd contracted a renewed debt to Burton in 1412, partly for the purchase of sheep and partly for a loan.[119] A debt of 2s. 3d. claimed by William de Stowe from Roger Walker in 1404 related to the weaving of some cloth, perhaps indicating that Roger was indeed a fuller.[120] When Robert Baxtere was impleaded by Nicholas Smith the issue concerned the shoeing of Baxtere's horses at intervals over the two years before the plea in 1412.[121] Even in 1430–31, occupational bynames seem still to be eponymous, as when (1431) John Walker in le Byggyng acknowledged a debt of 10s. for a pair of shearman's shears implicating him as a fuller and, in the previous year, John Walker in le Kirkgate admitted a debt of 1s. for the shearing of a dozen of cloth.[122] In 1430 also John Westerby conceded a debt of 8d. to John Cartwright for the supply of a pair of wheels.[123]

The persistence of some occupational bynames eponymous with their trades after the middle of the fourteenth century is not unusual. Fransson's remarks about the transition from unstable occupational bynames to family surnames should only be taken as a general rule of thumb.[124] In some rural villages, some individual occupational bynames seem to have continued to be associated with the *métier*, in particular Miller and Brewster. In some few circumstances, the trades seem to have been inherited, which explains the continued association of byname and activity in the later middle ages. Nevertheless, a much wider range of occupational bynames seems to have remained eponymous in Loughborough through to the end of the fourteenth and even into the early fifteenth century.

Conclusion

The continuing level of occupational bynames and surnames in the two counties was around 20% of taxpayers. Whilst wool growing contributed to the distinctive surnames of eastern Leicestershire, woollen cloth production made less impact, except though the byname and surname Walker. As might be expected, the variety of occupational bynames and surnames was more extensive in urban centres than in the rural settlements, even in areas of higher incidence of by-employments.[125] In the small town of Loughborough a distinctive pattern was exhibited in the range of occupational surnames, but also the persistence of the identification of the surname with the occupation of its bearer — a very high correlation of surname and actual occupation. These eponymous surnames continued into the early fifteenth century, it appears. In some rural 'communities' too, a small number of occupational surnames in the later middle ages represented the actual employment of their bearers, but the relationship in Loughborough seems to have been much more conclusive and extensive.

References

[1] *AASR*, (1888–9); PRO E179/165/1, 21; PRO E179/133/35; *Tudor Rutland*; PRO E179/133/104–110, 112–118, 121–122, 124.

[2] As n.1 above.

[3] In this area, Bond is more likely to have derived from status as an unfree tenant than from the Anglo-Scand personal name Bondi: see 237.

[4] See generally, C C Dyer, 'Deserted medieval villages in the West Midlands', *Economic History Review*, 2nd ser., 35 (1982), 19–34 and E. King, 'D. The East Midlands' in chapter 2, 'Occupation of the land' in E Miller, ed., *The Agrarian History of England and Wales volume III 1348–1500*, (Cambridge, 1991), 76; more specifically, H S A Fox, 'The people of the Wolds in English settlement history' in M Aston, D Austin and C Dyer, eds., *The Rural Settlements of Medieval England*, (Oxford, 1989), 77–101.

[5] PRO E179/133/35.

[6] *AASR*, (1888–9); PRO E179/133/35.

[7] For Walker, see above 27–9.

[8] *RBL*, I; *passim*.

[9] Leicestershire Record Office, BRIII/4/70–73.

[10] Bodl. MS Laud Misc 625, fos. 186v–189r.

[11] R H Hilton, *English and French Towns in Feudal Society. A Comparative Study*, (Cambridge, 1992), 6–7; E Miller and J Hatcher, *Medieval England. Towns, Commerce and Crafts 1086–1348*, (London, 1995), 324–30; M K Dale, 'The City of Leicester: social and economic history', in R McKinley, ed., *Victoria History of the County of Leicestershire*, 4 (1959), 31–54.

[12] *RBL*, I, *passim*.

[13] See further below, 317–18, for a discussion of languages of names.

[14] G Fransson, *Middle English Surnames of Occupation 1100–1350*, (Lund Studies in English, 3, Lund, 1935), 162 (earliest reference, 1179); *RBL*, I, 92, 390, 393.

[15] *RBL*, I, 31.

[16] *RBL*, II, 244, 417, 425, 462; PRO E179/133/35; Fransson, *Middle English Surnames of Occupation*, 137.

[17] *RBL*, I, 64, 111, 136, 139, 209, 210, 212, 219, 222, 239, 251, 255, 311.

[18] *RBL*, I, 140, 142, 144.

[19] Fransson, *Middle English Surnames of Occupation*, 124; *RBL*, I, 17.

[20] *RBL*, I, 20, 23; W Rothwell, ed., *Anglo-Norman Dictionary Fascicle 5:*

P-Q, (London, 1988), 488; M-Th Morlet, *Dictionnaire Etymologique des Noms de Famille*, (Paris, 1991), 753 gives maker of *paniers*.

21 *RBL*, I, 23; L W Stone, W Rothell and T B W Reid, eds., *Anglo-Norman Dictionary Fascicle 3: F-L*, (London, 1983), 307; M-Th Morlet, *Dictionnaire Etymologique*, 414 suggests 'tart molle faite avec de la crème, de la farine et des oeufs, surnom de pâtissier', from *flaneau*.

22 *RBL*, I, 16–17, 21–2, 27, 300 (admission, 1198); the reference in L W Stone and W Rothwell, eds., *Anglo-Norman Dictionary Fascicle I: A-Cyvere*, (London, 1977), 55, is to the Year Books of Edward II, where it is explained as a collector of oats (by implication, purveyance).

23 Fransson, *Middle English Surnames of Occupation*, 113; *RBL*, I, 22.

24 Fransson, *Middle English Surnames of Occupation*, 179; *RBL*, I, 67.

25 *RBL*, I, 21, 142, 185, 190, 215; Fransson, *Middle English Surnames of Occupation*, 85.

26 *RBL*, I, 31; Fransson, *Middle English Surnames of Occupation*, 86.

27 *RBL*, I, 62; Fransson, *Middle English Surnames of Occupation*, 76.

28 *RBL*, I, 64 for the admission of le cunreur; Fransson, *Middle English Surnames of Occupation*, 123; below for the linguistic environment of the byname Curlewache; for cur-/cunreier, Rothwell and Stone, *Anglo-Norman Dictionary Fascicle 1: A-Cyvere*, 131, 136.

29 *RBL*, I, 14, 29, 60, 62.

30 Leicestershire Record Office, BRIII/4/70–73.

31 *RBL*, I, 191; cited by Fransson, *Middle English Surnames of Occupation*, 155.

32 Fransson, *Middle English Surnames of Occupation*, 70, recorded Oillemaker as early as 1220; *RBL*, I, 255.

33 *RBL*, I, 255, and II, 35–6; Leicestershire Record Office, BRIII/4/70–73.

34 *RBL*, II, 98.

35 *RBL*, II, 181, 268, 345, 350, but also William Matressmaker at 163.

36 HAM, Box 20, flders 7–8.

37 HAM, Box 21, flder 3.

38 HAM, Box 20, flders 6–7.

39 PRO E179/165/21, mm. 8, 9; E179/133/35.

40 *RBL*, I, 17, 25; PRO E179/133/35.

41 *RBL*, I, 312, 356.

42 HAM, Box 20, flders 2–3, 5–9, Box 21, flders 1–3.

43 HAM, Box 8; PRO DL30/80/1090–1101.
44 PRO E179/133/35; Bodl. MS Wood empt 7, fo. 67r; *AASR*, (1888–9), 236; *Oakham Survey*, 14.
45 PRO SC2/183/87; PRO E179/165/21, mm. 3–4; *AASR*, (1888–9), 298; PRO E179/133/121, m. 8; Bodl. MS Laud Misc 625, fo. 76r.
46 Fransson, *Middle English Surnames of Occupation*, 136.
47 HAM, Box 20, flders 1, 3–9 and Box 21, flders 1, 3.
48 HAM, Box 24, flders 2, 4.
49 HAM, Box 20, flders 3, 7–9, Box 21, flder 1.
50 *RBL*, II, 97, 164, 177.
51 PRO E179/133/35; PRO E179/165/21, m. 12.
52 *RBL*, I, 311, and II, 95; Fransson's earliest reference for Arowesmith is 1278: Fransson, *Middle English Surnames of Occupation*, 156.
53 *RBL*, II, 18, 20, 36, 43, 55, 58, 63–4, 69, 75–6, 79–85, 89, 91–3, 95, 102–4, 106, 109–10, 125.
54 *RBL*, II, 334.
55 Bodl. MS Wood empt 7, fos. 44r–46r; PRO DL30/80/1098.
56 HAM, Box 20, flders 1–2, 4–9, Box 21, flder 3; HAM, Box 8.
57 *RBL*, II, 94, 200, 371; PRO E179/133/35; Bodl. MS Laud Misc 625, fo. 92r.
58 PRO E179/133/122, m.7d; HAM, Box 20, flders 5–6.
59 PRO E179/133/35; PRO DL30/80/1102.
60 PRO DL30/80/1096–1098; HAM, Box 8.
61 PRO E179/133/116, m.5d; Bodl. MS Laud Misc 625, fo. 203v.
62 *RBL*, II, 63, 91, 97.
63 *RBL*, II, 29, 38.
64 *AASR*, (1888–9), 176; PRO E179/133/35; PRO E179/133/109, m.3; PRO SC2/183/87; PRO E179/133/115, m.4; HAM, Box 20, flder 2.
65 PRO E179/133/35; MM 6577; PRO E179/133/117, m.6; *Tudor Rutland*, 41.
66 HAM, Box 20, flder 7; PRO E179/133/35; PRO E179/165/21, m. 2.
67 MM 6384; HAM, Box 20, flder 4; Fransson, *Middle English Surnames of Occupation*, 57 maintained that muleward was a south-western form by comparison with milnere which pertained to the East Midlands.
68 *AASR*, (1888–9); Bodl. MS Laud Misc 625, fo. 62r; *Tudor Rutland*, 48.
69 PRO Chancery Miscellanea Bundle 66, File 4, item 107.

[70] PRO E179/165/1, m. 2; *Tudor Rutland*, 118.

[71] *AASR*, (1888-9), 165.

[72] *RBL*, I, 130, 312; II, 39, 97, 157, 182; Fransson, *Middle English Surnames of Occupation*, 189 discovered Blodleter as early as 1256.

[73] PRO E179/133/35.

[74] *RBL*, I, 138, 210, 256, 312; II, 95, 96, 99.

[75] *AASR*, (1888-9), 233; *RBL*, I, 256, 273, 311, 355; Fransson, *Middle English Surnames of Occupation*, 138.

[76] *RBL*, I, 138, 190, 210, 256.

[77] HAM, Box 20, flders 1-9; Box 21, flders 1-3.

[78] Bodl. MS Laud Misc 625, fo. 82r John Bocher 'alias vocatus Wynnall' held a messuage and virgate 'quondam W. Fleshewer'; PRO E179/133/35; *AASR*, (1888-9), 310.

[79] G Fransson, *Middle English Surnames of Occupation*, 29, 33-41.

[80] This matter has been documented quite extensively by P Glennie in a paper delivered at the Centre for Urban History in Leicester on prosecutions under the labour laws in the late fourteenth century.

[81] R Holt, *The Mills of Medieval England*, (Oxford, 1988), 90-106, esp. 105-6; the ascription of the source to the *Decameron* is at 91; but see also G F Jones, 'Chaucer and the medieval miller', *Modern Languages Quarterly*, 16 (1955), 3-15. The most recent exploration of the historical background of the *Tales* does not consider the *Miller's Tale*: P Brown and A Butcher, *The Age of Saturn. Literature and History in the Canterbury Tales*, (Oxford, 1991).

[82] L Patterson, *Chaucer and the Subject of History*, (London, 1991), 247-58. For the Brenner debate, T H E Aston and C H E Philpin, eds., *The Brenner Debate. Agrarian Class Structure and Economic Development in Pre-Industrial England*, (Cambridge, 1985).

[83] For all this, Helen Cooper, *Oxford Guides to Chaucer. The Canterbury Tales*, (Oxford, 1989), 95-101; J A W Bennett, *Chaucer at Oxford and at Cambridge*, (Oxford, 1974), chs. 1-2. For *Dame Sirith*, see now M W Walsh, 'Performing *Dame Sirith*: farce and fabliaux at the end of the thirteenth century', in W M Ormrod, ed., *England in the Thirteenth Century. Proceedings of the 1984 Harlaxton Conference*, (Nottingham, 1985), 149-65. For Chaucer's other sources, in particular the relationship of the *Franklin's Tale* to the Breton lays, L H Loomis, 'Chaucer and the Breton Lays of the Auchinleck Ms', *Studies in Philology*, 38 (1941), 14-33; K Hume, 'Why Chaucer calls the *Franklin's Tale* a Breton lai', *Philological Quarterly*, 51 (1972), 365-79; J B Beston,

'How much was known of the Breton lai in fourteenth-century England' in L Benson, ed., *The Learned and the Lewd. Studies in Chaucer and Medieval Literature*, (Harvard Studies in English, 5, Cambridge, Mass., 1974), 319–36; E K Yoder, 'Chaucer and the "Breton" Lay', *Chaucer Review*, 12 (1977), 74–7.

84 Cooper, *The Canterbury Tales*, 5.

85 G Fransson, *Middle English Surnames of Occupation* as n.79.

86 For the documentation of these trends, R McKinley, *The Surnames of Oxfordshire*, (English Surnames Series, III, 1977), 7–40; *idem, The Surnames of Lancashire*, (ESS, IV, 1981), 9–76.

87 PRO SC2/183/87; HAM, Box 8.

88 MM 6601.

89 PRO SC2/183/87; PRO DL 30/80/1102; HAM, Boxes 20–21.

90 MM 6404–6444.

91 'qui de dominis tenuit ad voluntatem secundum consuetudinem manerii unum cotagium cum communi furno in eodem de nouo edificato . . . [surrendered] . . . et super hoc veniunt omnes tenentes et ceperunt de dominis . . .'

92 Holt, *Mills*, 94–104.

93 PRO E179/133/35.

94 A Watkin, 'The woodland economy of the Forest of Arden in the later middle ages', *Midland History*, 18 (1993), 31.

95 PRO SC2/183/87–90.

96 For brewing in general, see Judith M Bennett, 'The village alewife: women and brewing in fourteenth-century England' in B A Hanawalt, ed., *Women and Work in Pre-Industrial Europe*, (Bloomington, Indiana, 1986), 20–36, and *eadem, Ale, Beer and Brewsters in England. Women's Work in a Changing World, 1300–1600*, (Oxford, 1996).

97 HAM, Boxes 20–21. The cases concern debt, whilst the rental locates the retail traders within the specialized areas of the town's market.

98 P Glennie as above, n.80.

99 'Abbas de bello Capite queritur de Willelmo Baxtere in placito debiti .vj.s.iiij.d. pro ordeo empto de procuratore suo apud W[ms torn] anno xvij^{mo} ad dampna &c.', HAM, Box 20, flder 2.

100 'in placito debiti .xx.s. pro blado ei vendito ... et dictus Willelmus venit in Curia et cognouit totum et erit in misericordia &c.', HAM, Box 20, flder 2.

101 'Robertus Baxtere queritur de Johanne del Grene in placito transgressionis de retraxione secte de communi furno quod tenet de domina ulteriori anno ad dampna .xij.d. et compertum

est per Inquisicionem quod culpabilis ad dampna .ij.d. & erit in misericordia &c.';' de retraccione secte de communi furno per unum annum et dimidium ad dampna .xij.d.', HAM, Box 20, flder 5.

[102] 'de eo quod in defectu suo habuit .vj. bussellos bladi predicti apud commune furnum ulteriori anno ad dampna .iij.s.iiij.d.', HAM, Box, flder 5.

[103] 'Et de firma communis furni de Lughteburgh dimissi Roberto Baxtere de Lughteburgh' ad voluntatem.', HAM, Box 20, flder 1.

[104] 'de eo quod ulteriori anno fecit Elenam uxorem eius emere .ij. quarteria frumenti pro .xxij.s. ad opus suum et postea nichilominus habere predictum frumentum ad dampna .x.s.', HAM, Box 20, flders 5–6 [and 1403].

[105] HAM, Box 20, flders 5–6.

[106] HAM, Box 20, flders 5–6.

[107] HAM, Box 20, flders 5–6.

[108] HAM, Box 20, flders 6–7.

[109] HAM, Box 20, flder 4.

[110] HAM, Box 20, flder 5.

[111] HAM, Box 20, flders 5–6.

[112] 'in placito debiti .vij.s.vj.d. pro bidentibus ei venditis ulteriori anno apud Loughtt' ad dampna .xij.d.'; 'pro bidentibus cum aliis animalibus ei venditis.', HAM, Box 20, flders 5–6.

[113] 'pro carne et aliis victualibus ei venditis per Willelmum Flesshewer nuper virum suum . . . ad dampna .xl.d.', HAM, Box 20, flder 6.

[114] HAM, Box 20, flder 6.

[115] HAM, Box 21, flder 3.

[116] 'Johannes Dextere queritur de Isabella que fuit uxor Lamberti Taylour executrice eiusdem Lamberti in placito debiti .xviij.d. quos idem Lambertus ei debet pro coloracione nigri panni ad dampna &c.', HAM, Box 20, flders 2–3.

[117] HAM, Box 20, flders 2–3.

[118] 'pro bidentibus ei venditis.', HAM, Box 20, flders 5–6.

[119] 'pro bidentibus ei venditis et pecunia ei acomodata.', HAM, Box 21, flder 1.

[120] 'pro textura panni linei.', HAM, Box 20, flders 6–7.

[121] 'pro ferura equorum ab eo recepta continue per .ij. annos apud Loughtt' ad dampna .vj.s.viij.d.', HAM, Box 21, flder 1.

[122] 'pro uno pari Shermansherres ab eo empto'; 'pro le sheryng .iij. duodenarum panni quos ei soluisse debuit.', HAM, Box 21, flder 3.

[123] 'pro .j. pari rotarum ab eo empto hoc Anno.', HAM, Box 21, flder 3.

[124] Fransson, *Middle English Surnames of Occupation*, 29, 33–41.

[125] But for the extent of specialization in the medieval rural economy, see P D A Harvey, 'Non-agrarian activities in twelfth-century English estate surveys' in D Williams, ed., *England in the Twelfth Century. Proceedings of the 1988 Harlaxton Symposium*, (Woodbridge, 1990), 101–12, and R H Britnell, *The Commercialisation of English Society 1000–1500*, (Cambridge, 1993).

CHAPTER 7

TOPOGRAPHICAL BYNAMES AND SURNAMES

As a consequence of the predominantly nucleated pattern of settlement in the two counties, the contribution of topographical bynames and surnames to the onomastic corpus here was relatively weak. Accordingly the range of topographical items in naming was also restricted. Nevertheless, some elements persisted as significant lexis in naming processes.

In the lay subsidy for Rutland in 1296, topographical bynames accounted for 12.9% of the total taxpayers, whilst in the Poll Tax of 1377 the proportion had declined to 7%.[1] In the early sixteenth century, the level was higher, with 9.4% of those males qualified in the muster roll of 1522, and 10.1 and 10.4% respectively of the taxpayers in the lay subsidy in 1524 and 1525.[2] By the Hearth Tax of 1665, topographical surnames constituted 9.5% of those assessed.[3]

A similar pattern was exhibited in Leicestershire during the later middle ages, commencing in the lay subsidy of 1327 with 7% of the taxpayers, decreasing slightly to 6.6% of the contributors to the Poll Tax in 1381, but increasing to 8.7% of taxpayers in 1524 and 7.5% in 1525.[4] Overall, therefore, topographical elements rarely exceeded 10% of the bynames and surnames of taxpayers in the two counties.

Moreover, by the middle of the nineteenth century, the contribution of topographical surnames had diminished even further, for, taking heads of households and those within households of independent status in the census of 1851, only 4% of this population in urban centres (Oakham and Uppingham) disported topographical surnames, whilst in the rural parishes of Rutland a slightly higher proportion, 5.8%.[5]

At least in Rutland, however, the range of elements expanded, inversely with the proportion of populations bearing topographical surnames. Although the lay subsidy of 1296 contained about 40 topographical elements in bynames, in the Poll Tax of 1377 the topographical elements consisted of fewer than 20 elements, but the range almost doubled by 1522. In 1665 again, the number of elements displayed was higher still, approaching 50, contracting to about 35 in the nineteenth century.[6] In this analysis, the ambiguous Cliff(e) has been interpreted as toponymic, deriving from King's Cliffe in Northamptonshire.

Consistently, a few elements were more frequent than others, particularly Green(e), Hill and Well(s), rather innocuous ones. Tabulated below are the most frequently recurring items.

Table 7.1

Most frequent topographical items: Rutland, 1296–1851[*7]

Item	1296	1377	1522	1665	1851
town (above the)	7	5			
hall	9	7	3		
bar	5				
cross	22	6			17
church/kirk	12		6		
well	24		14	14	
green	9		8	15	45
hill/hull	13	3	9	22	76
park	5				
bridge	11				
gate	6				
lane	14	3			14
wro/row	5	3			
style		3	3		
croft			3		
down			4		
grove			3		
pitt			7	12	
wood			5	16	53
dale				5	
holmes				10	
ley variants				6	31
broom					22
hay					41
yate (gate)					14
meadows					23
moor					20

Notes: Only items which exceed the mean are included; the means are: (1296) 4.4; (1327) 2.3; 1522 (2.4); 1665 (4.2); 1851 (13.25).

* This analysis excludes names with the prefix by-.

Particularly ambiguous is Towel(l), which did not appear in these records until 1851, when 35 of this population were recorded bearing this surname in the census. Its etymology may reside in the noun well with the syndetic preposition to-, but, if so, it is probably an introduction into Rutland, for in 1665 the exclusive form was Wells. Equally ambivalent is Brook, which might have been either topographical or toponymic, but its occurrence before 1851 was slight and then its frequency was 13 heads of household.[8]

Compounded forms of topographical byname and surname were rare in Rutland. Whilst the element -man was not unusual in the two counties, its occurrence in Rutland in composite topographical names was limited to Kirkeman (potentially occupational) in 1296 and Wileman and Holman (three) in 1851.[9] Topographical surnames with the suffix -er were absent except for a single occurrence in 1851 in the person of the John Weller, rector of North Luffenham, who had been born in Amersham in Buckinghamshire.[10]

Table 7.2

Most frequent topographical items: Leicestershire, 1327–1524.[11]

Item	1327	1381	1524
well	27	17	7
green	22	4	28
church/kirk	21	4	4
lane	18		
hull/hill	18	4	13
town	17	6	
hall	14	8	8
brook*	12		
wro/row	9	4	5
bridge	8	4	6
cross	6	6	6
yate	5		4
holme			5
lee			6
moor			10

Notes: Items are only included where they exceed the mean; the means are: 3.7 (1327); 3.2 (1381); 3.6 (1524).

* Brook is an ambivalent item, but is largely defined as topographical by the syndetic form atte. Heyne is omitted, since in Leicestershire the evidence is that it was derived from a personal name rather than topographical ME plural from heghen.

In Leicestershire, the late medieval pattern was replicated, although commencing with a much higher corpus of elements in 1327, some 70 in all, although there was considerable concentration in the most frequent items. The sequence is tabulated in Table 7.2.

Comparison with topographical bynames in adjacent counties provides some interesting contrasts and similarities. In Warwickshire, Derbyshire and Lincolnshire, the proportion of the taxable populations in the lay subsidies of 1327 and 1332 identified by topographical bynames was at a similar level to Leicestershire and Rutland. In Warwickshire, the range of elements amounted to about a hundred, much larger than the corpus in Leicestershire and Rutland, whilst, although more restricted in Derbyshire, some 50 items there still exceeded the corpus in the two counties. In southern Lincolnshire, the corpus expanded even further, extending to about 130 elements.[12]

Table 7.3

Most frequent lexis in topographical bynames in three adjacent counties, 1327–32

Warwickshire 1332		Derbyshire 1327		Lincolnshire 1332	
well	31	hill	15	green	90
hill	30	hall	8	church	57
green	23	green	7	well	39
gate	16	wood	6	be(c)k	35
abovetoun	16	well	4	hill	34
hall	16	townend	4	bridge	31
heath	15			hall	30
bridge	14			sea	23
moor	13			hirne	20
hurne	12			lane	20
mill	11			wra	19
cross	10			damme	11
				cross	11
				inthecroftes	10

Considerable consistency existed in the five counties in the recurring elements, with very little divergence from the dominant items in Leicestershire and Rutland. Green is prominent in all counties, even Derbyshire where the pattern of settlement in the northern part of the county was more dispersed. Despite this constancy, however, south Lincolnshire exhibited some difference in topographical bynames, principally in the localized importance of be(c)k and because of a very wide range of topographical items not encountered in Leicestershire and Rutland, such as in le Clay, atte wende, atte lund, atte slade, atte loft, atte kerre, atte flette and numerous others. In addition to its topographical difference, south Lincolnshire had received dialect topographical items from Scandinavian lexis which did not penetrate into Leicestershire and Rutland.

During the later middle ages, however, the composition of topographical bynames is complicated by the ambiguity of some forms which might have been occupational. Particularly is this the case in the Poll Tax of 1381 for Leicestershire. For example, at Stockerston Robert Attoparsons, Joan Attoparsons and Alice Attoparsons were described as *serviens*, from which it seems fairly conclusive that they were indeed household servants of the rector of Stockerston and that their *cognomina* were therefore occupational rather than topographical.[13] In a similar position was Agnes Atteparsons, a servant at Glooston, Thomas Atteparsons, servant at Gumley, Reginald Atteparsons, servant at Pickwell, and John Attoparsons, a servant at Galby, as well as Amice atto vikerus and James atto vikerus, servants at King's Norton, and John atto vikers, servant at Holt, who were presumably employed by the vicar. Similarly, Roger Atteprioris, a servant at Welham, may have been defined by his occupation. More conclusive was the case of Juliana Atteabbotys, a servant at Ingarsby, for the Abbey of Leicester held the manor, whilst Walter atte Abbotes, servant at Pickwell, was probably retained by the Abbey of Owston, which held a small property in Pickwell.[14] Such an interpretation might be extended to several of those described as atte Hall(e) in the record sources, particularly when their status is defined as servanthood. Examples include Helen Attohall, servant at Medbourn, Amice Attehall, servant at Fleckney, Ralph Attehalle and John Attehalle, servants at Knossington, Arabella Attehall, servant at Stretton Parva, and possibly also to Robert atte Syrhwys (shirehouse) servant in Glooston.[15]

Until the late fourteenth century, an association existed between topographical bynames and legal status, for, although the source material is limited, this form of byname seems to have been held predominantly by the unfree peasantry. Despite the difficulty of the record material, which is compounded by the sparsity of extensive manorial surveys which consistently define the status of the tenantry and also the comparative sparsity of topographical bynames, the relationship can be established. In manorial surveys, topographical bynames were almost exclusively attached to the unfree peasantry or small tenantry. Whilst, in the survey of the Bishop of Lincoln's estate in 1225x1258, few topographical bynames occurred, Alured *iuxta aquam* was a cottager at Caldecote (Rutland) and Ernis de la grene held a toft and virgate in customary tenure at Thurmaston (Leicestershire).[16] In 1305, in the survey of the soke of Oakham, Matilda Roo held a messuage and virgate in unfree tenure at Egleton.[17] More significantly, however, out of 54 tenures at Langham, 16 were held by tenants of customary status or cottagers with topographical bynames. Standard customary tenements were held by William in le Holme, Matilda *ad lap'* (attestones?), William Byeston, William atte Lane, Henry Benethegate, Simon [in] le Holme, Hugh a la Grene, Hugh atte Lane, William atte Lane, and Gilbert atte Grene, confirmed by cottages in the tenure of Robert atte Grene, William *ad Grenam*, Robert a la Barre and Emma atte Barre *orientale*.[18]

Supporting evidence of an anecdotal nature derives from the rental of the estate of Leicester Abbey in 1341. Whilst again topographical bynames were sparse in incidence, their occurrence was normally associated with the unfree peasantry. Thus at Anstey, Ralph *super le Grene* was enumerated as holding a messuage and half a virgate with some additional lands amongst the *nativi*.[19] Amongst the tenants *in villenagio* at Humberstone was Richard in le Mir', holding a messuage and virgate.[20] Moreover at Lockington, the *tenentes ad voluntatem* and *in villenagio* included Agnes in le Wroo, holding a messuage and virgate and a little additional land, and the following small tenants or cottars, William de Bovelton' (abovetheton?), William Hulle, Emma *super le Grene*, and William [in] le Wroo. Alice Attewelle, whose status was not defined clearly, yet appears to have been a customary tenant, for she held the standard customary holding of a messuage and virgate.[21]

The relationship is also visible in the topographical byname atte Pertre on the Abbey's manor of Stoughton in 1381. There, Adelina Pertre held a messuage and virgate *in villenagio*, complemented in the association by William, Thomas and Richard Attpertre, all cottars *ad placitum*.[22] The byname recurred in the Poll Tax of 1381, associated with a tenant *ad voluntatem*.[23] Although the status of Thomas Attepertre, a tenant of the Abbey at Hungarton in 1341, was not clearly identified, his holding of two messuages and two virgates with an additional half acre would suggest that he too was of customary status.[24]

Even in the late fourteenth century, the association of topographical bynames and unfree status was maintained, as is revealed by analysis of this form of byname in the Poll Tax of 1381 which recorded the status of the taxpayers. The relationship is tabulated in Table 7.4.

Table 7.4

Topographical bynames and legal status: Poll Tax for Leicestershire in 1381[25]

Free	TT	Cottars	Widow	Servants	*Cult'*	*Nativi*	TTAV	NTT
5	10	4	1	34	2	3	35	3

Notes: TT = terrarum tenentes; *Cult'* = cultivator; *TTAV* = terrarum tenentes ad voluntatem; *NTT* = nativarum terrarum tenentes.

In this table, all designations to the left of and including column six (*cult'*) contain either free (column 1) or ambiguous status, whilst columns seven to nine relate to those of unfree status or holding in unfree tenure.[26] Taking the unambiguously unfree association of columns seven to nine, at least 42.3% of the topographical bynames were associated with servitude. Moreover, the servants were of indeterminate status and should perhaps be excluded from the equation. Furthermore, at least 16 of the 34 bynames of servants were ambivalent, for they might have derived from occupational position, as described above. If the servants are omitted, 65.1% of the topographical bynames were associated with unfree status. By contrast, taking into account only the unambiguously free (column 1), only 5.2% of the bynames were unequivocally equated with freedom.

Whilst the relationship of topographical bynames and freedom was tenuous, topographical bynames intruded into small towns in the county, of which Melton Mowbray is an example. Their introduction resulted from two sources. First, although Melton had the status of a small market town with an urban centre, it also had an extensive agrarian hinterland within the parish. Furthermore, some townspeople derived from neighbouring rural parishes, whilst others acquired lands in those parishes. Thus in 1334 Walter de

Spiney of Melton conveyed to John Attecros of Melton one acre and half a rood in Melton, exmplifying these phenomena.[27]

Representative of these townspeople with topographical bynames, which were incipiently hereditary, was Margaret or Margery de la Hille. In a charter of 1317, Margery de la Hil *de Melton' nuper uxor Hugonis de la Hil* began, in her widowhood, to dispose of parcels of her holding. As Margery *relicta Hugonis del Hille de Melton'* in 1324, she released the full bovate, but before then Margery del Hil, by that style, had relinquished small parcels.[28] The byname, whether by relationship of kin or simply common formation, existed in the town through the fourteenth century, not least in the person of John del Hull or del Hill, who frequently attested charters relating to urban and rural property in Melton.[29] In contrast, it seems that William del Hil migrated to Melton from Grantham, but quickly acquired urban and rural property in Melton.[30]

Declining into a similar predicament, probably in her widowhood, Helen (*Elena*) *in venella*, was forced to resort to gage and sale of her real property in Melton. In 1317, she entered into a mortgage with Walter Prest (*Condicio Walteri Prest*), the condition of which was that Helen and her daughter, Agnes, were required to redeem to Walter 10 marks by 24 June 1319, the sum being duly acquitted in 1319. At that same time, however, Helen conveyed her messuage to Thomas de Belton, confirmation being required of her children, Walter, Agnes and John.[31]

Whilst the Attecros family was established within the town, kinship ties may have been maintained with Ab Kettleby, for in 1347 John Attecros of Ab Kettleby sold a messuage in Melton, his charter attested by William Attecros of Melton Mowbray.[32] William *ad crucem* had attested charters earlier in the fourteenth century.[33] John, however, was the most acquisitive in the small town, having acquired one acre and one and a quarter roods in 1333 as John Attecros of Melton and by the same style in charters small parcels of three quarters of a rood and three roods in rural Melton. As John Attecros of Melton he had also received two acres in Ab Kettleby, his charter attested by Henry atte Cros of that rural vill. In 1349, John atte Cros *de Melton'* bought the right in two *camere* and a brewery next to his own brewery in Melton.[34] John's father, Henry atte Cros, had earlier attested charters in Melton.[35]

Witness to a charter of 1326 relating to property in Melton, Hugh de Spineto had held land there in 1319.[36] Some time later, in 1333,

Walter de Spineto disposed of three selions in the town's fields, preceded by his sale, as Walter del Spiney, of one rood and a half in 1332.[37] A further three quarters of a rood were relinquished by Margery del Spiney of Melton in 1338.[38]

Persisting into the late fourteenth century, topographical bynames and surnames were not unusual in the small town of Melton, reflecting both the rural surroundings to the urban enceinte, but also the close relationship between small town and countryside. In 1394, a single charter was attested by John Inthezerd, Richard in the lane, and Thomas atte Cros, surnames representative of the topographical features of small towns.[39] Shortly before that date, Margery *quondam uxor Thome othe Sale de Melton'* confirmed the alienation by her late husband, Thomas, son of John othe Sale (*Thomas filius Johannis othe Sale de Melton'*).[40] Perhaps unlike the situation in larger boroughs, topographical bynames and surnames were an integral part of the vocabulary of naming in small towns.

In the borough of Leicester, topographical bynames, although existing from an early date, were not significant in the lexis of names in the borough. For example, in the lay subsidy of 1307, merely 2.6% (five) of the urban taxpayers, presumably burgesses, were identified by topographical bynames, but two of those bynames could have been occupational (*de bracina* and de le waynhous).[41] Similarly, only four (1.6%) of the contributors to the subsidy of 1311 were described by topographical bynames, two of which were also ambiguous (de whaynhouse again and *de abbatia*, probably occupational).[42] If bynames might have been associated with lower social status, such tax listings for the borough, comprising burgesses only, might under-represent topographical bynames in the borough. Unfortunately, there are few listings which comprehend townspeople who were not burgesses, although there are two potential sources, the *Nonarum Inquisitiones* and the rental of the urban property of Leicester Abbey of similar date.[43]

The rental of 1341 comprised over 180 tenants of the Abbey, including cottagers, in the north and east of the borough and its suburbs, but only 3.8% (seven) of these tenants were identified by topographical bynames, including several ambivalent forms (atthall, de la waynhous and *de camera*, all potentially occupational, and wodegate, probably a minor urban placename). More inclusively, the assessment for the *Nonarum Inquisitiones* of 1340–42, collected in four instalments, comprehended altogether about 700 urban inhabitants, but of whom only nine received topographical denominations. Moreover, of these nine, six were ambiguous, since three de le (othe) waynhous, one atte halle and another atte walshall, tend towards occupational bynames. To these examples might be appended Emma *de cimiterio*, Margaret *ad scalam* and Roger *de bracina*, who were assessed to the cannemol for brewing in the late thirteenth century, but inclusion in that list suggests that Roger's byname was occupational too.[44]

The earlier corpus of topographical bynames included some which reflected the urban topography. For example, contributions to the subsidy of 1271 were exacted from William *sub muro* and Richard *sub muro*, and in 1307 from Margery *sub muro*. Richard occurred in the records of the borough between 1258 and 1292.[45] At a much earlier time, Reginald *sub muro* was involved in a case of debt in the morningspeech court, whilst in 1254 the byname was transmitted across two generations on the admission to the gild merchant of Geoffrey *sub muro filius Walteri sub muro*. Onderwal, an unusual compound, occurred in 1302. Nevertheless, the byname Wall recurred only in the later middle ages, in the person of Robert Wall(e) (fl. 1492—1508).[46]

Amongst the earlier forms of topographical byname appeared also atte Crosse (*ad crucem*) or Cruke, apparently inherited across two generations in the form of John Cruke *filius Hugonis Cruke* in 1253, and relating almost certainly to an urban cross.[47] Other, apparent topographical forms were possibly occupational bynames, thus *ad solarium* (*de solario*), *de camera* (*de la chaumbre*), de la Bracina, *de aula* (atte halle), and the ubiquitous de le waynhous which was held by several urban inhabitants between 1271 and 1360. Yet other early forms were more properly minor urban placenames, such as de le wodegate (1242–1341) and de kyngeslane.[48]

Nevertheless, the preponderance of topographical bynames in the borough remained ambiguous in that they might have been either urban or rural, allowing for open spaces in boroughs. More particularly, that tendency increased during the later middle ages, so that it might be surmised that these names were being introduced into the borough from outside, perhaps from suburban parishes. From the late fourteenth century into the sixteenth, the corpus of topographical bynames included othe Grene (del Grene), which existed in the borough from 1373 through to 1508, del Frith (1377), de Forest (1379), Yates (1452–84), Hurst (1473–1507), at Legh and

Knolles in the late fifteenth century, and a large range of surnames of similar character.[49]

William othe Grene *alias* del Grene *alias* atte Grene was elected MP for the borough on several occasions between 1369 and 1382 and also acted as an affeeror and accountant. Less distinguished was his namesake who entered the gild merchant in 1499, but Thomas Grene, draper, (fl. 1446–59) had also acted as MP for the borough in 1450 and 1459. John Grene held urban property in the rentals of 1458 to 1495, whilst Margaret Grene was also enumerated in the rental of 1458. Having been admitted to the freedom in 1476, Robert Grene advanced to the office of auditor between 1478 and 1483, and was assessed in the subsidy of 1492. Listed in the subsidy of five years later, Annes (Agnes) Grene was again mentioned in 1505, concurrently with Stephen and Richard Gren(e). In 1508, another Thomas Grene (of Leicester) was admitted to the freedom.[50]

Moreover, some topographical names which entered the borough in the later middle ages were not ostensibly local forms. For example, Robert Knolles was admitted to the gild merchant in 1480 and contributed to the subsidies of 1492 and 1497, but this topographical item is not local. Equally, Hurst was not evident in the local lexis of topographical bynames and surnames, but Thomas Hurst, an auditor between 1479 and 1494, inhabited the borough from 1473 to 1507.[51]

Although the overall contribution of topographical elements to the lexis of naming in the two counties was limited, one or two topographical surnames survived to establish a larger impact in the nineteenth century. One of the principal forms was Green(e), which in the Hearth Tax of 1665 for Rutland accounted for 18 taxpayers in 10 parishes.[52] In the population census for the two main registration districts in the county in 1851, 42 households contained a Green, dispersed through 15 parishes, and of whom over half had been born within the county, 10 in Lincolnshire and a further five in Leicestershire.[53]

Nonetheless, topographical items had only a circumscribed impact on naming in the two counties, since settlement was preponderantly nucleated. In the case of Green, for example, the etymology seems more likely to have been habitation near the village green rather than an explanation in the development of new settlements called greens in wood-pasture areas in the north-west of the county. Certainly, the earlier distribution of Green as a byname would be

**FIG 15 DISTRIBUTION OF GRENE
AND VARIANTS IN LEICESTERSHIRE
IN 1524-5**

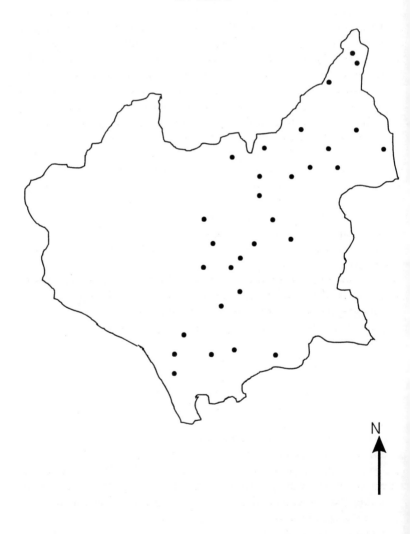

Scale 0   10

consistent with the former interpretation. In the Leicestershire lay subsidy of 1524–25, Grene and variants constituted the surnames of between 10 and 12% of the taxpayers with topographical surnames in each year.[54] The concentration of these taxpayers was located in north-east and east Leicestershire, with a smaller distribution in the south of the county, in *pays* where the etymon would accord more closely with village greens than colonization of new settlements. That predominantly nucleated nature of settlement in the two counties reduced the impact of topographical surnames.

Conclusion

As a result of the largely nucleated settlement of the two counties, topographical bynames and surnames did not develop on any scale nor have any large impact on the lexis of naming. Although there was some polyfocal settlement in some parishes, as in Barkby, and perhaps considerable dispersed settlement in the wood-pastures areas of Leicestershire, the proportion of taxpayers holding topographical bynames and surnames remained inconsequential. Consequently also, the range of topographical items was limited, and these elements were mainly conventional, particularly by comparison with, for example, adjacent parts of Lincolnshire. Within this restricted corpus in the two counties, only Green made had any serious import on naming. In general, an association existed between topographical bynames and status in the medieval country-side, these bynames seemingly related to the unfree peasantry. In the borough of Leicester, by contrast, where burgess status represented freedom, topographical bynames were scarce, although little can be discerned about the non-burgess population. Small towns, however, exhibited a greater familiarity with topographical bynames, if medieval Melton Mowbray was representative.

References

[1] PRO E179/165/1, 21. See generally M T Löfvenberg, *Studies on Middle English Local Surnames*, (Lund Studies in English, 11, Lund 1942) and S Carlsson, *Studies on Middle English Local Bynames in East Anglia*, (Lund Studies in English, 79, Lund 1989).

[2] *Tudor Rutland*.

[3] *Rutland Hearth Tax*.

4 *AASR*, (1888–9); PRO E179/133/35; PRO E179/133/104–110, 112–118, 121–122, 124.

5 PRO HO 107/2092–2093.

6 PRO E179/165/1, 21; *Tudor Rutland*; *Rutland Hearth Tax*.

7 PRO E179/165/1, 21; *Tudor Rutland*; *Rutland Hearth Tax*; PRO HO 107/2092–2093.

8 PRO HO 107/2092–2093.

9 PRO HO E179/165/1, HO 107/2092–2093.

10 PRO HO 107/2092 (North Luffenham, household 118).

11 *AASR*, (1888–9); PRO E179/133/35, 104–110, 112–118, 121–122, 124.

12 *The Lay Subsidy Roll for Warwickshire of 1332*, (Dugdale Society, 6, 1926); J C Cox, 'Derbyshire in 1327–8: being a lay subsidy roll', *Journal of the Derbyshire Archaeological and Natural History Society*, 30 (1908), 23–96; PRO E179/135/14–15 (Parts of Holland and Kesteven).

13 PRO E179/133/35.

14 PRO E179/133/35.

15 PRO E179/133/35.

16 The Queen's College, Oxford, MS 366, fos. 16v, 18v.

17 *Oakham Survey*, 25.

18 *Oakham Survey*, 29.

19 Bodl. MS Laud Misc 625, fo. 200r.

20 Bodl. MS Laud Misc 625, fo. 200r.

21 Bodl. MS Laud Misc 625, fo. 207v.

22 Bodl. MS Laud Misc, fos. 191v–192r.

23 PRO E179/133/35.

24 Bodl. MS Laud Misc 625, fo. 201v.

25 PRO E179/133/35.

26 PRO E179/133/35.

27 Bodl. MS Wood empt 7, fos. 40v–41r.

28 Bodl. MS Wood empt 7, fos. 4v, 5r–v, 6v, 7r–8r, 51v–52r. Hugh had been living in 1310, when he attested a charter: fo. 38v.

29 Bodl. MS Wood empt 7, fos. 13v–14r (1336), 18r–v (1352–53), 24r–v (1334–40), 40v (1333), 48r–49r (1349 and 1353), 69v–70r (as John othe Hill of Melton Mowbray in 1321).

30 Bodl. MS Wood empt 7, fos. 23v (1367, attestation as William del Hull), fos. 31v–32r (attestation as William super le Hill), fos. 37v–38r (acquisition of a house as William del Hil), fo. 38r (acquisition of a toft as William de le Hil de Graham), fo. 51r (attestation in the Latin form William *de monte*).

[31] Bodl. MS Wood empt 7, fos. 15v–18r.

[32] Bodl. MS Wood empt 7, fos. 40r–v.

[33] Bodl. MS Wood empt 7, fos. 12r, 20v (aš atte Crosse), 35r–36r, 74r–v (1311).

[34] Bodl. MS Wood empt 7, fos. 73r–74r, 75v–76r, 76r–77r.

[35] For example, Bodl. MS Wood empt 7, fos. 68v–69r (1329).

[36] Bodl. MS Wood empt 7, fos. 11r, 21r.

[37] Bodl. MS Wood empt 7, fos. 33r–v, 52v.

[38] Bodl. MS Wood empt 7, fos. 76r–77r.

[39] Bodl. MS Wood empt 7, fos. 77v–78r.

[40] Bodl. ME Wood empt 7, fos. 42r–v (1380).

[41] *RBL*, I, 255–7.

[42] *RBL*, I, 273–4.

[43] Leicestershire Record Office, BR III/4/70–73; Bodl. MS Laud Misc 625, fos. 185v–189r.

[44] Leicestershire Record Office, BR III/7/2.

[45] He was a *taxator* (affeeror or assessor) for the cannemol, toll on brewers: Leicestershire Record Office, BR III/7/2.

[46] *RBL*, I, 67.

[47] *RBL*, I, 67.

[48] *RBL*, I, 63, 141; II, 6. For Roger de Kyngeslane of Leicester, assessed on 16 sacks of wool in the purveyance of wool in 1343, PRO C260/54.

[49] *RBL*, II, 144, 147–8, 191, 258, 265, 268–9, 278–9, 307, 326, 330–3, 342, 344, 346, 348–9, 351 2, 352, 373–4, 381, 401–3, 415, 418–19, 422, 425–7, 429, 430, 432, 436–7, 445, 447–8, 451–5, 461, 464, 466–7 (Grene); 157 (Frith); 180 (Forest); 268, 278, 296, 348, 425, 429, 434, 448, 453, 463, 465 (Yates); 296, 330, 333, 350, 372, 441, 449, 452–6 (Hurst); 413–4, 448 (Legh); and 332, 334, 338, 351, 361, 372, 441, 444, 450, 464 (Knolles).

[50] As n.49.

[51] As n.49.

[52] *Rutland Hearth Tax*, 18, 22, 29, 30, 32, 33,, 40.

[53] PRO HO 107/2092–2093.

[54] PRO E179/133/104–110, 112–18, 121–22, 124.

CHAPTER 8

BYNAMES AND SURNAMES FROM PERSONAL NAMES

Generally, the development of bynames deriving from personal names was influenced in the two counties first by the transformation of personal names in the twelfth century and the relative persistence of insular Germanic personal names, secondly by the incorporation of specific personal names as bynames and surnames, and finally by the fortunes of individual kinship groups during the demographic transition after the mid-fourteenth century. The cultural influence of insular Germanic personal names — Old English and Anglo-Scandinavian items, which essentially comprised the preponderance of pre-Conquest forms — was attenuated. Almost certainly, the reason for their comparative insignificance in bynames from personal names was the eclipse of these personal names during the twelfth century by Continental-Germanic name forms and Christian names. By the time that bynames had assumed any widespread importance in the two counties, insular Germanic personal names had been substantially replaced by the newly introduced, post-Conquest forms, Continental-Germanic and Christian names.[1]

In the Burton Abbey surveys (A and B) of 1114x28 of the manor of Appleby Magna in north-west Leicestershire, within a generation of *Domesday Book*, two phenomena are evident. In Survey B, many villeins were still recognized by insular Germanic personal names, although there was a sprinkling of C-G names. In survey A, by contrast, some of the *censarii* or molmen — tenants whose services had been commuted and who contributed mainly money rents — had already assumed C-G names. Importantly, however, bynames had not developed amongst this tenantry.[2] From the insubstantial evidence of the manorial surveys of the Templar properties in Rutland (at Greetham and Empingham) in 1185, post-Conquest forms (including Christian) of name exceeded residual insular Germanic forms.[3] Nevertheless, only three of the 20 peasant tenants enumerated on these Templar properties were accorded bynames and those three probably as a reflection of their status; Ascelin *sacerdos* held a bovate as the solitary tenant of the Templars at Tickencote, whilst Odo *diaconus* a bovate at Empingham and Richard de Sewsterne half a carucate at Sewstern.[4]

Significantly, the tenants of the soke of Rothley in Scandinavianized Leicestershire in the survey of *c*.1245 were predominantly identified by C-G and Christian forms of personal name, with few exceptions.[5] Moreover, 465 of the 559 tenants were further attributed a byname, whilst the position of the remaining 94 was complicated by their status as joint tenants and thus potentially identifiable without reference to bynames.[6] That situation of almost universal peasant bynames might have existed earlier, for all 11 tenants in Worthington and Newbold in 1212 and in all 26 taxpayers in the lay subsidy for Stathern in 1232 had assumed bynames.[7]

Thus, as bynames were increasingly materializing amongst the peasantry of the two counties, so insular personal names were being comprehensively eclipsed by newer forms of personal name, principally C-G and Christian. Confirmation of that trend of substitution of new for old forms of personal name derives from the survey of the lands of the Bishop of Lincoln in the two counties in 1225x1258. For example, all 14 jurors at Lyddington were recorded with C-G names, 12 of whom were also accorded bynames. That tendency is further reflected in some patronymic forms in the same survey, such as Reginald *filius Terrici* and Hugh *filius Ascelini*, both patronyms incorporating West Frankish forms of personal name, particularly *Terricus* or Thierry, a significantly French hypocoristic form of Theodoric.[8]

Consequently, as bynames were becoming more customary amongst the peasantry of the two counties by the early thirteenth century, so insular personal names had been eclipsed by newer forms of name. Simultaneously, the general *corpus* of personal names in use contracted. Whilst there had been over 500 different male personal names of C-G derivation alone in the twelfth century in England, the use of forenames by the thirteenth century had become concentrated, including in the two counties, as reflected in the tables below.

Represented in Table 8.1 is that there were 64 different male forenames held by taxpayers in the lay subsidy for Rutland in 1296 and 59 in the taxation for Leicestershire in 1327, by comparison with the theoretically very much larger total *corpus* of C-G, Christian, and other personal names. The mean number of taxpayers per forename

Table 8.1

Descriptive statistics of forenames of male taxpayers in the lay subsidies for Rutland, 1296, and Leicestershire, 1327[9]

No. of forenames	mean	standdev	median	min	max	Q1	Q3
Rutland							
64	25.47	50.44	2.5	1	250	1	19
Leicestershire							
59	66.50	162.00	3.0	1	799	1	46

was about 25 in Rutland and 67 in Leicestershire, but the range was extremely wide, so that some bynames were held by a single taxpayer whilst the most frequent single name was held respectively in Rutland and Leicestershire by 250 and 799 of the assessed. Consideration should be directed, however, to the selective and exclusive aspect of the lay subsidies, which omitted a large proportion of the peasantry with the consequence that forenames in the taxation may reflect only the naming preference of the wealthier section of society. Since few extensive manorial surveys survive for the two counties before *c*.1300, controls on the nominal data in the subsidies are scarce, but two detailed, if small, comparative datasets are available.

A tithing listing for the manor of Kibworth Harcourt of *c*.1280 enumerated all males over the age of 12 within the manor, extending to 152 males, who held collectively 15 forenames, a mean of 10 per forename.[10] Comprehending a larger population in several vills, the survey of 'Oakham' in 1305 enumerated 254 different male peasant tenants, with 30 different forenames, a mean of 8.47 tenants per name (standard deviation 10.77) or a median of 3.5 (interquartile range of 3.5 to 12.25). The actual range extended from 11 forenames each held by a single tenant, to one forename accounting for 48 tenants.[11]

The rank order of forenames encompassed in the Oakham survey was a familiar spectrum, the most frequent names consisting of William (48 tenants), Robert (27), Henry (25), John (24), and Richard and Thomas (each with 16), six forenames thus comprehending over 60% of the male tenants.[12] Similar concentration is exhibited in the lay subsidies of 1296 and 1327 for the two counties, although it must be appreciated that the tax lists are more selective than the manorial surveys and tithing lists.

Table 8.2

Rank-order of forenames of male taxpayers in the lay subsidies for Rutland, 1296, and Leicestershire, 1327[13]

County	Forename	No. of taxpayers
Rutland	William	250
	Robert	175
	John	163
	Henry	154
	Richard	148
	Thomas	102

Percentage of all male taxpayers — 60.9

Leicestershire	William	799
	John	733
	Robert	530
	Richard	357
	Thomas	252
	Roger	213

Percentage of all male taxpayers — 73.5

The most common forenames were thus composed of a small concentration of six to eight names, largely C-G with two Christian, at the time when hereditary surnames were incipient. By comparison, the rank-order of bynames from personal names displayed a dissimilar composition, with little relationship to the six most frequent forenames, although the numbers of bynames from personal names are inconsiderable and thus allow a wide margin of stochastic difference.

Table 8.3

Rank-order of bynames from male personal names in the lay subsidies of Rutland, 1296, and Leicestershire, 1327[14]

Byname (stem)	No.	Origin	Actual forms
Rutland 1296 — (more than 6 occurrences)			
Erneys	9	C-G	
David	8	PCeltic	Daui
Bartholomew	7	Christian	Bate
Fulk	6	C-G	Faukes
William	6	C-G	diminutives

Byname (stem)	No.	Origin	Actual forms
Leicestershire — (more than 10 occurrences)			
Alan	20	PCeltic (Breton)	
Bartholomew	17	Christian	Bate (16)
Martin	17	Christian	
Adam	16	Christian	diminutives
Gamel	15	Anglo-Scand	
Gilbert	14	C-G	hypocoristic
Steyn	13	Anglo-Scand	
David	13	PCeltic	Davy (8)
Robert	12	C-G	diminutives
Simon	12	Christian	
Herbard	11	C-G	
Randolf	11	C-G	
Pain	11	C-G	
Sweyn	9	Anglo-Scand	

Note: For a discussion whether Sweyn was personal or occupational, see below.

In some measure, the forenames and bynames in the lay subsidies may have represented different generations, of which the bynames were the elder, so correlation between common forenames and common bynames need not be anticipated precisely. On the other hand, the fragmentary evidence of the earlier manorial surveys suggests that the six most popular forenames in the subsidies already constituted the most frequent names earlier in the thirteenth century. The dissonance exists then between the most popular forenames and the most frequent forenames incorporated in bynames from personal names; the most frequent forenames did not constitute the most common bynames from personal names in the late thirteenth and early fourteenth centuries. In fact, by contrast, personal names incorporated in bynames were not the most frequent forename.

The longer-term perspective during the later middle ages is represented in Table 8.4, but consideration again should be directed to the low numbers which allow stochastic variation.

In some cohorts, the numbers of surnames is particularly small, allowing few conclusions to be adduced. For example, the Poll Tax for Rutland in 1377 provides a rank order of (first equal) Elias, John, Randolph and Toky, each with five occurrences, followed closely by Bartholomew (Bate) and Swain, each with four. In this and the

Table 8.4

Surnames from personal names during the later middle ages in Leicestershire and Rutland, 1377–1525[15]

Date	No. of stem names	No. of taxpayers/listed with surnames from personal names
Rutland		
1377	58	112
1522	64	254
1524	59	202
Leicestershire		
1381	120	418
1524	101	421

Note: This table comprises surnames from female as well as male personal names.

following rankings, the names relate to the stem rather than the actual form of the byname, that is, for example, Robert rather than differentiating Robert, Roberts, Hopkin and Hobb.[16]

Relatively more conclusive are the data in the equivalent tax list for Leicestershire in 1381, producing a rank order as follows: John (23 incidences); David (14); Alan and Swain (13 each); Adam and Richard (11 each); Cole (10); and Bartholomew (Bate), Robert, Roger and Walter (nine each).[17] The smaller corpus for Rutland in the early sixteenth century is again unconvincing, but constructs a rank order in 1522 of Col(l)e (14), Robert (nine), Andrew (eight), William, Edmund and German (seven each), Allen, Simon, Wymark, Laurence and Nicholas (six each). Whilst that list comprehended all males over the age of 16, the lay subsidy of 1524 was a taxation assessed on eligibility to taxation, but it largely confirms the rank order: Cole (13); Andrew and Robert (10 each); Nicholas (eight); William (seven); and Laurence and German (six each).[18] Extending the analysis to 1665, the rank order in the hearth tax for Rutland consisted of Allen (27), Cole and variants (27), Andrew (19), Royce and Sewell (15), Bartholomew (Bate[s], Bett) (13), Christian (11), and Martin, Robert and Thomas (10 each).[19]

To some extent, then, change occurred during the later middle ages, for, whilst before the mid-fourteenth century, surnames from personal names did not correlate with the most frequent forenames, in sources from the later middle ages those more common forenames featured more strongly in the most frequent bynames from personal names, such as bynames from William or Robert. That pattern was replicated in Leicestershire, for which the lay subsidy of 1524–5, whilst including surnames from lower ranked forenames such as David (17 incidences), Cole (14), Bartholomew (Bates, Batte, Bett) (10), and Benedict (Benet) (nine), contained also those from the most common forenames Walter (Watte[s]) (16), Adam (15), Robert (14), and William (seven).[20]

Part of this discrepancy may be attributed to the sources, since it is possible that the earlier lay subsidies, exclusive by wealth, may have omitted bynames from common forenames if those forms of byname were more strongly associated with a lower socio-economic tranche of the peasantry. A second possibility is that the earlier listings reflected an earlier and wider active corpus of personal names still recently in use whilst bynames were still flexible, which was replaced, slightly before bynames developed into hereditary surnames, by bynames derived from a more narrowly restricted functional stock of personal names.

Excluding the influence of a small number of Anglo-Scandinavian personal names, however, little regional distinctiveness is displayed in this corpus of bynames from personal names.[21] One of the possible explanations is that East Midlands regional naming, like the corresponding dialect, developed a uniformity and standard over a fairly large area. Certainly, the lexis of personal naming discloses very little the intermediate relationship of the two counties between Midlands and lower North.[22] Before the middle of the fourteenth century, the high position of David (Daui, Dauy) in the rank order is somewhat unusual and Alan requires some comment on PCeltic/Middle Brettonic names in the East Midlands.

In 1296, the hypocoristic Daui, the consistent form of byname from David, was the second most frequent byname from a personal name in Rutland, with eight incidences, whilst forms from David, including Davy, were sixth in the rank order in Leicestershire in 1327.[23] There also bynames incorporating forms of Alan (principally Aleyn) were second most frequent amongst bynames from personal names in 1327.[24] Although bynames from insular PCeltic personal names existed in Rutland in 1296, such as Cade (three and also three in Leicestershire in 1327) and Murdak (one), some recurring forms were almost certainly Middle Brettonic ones introduced after the Conquest.[25]

In adjacent Lincolnshire, in the Parts of Holland and Kesteven, Brettonic influence was evident, perhaps an extension of the earl of Richmond's influence. Bynames from personal names in the lay subsidy of 1332 for these Parts included five Conayn and a Conyng and a sprinkling of Bryan, as well as Conan *faber*, reflecting the occasional use of the forename.[26] By far the most prevalent PCeltic name in bynames, however, was Alan, most predominantly as a Latin patronym (*filius Alani*), amounting to 23 taxpayers in patronymic form and five Alayn. By comparison, however, bynames from forms of David were relatively rare in these Parts, perhaps no more than half a dozen instances, comprising Dawis, Daw, and Daues, as well as Dauy.[27] Hypothetically, this distribution would suggest that bynames from Alan were introduced by Middle Brettonic influence, but those from David may have been of insular PCeltic derivation.[28]

Superior Breton influence was not established in the two counties in *Domesday*, represented in Leicestershire by only Mainou *Brito* and Oger *Brito*, the former holding more substantial lands in Lutterworth, Misterton and Catthorpe, but Oger only two-thirds of a hide in Kilby.[29] Whilst the byname Orger appeared in Melton Mowbray from at least *c*.1245 and through into the late thirteenth to fifteenth century, associated with a principal kinship in this small town, its origin from Breton lordship is implausible, particularly given the geography of the Breton estates in 1086.[30] Whilst Alan was a Breton comital forename, it was exogenous to Leicestershire, so that its existence must have owed something to introduction to the peasantry of the county from an external source, perhaps Lincolnshire.

Bynames and surnames from Anglo-Scandinavian
personal names

The intricate problems of Scandinavian forms of personal names have been outlined above, if only briefly.[31] First, the differentiation of some forms of Scandinavian names from cognate West Germanic or Old English forms presents considerable problems. Secondly, there ensues the difficulty of distinguishing Norman Scandinavian forms from late Anglo-Scandinavian ones. The principles described below have been followed as much as possible to elucidate differences of etymology, but the interpretation is not entirely conclusive. What, then, is the benefit of this inconclusive exercise?

Principally, the investigation is concerned with the extent of the cultural impact of Scandinavian influence by the eleventh century and afterwards. Leicestershire and Rutland composed part of the area of the Five Boroughs on the southern fringe of the Northern Danelaw, but subjected too from the west and south-west to the intrusion of Old English (West Saxon) cultures. The composition and distribution of placenames and placename elements in the two counties attests a high level of cultural impact, in Scandinavian generic elements, such as -thorp and -by, as well as specific elements, and also in the Grimston hybrids.[32] The cultural impact of personal naming may, however, modify the extent of that legacy.

Equally, a regional variation in Scandinavian personal names has been detected.[33] Whilst some Scandinavian personal names had a more generalized distribution — that is, were more common throughout areas which had come under Scandinavian influence and in some other areas too — such as variants from Gamall, Þorsteinn and Úlfr, other forms had a greater regional concentration, such as Anundr, Bondi and Hogni in Norfolk, or Ormr in Lancashire and Yorkshire.[34]

The principles generally adopted here to differentiate etymologies, which, it must be emphasized, have not been conclusive, are as follows. Syncopation has been used as a partially diagnostic criterion. More usually, this feature relates to the deuterotheme in compounded names, for example in -ketel. Where, for example, the second element -ketel has been elided to -kell or -kil, the name form has been assumed to have developed before the Conquest in the area of the Five Boroughs. When the full form of the element (-ketel) is preserved, however, there is a problem. The form may either have derived from East Anglia, where this form was more conservative, or it may be a Norman Scandinavian form.[35] In some names, the Norman Scandinavian form may be ascertained by the replacement of Anglo-Scand initial Ás by Frankish Ans (Ásketill by comparison with Ansketill).[36] Phonemic changes explain some other differences of Norman Scand forms, as in T(h)urstin, Anschetin and Astin, both Norman forms.[37] In some cases, Anglo-Scandinavian forms can be verified lexically, since the names were rare or did not occur in Normandy.[38]

Sufficient contentious areas, however, remain. In particular, phonemic changes cannot be depended upon as incontestable. The perceived differences in phonemes between West Germanic and Scandinavian forms of names are not totally reliable. For example, the distinction between initial Ás- and Os- could result from the difference of Scand and direct WG etymology, but might equally emanate from late Anglicization of Scand forms, more particularly in place-names but perhaps also in personal names.[39] In the immediate post-Conquest period, in early Anglo-Norman, the extent to which the phonemic construction of names might have been corrupted in the written record is debatable.[40] Some names will therefore continue to be contentious, perhaps of several origins.

Whilst taking into consideration these ambiguities, however, it can be fairly concluded that the enduring cultural impact of Scand personal names on English personal naming was relatively light in these two counties and probably throughout most of England. The reason, it will appear, is the relatively expeditious displacement of insular personal names in general in the twelfth century at the time of the introduction and formation of bynames. That decline will be discussed first, followed by a consideration of the corpus of Scand personal names incorporated in bynames and surnames in Leicestershire and Rutland.

In 1066, the personal names of thegns of Scand extraction comprised Arkell (syncopated), Haldane, Swein, Oswulf, Osmund, Toki, Ulf, Thorkell (syncopated), Auti and Ulfketel; four of those names recurred in 1086 held by mesne tenants, Swein, Osmund, Ulf and Thorkell. Additionally, in 1086, occurred Frienday, Ketelbern, Osbern, Thurstan, Riculf, Grimbald, Feggi and Thorold.[41] In 1086, Ulf in particular recurred in the contexts of sub-tenancies at Swinford, Willoughby Waterless, Enderby, and Walcote.[42]

The recorded instances of Scandinavian personal names in twelfth- and early thirteenth-century Leicestershire and Rutland are not abundant, but include a Toki at Appleby Magna in the second decade, Gamel at Asfordby 1225x1258, a Turkil *filius Alwini* who held a toft and croft in Leire, and another Turkil who held a messuage at one of the Dalbys.[43] In the custumal of Rothley soke, comprehending tenants in about a dozen vills in north-east Leicestershire *c.*1245, the area of greatest Scandinavian influence in the county, and which enumerated over 500 tenants, only Oky and Gamel unambiguously, and Osmund and Cole less certainly, occurred as Scandinavian personal names, each held by a single tenant.[44] Additionally, some memoranda about undated charters and gifts to Leicester Abbey, compiled at a later time, refer to a few Scandinavian personal names. Thus amongst the small donors of lands in Barkby was included Adam *filius Johannis filii Ketilbern'* and Peter *filius Thurstani de Barkeby*, whilst at Blaby, William de Diua contributed the attornment of the services of William *filius Horm'* [hypercorrect Orm], and at one of the Bosworths land was described as next to that of Geoffrey *filius Sweyn'*.[45]

The long-term influence of Scandinavian name forms on bynames and surnames in the two counties is tabulated below.

Table 8.5

Bynames and Surnames derived from Anglo-Scand personal names, 1296–1665[46]

| Date | Total 'population' | No. with pers | Anglo-Scand personal names | | |
			No.	%all	%pers
Rutland					
1296	1868	197	18	1.0	9.1
1377	806	112	15	1.9	13.4
1522	1661	254	20	1.2	7.9
1524	1400	202	17	1.2	8.4
1665	2919	568	58	2.0	10.2
Leicestershire					
1327	4216	742	78	1.9	10.5
1381	2060	418	49	2.4	11.7
1524	2683	421	18	0.7	4.3
1525	3879	679	46	1.2	6.8

Notes: Total 'population' relates to the total number of taxpayers; 'No. with pers' consists of the number of taxpayers with bynames or surnames derived from personal names; under Anglo-Scand personal names, No. enumerates the number of taxpayers with bynames or surnames from Anglo-Scand personal names, '%all' expresses the No. of taxpayers with bynames or surnames from Anglo-Scand names as a percentage of all taxpayers; and '%pers' expresses the same taxpayers as a percentage of taxpayers with bynames or surnames from personal names.

These figures, however, should be considered cautiously. As the numbers are low, stochastic variation will have an important effect. Additionally, the Poll Tax for Leicestershire comprised solely Gartree Hundred, in the east of the county, where Scandinavian settlement might have had its greatest impact, so the figure may be higher than the level for the county as a whole.[47]

The two lay subsidies, as explained above, omitted a significant proportion of the real population, since it fell below the taxable threshold. It is not possible accurately to assess the consequence, but the intimation is that bynames and surnames from Anglo-Scand personal names may been associated more with lower social groups. The mean assessment on taxpayers with such bynames in Leicestershire in 1327 was 30.64*d*. (standard deviation 24.57, whilst the median was 24*d*.; for the entire taxable population (4,216 taxpayers), the mean was higher, at 32.64*d*). The lay subsidy of 1327 may thus conceivably omit a larger proportion of the peasantry with bynames from Anglo-Scand personal names.[48]

Nevertheless, the long-term trend of the figures in Table 8.5 suggests that Anglo-Scand personal names had only a modest impact on the composition of bynames and surnames in the two counties. Their impact was sustained in Rutland, which might have been expected *a priori*, since the county was located more securely in the area of Scandinavian influence. By contrast, the content of Anglo-Scand personal names in surnames declined in Leicestershire over the later middle ages; either bynames of 1327 were abandoned or the fortunes of individual families and kinships over the later middle ages affected the Anglo-Scand material.

Bynames and surnames with an Anglo-Scand content were borne by only a small proportion of the taxpayers assessed — between 0.7 and 2.4% at any time. In that context, their significance was minimal. As a proportion of bynames and surnames from personal names, their importance was more substantial, although they still comprised in general less than 10%.

Another perception, however, should be considered, that is, not the proportion of individuals possessing this form of name, but the proportion of different bynames and surnames which consisted of those with Anglo-Scand forms. The namestock of the taxpayers in the lay subsidy for Leicestershire in 1327 consisted of some 230 different bynames from personal names, although this figure should be conceived as very approximate because of the complexity of differentiat ing different forms of byname. About 10% had Anglo-Scand etymology (24 different bynames). The reduced content of Anglo-Scand forms at the end of the middle ages is reflected by only six different Anglo-Scand forms of surname from a total of 97 different bynames from personal names in the Rutland militia list of 1522.[49]

FIG 16 DISTRIBUTION OF BYNAMES FROM
ANGLO-SCAND PERSONAL NAMES IN 1327

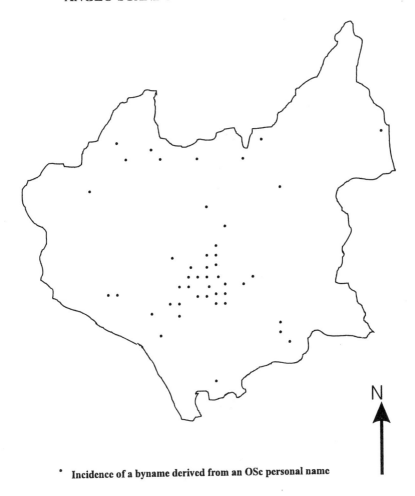

•   **Incidence of a byname derived from an OSc personal name**

N

Scale 0 ——————————— 10

Within that corpus, some particular names achieved a greater concentration. The numbers of different bynames with Anglo-Scand content prevailed as follows: 10 in Rutland in the lay subsidy of 1296, seven in the Poll Tax of 1377, six in the militia list of 1522, three in the lay subsidy in 1524, and 12 in the Hearth Tax of 1665;[50] and in Leicestershire in the respective listings 24 in 1327, 13 in 1381, and eight in 1524.[51] In the rank-order of bynames and surnames from personal names, however, some names of Anglo-Scand derivation performed highly. In the lay subsidy for Leicestershire in 1327, the mean of taxpayers per byname was 3.267, but Gamel, third in the order of frequency, was borne by 17 taxpayers; whilst Steyn (sixth) was associated with 13 of the assessed, another 11 were identified by the byname Sweyn (joint eighth).[52] Toky was joint most frequent in Rutland in 1377 and Swain joint second.[53] Correspondingly, Swain was joint third in frequency of bynames and surnames from personal names in the Poll Tax of 1381 for Leicestershire, whilst Cole was fifth.[54] In the listings of 1522 and 1524 for Rutland, variants of Cole were again highly represented, first in frequency.[55] In 1665 this level was replicated by variants of Cole, followed by Gamble with eight taxpayers and Swan(n) with seven. Cole was, nevertheless, an ambiguous name, with conflicting etymologies; whilst it might be expected that in this area of Scandinavian influence it originated from Scand Kolí or Kolr, that still remains supposition, and the variant forms are particularly ambiguous.[56]

Since the numbers of these names and their bearers lack any real significance, suggestions of regional differentiation are hazardous. In all sources, discounting the ambivalent Cole, Gamel assumed the most importance, but this name is acknowledged as the most common Anglo-Scand name. Its distribution was contained more within the Northern Danelaw.[57] Its extensive occurrence in 1327 in the Leicestershire lay subsidy is noted above, although one explanation for its success may have been kinship groups in some vills where it was held by several taxpayers, such as Worthington with three Gamels, Burton Overy with two Gamils, and Peatling Magna with three Gamils.[58] By 1525, variant forms of Gamel accounted for 39% of surnames from Anglo-Scand personal names. Its abundance again owed something to kinship groups or concentrations in 1525, with the persistence of three Gamolls at Burton Overy and the enumeration of seven Gambulls at Saxilby.[59] Additionally, it occurred in the lay subsidy of 1525 at Grimston (Gamble), Asfordby (Gambull), Rotherby (Gambull),

Kibworth Beauchamp (Gamall), Ashby Magna (Gambull), Bruntingthorpe (Gamull), and Fleckney (Gamull).[60]

Its persistence at Burton Overy over the late middle ages
contributed to the small proportion of cases of continuity of
bynames and surnames in specific 'communities' at that time. Three
Gamels were listed intermediately between 1327 and 1524–25, in
the Poll Tax of 1381 in Burton Overy.[61] The byname evolved at an
earlier time in the county, represented by Ralph Gamel of Barnsby
in *c.*1245, one of the jurors of the custumal of Rothley.[62] Contemporaneously, Richard Gamel was one of the Bishop of Lincoln's tenants
at Asfordby in 1225x1258.[63] Its distribution was probably wider
than attested in the taxation listing, for court rolls and a rental of the
later middle ages disclose other occurrences: at Saxilby (1497); at
Prestwold (1403–4); Kibworth Harcourt (1527); Loughborough
(1411–12); Stoughton (1477); and Barkby (1409).[64]

The phonemic evolution of the surname is illuminated by the
miscellany of records during the later middle ages. One particular
aspect was the vowel change; whilst the form was consistently Gamel
up to and including the lay subsidy of 1327, other variants such as
Gamil, Gamyl, Gamoll and Gamul, were generated in the late middle
ages. These forms persisted into the early sixteenth century, but in
the lay subsidy of 1524–25 was introduced a new form with an inter-
polated /b/, as Gambull in Saxilby and Rotherby (and similarly Gambell
in Pisbrook in Rutland in the militia list of 1522) and the
recognizably modern Gamble at Grimston.[65]

Other Anglo-Scand forms exerted less impact than Gamel, but did
introduce some interesting and perhaps, in some cases, unexpected
forms. Arketill occurred at Great Easton in 1290 and 1381 in its
unsyncopated guise. Either it was a Norman introduction, or,
perhaps more likely considering the location of Great Easton, it had
been received from East Anglia. The kinship group at Kibworth
Beauchamp, the Asteyns, who consisted of at least eight (male) members
recorded in the lay subsidy, Poll Tax and court rolls between 1327
and 1381, present a complexity.[66] Superficially, Astin would be
expected to be a Norman form, but the retention of -steyn complicates
the issue.[67] The Norman personal name did occur in charters relating to
Gaddesby in the patronym *filius Astini*.[68]

Asty is represented in various records in a number of places in the
fourteenth century — Thringstone, Croxton, Loughborough, and
Dalby on the Wolds. By contrast, the 'curiously quite uncommon'

name Eyrik remained, excluding the borough of Leicester, localized in the middle ages in Great and Little Stretton, revealed only in charters of the late thirteenth century and the lay subsidy of 1327.[69]

Grym occurred sporadically in the records, the earliest occasion being a foot of fine of 1202 relating to land in Seale.[70] It recurred in charters of the thirteenth century at Thornton and Kirby Bellars. In the lay subsidy of 1327, four taxpayers were associated with the byname, in east and north Leicestershire, whilst, shortly afterwards, it was recorded in Swannington in 1336. An account for Loughborough included the name in 1474, and John Gryme was assessed at Melton in 1524.[71]

Halfdan appeared in the records most frequently as Haldeyn, but twice as Halden, once as Haldane, three times as Heldyn, and on single occasions as Holdein and Holdyn.[72] These records principally related to Mowsley in the late thirteenth and early fourteenth centuries.[73] Ilyff(e) constituted an unusual name which seems to have been introduced into Leicestershire in the later middle ages, concentrated in the south of the county. From two Iliffs at Saddington in 1381, it seemingly expanded to Ilyfs and Ilyffes (Yliffes) in Kibworth Harcourt, Great Glen, Foxton, Theddingworth, Arnsby, Gilmorton, Foxton and particularly Kimcote and Walton.[74]

Surprisingly, Ketel made no great impression, with but isolated incidence, although it persisted at Great Casterton from the lay subsidy of 1296 through to the Poll Tax of 1377.[75] Its principal concentration was in Castle Donington and Loughborough in the later middle ages, at Castle Donington from 1458 through until at least 1516, and in Loughborough from 1550, in the forms Ketill, Kettell, Kettull and Kettyll, but with the presumed Norman orthography Cheytyll at Leire in 1524-25.[76] In compounded form, it occurred in Ketilbern at Thurmaston in 1341 and (Ketylbarn) at Wanlip in 1524-25. Oky as a byname or surname occurred only at Seale in the lay subsidy of 1327.[77]

Although Orm has been associated with the North of England, it obtained a small incidence in Leicestershire, represented at an early date by William *filius Orm'* in the Pipe Roll of 1184.[78] It was transferred over two generations at Blaby in the early thirteenth century in hypercorrect form, from William *filius Orm'* to Geoffrey Horm of Blaby, who attested a charter relating to land in Aylestone in 1237x1262.[79] It apparently continued in Blaby through the later middle ages, for Richard Orm inhabited the vill, Joan *filia Willelmi Orm* was a tenant of Leicester

Abbey there in 1341, and she was succeeded by William Orm who had held a virgate there as reflected in the rental of 1477.[80] This surname too migrated into Castle Donington and Loughborough towards the end of the middle ages, at Loughborough from 1474 to 1526 and at Castle Donington in 1539.[81]

Whilst Osmond or Osmund presented only a feeble presence in the counties, mainly at Foxton in the early fourteenth century (1315-17) and at North Marefield in 1280, Steyn(e) was more widespread, in six vills mainly concentrated to the south-west of Leicester — Cosby, Stormsworth, Shearsby, Whetstone, Enderby, and Fleckney.[82] From 1296 to 1346, it was a family surname in Kibworth Harcourt.[83] By 1524-25, its presence was located in east Leicestershire, at Skeffington, Billesdon, and Loddington, but also Carlton Curlieu.[84]

The widest distribution was reserved to Swein, although its etymology is complex. That complication is illustrated by John le Swon, taxed at Newbold Verdon in 1327, and Stephen le Swon, a cottager holding *ad placitum* from Leicester Abbey at Stoughton in 1341, reflecting one origin as an occupational byname.[85] Swon existed in the late fourteenth century in asyndetic form in east Leicestershire and Rutland, at Owston, Stretton Parva, Lyddington, North Luffenham, and Medbourne. Sweyn and Swayn were recorded in many places in the counties in the thirteenth and fourteenth centuries, at Kibworth Beauchamp, Broughton Astley, Brooksby, Wigston Magna, Ketton, Lockington, Shepshed, King's Norton, Smeeton Westerby and Gaddesby.[86] The derivation of these forms must be unambiguous, particularly as in 1212 a fine referred to Thomas *filius Swein'*, and the Pipe Rolls of 1195 and 1199 alluded to fines paid by Richard *filius Suein'*.[87]

Less certain is Swan, an extremely frequent form, consistently employed in the court rolls of Kibworth Harcourt from the late thirteenth century to 1354 and at adjacent Kibworth Beauchamp from 1346 to 1381, associated with a kinship group which may have been connected over the two 'communities'. No fewer than 75 entries in the court rolls of these two manors applied the form Swan, as did the lay subsidy of 1327 and the Poll Tax of 1381, but in 1346 Swayn was twice preferred in the court roll and Juliana of this kinship was attributed the surname Suane in the Poll Tax of 1381.[88] Other vills included their Swans in the fourteenth century, in kinship groups as at the Kibworths, Wigston Magna, Houghton, and Lubbenham.[89] Juliana's surname provides some intimation of the origin of Swan and it may be confirmed by a charter relating to land in Gaddesby which referred to Walter *filius Suani*.[90] Swan may uncertainly have resulted from the Latin form of the Anglo-Scand personal name. Kibworth Harcourt was the *locus* for another Anglo-Scand personal name represented by a kinship group, Thort, Thorth or Thurt, which seems to have been confined to this vill and persisted there from *c*.1280 to 1349.[91]

In contrast, Tok(e)y was more concentrated in Rutland, and certainly in the east. Represented by Richard Toky in North Luffenham in the lay subsidy of 1296, this byname continued there in 1377 in Robert and John Toky and John junior, migrating into contiguous South Luffenham in 1522 and 1524 with another John Toky.[92] In 1377, Peter Toky was assessed at neighbouring Pilton, whilst in 1522 Jane Toky was listed in adjacent Seaton succeeded by Henry Tokey there in 1524.[93] Although in the Leicestershire lay subsidy of 1327 the byname was borne by two taxpayers in Sheepy Parva in the west of the county and by a single taxpayer at Croft to the south of Leicester, its only occurrence by 1525 was at Frisby by Galby in the east.[94] Since Tooley was a byname more distinctive of the eastern Danelaw, it was largely unrepresented in Leicestershire and Rutland.[95] There is, however, firm evidence of its existence as a personal name in the early thirteenth century, for in 1204 and 1206 Anketil *filius Toli* and Simon *filius Toli* were mentioned in the pleas before the justices of assize.[96] Thereafter, only John Toly of Lyddington, assessed in the Poll Tax of 1377, personified this name.[97]

Ulf or Wlf exemplified those Anglo-Scand forms of personal names in bynames which were highly localized and transitory. Confined apparently to Barkby, this byname was held by four tenants, two male and two female, between 1279 and 1296, although the *Novum Rentale* of Leicester Abbey referred back to a Richard *filius Ulfi* at Owthorpe at some indeterminate date.[98]

By the early modern period, the legacy of Anglo-Scand personal names had become even more defined. In the Hearth Tax for Rutland in 1665, that endowment consisted of heads of household called Gamble in six different townships, including three in Oakham, one called Iliffe in Uppingham, a Ketle in each of Barrow and Market Overton, Swan(n) heads of household in Morcott (four heads), North Luffenham, Uppingham and Oakham, a Thirkill in Ryhall, and Tookeys in South Luffenham (two), Belton and Hambledon.[99]

Consequently, the taxation lists provide only partial evidence of the existence and re-distribution of bynames from Anglo-Scand personal names in the two counties in the later middle ages. Court rolls, custumals and rentals, and charters, extend the corpus of personal names and illustrate the extreme localization of some and the wider distribution of others. Furthermore, some geographical patterns are clarified, for, whilst the lay subsidy of 1327 has a concentration of bynames from Scand personal names in an area south of Leicester, the more inclusive records divulge these bynames in other areas, particularly north Leicestershire, in the later middle ages. That pattern is also substantiated by the more comprehensive lay subsidies of the early sixteenth century. The cultural impact of Anglo-Scand personal names in the personal naming processes of the two counties remained, however, modest and moderate, by comparison with the continuing legacy of Scand elements in placenames.

Table 8.6

The continuing legacy of Anglo-Scand personal names in Rutland, 1665[100]

Surname	Total occurrence	Distribution
Co(a)l(e)s	20	13
Colson	2	2
Gamble/Gambell	8	6
Grime(s)	2	1
Hack(e)	8	2
Hammond	2	1
Holden	1	1
Iliffe	1	1
Ket(t)le	2	2
Steanes	1	1
Swan(n)	7	4
Tirkill	1	1
Tookey	4	3
Toly	4	3

Notes: Total occurrance represents the number of instances of the surname and distribution the number of parishes in which the surname was recorded. Coles and its variants, Hack(e) and Swan(n) are ambivalent, whilst omitted from the calculation are Collin and Cooley. Cole(s) was concentrated in Langham, where Coale and Cole were concurrent.

Nonetheless, that inheritance from Anglo-Scand personal names was continuing, albeit at an inconsiderable level. Table 8.6 encapsulates the data from the Hearth Tax of 1665, relating to the surnames of heads of household responsible for contributing to the Hearth Tax, of whom there were 2,920. Of those assessed or exempted as not chargeable, 568 (19.5%) held surnames from personal names, 63 of which had Anglo-Scand origins. Thus 11.1% of the Hearth Tax payers with surnames from personal names had surnames derived from Anglo-Scand forms.

Extending the analysis later, Table 8.7 presents data from the population census of 1851 for a significant part of the county (two of the registration districts, excluding that which centred on Stamford).[101] For this purpose, it is possible to add an additional circumstance, whether the bearer of the surname was born within or outside the county and thus whether the accretion of surnames of Anglo-Scand origin was still internally generated or influenced from outside. In this table, the occurrences relate to heads of household or others of independent status within households with surnames which differed from the head. For rural parishes, excluding Oakham and Uppingham, the total of this population of bearers of surnames is 7,280, whilst for the two small towns it amounts to 2,676.

Table 8.7

The legacy of Anglo-Scand personal names in surnames in Rutland in 1851[102]

Surname	Occurrences	Distribution	Immediate origin	
Asmand	1	1	Lincolnshire	1
Cole(s)	19	10	Rutland	14
			Northamptonshire	5
Coulson	18	8	Rutland	10
			Lincolnshire	4
			Leicestershire	2
			Northamptonshire	2
Gamble	25	9	Rutland	17
			Leicestershire	3
			Lincolnshire	2
			Middlesex	1
			Bedfordshire	1
			Northamptonshire	1

Surname	Occurrences	Distribution	Immediate origin	
Gunnill/	3	1	Northamptonshire	2
Gunnell			Lincolnshire	1
Herrick	1	1	Nottinghamshire	1
Iliffe	4	3	Rutland	3
			Lincolnshire	1
Kettle	23	7	Rutland	13
			Leicestershire	5
			Lincolnshire	4
			Nottinghamshire	1
Orme	1	1	Lincolnshire	1
Sturges	5	3	Rutland	2
			Northamptonshire	2
			Lincolnshire	1
Swan(n)	32	12	Rutland	28
			Lincolnshire	2
			Northamptonshire	1
			Middlesex	1
Thorold	4	1	Rutland	3
			Lincolnshire	1
Tookey	10	7	Rutland	5
			Lincolnshire	3
			Leicestershire	2

Notes: Immediate origin relates to the place of birth of the bearer.

Immediately evident is the high proportion of these surnames resident within the county, since only an inconsequential number of the bearers was born outside the county. Moreover, it is probable that many of those born outside the county were nonetheless kin. Despite the generally wide distribution of the surnames through the county, two concentrations existed, for 18 of the 29 Swan(n)s were resident in Barrowden and 10 of the 20 Kettles inhabited Whissendine. The Anglo-Scand legacy to surnames in Rutland was thus persistent and enduring, although quantitatively not exceptional.

Bynames from Old English personal names

Besides the Anglo-Scandinavian contribution to bynames from insular personal names, Old English personal names augmented the corpus of *cognomina* marginally. Comparison of the relative corpora of bynames from personal names in Leicestershire and Rutland and adjacent counties introduces some interesting contrasts. In the lay subsidy of 1296 for Rutland, some 10 bynames from OE personal names were comprehended, mainly fairly common forms such as Alwin, Edelm, Edward, Godwin, (ambiguously) German and Loueric (*sc* Leueric from Leofric), but including also some less frequent items such as (ambiguously) Podding, Sebern, Wolwyne and Wygeyn. Slightly higher, the count of such names in Leicestershire in the subsidy of 1327 comprised similarly common forms such as Ailmer, Alwin, Edmund, Edwin, and Godwin (most common with five taxpayers), but complemented by some less usual forms, such as Blacwyne, Derlyng, Derman, Ordwy, and Wygeyn.[103]

In contrast, the taxation list of the same year for southern Lincolnshire contained a much wider range of these bynames, extending to 39 different items, although fewer than 120 taxpayers bore bynames from OE personal names. Accordingly, the extent of more unusual items was more pronounced, incorporating, for example, Leffy, Utwy, Wygot, Herwy, Osgot and several others.[104] In particular, the corpus in the southern Parts of Lincolnshire — Holland and Kesteven — included names which were more identifiably northern — for example, bynames from Uchtred and Utting.[105] Indeed, the most frequent bynames from OE personal names consisted of Osgot (seven), variants of Outred from Uchtred (10), variants of Elrych (seven) and Utting (seven).[106] In complete contradistinction again, the taxpayers for that year in Derbyshire exhibited only two bynames from OE personal names, from the common forms Godric and Osbern.[107] The corpus in Warwickshire in 1332 was more extensive than Leicestershire, Rutland and Derbyshire, consisting of some 20 bynames from OE personal names. Moreover, these taxpayers in Warwickshire also exhibited forms associated with the north, such as Dolfin, Unewyne, and Outred.[108]

To the north-east, therefore, the pattern of bynames from OE personal names in Lincolnshire reflected quite a strong affinity with northern England. Those features were largely absent from Leicestershire and Rutland, as well as Derbyshire, but reappeared in Warwickshire in isolated examples. In Leicestershire and Rutland, more conventional items were characteristic within a fairly restricted currency of bynames from insular personal names.

The contrast with the more northerly influence in south Lincolnshire was further exhibited in phonemes or allophones in these bynames in Lincolnshire, at least in the forms as they were interpreted in the tax lists. In particular, palatal c assumed the form /k/. Consequently, the forms Elrych(e) and Elryke occurred, as did Ederyche and Edryk, but only Goderyck and Leueryk, through presumed Scandinavian influence. Secondly, Æ (aesc) was reduced in Lincolnshire to E rather than A(i), reflected in the predominant forms of Elryche (Elryk), Eylward, Elstan, Elsi (but one Ailsi), Elger, Elred(d), Elwyn, and Edelward, although there was a single Ailmer.[109] Finally, more forms assumed hypercorrection in these parts of south Lincolnshire, such as Heylward, Hutting and Houtred (Houtered).[110] Comparable forms in Leicestershire and Rutland did not reveal these features.

During the later middle ages, the slight impact of OE personal names on bynames receded even further, as reflected in Table 8.8.

Table 8.8

Taxpayers with bynames from OE personal names[111]

	Total personal bynames	Total OE bynames
Leicestershire		
1327	742	51
1381	418	22
1524	421	7
Rutland		
1296	197	24
1377	112	4
1522	254	0
1524	202	1

Notes: In this table, total personal names represents the total number of taxpayers bearing bynames derived from personal names, whilst total OE bynames encompasses the number of taxpayers with bynames incorporating OE personal names.

Accompanying the decline was a restriction of the corpus to more conventional or frequent forms of OE personal names, such as Godwin.

In the late thirteenth and early fourteenth century, taxpayers with bynames from OE personal names were taxed at a substantially lower level than the mean — at levels of 28.12*d.* (standard deviation

17.10) in Leicestershire in 1327 and 32.57d. (stdv 20.04) in Rutland in 1296 and thus perhaps at about 80% of the level of other taxpayers.[112] Intriguingly raised then are the questions of whether the tax list is an under-enumeration of this form of byname and whether the exempt correspondingly had a greater association with such bynames.

Equally, it might be enquired whether there was a relationship between bynames from OE personal names and the unfree peasantry in the early development of bynames. Unfortunately, the investigation for Leicestershire and Rutland is likely to remain inconclusive, because of the reticence of the record sources. Although there is a small corpus of surveys which differentiate the peasantry according to legal status, the incidence within them of insular personal names is insignificant. Contrary evidence occurred in the survey of the soke of Oakham in 1305, for here the bynames from insular personal names are associated with the free peasantry. In Oakham, Margery Wygeyn held a small free tenure, whilst William Wygeyn held a burgage tenement. At Egleton, Robert Godwyn, however, was a bond tenant.[113]

Certainly of unfree status was the Godwin (Gudewene, Godweyn, Goduine, Godwyn[e], Gudwen, Gudwine) kinship in Kibworth Harcourt in the late thirteenth and the fourteenth century.[114] Hugh Godwin was frequently involved in personal actions in the manorial court and view of frankpledge between 1280 and 1291 and, in the rentals of unknown date, he was listed as a customary tenant or *nativus* of half a virgate.[115] He was succeeded by his son, Richard, in 1295-96.[116] At that date, Richard may have been aged at least 26, for he was in tithing in 1282. Married to Avice, Richard died in 1327, and in 1334 Avice was described as a widow; they seemingly had issue Matilda, who was involved in a hue and cry in 1326, and John. Confirmation of the unfree status of the Godwins is provided by the illicit tonsuring of John, presumably when he took the first tonsure at the age of seven, probably in 1314–15.[117] Sir John Godwin first appeared in the court rolls in 1331 in a case of the hue, perhaps then aged about 24. His appearances in the rolls were more frequent between 1338 and 1346, and he was described as the tenant of a quarter of a virgate and a cottage, but he succumbed in 1349, when the list of heriots included a cow for Sir John Godwyne, as well as another for Adam Godwyne.[118] Adam Godwin had been the tenant of half a virgate. Other Godwins mentioned in the rolls included Nicholas (1343),

Agnes (1348), Mabilia, who held a quarter of a virgate, William a cottage, and Amice (1280, 1298). The William listed as holding a cottage in a rental of indeterminate date was probably eponymous with the William *filius Godyn'* who held a quarter of a virgate in 1294 and may have been a son of Hugh Godwin. In the Poll Tax of 1381, Robert Godwyne, a singleton, contributed 6*d.* in Kibworth Harcourt.[119]

An unusual survival, although only small in incidence, was Dorman (OE Deormann).[120] Although this byname also occurred at Kibworth Harcourt, represented fleetingly in 1343-48 by John and Matilda Derman, both presented in the manorial court only for brewing, and William Derman who held a *placea* in 1344, its earliest occurrence was in the lay subsidy of 1327, in which John Derman and Henry Dermon contributed 1*s.* and 2*s.* respectively. If Henry's byname was truly dialectal, an origin in the West Midlands may be indicated, but imposing such an interpretation on an entry in a lay subsidy is precarious. During the later middle ages, the byname Dorman was represented again at Fleckney in the Poll Tax of 1381, where it persisted in 1603-04, as well as at Evington in the same taxation, at Loughborough in 1428, at Stoughton by a tenant of two virgates in the rental of 1477, and in the lay subsidies of 1524-25 repeated in Fleckney in the taxpayers Edmund, Henry, Thomas and William Dorman, taxed on goods valued at £2 and £5, and at Arnsby by Isabel Dorman.[121] Although no Dormans were assessed for the Hearth Tax in Rutland in 1665, by 1851 six households contained the surname in Uppingham, with a further two in Whissendine and an equal number in Langham.[122]

Nonetheless, the legacy of OE personal names to the corpus of bynames and surnames in Leicestershire and Rutland was extremely light and conventional in range. In 1665, Goodwyns contributed to the Hearth Tax at Egleton (three households), Barrow (a single household) and Uppingham (one), with a German household in Belton and an Edmonds at Ketton. In 1851, Goodwins were enumerated in three households in Uppingham, in two in Ridlington and similarly in Belton, and in single households in Belton, Wardley, Preston, Ayston and Seaton. More ambivalently, Ailmores (etymon Ailmer?) appeared in 1851 in Stretton (one household), Greetham (three), Exton (one) and Uppingham (one). The contribution to surnames in the county thus remained rather insignificant.

Bynames and surnames from personal names in the medieval borough of Leicester

The concentration of personal names evident amongst the medieval taxpayers of the countryside of Leicestershire and Rutland by the late thirteenth and early fourteenth century, evolved to the same degree within the borough of Leicester, perhaps at an earlier time. Examination of the admissions to the gild merchant up to the middle of the thirteenth century, when burgesses' bynames were becoming hereditary, reveals the extent to which personal names had become restricted in their range. Nonetheless, the townspeople encompassed by the freedom were probably a selective proportion of the urban population, so that, once again, only the names of the higher status of inhabitants of a 'community' are involved, so accordingly it is possible that the non-burgess population of the borough exhibited a different corpus of personal names, perhaps including more archaic forms.

Between 1196 and 1257, 1,040 inhabitants of Leicester were admitted to the freedom, for whom statistics of personal names are represented in Table 8.9. By 1196, the personal name stock of newly-admitted burgesses had already developed its future characteristics, both in the degree of concentration and in the corpus of common personal names. Between them, these 1,040 burgesses shared 88 personal names, of which merely 15 derived from insular tradition: Stein; the ambiguous Swein; Osin; Hamund; Alured; Aswi; Alwin; Ailrich; Harding; Gamel; Edward; Osmund; Hereward; Ketelburt (*sic*) and a suspended personal name with a diagnostic digraph, Ealf — thus mainly OE with a substantial minority of Anglo-Scand. These insular names were attributed to 21 new freemen.

Moreover, the significance of these names seems to have evaporated, for two were combined with a French byname in the persons of Alwin Mercer (1199) and Swein *filius Roberti le Macun* (1214). That last burgess represents another aspect of the possible loss of insular tradition in the names, since his father's name was C-G. Whilst none of the patronyms of these burgesses with insular personal names comprised an insular name for the father, three patronyms consisted of new names (*filius Thome, filius Reginaldi* and *filius Roberti*). Finally, some of these insular personal names may have been imported into the borough from rural settlements, for seven of these burgesses had toponymic bynames relating back to their rural origins, such as Gamil de Houtheby and Hereward de Roleya, whilst one other was

more clearly an immigrant or foreign member of the gild, Ketelburt
(*sic*) *aquarius de Ravensthorpe* (1221).[123]

Table 8.9

*Descriptive statistics of the personal names of burgesses (admitted to the
freedom), 1196–1257*[124]

No. of names	mean	trmean	stdv	min	max	median	Q1	Q3
88	12	7	27.16	1	184	2	1	6

Notes: No. of names represents the number of different names; mean the
mean number of burgesses per name; trmean the trimmed mean of same
(removing top 5%); stdv the standard deviation; min the lowest number of
burgesses for a particular name; max the maximum in the same manner;
Q1 the first quartile; and Q3 the third quartile.

The descriptive statistics suggest a small number of extremely frequent
names and a very large number of infrequent names, which is
confirmed by the rank order of names established in Table 8.10. In this
table, the characteristics of rural naming in later generations are
already exhibited.

Table 8.10

Rank order of personal names of burgesses, 1196–1257[125]

Name	No. of burgesses	% of burgesses
William	184	17.7
Robert	118	11.3
John	77	7.4
Richard	73	7.0
Ralph	58	5.6
Roger	51	4.9
Henry	43	4.1
Hugh	43	4.1
Geoffrey	36	3.5
Simon	34	3.3
Total	674	64.8

Fully 65% of burgesses were thus encompassed by 10 personal
names, mainly C–G, but with the intrusion of two Christian names.
At the other end of the scale, 37 personal names accounted each for
only one burgess and a further 15 only two burgesses each; these 52

personal names thus comprehended only 67 (6.4%) of the burgesses in the late twelfth and early thirteenth century.

The familiarity of the 'new' names is reflected by hypocoristic forms not only in the bynames, but more particularly in the forenames, such as Wilke smalbon.[126] Accordingly, Wilke recurred eight times, Robin seven, and Hiche and Bate once each as forenames. Moreover, distinctively French hypocoristic forms of personal names occurred as forenames in the persons of Colin de Faleuille (1196) and Beher *frater Colini*, a short form of Nicholas, Viel *filius Ailwini de derbi*, a French form derived from classical Vitalis, and Astin clei, a Norman syncope of Scand Ansketin.[127] The fortition which occurred so frequently in Galterus in 1196 and the lenition in Baudwine (for example, 1199), both as forenames in the gild merchant rolls, further suggest French influence, clerical if not conclusively environmental and social.[128] Furthermore, the personal name Rocelinus, whose bearer had no byname and was admitted to the freedom in 1198, was also a particularly French form and presumably the etymology for the byname Russel in the borough (for example, 1211).[129] The early occurrences of the byname Teri or Terry, in the gild rolls in 1199 (Ralph), 1211 (Robert) and 1220 (William *filius Walteri terry*) confirm the impression of a French influence, as does the French form of Stephen, with a prosthetic E, on the admission of John *filius Estephani* in 1196.[130]

Nevertheless, despite this familiarity with C-G personal names in particular, bynames derived from personal names in the borough did not evolve out of the most common forenames. In contrast, the most frequent bynames from personal names incorporated the least frequent forenames of burgesses. The following data confirm several aspects of burgesses' names: first, the extreme concentration of forenames at the time when bynames were becoming hereditary; second, the formation of bynames from the less frequent forenames; and thirdly, the relatively low proportion of burgesses with bynames from personal names.

In the internal borough subsidy of 1286, the 10 most frequent male forenames accounted for 76% of the burgess taxpayers, whilst in 1318 that proportion had increased to 85%, around which level it stabilized in the *Nonarum Inquisitiones* of 1340–42 (84%) and the subsidy of 1354 (85%).[131] The Spearman rank correlation coefficient between these four lists (1286, 1318, 1340, 1354) of 10 most frequent taxpayers produces a coefficient of 0.962.[132]

Table 8.11 relates the statistics of the 10 most frequent male forenames in the internal subsidies. Although some bynames were formed from female personal names, there is insufficient data of female forenames to integrate into the discussion.

Table 8.11

Statistics of the most frequent male forenames in internal subsidies, 1271–1354[133]

Name	1271		1286		1318		1340		1354	
	R	N	R	N	R	N	R	N	R	N
John	2	80	2	55	2	73	1	84	1	110
Geoffrey	*	*	7=	15	7	20	*	*	*	*
Henry	4	49	5	19	5=	22	6	16	6	28
Hugh	*	*	*	*	8	17	7	12	9	10
Richard	5	47	4	36	3	51	3	40	3=	39
Robert	3	64	3	37	4	41	4	35	3=	39
Roger	7=	27	7=	15	9=	12	8	11	7	26
Simon	*	*	8=	14	10	11	*	*	*	*
Thomas	7=	27	6	18	5=	22	5	19	5	31
Walter	*	*	8=	14	*	*	*	*	*	*
William	1	110	1	86	1	96	2	77	2	87

Notes: * not within the top ten in this year.

Emerging from this table is the consistency of the most popular forenames, a widely acknowledged pattern from which the borough of Leicester exhibited no difference. As far as individual personal names are concerned, principal changes involved the superseding of William by John in the middle of the fourteenth century, the position of Hugh, perhaps reflecting a wider influence in the diocese of Lincoln, and the relative absence of Walter, a forename which had associations of baseness and which might have been deliberately avoided by burgesses as a dishonourable name.[134]

In Table 8.12, the statistics of these names are presented in a different manner further to emphasize the extreme concentration of the most frequent names, with the caveat that the different tax lists embraced a different proportion of the male burgesses depending on the mode of assessment. That variable might have influenced the numbers of different forenames revealed in each tax list.

Table 8.12
Descriptive statistics of forenames of male taxpayers in internal subsidies,
1271–1354

Date	No. (forenames)	mean	trmean	stdv	median	min	max	Q1	Q3
1271	56	11	*	21.37	2	1	110	1	10.00
1286	42	10	7	16.58	3	1	86	1	13.25
1318	29	15	12	23.00	4	1	96	1	18.50
1340	31	12	7	20.69	3	1	84	1	11.00
1354	32	14	9	25.06	3	1	110	1	12.25

Notes: Mean and trimmed mean (trmean) given to the nearest integer.
Source as Table 8.11. * Not calculated.

Although the taxable male population varied between the lists, the
decline in the number of different forenames of male taxpayers was
probably not primarily affected by that variable, for the number of
taxpayers was higher in 1354 than in some earlier years. Consequently,
it appears that there was a real narrowing in the popularity of
forenames. Conversely, a number of forenames were held by a
single taxpayer in the listings — 19 forenames in 1286, eight in 1318,
and 11 in both 1340 and 1354. The immense concentration in the
burgesses' active corpus of forenames is thus established, parallelling
the same development in the countryside.

Contained within the tax lists of 1286–1354 were 65 different
bynames from personal names, but including five names from
female personal names (such as Sabyn, Amys, Aldyth and Mildrith).
None of these 65 bynames related to the 10 most frequent
forenames in the borough between 1271 and 1354. The fundamentals
of that pattern of forenames had been established between 1196 and
1258, if not at an earlier time, from the evidence of the forenames of
burgesses admitted to the freedom over that time. Five bynames
from personal names persisted through all the tax lists, including
Ace, Nor(e)man, and Martyn, whilst another three continued from
1318 through to 1354 (Mayhu, Herbert and Swain). None of the
most popular forenames contributed to this corpus of bynames
from personal names. The relationship was inverse, in fact, for all
the 65 bynames from personal names originated from forenames
which were apparently rarely employed in the borough.

Comparing the bynames from personal names contained in the

tax list of 1286 with the forenames of burgesses admitted to the freedom before 1260, 13 of 28 bynames in the taxation had not appeared as forenames in the admissions. The byname Ace had been represented by its cognate personal names (Aco, Azo) in four admissions, Baudwine (Baldwin) and Tebbaud (Theobald) each in two, Martyn in six, Aleyn in 11, Osemound, Gamel, and Bate (Bartholomew) each in three admissions, and Nor(e)man, Jordan, Walrand, Ingram, Olyuer, Benet(h) (Benedict), and Steyn each in one.

Extending the analysis back to the late twelfth and early thirteenth century, only 52 of the 1,040 burgesses admitted to the gild merchant before 1260 were attributed a byname from a personal name, comprising 42 different personal names. None reflected the evolving concentration of popular forenames in the early thirteenth century. Diglossic patterns were reflected in this corpus of bynames from personal names, as 12 insular names were held by 14 burgesses as bynames, including the rather unusual Anglo-Scand Erec, alongside the characteristically French forms in bynames such Teri (two) and the lenition of Baudwine.[135]

Before 1350, some 7% of burgesses admitted to the freedom were ascribed bynames from personal names, but from 1260 to 1510 the proportion increased to about 10%, some 200 of a total of 2,031. Between 1260 and 1510, the 200 burgesses held 122 different bynames from personal names (with an unusual resurgence in bynames from insular personal names, of which there were 19 different names held by 34 burgesses, including ones not ostensibly in the borough or visible at an earlier time, such as Dorman, Derlyng, Edrytch, and Lewyn).[136]

Amongst these later medieval burgesses' bynames from personal names, there was little correlation with the rank order of forenames. For example, William was represented only in one occurrence each of Gillam, affected by continental fortition, and Willemote, whilst John did not exist in burgesses' bynames unless in the form Hayne or Heyn (two burgesses). Most frequently occurring were forms (fully hypocoristic and diminutive) from Gilbert, in Gill (one burgess), Gillot (four), Gelet (one) and Gilbert (three). Next in order was Martyn (six burgesses admitted) and the hypocoristic of Bartholomew, Bate(s) (five), followed by Norman, Aldyth, Andrew(e) and Herbert, all with four, equal with a single common forename in a byname, Roberd(e)s.

By comparison, the formation of some bynames from less frequent personal names, some archaic, can be illustrated. The byname Ace represented a presumed kinship in the borough in the late thirteenth and early fourteenth century, commencing in the records with William Ace, who contributed to the subsidies of 1271, 1286 and 1311. Another William was admitted as a burgess in 1314, subsequently assessed to the subsidies of 1318 and 1336 and in the *Nonarum Inquisitiones* of 1340–42. Other Aces were included in the internal subsidies, Alice in 1286, Richard in 1307 and 1311, Matilda in 1318, and Ralph, who entered the gild merchant in 1344, in 1354. Although the byname presumably derived from the personal name of Azo or Aco, it is difficult to pinpoint the precise *antecessor*, for Azo *filius Simonis de Petra* was admitted to the freedom in 1196, contemporaneously with Azo *filius Ricardi de Vuncha*, whilst Azo *filius Osolfi* received the same privilege in 1207 and, in the following year it was conferred on Azo *filius Osberni le ferur*. Furthermore, in 1208 and 1209 John *filius Aze de Sileby* and Roger *filius Aze Vinatoris* entered the gild merchant.[137] Later, Azo *cum barba* was mentioned in gild business in 1258 and contributed to the internal subsidy of 1271. That byname obviously derived from a C-G forename and might, in view of some of the bearers of the forename, have had continental origins; indeed, the mutation to Ace confirms that French influence was at work.[138]

In contrast, in the thirteenth and fourteenth centuries, a few bynames from OE personal names were attached to burgesses of some significance. In 1209, William *filius Leueric'* was described as alderman of the gild merchant.[139] In 1314–17, John, William and Richard Leverich were admitted to the same gild, of whom John was the first to serve as a distinguished burgess, elevated to the position of mayor in 1335–36 and also MP for the borough in the 1330s. William was elected MP in 1339, whilst Richard also served in that capacity, was mayor on two occasions and coroner.[140] Simon Leverich contributed to the subsidy of 1318, as did William, John and Henry to that of 1354. After that date, however, the kinship's fortunes declined in the borough and it became less visible. Their byname derived from OE Leofric (Latinized Leuericus).

In 1159, Amfred *filius Alsy* attested the charter of the Earl of Leicester in favour of the borough. Between 1260 and 1338, two burgesses called John Alsi monopolised burghal offices, including the mayoralty 10 times.[141] Although Amfred was almost certainly a C-G form, Alsi was definitely OE.[142] It appears that Alsi and these other bynames from archaic, insular personal names endured in the borough from the twelfth into the fourteenth century, but that the records, mainly the gild merchant roll and the subsidies, intermittently did not reveal their existence.

A further characteristic of the later middle ages was the transformation of the stock of bynames or surnames from personal names amongst the burgess 'community'. One indicator is that, whereas before 1350, the genitival -s was largely absent, in the later middle ages some 11 burgesses bore bynames of this kind (for example, Wattys and Harrys). Moreover, hypocoristic forms expanded in number as also, to a lesser extent, diminutive suffixes, both French -ot (Bartilot and Gillot) and ME -cok. Overall, the surname stock in the internal subsidy of 1492 was completely different from that in those of the early fourteenth century, up to and including 1354.[143] Common bynames and surnames from personal names in the two lists, at a remove of about a century and a half, did not exceed five names, although the taxation of 1492 comprehended 259 taxpayers.

Conclusively, therefore, the bynames of burgesses formed from personal names derived exclusively from forenames apparently less commonly used in the borough rather than from the most frequent. Nevertheless, bynames from personal names remained less frequent amongst burgesses than amongst the rural population. For the later middle ages, there is a strong presumption that the stock of urban bynames and surnames from personal names was replenished and expanded from the countryside through immigration, which might, to some extent, have imported some at least of the archaic names, although it is clear that a small corpus, such as Leverich and Alsy, persisted from the twelfth century.

Genitival -s

Generally, a distinction has been established between the 'North' in which patronyms and metronyms with the suffix -son were characteristic, and the south of England, where appositional patronyms and metronyms or bynames from personal names were an alternative form. These appositional genera assumed the forms William or Williams, the latter with the Middle English genitival inflection. Located at the conjunction of these two broad areas, Leicestershire contained all forms, patronyms and metronyms with -son and appositional patronyms and metronyms (or bynames from personal names) with and without the genitival inflection (-s).

FIG 17 DISTRIBUTION OF BYNAMES IN -SON AND GENITIVAL -S IN 1327

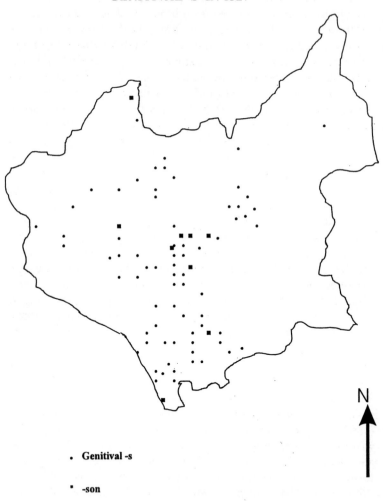

. Genitival -s

▪ -son

Scale 0   10

In the 1327 lay subsidy, about 3% of taxpayers were ascribed a byname with a final -s, although some were ambivalent and cannot be conclusively established as genitival forms. Twenty-four inflected bynames comprised other forms of bynames in the subsidy: Cokes (five incidences), le Clercks (five), Kynges (three), Prests (one), Knytes (two), Mongks (one), le Wardes (one), Carteres (two), le Baillyfes (one), Abbotes (two) and Ryperes (one).[144] Predominantly, however, the inflections occurred on personal names, such as the most frequent of these genitival bynames, Randolfes (eight occurrences), Adecokes (four), Elyotes (three) and Roulotes (three).

Fewer bynames of this composition occurred in the Poll Tax of 1381, although, since the only extant roll relates to Gartree Hundred in the east of the county, that paucity might be expected. Only eight inflected bynames were evident in this area in the late fourteenth century: Daueys; Howes; Jonys; Wattys; Robyns; Reues; Prestus and Parsons, although these last two are ambiguous in that they need not be genitival inflections.[145] When, however, a more comprehensive coverage is available in the lay subsidy of 1524–25, a significantly larger number of genitival forms appears; taking only those inflected on surnames from personal names accounts for 82 taxpayers, about 2% of those assessed.[146]

By contrast, genitival inflections remained much scarcer in Rutland to the east, only six taxpayers (0.3%) recorded with this form of byname in the lay subsidy of 1296 (Hoges — *bis*, Rogers, Willames, Willes and Wylymotes).[147] Significantly, these taxpayers with inflected bynames in 1296 were predominantly women, such as Cecily Rogers, Alice Willames, Alice Hoges and Cecily Willes. The rarity of the suffix -s seems concomitant with its gendered use and implications. Similarly, in the Poll Tax of 1377 merely three taxpayers out of 917 with independent bynames or surnames were attributed such a name (Tommys, Roberts and, less certainly, Balis).[148] By 1522, however, the proportion had increased considerably, attaining the same frequency as Leicestershire, as 1.9% of the adult male population (32 listed males) were identified by surnames from inflected personal names (that is, excluding inflections on other forms of byname).[149] Slightly fewer were encompassed in the lay subsidy of 1524; some 23 taxpayers (1.6% of all those taxed) bore bynames from personal names which were inflected, still appreciably higher than the proportion in the late fourteenth century. Moreover, by the Hearth Tax of 1665, the proportion of the assessed who had surnames from inflected personal names, had expanded further to 4.2%, some 122 assessed persons.[150]

Realistically, however, all these figures should be accepted as minima, since the inflection was customarily applied more frequently to certain forms of byname, most usually bynames from personal names and, to a lesser extent, occupational bynames. The potential for the application of the inflection did not extend without exception to all forms of byname.

Nevertheless, the lexical content of surnames with a final -s was transformed during the later middle ages in both counties. Before the middle of the fourteenth century, final -s was appended conventionally only to bynames from personal names and occupational bynames. By the early sixteenth century, the corpus of surnames with final -s contained a much wider composition of forms (which explains the restriction above to surnames from personal names in the discussion of inflections). Substantially, these new forms evolved out of three developments.

One strand derived from the more widespread replacement of Latin in the written records by Middle English in recording bynames and surnames combined with the transition from syndetic to asyndetic forms. The surnames Parsons and Prestus in the Poll Tax for Gartree Hundred in 1381 may represent this evolution as elisions from atte Parsons and atte Prestus and similarly Vycars in the lay subsidy for this county in 1524–25.[151]

More extensive, however, were topographical surnames with a final -s which might have been inorganic, not an authentic inflection. Assessed in the lay subsidy for Leicestershire in 1524–25 were taxpayers identified as Borowes (one, but potentially toponymic), Bryg(g)es (six), Downes (one), Mills or Mylles (three), Parsons (nine), Priors (two), Vycars (four), Towrsse (two), Watters (one), Welles or Wellys (12), Woodes (four), Wykys (one) and Yates (five). Similarly, in the musters roll for Rutland in 1522 the listed men included eight called Pitt(e)s or Pyttes, whilst others were identified by Barnes (Barnys), Bregges or Briggs, Burnes, Knolles, Waters, Ways, Well(e)s or Wellis, the last recurring eight times in the lay subsidy of 1524 as Well(e)s.[152] Thus, in the Leicestershire lay subsidy of 1524–25, 61 taxpayers were registered by topographical surnames with a final -s, whilst there were 19 in the Rutland musters of 1522, and 26 in the lay subsidy of 1524 for the smaller county. A sprinkling of toponymic surnames had been affected in the same way, such as Dolbys (one taxpayer)and

Pekes (one) in Leicestershire in 1524–25 and Keteryns (one) at the same time in Rutland.[153]

Combining all surnames with a final -s with the exception of those from personal names, 101 taxpayers in Leicestershire in 1524–25 were distinguished in this way — a further 2.6% in addition to those bearing surnames from personal names with the genitival inflection. In Rutland, in 1522 and 1524, the equivalent proportions were 1.5% and 2.2% in addition to the surnames from personal names with inflection. The overall representation of surnames with final -s was thus augmented from two sources: by an increase within the numbers of surnames from personal names which were authentically inflected and by the development of topographical surnames with final -s during the later middle ages. Scattered amongst these forms were inflected occupational surnames such as the 10 Kockes, Cokkes or Cokys in Leicestershire in 1524–25, as also some evidently exogenous inflected occupational surnames such as the five Greves, Grevis or Grevys.

Extending the analysis to the Hearth Tax of 1665 for Rutland, 94 of the 2,919 assessed (3.2%) had surnames with a final -s which did not incorporate a personal name and thus were additional to the 4.2% with inflected surnames from personal names. Of the 94, 72 consisted of topographical surnames, dominated by Wells (13 taxpayers), Pitts (12) and Woods (10).[154] The appendage of final -s to surnames thus embodied an enormous change from the middle of the fourteenth century.

One of the significant transformations of the later middle ages was the diffusion of inflected bynames from personal names into Rutland on a much larger scale. Their absence in the 1296 lay subsidy was not simply produced by the exclusiveness of the tax list, since the paucity was confirmed in the more comprehensive Poll Tax of 1377. Similarly the distribution throughout Leicestershire may have altered during the later middle ages. In 1327, according to Figure 17, despite some scattering in the north and east of the county, bynames with the genitival -s were concentrated in the south and west of the county. Their appearance in the west corresponds with their incidence in adjacent Staffordshire, where 1.5% of the taxpayers in 1327 had this form of inflected byname, significantly 60 males and eight females, reflecting that -s had no gendered implications there by that time.[155]

The virtual absence of bynames and surnames in -s during much of the middle ages in east Leicestershire is confirmed by the court rolls and rentals of Leicestershire manors, those extant relating largely to that part of the county. The continuous series for Barkby, five miles north-east of Leicester, produced seemingly only one byname or surname of this type through the late middle ages from the late thirteenth century into the sixteenth: William Stevyns (fl. there 1477–79).[156] On the other Merton College manor, Kibworth Harcourt in south Leicestershire, from the 1270s, few such bynames are in evidence before 1350.[157] In 1277, the court rolls referred to William and Robert Heyns in 1277 and to Robert Heyn(e)s in 1338, yet the continuous core kinship group was usually designated Heyn(e). Fleetingly, the rolls made reference to Huchenes in 1343, but the bearer was apparently not a long-term resident of the manor.[158]

The rental in 1341 of Leicester Abbey's estate, with consolidated manors at Stoughton in east Leicestershire and Lockington in the north of the county, contained no peasant tenant with a byname with a final -s, from a peasant population of 121 unfree tenants, seven free tenants, and 114 cottagers.[159] On the manors of Owston Abbey, rather more disparate, in east Leicestershire in the later middle ages, only two tenants with this kind of surname appeared in the court rolls, John and Martin Rawlyns (1440–67).[160] Of all the tenants enumerated in the rental of the town of Loughborough *c*.1370, only Agnes Drewes represented this form of surname until the occurrence of Dykouns and Hares in the court rolls of the manor respectively in 1428 and 1474.[161] At nearby Castle Donington, another small town, the fairly complete court rolls from 1454 introduce only one kinship group with a surname of this type, the family called Cokkes or Kockes, successively Thomas (1457–65), Henry (1476–82), John (1482), another Thomas (1510) and his widow, Margaret (1513).[162]

Two points emerge from these data. First, the genitival -s was unusual in east Leicestershire during the middle ages, and second, the progress of the wider distribution of surnames with final -s throughout areas of Leicestershire in the later middle ages was protracted. From the fragmentary evidence of court rolls and rentals, the more extensive dissemination of these surnames may not have been effected until the fifteenth and even early sixteenth century.

Patronyms and metronyms in rural settlements in the middle ages

Sørensen has suggested that patronymic and metronymic bynames which include the compound or suffix -son resulted from Scandinavian influence, the impact of which re-institutionalized the OE suffix *-sunu*, through approximation or accommodation, although the Scandinavian arrangement had a greater honorific and heroic significance. Whereas, therefore, in areas in the North of England subjected to Scandinavian settlement bynames and surnames in -son were assimilated, patronyms and metronyms of this formation were largely absent from the South of England, where there was little Scandinavian promotion.[162] In the South, elided, syncopated, appositional and genitival forms developed, such as William (appositional) and Williams (genitival).[164] Leicestershire and Rutland lie intriguingly at the junction of the two different onomastic regions on this criterion, with a considerable part of the two counties directly and strongly within the influence of the Five Boroughs and Scandinavian settlement.[165]

Encompassed by the term patronyms and metronyms here are both the Latinized forms, such as *filius Willelmi*, and the vernacular ME forms, such as Williamson, although it is fully recognized that the Latin forms might well have developed inconsistently into either genitival and appositional (inflected) forms or forms in *-son*. In contrast, the appositional and genitival forms, for convenience, are here designated bynames from personal names to distinguish them by a short term.

The overall development of all these forms in the two counties is represented in Table 8.13, but some clarification and circumspection is required. Since the data are all extracted from tax returns, it is necessary to elucidate the nature of those taxable populations. In this Table, furthermore, the terms patronyms and metronyms comprise both Latin and vernacular forms, although only vernacular forms (-son) are included in column seven (headed -son). Thus by way of further clarification, the Leicestershire lay subsidy of 1327 contained 403 taxpayers with patronyms and 13 with metronyms; of this total of 416 only 12 consisted of the ME element -son, whilst the majority comprised Latinized forms. Column seven thus refers to the aggregate number of taxpayers with forms in -son in columns three and five combined.

**FIG 18 DISTRIBUTION OF PATRONYMS AND
METRONYMS IN 1327
(LATIN AND VERNACULAR FORMS)**

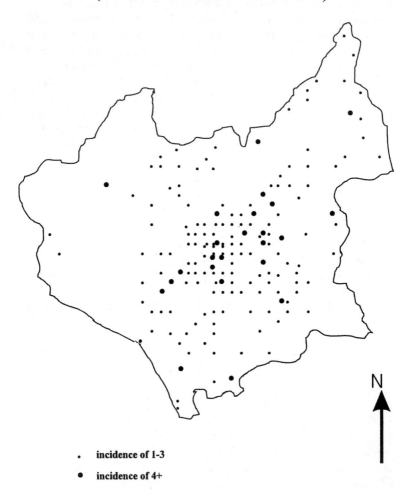

. incidence of 1-3

● incidence of 4+

Scale 0 ⎯⎯⎯⎯⎯⎯ 10

Addditional considerations are concerned with the geographical extent of the Poll Tax of 1381 for Gartree Hundred, which coincides with an area of Scandinavian influence where patronyms and metronyms in the vernacular might be expected. In contrast, the lay subsidy of 1524–25 is not extant for the south-west of Leicestershire, Sparkenhoe Hundred, in an area where a higher incidence of appositional and genitival forms might be anticipated.

Nevertheless, some conclusions can be elicited from the data, the first of which is that vernacular forms in -son were still only very incipient in the late thirteenth and early fourteenth century. Secondly, a large element of the Latinized forms must have transmuted into appositional or genitival forms since the Latinized forms in the earlier tax lists constitute a very much higher proportion of the taxable populations than the later vernacular forms with -son. This suggestion is compounded by two questions: first, the percentage of taxpayers with bynames from personal names did not increase radically amongst the total populations; and secondly the status of vernacular patronyms and metronyms was complicated by their instability.

Table 8.13

Proportions of taxpayers with patronyms and metronyms and bynames from personal names in tax lists of the later middle ages

	Pop (N)	Patronyms N	%	Metronyms N	%	-son N	Personal N	%
Leicestershire								
1327	4128	403	9.8	13	0.3	12	746	18.1
1381	2476	106	4.3	17	0.7	87	466	18.8
1524	2683	164	6.2	3	0.1	167	426	15.7
1525	3924	179	4.6	6	0.2	185	691	17.8
Rutland								
1296	1868	236	12.6	58	3.1	3	194	10.4
1377	917	39	4.3	6	0.7	6	115	12.5
1522	1661	86	5.2	0	0.0	86	237	14.3
1524	1401	89	6.4	0	0.0	89	201	14.4

Notes: It is important to remember that the tax lists constitute different types of population, so that the data can be used only to express or represent trends.[166]

Lay subsidies, however, omitted a large proportion of the population: those whose movable goods (personal estate) not required for subsistence fell below the taxable threshold.[167] If, as has been inferred in some areas, patronyms and metronyms were associated with the unfree and lower social groups, then these exclusions from the tax lists may have some significance, for the enumerations will thereby under-represent patronyms and metronyms.[168] That issue can only be partially addressed from other sources for Leicestershire and Rutland, since some of the manorial surveys and rentals describe legal status of tenants imperfectly or not at all.

The custumal of Rothley probably consisted mainly of customary tenants, in this case privileged villeins of ancient demesne status. The high proportion who bore patronyms and metronyms suggests that this form of byname may have had an association with this status, although the early date of the survey — c.1245 — was a contributory reason.[169] Many customary tenants in the rental of Leicester Abbey in 1341 held this form of byname, but the data are not sufficient for statistical analysis.[170] Paradoxically, the later rental of the Abbey's lands, for 1477, does allow statistical analysis, but by that date the association of type of byname and legal status may have declined.[171]

The custumal of Rothley reveals the widespread use of patronyms in Latinized form, antedating the evolution of the vernacular form in -son. Although it contains 559 tenants, the bynames of only 465 can be confidently analyzed, since many tenants were identified by their relationship as brother (*frater eius*) and coparcener because of the custom of partible inheritance.[172] Of the 465, 33% (N=155) bore patronyms or metronyms.

By 1341, the date of the earliest rental of the estates of Leicester Abbey, vernacular forms with son had been incorporated into written records, if they were not already in colloquial use. The raw data are presented in Table 8.14.

Precise definition of the tenantry of 1341 is hindered by inadequate description in the rental. In 1341, the unfree consisted of both *tenentes in villenagio* and *nativi*. Whilst the Abbey had 338 tenants throughout Leicestershire in 1477, the surnames of only 274 are analyzed here, since many tenants in that rental were also of indeterminate status. Although the rental differentiated between *tenentes ad voluntatem* and *tenentes libere* (or *liberi*), confusion between personal status and status of the land resulted from many customary tenants holding free land. For example, six of the 21 tenants at will in Lockington also held small parcels of free land.

Table 8.14

Forms of byname held by tenants of Leicester Abbey in 1341 and 1477[173]

| | Rental of 1341 | | | | Rental of 1477 | | | |
| | patr/metr | | personal | | patr/metr | | personal | |
Status	No.	%	No.	%	No.	%	No.	%
Unfree	27	22	25	21	11	4	21	8
Free	0	0	2	1	2	1	18	7
Cottagers	10	9	15	13	0	0	0	0

Notes: No. of all tenants in 1341: free 7, unfree 121, cottagers 114; No. of all tenants in 1477: free 109, unfree 139, cottagers 26.

In the rental of 1341, a considerable proportion of the patronyms and metronyms were constructed in the vernacular (ME) form -son; 14 of the 27 tenants with this form of byname had ME -son (eight at Stoughton and four at Thurnby, both vills located in east Leicestershire). By the rental of 1477, however, the proportion of patronyms had diminished considerably, as at Stoughton where only two tenants remained with patronyms, both Saundreson. Although demographic decline may have been one influence for the reduction, other causes were probably at work. A number of Latinized patronyms and metronyms may have become translated into bynames from personal names. On the other hand, a large number of the patronyms and metronyms in 1341 were already in the vernacular form (-son), so it seems reasonable to deduce that it was the inherent instability of forms in -son which engendered the decline, and such a suggestion may be substantiated by the changing nature of the protothemes (first elements) over the late middle ages.

The corpus of the earliest occurring patronyms and metronyms can be constructed from the lay subsidies, survey-type documents, court rolls of specific manors and poll taxes. These earliest compounds, before *c*.1350, contained a wider range of protothemes than in the later middle ages. About 63% of these earlier forms consisted of less usual personal names, that is those which did not belong to the 10 most frequent forenames; this less usual corpus included, for example, Batesone, Daykynsone, Hughesone, Iuesone, Juddeson, Kittesone, Matheusone and Tibbesone. In only a few instances was the element -son not compounded with a forename, unambiguously in le Reuesone and le Smythessone, less unequivocally in Kingessone and Wodardsone *alias* Wodatsone, since the last might have represented an office (woodward) or a very uncommon Continental-Germanic personal name. At Owston, also in the east of the county, some unusual forms persisted into the early fifteenth century, however, such as John Cassotsone, Robert Colleson and Richard Ameson. At Castle Donington, a decayed borough, occurred in the mid fifteenth century William Gybbonson, whose surname incorporates a French hypocoristic and diminutive.[174]

The variety of the earliest forms can be compared with the similarly eclectic characteristics of patronymic and metronymic bynames in the lay subsidy for Lincolnshire in 1332. Although the corpus in Lincolnshire displayed an almost completely different composition, the name elements were derived from unusual personal names, although greyueson, incorporating an office, was reasonably widespread.[175] Although a small number of these bynames was compounded with Scandinavian personal names, particularly Gun- (Gunnilda), but also Ing-, most items consisted of hypocoristic forms of less usual personal names.[176] Excluding these items, the composition consisted of Nalleson, Serson, Whytenelson, Bettesone, Tiddesone, Dussone and Douzesone, Lissone (perhaps relating to Leeson in nineteenth-century Rutland, derived perhaps from a hypocoristic of Lettice or Leticia), Goldesone, Peyneson, Kyppeson, Moldeson, Benetson, Pelleson, Magsoun, Simson, Catson, Gereson, Gregeson and Ammyson.[177]

All these compounds with less usual personal names were transient in their communities. Their ephemeral nature is epitomized by the metronymic byname Pelleson in Barkby. Petronilla de Thorp was mentioned in the court rolls for that manor between 1340 and 1348, twice by her full description, once as Pelle de Thorp and once simply by the hypocoristic form of her forename, Pelle. Her son, Richard, appeared between 1348 and 1353, having inherited her bovate in 1348:

> Radulphus [*sic*] Pellesone de Thorp venit in plena Curia
> et de licencia domini petit se admitteri ad tenenciam
> unius mesuagii et unius bouate terre cum pertinenciis
> post decessum Pelle matris sue et admissus est . . .[178]

This byname did not thereafter recur in the manor.

The implication of the data presented above is that patronyms and metronyms with the element -son did not occur in Leicestershire before the 1340s. This inference can be substantiated with evidence from the court rolls for two manors of Merton College, Oxford, at Barkby and Kibworth Harcourt. Both series commence in the 1270s, but there is a break in the early fourteenth century for Kibworth, although the series recommences fully from 1324. The vernacular forms in -son first appeared in written form in the Barkby court rolls and rentals in the 1340s. The earliest incidences, occurring in 1341, referred to Henry Daukynson and John Harrysone *alias* Henrison, and were followed by Henry Siwoteson (1346), William Amyssone (1347), Henry Auotesson (1349), John Iueson (1349), William Dyson (1354) and Roger Denoteson (1359). A similar chronology is revealed in the rolls for Kibworth: Adam Iuessone (1338); John Watteson(e) (1338-44); Hugh Hughesone (1343); Robert Sibilesone (1343); John Heynesone (1343-46); John Iuesone (1343-48), William Wodardsone *alias* Wodatsone (1344-46); Robert Tibbesone (1345); John Jackesone (1346); John Youngrobynsone (1346-48); Henry Nicholesone (1348); and William Emmesone (1348).

Double patronyms occurred rarely. In the early fifteenth century, Richard Thomson Rogerson married Emma daughter of John Carter, *natiua domini*, but at the next court he was identified simply as Richard Thomlynson. Similarly, William Jacson Heyneson appeared only fleetingly under that guise. Other forms of compounded patronym were equally unusual, although Robert Tibbesonbonde and William Hyuessonpolle transiently appeared in the manorial court rolls for Kibworth.

Some interesting characteristics emerge from prosopographical information about the bearers of these bynames since they were mainly, although not exclusively, drawn from the margins of their local societies. By and large, they did not belong to the core families within their 'communities'. Their bynames were transient within the records of their manors, disappearing from the record quite quickly after their initial appearance. In contrast, those patronymic bynames which became established surnames belonged to core families within the 'community' and were formed later.

The principal example at Barkby was Johnson and its variants. Henry *filius Johannis* continued to be so known in the manorial records from 1349 to 1381, although from 1371 he was also designated Henry Jonson (1371-99). This kinship group later comprised several core tenants, such as Ivo Johnson *alias* Jakson (1420-44), Thomas Jakson (1450-78), John Johnson (1390-1437), and Robert Jonson *alias* Jankynson (1420-40). Also continuous, but less influential, were the Richardsons, whose *antecessor*, John *filius Ricardi*, was described in this form in the court rolls from 1346–59 (18 incidences), although on four occasions as John Richardsone. He was succeeded by William Rychardson (1391–1413). Stable patronyms thus seem to have been formed only later and then in association with core families. Patronyms formed at an earlier time seem to have related to marginal individuals, were transient and unstable, and had a wider and less common range of protothemes.

Additional data from other manors confirm the patterns described above. In Kibworth Beauchamp, adjacent to Harcourt, patronyms and metronyms seem to have occurred first in the local manorial court rolls in 1348–49 (John Iuesson, John Moldesson, Robert Tymmeson and Isabella *filia Rogeri Maggeson*). In Breedon on the Hill, in the north-west of Leicestershire, Isolda Hulleson was involved in a case of trespass in *c*.1339, at about the time when John *filius Roberti Watteson* was a *nativus* and *fugitivus* from the same manor.[179] [Hulle is possibly a hypocoristic of Hugh.]

These processes are, however, complicated. First, it should be remembered that the manorial court rolls, although probably produced locally, may not have been truly reflective of the *parole* of the speech community. The language of naming in the court rolls may have assumed a higher register — of Latinized form — and only later adopted the lower register of the speech community. It is thus possible, and perhaps quite probable, that colloquially patronyms and metronyms were in common usage, and that what has been documented here is simply the introduction of those colloquial forms into the more formal written record.

Moreover, the processes were compounded by the transformation of some Latinized patronyms and metronyms into bynames from personal names. For example, although there are isolated instances of Sibilesone in Kibworth Harcourt, the byname from *filius Sibile* was almost consistently Sibile, pertaining to the core family there. The homonymous (if this is not an infelicitous term) Sibile (Sybil) was a widow there in the later thirteenth century.

The processes can be perceived in north-east Leicestershire, where most Latin forms stabilized into vernacular forms in -son. Thus at Gaddesby *filius Alexandri* became Saundreson and there too occurred Hanson (1366) (possibly homonymous with Heyneson elsewhere in the county), Stywardson (1392–1412) and Wilkynson (1421). Rogerson (1399), Perysson (1399) and Jankynson (mid-fifteenth century) existed at nearby Wartnaby. At adjacent Frisby-on-the-Wreake, from the

1390s through into the fifteenth century, occurred Hopkynson, Thomasson, Rowesone, Heyneson and Wilkokson. By contrast Henry *filius Jordani*, who was involved in many charters relating to lands in Gaddesby in the late thirteenth century, was also known, as in a charter of 1275, as Henry Jordan, which byname persisted in Gaddesby through to the fifteenth century.[180]

More evidence is available in the manorial court rolls of Kibworth Harcourt, where, for example, *filius Alexandri* (1277–98) seems to have transmuted into Saunder, just as *filius Reginaldi* (1289–98) became Reynald. There also an important kinship group, the Scolaces, succeeded Scolasse or Scolastica, who was a widow on the manor in the late thirteenth century. Her sons were identified in the record as Thomas *filius Scolace* [*sic*], John *filius Scolacie* and Hugh *filius Scolasse* or *Scolastisse* (1277–99), but the surname of the family became stabilized as Scolace *alias* Scolas. Similarly at Barkby, the descendants of a Milicent assumed the surname Milisent.[181]

It has been suggested above that patronyms and metronyms were initially more unstable than other forms of byname. There is, in fact, evidence to suggest that some patronyms retained an element of instability in Leicestershire into the late middle ages. A clear example concerned the manumission of several *nativi* of one kinship group at Anstey in 1420. Those manumitted comprised William Edson, the son of John Sareson, and his sons who were identified as John Wylson, Thomas Wilson, Robert Wilson, Richard Wilson and William Wilson, reflecting the changes in patronymic forms over generations.

> Memorandum quod iij° die mensis Maij anno Regni regis Henrici quinti post conquestum anglie octauo venerunt ad curiam domini Abbatis Willelmus Edson de Ansty filius Johannis Sareson nuper de eadem Johannes Wylson senior filius predicti Willelmi Edson Thomas Wilson filius predicti Willelmi Robertus Wilson filius eiusdem Willelmi Johannes Wilson filius Willelmi Ricardus Wilson filius eiusdem Willelmi et Willelmus Wilson filius predicti Willelmi Edson de Ansty qui attachiati fuerunt per corpora sua causa natiuitatis Et postea in curia omnes predicti scilicet Willelmus Edson &c per Ricardum Rotheley Abbatem cum Assensu tocius conuentus manumissi in libertatem pro qua uero manumissione fecerunt finem cum dicto Abbate et conuentu pro C marcis.[182]

Undoubtedly exceptional, since most patronyms and metronyms had become stabilized in this area by this late date, the event reflects the greater potential of patronyms and metronyms for instability. It might be speculated that metronyms were more unstable, but no evidence is available from the two counties to confirm that speculation.

Patronyms and metronyms in a medieval small town

Although abundant material is not available for the small town of Loughborough until the late fourteenth century, it enables some perception of the development of these surnames in the late middle ages. Situated near the county boundary with Nottinghamshire, Loughborough may have been receptive to the introduction of patronymic and metronymic surnames from more northerly areas. In the rental of the town's property of c.1370, John Hulleson held a cottage, whilst Henry Watesone a messuage.[183] Debt litigation in the manorial court in 1398 involved William Steuenson.[184] In 1403, William Daweson was presented as a brewer as well as for default of suit of court, whilst Robert Milleson was licensed as a common brewer and John Dawson held the office of aletaster. John Malenson was in that year involved in a case of battery. In a case of debt, John Hogeson impleaded John Fleshewer. In the following year, William Steuenson and William Daweson were heavily fined for nightwalking; then too Robert Mylleson repeated his fine as a common brewer. Appurtenant to the manor of Loughborough was a messuage and virgate in Prestwold, held by Richard Jonson Dawe. From Costock, Nicholas Denson trespassed in the lord's meadow at Loughborough with two carts.[185]

In the same court in 1411, Henry Steuenson was arraigned for trespass and a year later William Herryson in a case of debt. At that time, John Edmundson was a chief pledge and aletaster for the townships of Knightthorpe and Serlethorpe within the manor.[186] For the appurtenances in Prestwold, Thomas Iueson was chief pledge in 1429–30. The chief pledges in 1430 for Loughborough and Knightthorpe included Nicholas Jonson and James Williamson. In the court of 1431, a case of detinue was brought by William Sauncesone of Hoby concerning a coverlet valued at 2s. Other cases of debt in 1430 involved John Nicolasson, James Williamson, Robert Steuenson and Laurence Tomlynson. Consequently, by the early fifteenth century patronymic and metronymic surnames had become customary in the small town.[187]

During the early sixteenth century, their frequency in the town expanded further, for in the rental of 1526 tenements in the Bigging were held by William and John Sareson. In Woodgate, tenements were in the tenure of Thomas Tomson and a Mayson, whilst Agnes Colson held another in Hallgate. Land at Swannys Nest and Gose Hoke was farmed by John Heryson of Stanford on Soar.[188] A generation or more later, in the rental of 1559, the number of townspeople with patronymic or metronymic surnames had increased again. Not least of these tenants was Isabella Gibson, widow, who leased *per indenturam* three water mills called Sore Mylles and another called Shep Belck Myll, as well as meadow. On a smaller scale, Richard Iueson was tenant of three acres of meadow. Messuages were held by Richard Sison, in the market stead (the George), Nicholas Jackson in the Bigging, and William Iueson in Baxtergate. Cottagers included John Iueson in Baxtergate, John Sareson in the Bigging, Anne Dobson widow, and Anna Johnson in Highgate. A *hospicium* (inn?) was in the tenure of Elizabeth Jenkinson and a tenement at the head of the market place was ascribed to Thomas Johnson. Joan Richardson widow, Henry Dawson, James Sareson and Anna Dobson all held land in the townfields.[189]

Subsequently, the court rolls of the manor disclose other references to patronymic and metronymic surnames. For example, three of the 14 jurors of the homage in 1559 comprised Thomas Johnson, also an aletaster, John Sareson and John Gibson. One of the two chief pledges for the township of Woodthorpe was Robert Palser *alias* Allynson and for Loughborough township John Tompson was one of the five chief pledges. The bakers presented included Nicholas Jackeson, Richard Hucchenson, and in 1559 and 1560 John Gibson and Thomas Johnson. Amongst the brewers presented were the wives of John Sareson, Nicholas Jackeson, Richard Hucchenson, John Gibson, Thomas Johnson and Henry Daweson. John Sareson, moreover, had been elected *tastator victualium et mercati*, whilst the vendors of foodstuff included the butchers James Iveson and William Dixson in 1559 and 1560 (the latter of Melton) and in 1560 James Judson and the vendor of fish in 1559 and 1560, Thomas Jepson. In the latter year, Henry Sargenson was arraigned for an 'affray'.[190]

The court roll of 1564 confirmed the presence of these forms of surname, reflected in the appointment of William Dixson as a chief pledge for Loughborough township and as an aletaster. Presented amongst the bakers were Thomas Johnson, Roger Tompson and Robert Dixson, amongst the brewers the wives of Thomas Johnson,

Henry Dawson, James Sareson, William Dixson, Roger Tompson, John Sareson, and John Gibson, as a butcher John Tompson and as a fishmonger Robert Jepson. Of the officers, Henry Dawson was elected one of the two field wardens (*guardiani camporum*) in 1560 and 1564.[191]

Although not prolific, these surnames had become frequent in the urban environment of Loughborough, recurring in the records of the manor, its constituent townships and appurtenances. The common currency of patronymic and metronymic surnames in the manor was confirmed by the significance of their bearers, who continued to be retailers of food and office holders.

Patronyms and metronyms in the medieval borough of Leicester

The development of these forms of bynames and surnames in the medieval borough of Leicester represents some similarities with and some differences from the rural pattern.[192] Table 8.15 reveals the overall progress in the urban environment, showing that these forms were exotic in 1318 and 1354, encompassing less than 1% of the burgesses who contributed to the tallages. In previous taxations, between the loan of 1252-53 and the subsidy of 1311, no such bynames had occurred. These earlier lists, with the number of taxpayers in parenthesis, comprise the loan of 1252-53 (93), which was obviously very selective, and the tallages of 1271 (685), 1286 (404), 1307 (187) and 1311 (242). By the subsidy of 1492, however, 5.1% of contributing burgesses bore patronyms or metronyms, increasing to 5.5% in that of 1497 and 7.5% in the brokage roll of 1505. The rental of Leicester Abbey in 1477, the *Novum Rentale*, comprised properties from which the Abbey received rents in parts of the borough, mainly St Leonard's parish and the area adjacent to the Abbey. Of the tenants enumerated in the rental, 4.7% bore patronyms.[193]

Table 8.15

The frequency of patronyms and metronyms in the medieval borough of Leicester, 1318–1505

Date	Document	'Population' (N)	Patronyms/metronyms	
			No.	%
1318	tallage	463	1	less than 1
1354	tallage	482	2	less than 1
1477	rental	193	9	4.7
1492	subsidy	276	14	5.1
1497	subsidy	181	10	5.5
1505	brokage	320	24	7.5

Forms in -son were thus unusual in the borough before the fifteenth century and seem to have been introduced into the urban environment much later than in rural areas of the counties. Nevertheless, admissions to the gild merchant from the late twelfth century had included a large number of patronymic descriptions of freemen because of the emphasis on inherited freedoms or patrimony (*habet sedem patris*), one of the principal methods of qualification.

Such forms in Latin failed to materialize in the vernacular (ME), which may suggest that they lacked dignity and were not considered commensurate with burghal status. Admissions to the gild merchant and the freedom allow a quite precise chronology of the introduction of surnames in -son into the borough for this selective social group which comprehended only part of the burghal population.[194] A few exceptional entries occurred in the fourteenth century: Adam Huggesone in 1336; Adam Sareson in 1342; William Pelson of Groby (explicitly exogenous) in 1363; and Thomas Kyngson in 1378. The real influx did not happen until the mid-fifteenth century: in 1466, Thomas Jacson, William Colynson and William Gybson were admitted. In subsequent years, new freemen with this form of surname were recorded as follows: 1467 (one); 1474 (four); 1475 (two); 1476 (one); 1480 (one); 1481 (one); 1482 (one); 1483 (two); 1488 (one); 1490 (two); 1491 (three); 1492 (one); 1496 (three); 1499 (three); 1500 (one); 1501 (one); 1503 (four); 1505 (one); 1508 (10) and 1509 (one).

Surnames in -son thus achieved a foothold in the borough much later than in rural areas in the north-east and east of Leicestershire and, equally, they seem to have been exogenous rather than endogenous forms. In support of this latter notion, Pelson was evidently from Groby, Oliver Chobeson was a denizen of Melton when admitted to the gild merchant in 1505, Walter Dyatson was a clerk and perhaps from outside the borough, and so also was Mr William Gibson.[195]

As in the county, the earliest forms constituted the more exotic and transient, exemplified by the unusual forms Huggesone, Sareson and Pelson, which occurred in the admissions in 1336, 1342 and 1363, and Leveson in the tallage of 1354. Some less usual forms also occurred in the late fifteenth century, such as Tys(s)on (1452 and 1475), Sybson (1477), Goulson or Gouldeson (from 1477), Serleson (1482), Dyatson or Diotson (in the 1490s), Hampson (also in the 1490s), Genyson (1497) and Lawson (1505), but the later corpus predominantly consisted of the very common names Dawson, Jacson, Jonson, Tomson, Wilson, Robynson and Rychardeson.[196]

By the late fifteenth century, these forms and their bearers had become accepted within the borough, reflected in office-holding. John Gouldson or Goulson, for example, was one of the chamberlains in 1477, an auditor of the accounts of the south quarter and swinemarket in 1481 and 1489, and flesh and fish taster in various years between 1478 and 1492.[197] Mr William Gibson, who entered the gild merchant in 1466 and was then described as a *magister*, is another example.[198] In the subsidy of 1492, he resided in the south quarter and contributed 2*s*.8*d*., described there as a notary. He was elected mayor in 1492 and 1501 and was one of the auditors of the accounts for his quarter in nine years between 1491 and 1507. Only slightly less conspicuously, Hugh Tomson (occasionally T(h)omkyn(g)son) acted as chamberlain in 1493 and 1507, auditor for the accounts of the north quarter in 1495, 1497 and 1503, for the east quarter in 1509, as a leather tester in six years between 1487 and 1505, held a tenement in the parish of St Margaret in 1477, and had been admitted to the freedom in 1474.[199] This prosopography suggests that surnames in -son were no longer alien to the urban 'community' by the late fifteenth century. Nevertheless, even in the Hearth Tax for the borough of 1664, merely 5% of contributors, 48 out of 969, were identified by patronymic or metronymic surnames.[200]

Patronyms and metronyms in Rutland in 1665 and 1851

The subsequent development of patronyms and metronyms in Rutland entailed the stabilization of the proportion of the population with this form of surname. Whilst in the Hearth Tax of 1665 6.3% of contributors were identified by this form of surname, the proportion of households with the same form in the census of 1851 was slightly lower at 4.5% in rural parishes and 4.6% in urban places (Oakham and Uppingham).[201]

By the seventeenth century, the etymons — the forename elements in the names — had become quite restricted, but it is necessary first to establish real patronyms and metronyms and differentiate out some toponymic surnames. Branson, for example, was almost certainly a toponymic surname derived from one of the Braunstons or Branston either in these two counties or other Midland counties. Orson, similarly, is suggestive of a toponymic surname, perhaps related to Orston (possibly Nottinghamshire). Illson certainly pertains to Ilston on the Hill (Leicestershire), Beeson probably to Beeston (possibly Nottinghamshire), Elson to Elston (Nottinghamshire) and Syson to Syston (Leicestershire). Although those surnames occurred only sporadically, Musson and Crowson appeared very frequently in both sources. Both represent placenames in Leicestershire, Muston in the north-east and Croxton in the east of the county, but the latter ambivalently since the placename occurred in Lincolnshire also.[202]

In 1665, the corpus of etymons was limited to 22 names and in 1851 25, mostly consisting of the most common forenames such as John, Thomas, Walter, William, Robert, and Richard. The total of different surnames in patronymic and metronymic form comprised 47 in 1665 and 58 (rural and urban) in 1851. With the exception of a single Widdowson, an apprentice plumber at Oakham born in Melton, Leicestershire, all the surnames were compounded with personal names. In 1665, the most significant, in terms of frequency, consisted of Richardson, T(h)om(p)son, Johnson, Jackson, Robinson, Gibson, Harrison, and Simpson, with Hudson not quite as prominent. In rural parishes in 1851, the rank-order was partly consistent with the earlier pattern, but with some new, frequent forms. Thus, whilst Robinson, T(h)om(p)son, Jackson, and Johnson exhibited persistently high numbers, these surnames were joined by Williamson, Wilson, Stimson, Stephenson, Richardson and Dawson. Although in the borough the same corpus of patronymic and metronymic surnames existed, the most frequent consisted of Hudson, significantly in advance of the rest, Stimson, and then Robinson, T(h)om(p)son and Jackson. With few exceptions, however, the range of both the surnames and their etymons was restricted, with the most frequent surnames and etymons consisting of very common forms.

Conclusion to patronyms and metronyms

Although located in an area of some considerable Scandinavian influence, the two counties do not reveal an enormous propensity to patronymic and metronymic naming. Nevertheless, the level of these forms of names was higher than in counties to the south and west, outside the main impact of Scandinavian influence. In their earliest formation, these bynames exhibited an association with base legal status, combined with transience. Moreover, the earliest formations were compounds of less usual forenames, but the later stabilization and persistence of patronymic and metronymic surnames resulted from a more restricted and circumscribed corpus of etymons, most usually drawn from the common stock of forenames. Almost without exception, patronymic and metronymic surnames which endured were compounds of personal names rather than other protothemes, such as occupational items or elements.

References

1 For some thoughts on the process, C Clark, '*Willelmus Rex? vel alius Willelmus*', *Nomina*, 11 (1987), 7–33 and G Fellows-Jensen, 'The names of the Lincolnshire tenants of the Bishop of Lincoln *c.*1225', in F Sandgren, ed., *Otium et Negotium*, (Acta Bibliothecae Universitatis Stockholmiensis, 16, Stockholm, 1973), 85–95.

2 Burton Surveys; for the other properties of Burton Abbey, C Clark, 'Women's names in post-Conquest England: observations and speculations', *Speculum*, 53 (1978), 238.

3 *Templars*, 112–13.

4 See D Postles, 'Notions of the family, lordship and the evolution of naming processes in medieval English rural society: a regional example', *Continuity and Change*, 10 (1995), 179.

5 Rothley, 89–130; the date is assigned by reference to PRO C260/86.

6 Postles, 'Notions of the family', 181.

7 *AASR*, 34 (1917–18), 170 (no. 157) and E Niermeyer, 'An assessment of the fortieth of 1232', *English Historical Review*, 24 (1909), 733–5.

8 For these two names, T Forssner, *Continental-Germanic Personal Names in England in Old and Middle English Times*, (Uppsala, 1916), 38–9, 231–3.

9 PRO E179/165/1; *AASR*, (1888–9).

10 MM 6376. For the significance of this type of listing, L R Poos, 'Population turnover in medieval Essex' in L Bonfield, R Smith and K Wrightson, eds., *The World We Have Gained. Histories of Population and Social Structure*, (Oxford, 1986), 1–22.

11 *Oakham Survey*.

12 For comparative data, P Franklin, 'Normans, saints and politics: forename choice among fourteenth-century Gloucestershire peasants', *Local Population Studies*, 36 (1986), 9–26.

13 PRO E179/165/1; *AASR*, (1888–9).

14 PRO E179/165/1; *AASR*, (1888–9).

15 PRO E179/165/1, E179/133/35; *Tudor Rutland*; PRO E179/104–110, 112–118, 121–122, 124.

16 PRO E179/165/1.

17 PRO E179/133/35.

18 *Tudor Rutland.*

19 *Rutland Hearth Tax.*

20 PRO E179/133/104–110, 112–118, 121–122, 124.

21 For the Scandinavian names, see below, 236–49

22 For the concept of a lower North, H Jewell, *The North-South Divide. The Origins of Northern Consciousness in England*, (Manchester, 1994).

23 PRO E179/165/1; *AASR*, (1888–9).

24 *AASR*, (1888–9).

25 For Cade, O von Feilitzen, 'Some Old English uncompounded personal names and bynames', *Studia Neophilologica*, 40 (1968), 5.

26 PRO E179/135/14–15; for Conan *faber* E179/135/14, m. 13. Brian was almost certainly Middle Brettonic rather than OIr or Godoillic.

27 For example, PRO E179/135/14, mm. 11 (Dawis), 17 (Daw); E179/135/15, mm. 5 (Daues), 16, 27 (Dauy). For the possibility that Dawe(s) derived from Ralph (Rawe[s]), P McClure, 'The names of merchants in medieval Dublin', *Nomina*, 19 (1996), 63.

28 In any case, Alan and its variants do not seem to have featured as Welsh surnames. Welsh forms of surnames from David assumed the full form or the hypocoristic Dewi; the indigenous form Daffyd might have evolved to Davy by loss of the final -dd, visible by the early fourteenth century: T J Morgan and Prys Morgan, *Welsh Surnames*, (Cardiff, 1985), 43, 81–5, esp. 81.

29 *Domesday Book*, I, fo. 236.

30 Bodl. MS Wood empt. 7, fos. 4v–91r, 120; for the personal name, Forssner, *Continental-Germanic Personal Names*, 197, citing sources from Leicestershire and Lincolnshire, but it might more reasonably have been an Anglicization of Audgeirr (Scand) rather than a Continental form of West Germanic name.

31 See above, 3–4. In this section, I largely rely on J Insley, *Scandinavian Personal Names in Norfolk. A Survey Based on Medieval Records and Place-Names*, (Acta Academiae Regiae Gustavi Adolphi LXII, Uppsala, 1994), as the most recent exposition of Scandinavian personal names, supplemented by other works listed below.

[32] Most recently, G Fellows-Jensen, 'Place-names in -þorp in retrospect and in turmoil', *Nomina*, 15 (1991-2), 35-51.

[33] J Insley, 'Some aspects of regional variation in early Middle English personal nomenclature ', *Leeds Studies in English*, n.s. 18 (1987), 183-99; 'Regional variation in Scandinavian personal nomenclature in England', *Nomina*, 3 (1979), 52-60; 'Some Scandinavian personal names from South-West England', *Namn och Bygd*, 70 (1982), 77-93; *Scandinavian Personal Names in Norfolk*, xxxvi-xxxvii.

[34] Insley, *Scandinavian Personal Names in Norfolk*, xxxvi-xxxvii.

[35] Insley, *Scandinavian Personal Names in Norfolk*, xxxviii, 23, 48-60, 414-19, 437; J Adigard des Gautries, *Les Noms des Personnes Scandinaves en Normandie de 911 à 1066*, (Nomina Germanica, 11, Lund, 1954), 164-25, 287-94, 322-6, 429.

[36] Insley, *Scandinavian Personal Names in Norfolk*, 39, 41, 59.

[37] Insley, *Scandinavian Personal Names in Norfolk*, xxxvi, 59, 425-30, although Astin may be the replacement of -ill by -in perceived to be alternative diminutive forms.

[38] By reference to Adigard des Gautries, *Noms des Personnes Scandinaves en Normandie*.

[39] Insley, *Scandinavian Personal Names in Norfolk*, xxxvii-xxxviii.

[40] C Clark, 'Onomastics' in N Blake, ed., *The Cambridge History of the English Language*, vol. II, *1066-1476*, (Cambridge, 1992), 548-50.

[41] *Domesday Book*, fos. 230d, 231a, 232a, 232c-d, 233a, 233d, 234a-b, 235a-c, 236a-d, 237a-b (with a concentration of tenants of the Countess Judith). For Ulf as Anglo-Scand rather than OE monothematic Wulf, Insley, *Scandinavian Personal Names in Norfolk*, 437-40, esp. 440. For Arkil as a syncopated form of Arnketil, *ibid.*, 19-23; only in Herefordshire Db is -ketel unsyncopated (22) and in Normandy the full form (-ketel) is usual (23). For Ketelbern, *ibid.*, 254-6. Swein is perhaps more ambiguous: *ibid.*, 356-60; for occurrences in Normandy and Brittany, *ibid.*, 358, Adigard, *Noms des Personnes Scandinaves en Normandie*, 145, 318; and for the possibility of OE swan or its influence, Insley, *Scandinavian Personal Names in Norfolk*, 360, which, however, can be discounted here, as the influence would be OE Swan, and Svein seems more likely as a personal name in *Domesday Book*. Osmund is particularly difficult, with Norman Scand, OE or Anglo-Scand etymologies, with the further possibility of Anglo-Scand assimilation of OSc Ásmundr to OE Ōsmund; Insley concludes that in the Danelaw the origin is more likely to have been Anglo-Scandinavian: *ibid.*, 66-73, esp. 70.

Thorkell was usually syncopated in the Danelaw, but the Norman form unsyncopated: Insley, 414–19; Adigard, 164–25, 322–6, 429. For Feggi, Insley, 121; G Fellows-Jensen, *Scandinavian Personal Names in Lincolnshire and Yorkshire*, (Copenhagen, 1968), 81. Thurstan would appear to be an Anglo-Scand form, as opposed to Norman Turstin: Insley, 425–30; Adigard, 168–9, 326–40, 431; Fellows-Jensen, 313–17. Auti was less complicated: Insley, 86–7 and Fellows-Jensen, 44.

42 *Domesday Book*, fos. 231a, 232c, 234b.

43 Burton Surveys, 244–6; The Queen's College, Oxford, MS 366, fos. 16r–17r, 19r; *Berkeley*, 17, 43, 61, 64 (nos. 32, 109, 175, 184). For the sources consulted, D Postles, 'The changing pattern of male forenames in medieval Leicestershire and Rutland to *c*.1350', *Local Population Studies*, 51 (1993), 54–61.

44 Rothley, 89–130; the date is attributed here by comparison with PRO C260/86. For Oky, Insley, *Scandinavian Personal Names in Norfolk*, 2–4; for the ambiguity of Cole, *ibid.*, 275–7.

45 Bodl. MS Laud Misc 625, fos. 17v, 29v, 31r. Orm, as elaborated further below, is an interesting incidence, since the name has been associated with the North, in particular Lancashire and Yorkshire: Insley, *Scandinavian Personal Names in Norfolk*, xxxvi; but see also the Orm in the Burton Abbey surveys and charters of the early twelfth century in Staffordshire: D Postles, 'Monastic burials of non-patronal lay benefactors', *Journal of Ecclesiastical History*, 47 (1996), 628.

46 PRO E179/165/1, 21; *AASR*, (1888–9); *Tudor Rutland*; PRO E179/133/104–110, 112–118, 121–122, 124; *Rutland Hearth Tax*.

47 PRO E179/133/35.

48 *AASR*, (1888–9).

49 *AASR*, (1888–9); *Tudor Rutland*.

50 PRO E179/165/1 and 21, *Tudor Rutland; Rutland Hearth Tax.*

51 *AASR*, (1888–9); PRO E179/133/35; PRO E179/133/104–110, 112–118, 121–122, 124.

52 *AASR*, (1888–9).

53 PRO E179/165/21.

54 PRO E179/133/35.

55 *Tudor Rutland.*

56 Insley, *Scandinavian Personal Names in Norfolk*, 275–7; for Cole possibly as a French hypocristic form of Nicholas, Clark, 'Onomastics', 565.

57 Insley, *Scandinavian Personal Names in Norfolk*, 130–1.

58 *AASR*, (1888–9),,132, 258, 269.

59 PRO E179/133/109, m.4, 116, m.8d.

60 PRO E179/133/115, m.1, 116, mm.6d, 7, 117, m.5d, 121, mm.10, 13.

61 As n.58–9 and PRO E179/133/35.

62 Rothley, 106.

63 The Queen's College, Oxford, MS 366, fo. 19r.

64 PRO C244/144 (jurors called William and Thomas Gamill, both of Saxilby); HAM Box 20, flder 7, Box 21, flder 1; MM 6439; MM 6590; Bodl. MS Laud Misc 625, fo. 131r.

65 PRO E179/133/116, m.7, 117, m.5d; *Tudor Rutland*, 47.

66 *AASR*, (1888–9), 237; PRO SC2/183/76–77; PRO E179/133/35.

67 Insley, *Scandinavian Personal Names in Norfolk*, 59.

68 Bodl. MS Wood empt 7, fos. 109r–v (Reginald *filius Astini*, Astin *filius Christiane*, and Roger *filius Astini*; see also, *ibid.*, fo. 124r ('iuxta selionem Astini Palmere' (n.d.).

69 Insley, *Scandinavian Personal Names in Norfolk,* 116; O von Feilitzen, *The Pre-Conquest Personal Names of Domesday Book*, (Nomina Germanica, 3, Uppsala, 1937), 246; *AASR*, (1888–9), 249; Bodl. MS Charters Leics A1, no. 25. It occurred as Herrick in the borough over a long period of time.

70 W G D Fletcher, 'Some unpublished documents relating to Leicestershire preserved in the Public Record Office. Second Series', *AASR*, 23 (1895–6), 396 (no. 60).

71 *Hastings MSS*, 42; *AASR*, (1888–9), 258, 275; HAM Box 58b; PRO E179/133/108, m.2.

72 For the -ein form, Insley, *Scandinavian Personal Names in Norfolk*, 189–91.

73 For example, PRO SC2/183/76 (Alice Haldane *alias* Haldeyn, 1346–7).

74 PRO E179/133/35; PRO E179/133/109, mm. 5, 6, 9, 13; PRO E179/133/121, mm. 6, 8, 14d; MM 6375. In the taxation of 1603–4, Simon and Richard Iliffe contributed at Gumley in the same area: H Hartopp, 'Leicestershire lay subsidy roll, 1603–4', *AASR*, 24 (1897–8), 625.

75 PRO E179/165/1, m.1, 21, m.9.

76 PRO DL30/80/1090–1101; HAM Box 8; HAM Box 24, flders 4 and 6–7; PRO E179/133/121, m.15.

77 Bodl. MS Laud Misc 625, fo. 205r; PRO E179/133/104, m.6d; *AASR*, (1888–9), 133.

78 *Great Roll of the Pipe for the 30th Year of Henry II*, (Pipe Roll Society, n.s. 33, 1912), 46.

79 *Hastings MSS*, 56.

80 Bodl. MS Laud Misc 625, fos. 29v, 196r.

81 HAM Box 24, flder 2; PRO DL30/80/1097-1098.

82 M J Franklin, ed., *The Cartulary of Daventry Priory*, (Northamptonshire Record Society, 35, 1988), 297—8; Bodl. MS Rawl 350, 42; for Osmund at N Marefield *c.*1245, Rothley, 112; *AASR*, (1888-9), 244, 288-9, 291, 294, 311.

83 MM 6391-6406.

84 PRO E179/133/104, mm. 2, 3; 109, m.8; 115, m.2.

85 *AASR*, (1888-9), 284; Bodl. MS Laud Misc 625, fo. 192r.

86 For example, Reginald and Robert Swein, the former a tenant *ad voluntatem et in villenagio* the latter a cottager, at Lockington: Bodl. MS Laud Misc 625, fos. 207v, 208r.

87 *Great Roll of the Pipe for the 7th Year of Richard I*, (Pipe Roll Society, n.s. 6, 1929), 192 (there also Suein *filius Lefwin'*); *Great Roll of the Pipe for the 1st Year of King John*, (Pipe Roll Society, 48, 1933), 20.

88 PRO E179/133/35; MM 6367-6406; PRO SC2/183/76-77, *AASR*, (1888-9), 237.

89 P R Reaney, *The Origin of English Surnames*, (London, 1967), 329; *AASR*, (1888-9), 255.

90 Bodl. MS Wood empt 7, fo. 108r.

91 Insley, *Scandinavian Personal Names in Norfolk*, 401-2; MM 6367-6400.

92 PRO E179/165/1, m.11; PRO E179/165/21, m. 2; *Tudor Rutland*, 44-25, 89.

93 PRO E179/165/21, m.10; *Tudor Rutland*, 89.

94 *AASR*, (1888-9), 283, 299; PRO E179/133/109, m.10.

95 C Clark, 'English personal names *ca.*600-1300: some prosopographical reflections', *Medieval Prosopography*, 8 (1987), 45.

96 D M Stenton, ed., *Pleas before the King or His Justices 1198-1212*, vol. III, (Selden Society, 83, 1966), 224, 260.

97 PRO E179/165/21, m. 3.

98 MM 6563-6567; Bodl. MS Laud Misc 625, fo. 112r.

99 *Rutland Hearth Tax*, 15, 16, 17, 18, 20, 22, 23, 24, 29, 33, 36, 38, 39, 40, 41, 43.

100 *Rutland Hearth Tax*.

101 PRO HO107/2092-2093.

102 PRO HO107/2092–2093.
103 For the concentration of insular personal names in the eleventh century, particularly Godwin and Godric, C Clark, '*Willelmus Rex? vel alius Willelmus*', *Nomina*, XI (1987), 10–11.
104 PRO E179/135/14, mm. 15 (Leffy) (perhaps referent to East Anglia), E179/135/15, mm. 5 (Utwy), 18 (Herwy), 21 (Wygot). Osgot is ambiguous, but was presumably either OE or an Anglicization (Os-) of Scand As-: Insley, *Scandinavian Personal Names in Norfolk*, 38; von Feilitzen, *Pre-Conquest Personal Names in Domesday Book*, 164–5.
105 G W S Barrow, 'Northern English society in the twelfth and thirteenth centuries', *Northern History*, IV (1969), 5.
106 PRO E179/135/14, mm. 1, 5–7, 11, 15; E179/135/15, mm. 3, 17, 21, 31.
107 J C Cox, 'Derbyshire in 1327: being a lay subsidy roll', *Journal of the Derbyshire Archaeological and Natural History Society*, 30 (1908), 23–96.
108 *The Lay Subsidy Roll for Warwickshire of 1332*, (Dugdale Society, 6, 1926).
109 PRO E179/135/14–15. Compare, G Kristenssen, *A Survey of Middle English Dialects 1290–1350. The Six Northern Counties and Lincolnshire*, (Lund Studies in English, 35, Lund, 1967), 38–57.
110 PRO E179/135/14, mm. 5 (Heylward), 11 (Houtred), 15 (Houtared); E179/135/15, m. 17 (Hutting).
111 *AASR*, (1888–9); PRO E179/133/35; PRO E179/133/104–110, 112–118, 121–122, 124; PRO E179/165/1, 21; *Tudor Rutland*.
112 *AASR*, (1888–9); PRO E179/165/1.
113 *Oakham Survey*, 14, 15, 19, 25.
114 What follows is based on MM 6367–6404.
115 MM 6367 lists the tenure.
116 MM 6205: 'Et de Ricardo filio Hugonis Godvine pro terra patris sui. . .' an entry fine of 13s. 4d.
117 MM 6219: 'Et de Johanne filio Ricardi Godewene coronato contra voluntatem domini' a fine of 6s. 8d.
118 MM 6243: the list of heriots received.
119 PRO E179/133/35.
120 Von Feilitzen, *Pre-Conquest Personal Names of Domesday Book*, 223: only one incidence of this personal name in *Domesday Book*, in Warwickshire.
121 *AASR*, (1888–9), 244; MM 6404; Bodl. MS Laud Misc 625, fo.

130v; HAM Box 21, flders 2-3; PRO E179/133/35, E179/133/109, m.5, E179/133/121, m.14d; H Hartopp, 'Leicestershire lay subsidy, 1603-4', *AASR*, 24 (1897-98), 619.

122 PRO HO107/2092 322, 328, 355; 107/2093 66, 76, 80, 91.

123 *RBL*, I, 23, 25, 46, 64.

124 *RBL*, I, 12-75.

125 As n.124.

126 *RBL*, I, 14.

127 For Astin, Insley, *Scandinavian Personal Names in Norfolk*, 74; *RBL*, I, 14, 17, 19.

128 *RBL*, I, 12.

129 Forssner, *Continental-Germanic Personal Names*, 221, *s.n.* Rozelin; *RBL*, I, 16.

130 Forssner, *Continental-Germanic Personal Names*, 228, 231-2, for Terri (*s.n.* Theodric); *RBL*, I, 13, 17, 23, 24.

131 *RBL*, I, 128-45, 208-11, 250-7, 272-4; II, 93-9; Leicestershire Record Office BR III/4/70-73.

132 For the statistics of naming in the internal subsidy of 1271, see D Postles, 'The changing pattern of male forenames in medieval Leicestershire and Rutland to *c.*1350', *Local Population Studies*, 51 (1993), 57-8.

133 *RBL*, I, 128-45, 208-11, 250-7, 272-4 and 309-13.

134 C Clark, 'Socio-economic status and individual identity: essential factors in the analysis of Middle English personal-naming' in C Clark, *Words, Names and History. Selected Papers* ed. P Jackson, (Woodbridge, 1995), 109.

135 Insley, *Scandinavian Personal Names in Norfolk*, 116, remarks on Erec's infrequency in England.

136 *RBL*, I-II, *passim*.

137 *RBL*, I, 12, 19, 20, 21, 256, 273; II, 37, 58, 94, 98, 130, 202; Leicestershire Record Office BR III/4/70-73.

138 For Azo, Forssner, *Continental-Germanic Personal Names*, 39-40.

139 *RBL*, I, 21.

140 C J Billson, *Mediaeval Leicester*, (Leicester, 1920), 154. A Richard Leuerych of Market Harborough was assessed at £6 for a sack of wool in the caption of wool of 1348: PRO C255/2/9.

141 Billson, *Mediaeval Leicester*, 21.

142 For Ansfred and variants, the most cogent treatment is Insley, *Scandinavian Personal Names in Norfolk*, 34-5.

143 *RBL*, II, 331-4.

[144] *AASR*, (1888–9).

[145] PRO E179/133/35.

[146] PRO E179/133/104–110, 112–118, 121–122, 124.

[147] PRO E179/165/1.

[148] RO E179/165/21.

[149] *Tudor Rutland*

[150] *Tudor Rutland*; *Rutland Hearth Tax*.

[151] PRO E179/133/35, 104–110, 112–118, 121–122, 124.

[152] PRO E179/133/104–110, 112–118, 121–122, 124; *Tudor Rutland*, 21, 23, 25, 27–9, 31, 35–7, 42, 47, 55, 57, 60, 63, 67, 69, 73, 78, 81, 83, 84–6, 89, 92–3, 97–9, 102, 105–6, 110–16, 119.

[153] In the lay subsidy for Leicestershire in 1603–04, which comprehended a very much smaller taxable population, surnames with -s were as frequent as surnames with -son, despite the geographical area covering the east of the county where a higher proportion of patronyms and metronyms might have been expected: H Hartopp, 'Leicestershire lay subsidy roll, 1603–4', *AASR*, 24 (1897–8), 603–27.

[154] *Rutland Hearth Tax*.

[155] G. Wrottesley, 'The lay subsidy roll of AD 1327', *Collections for a History of Staffordshire*, (William Salt Archaeological Society), VII (1886), 197–254.

[156] MM 6622.

[157] MM 6367–6406.

[158] MM 6376, 6404.

[159] Bodl. MS Laud Misc 625, fos. 191v–211r.

[160] PRO SC2/183/89–90.

[161] HAM Box 20, flder 4; Box 21, flder 2.

[162] HAM Box 8; PRO DL 30/80/1090–1101.

[163] J K Sørensen, *Patronyms in Denmark and England*, (Dorothea Coke Memorial Lecture, 1982, (London, 1983).

[164] This section is largely reconstituted from D Postles, 'At Sørensen's request: the formation and development of patronyms and metronyms in late medieval Leicestershire and Rutland', *Nomina*, 17 (1994), 55–70. For the broad onomastic division, see also C Clark, review of R McKinley, *The Surnames of Oxfordshire*, *Nomina*, 3 (1979), 113–14, and *eadem*, 'Onomastics' in N Blake, ed., *The Cambridge History of the English Language*, II, *1066–1476*, (Cambridge, 1992), 567–9.

165 K Cameron, 'Scandinavian settlement in the territory of the Five Boroughs' in *idem*, ed., *Place-Name Evidence for the Anglo-Saxon and Scandinavian Settlements*, (Nottingham, 1977), 115–71.

166 For analysis of the Poll Tax data, C Fenwick, 'The English Poll Taxes of 1377, 1379 and 1381', unpublished PhD thesis, University of London, 1983, 445–60 (for Leicestershire). The sources of data are: *AASR*, (1888–9); PRO E179/133/35, 104–110, 112–118, 121–122, 124; E179/165/1, 21; *Tudor Rutland*.

167 J F Willard, *Parliamentary Taxes on Personal Property 1290–1334. A Study in Mediaeval Financial Administration*, (Cambridge, Mass., 1934), 81–5; J R Maddicott, 'The English peasantry and the demands of the Crown, 1294–1341', in T H Aston, ed., *Landlords, Peasants and Politics in Medieval England*, (Cambridge, 1987), 294.

168 R A McKinley, *The Surnames of Oxfordshire*, (English Surnames Series, III, London, 1977), 199–200.

169 Rothley; the probable date is contained in PRO C260/86.

170 Bodl. MS Laud Misc 625, fos. 186r–211r.

171 Bodl. MS Laud Misc 625, fos. 1–180. Interestingly, however, the relationship between free status and toponymic surnames persisted.

172 See R Faith, 'Peasant families and inheritance customs in medieval England', *Agricultural History Review*, 14 (1966), 77–95.

173 Bodl. MS Laud Misc 625.

174 MM 6376–6406 and 6556–6573 (Kibworth Harcourt and Barkby court rolls and surveys); see also C Howell, *Land, Family and Inheritance in Transition: Kibworth Harcourt 1280–1700*, (Cambridge, 1981); PRO SC2/183/87–88, DL30/80/1090 and HAM Box 8 (Owston and Castle Donington court rolls). For Wodard, Forssner, *Continental-Germanic Personal Names*, 237.

175 For Greyueson and variants, PRO E179/135/14, mm. 1, 17, E179/135/15, mm. 15, 25.

176 For Gunneson, Swaynson and Ingson, PRO E179/135/14, mm. 10, E179/135/15, mm. 9, 12, 16, 17, 26.

177 PRO E179/135/14, mm. 3, 5, 6, 12, 14, 17, 18, E179/135/15, mm. 6, 9, 15, 18, 28.

178 MM 6571.

179 PRO SC2/183/51–52, 76.

180 Bodl. MS Wood empt 7, fos. 107v–126v, 129v–131r, 137r, 146r–v, 170r–182v.

[181] MM 6376–6406.

[182] Bodl. MS Laud Misc 625, fo. 14r.

[183] HAM Box 20, flder 4.

[184] HAM Box 20, flders 2–3.

[185] HAM Box 20, flders 5–7.

[186] HAM Box 21, flder 1.

[187] HAM Box 21, flder 3.

[188] HAM Box 24, flder 2.

[189] HAM Box 24, flders 6–7.

[190] HAM Box 24, flders 6–7.

[191] HAM Box 24, flders 6–7.

[192] Data file Leibor.dbf (dBase IV) mainly extracted from *RBL* I, II.

[193] Bodl. MS Laud Misc 625, fos. 91r–97v.

[194] M Kowaleski, 'The commercial dominance of a medieval provincial oligarchy: Exeter in the late fourteenth century', in R Holt and A G Rosser, ed., *The Medieval Town. A Reader in English Urban History 1200–1540*, (London, 1990), 186.

[195] *RBL*, II, 331–2, 334, 338, 444, 466.

[196] *RBL*, II, 49, 96, 133, 351–2, 371, 428, 436–7, 464–5.

[197] *RBL*, II, 449, 454–8, 463.

[198] *RBL*, II, 442–4, 449, 452, 454–7, 463.

[199] *RBL*, II, 456, 458–9.

[200] H A Hartop, ed., *The Leicester Hearth Tax 1664*, (Leicester, 1912).

[201] *Rutland Hearth Tax*; PRO HO107/2092–2093.

[202] See above, 44–5.

CHAPTER 9

BYNAMES AND SURNAMES FROM NICKNAMES

Although insignificant quantitatively, bynames and surnames derived from nicknames also possess considerable and multivalent interest from the linguistic and social perspective.[1] Not least in importance is their reflection on colloquial aspects of naming, perhaps the closest to the use of the speech community. Inherent in that aspect are both irony, which renders the precise etymological content of these names ambiguous, and also language and the use of language.[2] The last question is considered below both generally and in so far as nickname bynames are possibly one of the most poignant indicators of the use of language. Conversely, however, a large proportion of the nickname bynames failed to persist in any number and were effectively transient, perhaps precisely because of their nature as terms used by the speech community or colloquially.

The contribution of nickname bynames and surnames to the naming pattern of Leicestershire and Rutland was not inconsiderable and remained largely stable during the later middle ages. In Rutland in 1296, over 17% of taxpayers bore this form of byname, consistent with the level in the Poll Tax of 1377, at just over 18%.[3] Despite an apparent decline in the musters of 1522, to 16.5%, larger numbers of taxpayers were identified by nickname surnames in the lay subsidy of 1524-25, at 18-21%.[4]

A comparable pattern can be detected in Leicestershire, where, in the lay subsidy of 1327, 17% of taxpayers were thus designated, apparently reducing to just over 14% in the Poll Tax of 1381, but increasing to 20-22% in the lay subsidy of 1524-25.[5] By the Hearth Tax of Rutland of 1665, still over 18% of contributors or exempt were identified by nickname surnames, maintaining a consistent level.[6]

By the seventeenth century, the corpus of nickname surnames had narrowed considerably, dominated by some names common in other areas of England. Amongst the most frequent names were Brown(e) (36 heads of household) and Sharpe (34), each twice as common as the next most frequent nickname surname with 14 occurrences.[7] The pattern was replicated amongst heads of household in the 1851 population census for rural parishes in Rutland, in which 75 heads held the name Brown(e), the highest incidence of a nickname surname, followed by Sharpe which comprehended 50 heads. The association between rural parishes and the two market towns, Oakham and Rutland, remained close as the pattern of nickname surnames corresponded in the towns with the rural parishes. In Oakham and Uppingham, Brown represented the most common nickname surname (43 heads), followed again by Sharp(e) (26). Moreover, there was a close association in the pattern of all nickname surnames, the same ones replicated in similar proportions in town and country.[8]

Compounds

Compounded forms of nickname bynames existed from the twelfth century in Leicestershire and Rutland, in ME as well as French form, comprising both 'Shakespeare' (so-called 'imperative') compounds and 'Bahuvrihi', of which the former consisted of a verb and noun and the latter of an adjective and noun.[9] Not all the issues surrounding these forms can be addressed, although the question of the use of language is discussed below. The persistence of forms in different codes into the sixteenth century is considered further here, but also mentioned below.[10] Less easily defined is the relationship of status and language, whether French nickname bynames were more closely associated with the free, whilst the unfree were more usually attributed nickname bynames in ME.[11]

In litigation in the common law courts in 1219, in which the issue was property in Leicester, William Wagstaffe impleaded Alexander Costeyn.[12] Previously, the Pipe Roll of 1177, under offences of the forest, included Simon Lieuelance.[13] Both ME and French codes were thus in evidence from an early date and, moreover, both nickname bynames had the imputation of sexual innuendo.[14]

This employment of compounds and both codes was continued in the Rothley custumal of *c*.1245, in which about eight of the peasant tenants, of all levels, were attributed compounded nickname bynames.[15] Thus, Robert Waytegood held merely a toft jointly with another tenant in Rothley.[16] No clear association was intended between code and status, however, for another tofter in Rothley, Ivo Belamy, was described in the French code.[17] In contrast, Richard Godtid was the tenant of a virgate in the same vill, but more substantial still was

Henry Wiseman, tenant of 3½ bovates.[18] Another tofter, however, was Gilbert Wytheved.[19]

Two potential, but perhaps speculative, indications ensue from these peasant tenants in *c*.1245. The possibility of incipient heritability of compounded nickname bynames is presented by Walter Wategood, tenant of a toft in Rothley, but perhaps more strongly by Henry Belamy, formerly the tenant of a messuage.[20] Secondly, ME seems, on this slender evidence, to have become more dominant than French amongst the peasantry, assumed here to be villein sokemen or privileged villeins of ancient demesne.[21]

The use of compounded nickname bynames in the early thirteenth century is confirmed by Hugh Brekeweni, who held a half-virgate at Asfordby, in 1225x1258, and the metonymic Robert Witbred, who also held a virgate of the Bishop of Lincoln in the same survey.[22] Further affirmation derives from Anselm Porteioye of Cottesmore, who, because he attested a charter, was presumably free, but that association between attestation of charter (in *c*.1257), language and free status, is subverted by Hugh Skerehare of Luffenham, who witnessed another charter of similar date (1257x1263).[23]

Although held only by a small proportion of taxpayers, a fairly wide variety of compounded surnames persisted into the early sixteenth century, amongst whom the most eclectic might seem to have been Throston Thonderforth, assessed at 40*s*. for goods at Stoughton in the lay subsidy of 1524–25.[24] In that same subsidy, taxpayers were identified by the surnames Shorthose,[25] Hor(e)top(e),[26] Lechgood,[27] Dubulday,[28] Feyrwythe,[29] Passant (presumably a syncope of Passavant),[30] Schershake,[31] Makdans,[32] Cronkhorn,[33] Wyghtbrest,[34] Guddland,[35] Tracelove and Truelove,[36] Whithed,[37] Sha(u)kespere,[38] Spenluff,[39] Honyluffe,[40] and Peybodye.[41]

The rentals and court rolls of Loughborough supplement this list of compounded surnames which existed in the early sixteenth century. Henry Skattergood was a baker there in 1560 and 1564, his wife a brewer, as was Mary Barfoote in 1560, whilst William Swetefote was presented for overstocking in 1560.[42] In the rental of 1526, John Waitgod was recorded as the previous tenant of a tenement in the Bigging, where Thomas Paternoster held a tenement also; in the Hallgate, the rental enumerated a tenement held by Silvester Barefoote.[43] The rental of 1559 contained William Shackspeare, tenant of a piece of meadow, and Mary Barefoote, widow.[44]

From all records examined for the sixteenth century, mainly the first three decades and principally lay subsidies, some 76 different compounded surnames occurred in the two counties. The code of these surnames was predominantly ME, with the survival of merely half a dozen French forms and two with mixed codes, such as Makdans, a surname which occurred earlier in the person of John Makedaunce who held a messuage and 40a. at Gaddesby in 1445.[45]

By comparison, all the records consulted before *c*.1550 yield about 192 different compounded bynames and surnames. Comprehended in this wider corpus during the later middle ages was a number of French compounds and code-mixtures: Beaufitz (Croxton, 1327),[46] Belamy (Rothley, 1245, and Kibworth Beauchamp, 1346),[47] Blankamy (Loughborough, 1398 and 1430),[48] Bonemour (Somerby, 1524–25),[49] Bonyfaunt (Leicester suburb, 1327),[50] Cacchepol (Cotes, 1398),[51] Duredent (South Luffenham, 1296),[52] Foliame (Caldecott, 1522),[53] Foliaunte (Castle Donington, 1477),[54] Grauntsack (Freeby, 1327),[55] Horrteste (code-mixing, Scraptoft, 1469),[56] Magdaunce and variants (code-mixture),[57] Maleherbe (Shepshed, 1411),[58] Maudust/Mauduit (Wing and Market Overton in 1296),[59] Maufras (Buckminster, 1327),[60] Mosendieu (Bisbrooke, 1296),[61] Pardeu (Saddington, 1381),[62] Parlebeyn (Castle Donington and Kegworth, 1516–19),[63] Passelew (Stapleford, 1327),[64] Passauaunt (Breedon on the Hill 1342),[65] Paswater (code-mixture, Blaby, 1477),[66] Plauntefolye (Weston, 1296),[67] Porteioye (Greetham, 1296),[68] Prodhomme (Empingham, 1296),[69] and Makehayt (code-mixture, Blaston, 1327, and Essendine, 1296).[70] Few of these French compounded surnames consequently survived into early modern Leicestershire and Rutland, the principal exception being Belamy, which reappeared at Whitwell and Whissendine in 1522–24.[71]

Moreover, a significant proportion of these French bynames and surnames, but less so the code-mixtures, was conventional in the sense of fairly widespread. For example, Parlebeyn was, for a French nickname byname, quite well distributed, not least in Lincolnshire.[72] By contrast, some late medieval ME compounds seem to have been more vigorous in their composition and their construction. Joan Drawsper *alias* Drauspere, a widow, was presented as a baker and brewer in the manor of Hallaton in 1378–82 and she contributed 1*s*. in the Poll Tax of 1381 there, her name consisting of a 'Shakespeare' form, but also fairly unusual.[73] This surname was also located in adjacent Huntingdonshire, localized in Forcet and Woodstone.[74] At Hallaton too appeared Alan Goldynheude, John Syngalday, holding a small amount of land, Alice Gyldenhed, a cottager, and William Cruschecob, who held a messuage for the term of his life.[75] Nevertheless, the only ME compounded surname of this type with sexual connotations was William Longstaf of Husbands Bosworth, in the Poll Tax of 1381, unless Drawsper had similar imputations.[76]

From the sixteenth century, however, the variety of these compounded forms declined, as also their distribution. In the Hearth Tax of 1665 in Rutland, fewer than 40 taxpayers were identified by this sort of surname. The corpus, moreover, was very restricted, comprising merely Whitehead, Fairchild, Goodlad, Harfoote, Hallowday/Holliday, Bellamy (the sole French survivor other than Tillewast which had been associated with the lower nobility), Longfoote, Goodale, Merryman and Lightfoote.[77] Most of these surnames were held by only one to three taxpayers, although Whitehead was associated with six in six different parishes and Fairchild with seven in six parishes.[78] Further concentration had occurred by 1851, at which point the compounded surnames consisted mainly of Whitehead, Bellamy, and Fairchild. Bellamy was contained in households in Oakham and Whissendine (four households), Fairchild in five households in Barrowden, and in one household in each of Oakham, Ketton, Hambleton and Wing, and Whitehead in one or two households in each of Lyddington, Seaton, Morcott, Barleythorpe, Whissendine, Empingham, Hambleton and Uppingham.[79]

Baines

One particular surname which appears to have expanded in distribution from the early modern period was Baines. Given the potential ambiguities of its etymology, no clear connections can be established for its longer-term development.[80] In 1277, Robert Bayns was transiently recorded in the manorial court of Kibworth Harcourt, whilst Geoffrey Bane had attested a charter relating to Seagrave earlier in the thirteenth century (before 1241).[81] The surname does not, however, recur in the late middle ages in any documents used here. In records of the early sixteenth century, nevertheless, it reappeared, in the guises of Thomas Banes of Braunston in 1522 (Rutland), Hugh Banys of Wing in 1524, Thomas Banys of Manton also in 1524, and Thomas Baynes at some illegible place in Gartree Hundred in the lay subsidy for Leicestershire of 1525, and thus concentrated in the eastern part of the two counties.⁸² By 1665, in the Hearth Tax for Rutland, the surname Ba(i)ne(s) comprehended 16 households.⁸³ Its expansion continued for in the 1851 census 36 rural households and 17 urban contained a head or other occupant with this surname, now consistently Baines.⁸⁴

Berridge

Amongst these nickname bynames and surnames, Berridge evolved as one of the more frequent (if ambivalent) nickname items in Leicestershire and Rutland. Its classification as a nickname byname is ambiguous, since its etymon might have been a compounded exocentric nickname byname such as makebeuerage, thus signifying an occupational interest, or it might have evolved as a metonym.⁸⁵

During the later middle ages, the surname became established in Barkby amongst the core tenantry of Merton College in the vill. Apparently occurring first in the court rolls in 1449, represented by Richard Berege both on the homage and as an affeeror, it persisted there through the early modern period.⁸⁶ Since Richard had been elected affeeror, it seems most probable that the surname had been introduced into the vill at an earlier time. Thereafter, Bereges were continuously represented on the homage throughout the fifteenth and sixteenth century, for example by John Barage and Richard Barage in 1455 and John Beregh junior and senior in 1474–75.⁸⁷ In 1464, John Berrage took from the lord a cottage and garden *nuper in tenura Ricardi Berrage* for an entry fine of 4s.⁸⁸ In 1542, when John Beregg was included on the homage, Anthony Beregg became tenant of a messuage and half a virgate for a term of six years for an entry fine of 5s.⁸⁹ Two years later, on the death of an elder John Beregg, his son, John, was admitted to a messuage and bovate of copyhold for term of years.⁹⁰

Although most visible at Barkby, the byname and surname was more widely distributed in the two counties. In 1296, a Beueriche contributed tax at Seaton.⁹¹ In that taxation, William Beuerech was listed at Oakham and he recurred as a tenant of a shop in the market there in the survey of 1305.⁹² Within the soke of Oakham, in the survey of 1305, were enumerated Beatrix Beuerech, a cottager, at Langham and Matilda Beuerage, a free tenant who held a shop in the market at Oakham.⁹³ The Poll Tax of 1381 recorded Bereches, Bereges or Beryches at East Langton, Kibworth Beauchamp, Fleckney, and

Ilston.[94] Beruges were listed in the musters roll for Rutland in 1522 at Ridlington (John and Agnes) and Seaton, and, as Beryge and variants, in the lay subsidy of 1524 for the county at Ridlington, Seaton and Whissendine.[95] The surname had been established in nearby Melton Mowbray at the end of the fourteenth century, for, in 1398, John Beuerage of Melton, ironmonger, acquired with John Muskham of Melton, a shop in that market town, which Beuerage on his own conveyed to Henry Wright in 1400.[96] It would seem to be fairly certain that this John is to be identified with the John Berege who attested local charters at about the same time; in 1398 and 1399, he witnessed a transaction relating to a messuage in Melton, possibly as a neighbour, since the property seems to have been in the vicinity of that which he had acquired in 1398.[97] In the late fifteenth century, John Beregge of Thurnby was one of the jurors in an inquisition in a case of clerical rape.[98] Wanlip, a few miles from Barkby, was the locus for the taxation of William Berryge in 1524-25.[99] In 1603-04, John Beridge was assessed for the lay subsidy in Tugby.[100]

Nonetheless, the byname was extensively represented throughout the East Midlands. In the Huntingdonshire lay subsidy of 1327, for example, just south of Rutland, Beueriches were assessed in Old Weston (Adam, William and Thomas), Spaldwick (Richard and Roger), Abbotsley (Roger, Robert and Hugh) and Alconbury and Weston (Alexander).[101] Just to the north, in Lincolnshire, a Berege and Beuereges contributed to the lay subsidy of 1332 at Aswardby (one taxpayer) and Binnington and Foston (three contributors).[102] Despite these ostensible concentrations, however, the nickname was to be found amongst the taxpayers in lay subsidies of this time in many other areas of the country, including adjacent Warwickshire (at Tysoe and Kineton), Wiltshire (although only a single taxpayer), and in the eastern counties of Essex (two taxpayers called Beverache) and Suffolk (three Beueriches).[103]

Significantly, however, the surname persisted in Rutland from its occurrence in Seaton in 1296 through into the nineteenth century. Although Berridges were sparsely listed in the Hearth Tax of 1665, assessed only at Barrow (one household) and Exton (two), by the middle of the nineteenth century the distribution was much wider.[104] In that census, households containing Berridges were enumerated at Oakham, where there were two such households, but a further family in the workhouse. In the rural parishes, Berridges existed in single households at Greetham, Cottesmore, Barrow, Exton,

Barleythorpe, Bisbrooke, Seaton, and North and South Luffenham, in two households at Whissendine, Preston and Lyddington, and in four in Glaston, whilst at Empingham seven households were recorded with this surname. The surname had thus expanded from three households in 1665 to encompass 38 in rural Rutland in 1851 with additionally six Berridges in Oakham and Uppingham combined.[105]

Two principal points may consequently be elicited about this nickname byname. Geographically, it was concentrated in the late middle ages in Rutland and east Leicestershire, and the distribution and incidences at that time suggest that in this region Berridge was closely associated with Beverage.[106]

Conclusion

Although nickname bynames offer, for the medieval period, a window on colloquial aspects of naming, by comparison with the formality of the written record, this type of byname and surname became as concentrated as other forms, dominated by the seventeenth century by common items. In particular, compounded nickname bynames, which through their vibrancy and vigour reflected more closely the speech community, declined during the later middle ages and by the seventeenth century contributed but little to the corpus of naming in the two counties. That pattern of domination by a small number of common items was characteristic too of the nineteenth-century composition of nickname surnames in Rutland, both in rural settlements and small urban centres.

References

[1] P McClure, 'The interpretation of Middle English nicknames', *Nomina*, 5 (1981), 95–104.

[2] McClure, 'The interpretation of Middle English nicknames'; G Fellows-Jensen, 'On the study of Middle English by-names', *Namn och Bygd*, 68 (1980), 102–15.

[3] PRO E179/165/1, 21.

[4] *Tudor Rutland*.

[5] *AASR*, (1888-9); PRO E179/133/35, 104–110, 112–118, 121–122, 124.

[6] *Rutland Hearth Tax*.

[7] *Ibid*.

[8] PRO HO107/2092–2093.

⁹ For a brief explanation of these periphrasal forms of nickname byname, C Clark, 'Onomastics' in N Blake, ed., *The Cambridge History of the English Language*, vol. II, *1066-1476*, (Cambridge, 1992), 576-7. For criticism of the term 'imperative', D Burnley, 'Lexis and semantics' in *ibid.*, 443. B Seltén, *Early East Anglian Nicknames: 'Shakespeare' Names*, (Lund, 1969); J Jönsjö, *Studies on Middle English Nicknames I Compounds*, (Lund, 1979); B Seltén, *Early East Anglian Nicknames: 'Bahuvrihi' Names*, (Lund, 1975); I Hjertstedt, *Middle English Nicknames in the Lay Subsidy Rolls for Warwickshire*, (Acta Universitatis Upsaliensis, 63, Uppsala, 1987).

¹⁰ See below.

¹¹ Fellows-Jensen, 'On the study of Middle English by-names', 107-9.

¹² A H Thompson, 'Leicestershire documents temp. King John', *AASR*, 34 (1917-18), 333.

¹³ *The Great Roll of the Pipe for the 23rd Year of Henry II*, (Pipe Roll Society, 37, 1915), 33.

¹⁴ See generally, McClure, 'The interpretation of Middle English nicknames'.

¹⁵ Rothley, 99, 100-1, 120.

¹⁶ Rothley, 99.

¹⁷ *Ibid.*, 99.

¹⁸ *Ibid.*, 100.

¹⁹ *Ibid.*, 120.

²⁰ *Ibid.*, 100-1. Two tenants contributing foreign rents are excluded, Ralph Makebred and Henry Corleuach, since they appear to have been burgesses of Leicester: *ibid.*, 121.

²¹ For this status, R S Hoyt, *The Royal Demesne in English Constitutional History 1066-1272*, (Ithaca, New York, 1950), 192-207; M K McIntosh, 'The privileged villeins of the English ancient demesne', *Viator*, 7 (1976), 295-328. See C Clark, 'Some thoughts on the French connection of Middle English nicknames', *Nomina*, 2 (1978), 38-44.

²² The Queen's College, Oxford, MS 366, fos. 18v, 19r.

²³ E Mason, ed., *The Beauchamp Cartulary Charters 1100-1268*, (Pipe Roll Society, n.s. 43, 1980), 146-7 (nos. 255-6).

²⁴ PRO E179/133/109, m.14.

²⁵ PRO E179/133/104, m.2, 110, m.3.

²⁶ PRO E179/133/104, m.3, 108, m.3, 116, m.4, 117, m. 8d (Robert at Ashby Folville, Richard at Burton Lazars, and John at Quorndon).

²⁷ PRO E179/133/104, m.5d.

[28] PRO E179/133/108, m.1, 108, m.7, 7d (John at Barston, Robert and Thomas at Harby).

[29] PRO E179/133/108, m.1, 7d.

[30] PRO E179/133/108, m.3.

[31] PRO E179/133/108, m.5.

[32] PRO E179/133/108, m.5d.

[33] PRO E179/133/108, m.8, 112, m.1.

[34] PRO E179/133/108, m.8, 112, m.1.

[35] PRO E179/133/109, m.3 (possibly occupational).

[36] PRO E179/133/109, mm. 5, 7, 13, 122, mm. 1d and 6,   124, m. 6.

[37] PRO E179/133/109, m.10 (Robert, William and John at Lubbenham), 117, m. 5d (Thomas Whytehedde at Dalby on the Wolds).

[38] PRO E179/133/116, m.2, 117, mm. 6, 6d.

[39] PRO E179/133/116, m.4d.

[40] PRO E179/133/122, mm. 8, 9 (Thomas at Claybrooke and John at Knighton).

[41] PRO E179/133/122, m.9d.

[42] HAM Box 8.

[43] HAM Box 24, flder 2.

[44] HAM Box 24, flder 6.

[45] Magdaunce at Ridlington in 1522, Makdans at Wymondham in 1524-25, and Makedaunce at Whissendine in 1524: *Tudor Rutland*, 19, 64, 107; Bodl. MS Wood empt 7, fo. 139v.

[46] *AASR*, (1888-9), 157.

[47] PRO SC2/183/76; Rothley, 99-100.

[48] HAM Box 20, flders 2-3, Box 21, flder 3.

[49] PRO E179/133/112, m.9.

[50] *AASR*, (1888-9), 234.

[51] HAM Box 20, flders 2-3.

[52] PRO E179/165/1, m.9.

[53] *Tudor Rutland*, 55 (James Foliame, a labourer).

[54] HAM Box 8.

[55] *AASR*, (1888-9), 227.

[56] Bodl. MS Laud Misc 625, fos. 73r-v.

[57] See above, n.45.

[58] HAM Box 21, flder 1.

[59] PRO E179/165/1, mm. 5, 7.

[60] *AASR*, (1888-9), 218.

61 PRO E179/165/1, m. 10.

62 PRO E179/133/35.

63 PRO DL30/80/1094.

64 *AASR*, (1888–9), 215.

65 PRO SC2/183/51.

66 Bodl. MS Laud Misc 625, fo. 29v.

67 PRO E179/165/1, m. 5.

68 PRO E179/165/1, m. 8.

69 PRO E179/165/1, m. 1.

70 *AASR*, (1888–9), 249; PRO E179/165/1, m. 2.

71 *Tudor Rutland*, 19, 25, 114 (Bellamy).

72 For example, PRO E179/135/15, m. 8 (Parleben at Pointon and Millthorpe).

73 PRO E179/133/35; PRO SC2/183/89.

74 J A Raftis and P M Hogan, eds., *Early Huntingdonshire Lay Subsidy Rolls*, (Pontifical Institute of Mediaeval Studies, Subsidia Mediaevalia, 8, Toronto, 1976), 185–6, 251, 155–6.

75 PRO SC2/183/89.

76 PRO E179/133/35.

77 *Rutland Hearth Tax*.

78 *Ibid.*, 14–17, 22, 27, 29, 35, 38, 41, 44.

79 PRO HO107/2092–2093.

80 P H Reaney, *A Dictionary of British Surnames*, (2nd edn., repr. London, 1987), 20–1, suggests that the name might represent a northern variant of bones, dependant on the vocalic exchange of northern ME /ā/ and southern /ō/, perhaps with the implication of upright or stiff gait.

81 MM 6376; *Berkeley*, 89 (no. 265). The attestation, however, does not prove residence in Leicestershire.

82 *Tudor Rutland*, 82, 102, 105.

83 *Rutland Hearth Tax*, 34–6, 38, 42–4.

84 PRO HO107/2092–2093.

85 See, for example, C Drinkwater, 'The merchant gild of Shrewsbury. Seven rolls of the thirteenth century', *Transactions of the Shropshire Archaeological and Natural History Society*, 2nd ser., 12 (1900), 250 (1252), for makebeuerage.

86 MM 6604.

87 MM 6615, 6625.

88 MM 6616.

89 MM 6614.

[90] MM 6629: 'Johannes Beregg' qui de domino tenuit per copiam secundum consuetudinem manerii pro termino annorum nondum determinando unum mesuagium et unam bouatam terre ... diem clausit extremum et non debet domino herietto secundum consuetudinem ibidem. Et quod Johannes Beregg' filius predicti Johannis venit in Curia et petit Admiss' ... pro residuo Annorum in predicta copia specificatorum secundum consuetudinem manerii ibidem.'

[91] PRO E179/165/1, m. 10.

[92] *Oakham Survey*, 22; PRO E179/165/1, m. 3.

[93] *Oakham Survey*, 20-1, 31.

[94] PRO E179/133/35.

[95] *Tudor Rutland*, 28-9.

[96] Bodleian Library MS Wood empt 7, fos. 24r-v, 46r.

[97] *Ibid.*, fo. 43r (two charters).

[98] PRO C244/152: the accused was Robert Thyknall of Wymondham, chaplain.

[99] PRO E179/133/104, m.6d.

[100] H. Hartopp, 'Leicestershire lay subsidy roll, 1603-4', *AASR*, 24, (1897-8), 613.

[101] Raftis and Hogan, *Early Huntingdonshire Lay Subsidy Rolls*, 160-2, 204-25, 215.

[102] PRO E179/135/15, mm. 20, 30.

[103] Hjertstedt, *Middle English Surnames in the Lay Subsidy Rolls for Warwickshire*, 65; D A Crowley, ed., *The Wiltshire Tax List of 1332*, (Wiltshire Record Society,45, 1989), 64; J Ward, ed., *The Medieval Essex Community. The Lay Subsidy of 1327*, (Essex Record Office, Essex Historical Documents, 1, 1983), 35, 109; E Powell, ed., *Suffolk in 1327 being a Lay Subsidy Return*, (Suffolk Green Books, 9, vol. 11, Woodbridge, 1906), 70, 115, 207.

[104] *Rutland Hearth Tax*, 28-9.

[105] PRO HO107/2092-2093.

[106] P H Reaney, *Dictionary of British Surnames*, (2nd edn., repr. London, 1987), 30, implied that this connection applied only in Scotland.

CHAPTER 10

WOMEN'S BYNAMES AND SURNAMES

Recently, particular interest has been directed to the naming of women, in particular the 'forename' (*nomen*), but also to bynames and surnames.[1] To some extent, this discussion, as with so many aspects of women's position, has revolved around the general effects of a patriarchal society and the extent of women's agency.[2] In the case of bynames and surnames, it has been remarked that wives did not, for much of the medieval period, necessarily receive the bynames and surnames of their husbands.[3] It may be that the change to women acquiring the bynames and surnames of their husbands reflected more generally on the social position of women and the changes of gendered relations.[4]

The descriptions of women in medieval records may partly be attributed to the general instability of naming before the development of surnames, although women were still described in a variety of conventions after males were more formally recorded by surnames in the later middle ages. Moreover, it should be emphasized that the record sources provide only formal descriptions of women or, at least, forms very often in Latin, rather than divulge how women were colloquially known, certainly outside the north of England.

Despite the seemingly overall flexibility of women's descriptions, some principles, conventions or norms do seem to have operated. First, women, throughout their life-cycle, were described in relation to a male and, in some circumstances, to land associated with males. In this sense, there is little difference in the stages of the life-cycle: adolescence (as a dependant or daughter); marriage; and widowhood. Whereas, in many other spheres of female life, widowhood introduced some notion of public responsibility, widows at certain historical times continued to be described in relation to a male. Nevertheless, the precise nature of the relationship during marriage or widowhood depended on circumstances and the nature of the record. Particularly in charters was this so; if the land at issue was inherited or *maritagium*, then a wife or widow was given a style in relation to her father or any other male who provided the real property or

305

from whom it had been inherited. If, however, the land in the transaction was dower, the widow received a style related to her late husband. Charters too best reflect the consequences of hypergamy, where the lineage of a wife was superior to that of her husband, with its consequent effect upon naming processes.

In other records, however, such as manorial surveys and court rolls, a progression of descriptions is reflected, which may have significance for the position of women. One problem here, however, is that, because women featured so much more infrequently than men in these records, as a result of their public incapacity, their identification was easier and could be more cryptic. By comparison with men, it was possible to identify women for manorial purposes by a very simple description. The following discussion of manorial records concerns women of peasant status. It is probable that those women enumerated in the lay subsidies were also of peasant status, if from the wealthier echelon. The female contributors to the Poll Taxes more certainly belonged to the general ranks of the peasantry.

In the Templars Inquest of 1185, only two women occurred, Matilda and Wulwiet, the former of whom held a bovate at Empingham. She was ascribed no *cognomen* in the survey; no male tenants, however, were attributed a byname either.[5] Female tenants in the survey (1225x1258) of the lands of the Bishop of Lincoln had a uniform description: eight of the 10 were described by their forename and the affix *vidua* (Matilda *vidua* at Thurmaston) whilst only one (Matilda Geue) had an independent byname.[6] Greater complexity was exhibited in the custumal of the soke of Rothley *c*.1245, although of the 34 female tenants 11 were simply recorded by a forename and the affix *vidua*. The survey referred to the other widows as: Alice *relicta Balke*, Alice *que fuit uxor Seamon (sic), uxor Willelmi clerici* (without a forename), Alice *vidua Willelmi filii capellani*, and *uxor Walteri filii capellani* (without a forename). By contrast, nine, seemingly independent, women tenants were accorded bynames (for example, Matilda la Carter). Although five were enumerated only by their *nomen* with no byname or affix, three were easily identified because they were joint tenants of two thirds of a virgate and thus required no more complex identification. The remaining four were daughters and so described in relation to their fathers.[7]

To some extent, these manorial records were localized, although the survey of the Templars' properties extended throughout the country and that of the Bishop of Lincoln's lands throughout his diocese. Although the assessment to lay subsidies was conducted locally, the final records of lay subsidies were centrally enrolled. Their recording of women is thus likely to reflect wider cultures of naming than particularly local. Furthermore, the taxation was wealth-specific, excluding those below the level of assessment, so that the women included in the subsidies are likely to have belonged to the peasant elite.

The lay subsidy for Rutland in 1296 included nine women described by a forename and the affix *relicta*, 37 by a forename and the descriptive phrase *uxor* of AB, and 16 by a forename and the unqualified affix *vidua* (for example, *Johanna vidua*). The remainder of the 195 assessed women were either known by their status as daughters or by their own byname.[8] The lay subsidy of 1327 for Leicestershire reveals a similar pattern, for, of 251 female taxpayers, seven were known as Y *vidua* (but one other in the French vernacular (*la vedue*)), 24 as Y *uxor* of AB, and 13 as Y *relicta* of AB.[9] Excluding the daughters, it is alluring to consider the women taxpayers with their own bynames as independent, unmarried women, but such a supposition, although probable, may not be entirely correct.

The Poll Taxes were regressive, levied *per capita*, so that they are comprehensive. The analysis below is concentrated on women who occurred as singletons in the Poll Tax listings or as servants with their own bynames or surnames and not ostensibly related (by name) to the head of the household. Only the Poll Tax for Gartree Hundred in 1381 contains data of this quality.[10] Of all these women taxpayers, 56 were known simply by forename and byname or surname, 37 by forename, byname (or surname) and the affix *vidua* (as, at Hallaton, Joan Drawsper *vidua*), three by a forename and the term *vidua* without a byname (for example, Denise *vidua* at Tur Langton), and three by a forename and the phrase *uxor* of AB. Eighty-seven of the female servants, moreover, were also attributed a byname as well as the description *seruiens*.

The culture of women's naming had thus been modified quite considerably over the fourteenth century, although that transformation was not complete. By the late fourteenth century, most women were identified by a more complex description, a real byname or surname, rather than a lexical term or phrase such as *vidua* of *relicta/vidua* of AB. That progression, however, was only one aspect of the development of women's names, which was still more involved.

Hypergamy and its effect on naming processes might have occurred at all levels of society, although it is more evident at the higher levels. In Leicestershire, the most visible was the Basset-Ridel marriage in 1123. Ralph Basset was elevated by his service to Henry I, as one of the *novi homines* or *curiales*, in the words of Orderic Vitalis 'raised from the dust'. Orderic disparaged the size of the Basset fees in Normandy. Maud Ridel was the daughter of Geoffrey Ridel, another of the *curiales* of Henry I, who died in the White Ship in 1120. Maud's mother, Geva, however, was the daughter of Hugh, late earl of Chester, and the marriage of 1123 was probably arranged by Maud's first cousin, Ranulph, earl of Chester.

After the marriage, Maud continued to be known by her *cognomen* Ridel; thus, whilst her husband, Richard Basset (I) accounted in the Leicestershire Survey of *c*.1130 for the Basset fees, Maud Ridel responded for the original Ridel honour. The eldest son of the marriage, Geoffrey, assumed the *cognomen* Ridel rather than Basset.[11] In two royal writ-charters, shortly after his inheritance, Geoffrey was addressed by a more complicated style: Geoffrey Ridel *filius Ricardi Basset*.[12] The superiority of the lineage of Maud thus influenced her use of *cognomen* and also that of the eldest line from the marriage which inherited the honour of Weldon.

Similarly at the highest social level, the *cognomen* of the female line assumed precedence over the husband's lineage on the union of Aubigny and Mowbray families. Nigel d'Aubigny was the landless son of a minor Norman baron, whose prestige accrued from his marriage to Matilda de Laigle, the widow of Roger de Mowbray. The eldest son of the issue, Roger, assumed the *cognomen* of his mother's first husband, associated with the honour, de Mowbray, in preference to Albini or d'Aubigny.[13] In this circumstance, it was the *cognomen* of the first marriage which persisted, but effectively it continued first because of the association of the name with the honour and second as a consequence of the inferiority of the husband's lineage.

Occasionally, analogous events happened in peasant society. Sometime before 1350, Matilda sister and heir of Gilbert del Graue, chaplain, married Geoffrey Daunsot, a *nativus* of the lord of Kibworth Beauchamp. The lands inherited through Matilda were confiscated by the lord of the manor as his free tenement, and restored. The restoration was to John del Graue, *nativus domini*, the issue of the marriage. The implications are that, apart from the lord's concern to protect the status of his lands and tenants, Matilda was of free condition, whilst Gilbert was unfree. The issue of the marriage was deemed to be unfree. Nevertheless, because of Matilda's superior status, the issue of the marriage received her byname, that associated with her family, lineage, and, importantly, the tenement.[14]

Many similar instances can be discovered, particularly in charter material, for both rural and urban liaisons, but the circumstances cannot be fully elicited. In some cases the full events are not revealed and all that is demonstrated (for example by the style of husband and wife or widow in a charter) is that man and woman were described in these particular arrangements by different *cognomina*. The possibility remains in the case of widows that they had remarried, explaining their different bynames or surnames at the time of their transaction.

Alice, widow of Thomas de Belton of Melton Mowbray, in her charter of 1352, transferred to her son, Hugh Banastre of Melton, the messuage which she and her husband, Thomas, had received from her brother, Robert Banastre.[15] The property was evidently a *maritagium*, associated with the Banastre line which may have determined the byname of the issue of the marriage if the Banastre's had been economically or socially more important than de Belton'. Property in Melton seems also to have had similar implications for another union. When John de Fontibus confirmed a toft in Melton, perhaps before 1290, it was to John Pestel of Leicester *et heredibus suis de Matillde de Foleuille uxore sua exeuntibus* (to his heirs issuing from his wife Matilda de Foleville).[16] This charter evidently involved the entailed *maritagium* which Simon de Foleville had conferred on the marriage of Matilda and John (as recited in the charter).

Similarly, in 1303, Margery Orger of Melton conveyed to Roger de Waltham of Melton two messuages in that town, all the lands and tenements once of her husband, Adam de Rameseye (*quondam Ade de Rameseye viri mei*) which she held in dower. Her transfer was confirmed by Ralph, son of Adam de Ramesey in 1304, referring to his brother homonymous with his father, Adam de Rameseye, and to Margery Orger the widow of his father, Adam (*uxor quondam Ade patris mei*).[17] In default of more information, at least two circumstances may be adduced of which the first is that Margery had remarried an Orger. The virtue of that explanation is that, since the land in question was dower, a norm would have been for Margery to use her husband's name, not just to refer to him. Nevertheless, the Orgers were a prominent family in Melton and it is equally possible that this marriage was another instance of hypergamy dictating a wife's separate *cognomen*. Correspondingly, the real significance behind several other instances of independently-named spouses in and around Melton cannot be determined: Peter de Thorp' *et Petronilla uxor eius le Palmer' manentes in Melton* (before 1290?), although a Palmer family existed in Melton; Edmund Picson of Barnsby and his wife, Matilda de Rakdale (after 1290?); and Petronilla de Rotherby *relicta Galfridi filii Roberti de Pyne de Houby* (after 1290?), Petronilla having moved to Rotherby, it seems, as the charter related to land there, which may have influenced how she was known.[18] Moreover, there is evidence, however slight, that in other circumstances widows in Melton retained the bynames of their deceased husbands, as in a charter of 1317, did Margaret (*sic*) de la Hil widow of Hugh de la Hil.[19]

A particularly interesting union happened in Great Easton (Leicestershire), in the late thirteenth century, before 1290. Emma Godʒer was the daughter of Walter Godʒer of that vill and she later married Robert Pacy. According to a later memorandum of Peterborough Abbey relating to the confiscation of their lands, both were unfree (*natiui — sic*). Robert *bercator* granted to Emma daughter of Walter Godʒer an acre in the vill and he (later) confirmed it to Robert Pacy and Emma Godʒer of Great Easton. It would thus seem likely that Emma acquired this small amount of land before her marriage and that it was confirmed by the grantor after her union. Husband and wife subsequently received more land, the charters styling them respectively as Robert Pacy and his wife Emma Godʒer, Robert Pacy and his wife Emma, and Robert Pacy and Emma Godʒer of Great Easton (in all, five acres and one rood).[20] The real circumstances behind the match are not revealed, but it may be important that Emma brought some of the land into the marriage herself by her own acquisition.

Other charter material presents the bare facts of different bynames of husband and wife, such as Adam, son of Thomas de Billesdone and his wife, Matilda Chaumpeneis, in Cottesmore (Rutland) (*c*.1257), although her byname may reflect superior status, and Agnes de Oleby *quondam uxor Hugonis de Saxelby*, but with the implication, since the land in question was in Welby (*Oleby*) that she had migrated to that vill.[21]

On the manor of Merton College at Barkby, there are equally unexplained divergences of names of marital partners amongst the customary tenants. When Richard Arnold died in 1279, his lands were taken into the hands of the lords (the Warden and Scholars) and then his widow, Alice le (*sic*) Wyte was admitted.[22] It seems clear that in this case his widow had not remarried. As late as 1362, Joan Hichebon took the messuage and half-virgate which her husband, Richard Bron, had held, giving the customary heriot on the death of a husband.[23] Again, the circumstances suggest that she had not remarried. Nevertherless, widows in Barkby did employ their late husbands' bynames. In 1279, the homage presented that Matilda widow of Henry Osbern had contracted to marry John Arnold, but the union was proscribed because of ecclesiastical censure; in 1287, Matilda Osbern paid merchet for the marriage of her daughter, Denise, on the lords' fee to Henry *filius Sampsonis*.[24]

In manorial records of the late thirteenth century, some peasant widows, of customary status, were described without specific reference to their deceased husbands, redolent of the twelfth-century pattern. That is especially the case with the customary tenant Scolastica on Merton College's manor at Kibworth Harcourt (Leicestershire). In the account for 1284, 18*d*. were received *de Scolastica vidua* whilst in the rental of *c*.1300 she was listed simply as Scolacia.[25] In yet other rentals and extents and in the court rolls, she was described as simply Scolasse, Scolac' *vidua*, Scholace le (*sic*) vediwe and Scolasse *vidua*.[26] Never was she attributed a byname or described by any relationship to a male.[27] On the other hand, sometimes women were considered in the court rolls *only* by relation to their husbands; in the list of brewers in 1290, those amerced included *uxor Iuonis mercatoris* and *uxor Roberti Nichol*, both without forenames, and the latter was merely listed as *femina Roberti Nichol* in the following year.[28] Throughout court rolls for manors in Leicestershire, through into the late fourteenth century, wives were frequently described by relation to their husband, as X *uxor* of AB, and widows in the same way to their deceased husbands, as X *quondam uxor* or *relicta* of AB.

The frequency of that sort of appellation, however, should not be comprehended as their exclusive form of address, certainly not in colloquial terms, nor entirely in the written record. These references may tend to obscure other forms of reference to wives. At Kibworth Beauchamp in 1347, John de Boudon and his wife, Alice, were fined for non-suit against John Mariot and Helen Mariot, in a case of debt, but in the previous year Roger Mariot had been involved in a hue and cry with Alice de Boudon.[29] There too, in the same court in 1350, Agnes *uxor Roberti Daunsot* was presented for being the *causa hutesii* in the proceedings of the view of frankpledge, but in the manorial court (*parva curia*) Robert Cibill impleaded Agnes Daunsot in a case of trespass.[30] In 1330, Isolda Osbern in a case of debt brought against her by Nicholas Polle at Kibworth Harcourt, brought an exception that she should not respond without her husband, Nicholas, and he was summoned to appear.[31] From 1320 through to 1359, however, she was constantly presented as a common brewer, consistently as Isolda Osbern, without reference to her husband and in 1335, as Isolda Osbern, she raised the hue on two occasions.[32] Another Osbern couple provide further evidence of the duality of naming of women at Kibworth Harcourt. In 1346, Richard Seluester proceeded in debt and trespass against William Osbern and his wife, Avice, yet in the same court Avice Osbern, by this style, was placed in mercy against Robert Saundr' in trespass and Robert Wodard in debt.[33] In the same court too, Isolda Osbern, in that form, was placed in mercy for taking away grain and for raising the hue twice, whilst in 1351 she appeared in a case of detinue in the hypercorrect form Isolda Hosebern.[34]

Still in the court rolls of Kibworth Harcourt, in 1366, Matilda *uxor Johannis Michel* raised the hue against Robert Smyth, but three years later she recurred in reciprocal dispute with Agnes atte Cros, this time in the form of Matilda Michel and in that guise too she was presented as a brewer.[35] By the late fourteenth century, indeed, it seems that wives and widows were increasingly designated in local manorial records by their husbands' surnames, as in the Poll Taxes. Indeed, cross reference between manorial court rolls and Poll Taxes establishes one example. In the court rolls of the manor of Hallaton, Joan Drausper(e) was presented as a brewer between 1378 and 1382, but without any reference to her marital status or her husband — that is, simply as Joan Drausper(e).[36] However, in the Poll Tax of 1381, she is listed by those names and as a widow.[37]

From those court rolls of Hallaton derives too further evidence of the use of husbands' surnames by married women. The following women were presented as brewers in the years in parenthesis in the form listed here: Margaret Selwyn (1378); Isabel Wryth (1378, 1380-81, 1383); Catherine (de) Caldewell (1378, 1380, 1381-82, 1383-84); Alice Smyth (1378-84); Agnes Bay (1378-83); Margaret (Magot) de Ilueston (1378, 1380); Mariora Masoun (1381-83); and Alice Tailour (1381). They were described by the forename and byname or surnames in the form above, without reference to any males. In intervening courts, however, males appeared for brewing with exactly the same bynames or surnames: Ralph Selwyn (1378); John Wryʒ or Writʒ (1382); William (de) Caldewell (1378-82, 1384-85); Robert Smyth (1378, 1382, 1384-85); William de Ilueston (1378-79; John Masoun (1381-82, 1384-85); and Thomas Tailour (1382, 1384).[38] These brewers of different gender with the same byname or surname did not appear in court simultaneously, but in alternating courts, suggesting very strongly that in some years husbands were appearing as responsible for the brewing and in other years their wives who were described with the byname or surname of the husband, but without other reference to him.

By the fifteenth century, this process of female naming was firmly established within peasant society. A charter of 1404, relating to land in Stathern (Leicestershire) was issued by Beatrice Sparlynge widow of John Sparlynge, reflecting the convention amongst the free peasantry.[39] In 1412, on the death of John Sandur senior, a customary holding in Kibworth Harcourt passed to his widow, Margaret; in the court rolls, under a marginal note *Capcio terre*, the lords in 1416 seized into their hands these lands of Margaret Sandur, so described, because of the ruined state of the buildings.[40] In 1392, another generation of Sanders substantiated the point, when a widow was described in the same court rolls as Alice Sander *Relicta Nicholai Sander* when she died and Robert Sander was admitted to the customary tenement.[41] In 1431 John Coltman, a cottager in that manor, died, the cottage passing to his widow, Alice, in customary tenure; in the same year, she, described as Alice Coltman, surrendered it to the lords.[42]

Parallel developments happened on the College's other manor in the county at Barkby, for here, when Reginald Playtour died in 1401, his widow, Amice, acceded to his messuage and bovate held in customary tenure; within four years, she, described as Amice Pleytour, surrendered the same holding to the lords and William Kynge was admitted.[43] This form of representation of married and widowed women was more prevalent, but not exclusive, as widows were still sometimes described by reference to their late husbands, as Joan *relicta Ricardi Colyer* when she surrendered the customary tenement to which she had succeeded after the death of her husband, or Matilda *relicta Ricardi Samson*, when she invoked the same course of action (the two events in 1417-18).[44]

By the late fourteenth century, the convention that married women and widows were known in the written records by their husbands' bynames and surnames, but without a specific reference to their relationship to their husbands (as *uxor* or *relicta*), was more widely established. Some evidence, suggests, however, that this had occasionally been the case in the written records at an earlier time, but this form of naming was concealed from view by the more frequent descriptive phrases of relationship. A significant transformation thus occurred in the records, both central and localized, listing women in Leicestershire and Rutland between the twelfth and fifteenth centuries, therefore, but those records reveal little about how women's names were constructed within the speech community and in colloquial language. Occasionally, an intimation is given, as when the court roll of Kibworth Harcourt in 1371 referred in the lists of brewers to Emma Hickeswyf, a form of ME vernacular and presumably colloquial naming which surfaced incidentally in Loughborough in the later middle ages, but which was exceptional in this region.[45]

References

[1] C Clark, 'Women's names in post-Conquest England: observations and speculations', *Speculum*, 53 (1978), 223–51; C Clark, 'Women's names' in N Blake, ed., *The Cambridge History of the English Language*, vol. II, *1066–1476*, (Cambridge, 1992), 583–7; M Bourin and P Chareille, eds., *Génèse Médiévale de L'Anthroponymie Moderne*, Tome II–2, 'Designation et anthroponymie des femmes', (Tours, 1992); D Postles, 'The distinction of gender? Women's names in the thirteenth century', *Nomina*, 19 (1996), 79–89.

[2] See, in general, R Karras, 'Introduction: Common women, prostitutes and whores', *Common Women. Prostitution and Sexuality in Medieval England*, (Oxford, 1996), 3–12.

[3] R McKinley, *The Surnames of Oxfordshire*, (English Surnames Series, III, 1977), 181–98.

[4] For the notion of a crisis of gender relations — not uncriticized — see D Underdown, 'The taming of the scold: the enforcement of patriarchal authority in early modern England' in A J Fletcher and J Stevenson, eds., *Order and Disorrder in Early Modern England*, (Cambridge, 1985), 116–36.

[5] *Templars*, 112.

[6] Queen's College, Oxford, MS 366, fo. 16r–19r.

[7] Rothley, *passim*.

[8] PRO E179/165/1.

9 *AASR*, (1888–9).

10 PRO E179/133/35.

11 D Postles, 'Notions of the family, lordship and the evolution of naming processes in medieval English rural society: a regional example', *Continuity and Change*, 10 (1995), 176–7; W T Reedy, ed., *Basset Charters, c.1120–c.1250*, (Pipe Roll Society, ns L, 1995), viii–xi.

12 Reedy, ed., *Basset Charters*, 25 (no. 47X, from Henry, duke of Normandy and Aquitaine and Count of Anjou, 1153), 25–6 (no. 48, from the Empress Matilda, 1146x1147).

13 R C De Aragon, 'In pursuit of aristocratic women: a key to success in Norman England', *Albion*, 14 (1992), 261, n.1; D E Greenway, ed., *The Charters of the Honour of Mowbray*, (British Academy Records of the Social and Economic History of England and Wales, 1972), xvii–xviii; *Leicestershire Survey*, 89.

14 PRO SC2/183/77: 'Compertum est per .xij. Juratores . . . que Matilldis desponsauit Galfrido Daunsot Natiuo domini . . . procreauit super eandem quendam (*sic*) Johannem del Graue Natiuum domini Et quia predictus Johannes est Natiuus domini predicta tenementa capta fuerunt in manus domini ut liberum tenementum domini et dimissa fuerunt dicto Johanni tenend' ad voluntatem domini . . .' The record was made when John died of the plague in 1350, so the events must have transpired some considerable time earlier.

15 Bodl. MS Wood Empt 7, fos. 18r–v: 'Sciant presentes et futuri quod ego Alicia quondam uxor Thome de Belton de Melton Moubray dedi concessi et hac presenti carta mea confirmaui Hugoni Banastre de Melton filio meo . . . quod quidem mesuagium dictus Thomas de Belton et ego habuimus de dono et feoffamento Roberti Banastr' fratris mei . . .'

16 Bodl. MS Wood Empt 7, fos. 21r–22r.

17 Bodl. MS Wood Empt 7, fos. 83r–84r.

18 Bodl. MS Wood Empt 7, fos. 84r, 136r, 189r–v.

19 Bodl. MS Wood Empt 7, fos. 6v: 'Sciant presentes et futuri quod ego Margareta (*sic*) de la Hil de Melton nuper uxor Hugonis de la Hil . . .' In all her other charters she was styled simply Margery (*sic*) del Hil.

20 C N L Brooke and M M Postan, eds., *Carte Nativorum. A Peterborough Abbey Cartulary of the Fourteenth Century*, (Northamptonshire Record Society, xx, 1960), 138–140 (nos.418–24); see also, C Clark, 'Women's names', in R Blake, ed., *The Cambridge History of the English Language*, vol. II, *1066–1476*, (Cambridge, 1992), 586.

21 E Mason,, ed., *The Beauchamp Cartulary Charters 1100–1268*, (Pipe Roll Society, n.s. 43, 1980), 146–7 (no. 256); *Berkeley*, 104 (no. 316).

22 MM 6563: 'Ricardus Arnold mortuus est ideo terra sua . . . capiatur in manibus dominorum . . . Et Alicia le Wyte uxor eius inueniet plegios . . . ad Custodiendum predictam terram et facere inde seruicia debita.'

23 MM 6575: 'que Ricardus Bron vir suus prius tenuit . . . [heriot of a ewe] ex consuetudine post mortem viri.'

24 MM 6563 and 6565: 'Matilda uxor quondam Henrici Osbern . . . capere virum qui vocatur Johannem Arnold et consideratum fuit per censuram ecclesiasticam quod dictus Johannes non potest ducere dictam Matildam in uxorem . . .';'Quia Matilda Osbern maritauit dyonisiam filiam suam super feodum dominorum sine licencia cum Henrico filio Sampsonis in misericordia.'

25 MM 6204, 6367.

26 E.g. MM 6370, 6385, 6390.

27 See, for example, MM 6376 (1282): 'Scolasse queritur de Johanne filio Roberti carpentarii . . .' in a case of trespass.

28 MM 6384, 6388.

29 PRO SC2/183/76 (1346–7).

30 PRO SC2/183/77.

31 MM 6398: 'Isolda dicit quod non debet respondere sine Nicholao marito suo.'

32 MM 6393–6403, but in view of the longevity of these appearances, perhaps there was a daughter Isolda as well in the later cases.

33 MM 6404.

34 MM 6404–25.

35 MM 6406.

36 PRO DL30/80/1102.

37 PRO E179/133/35.

38 PRO DL30/80/1102.

39 *Rutland MSS*, 9 (no. 34).

40 MM 6419: 'Margareta Sandur natiua dominorum que de dominis tenuit in villenagio . . .'

41 MM 6407.

42 MM 6419.

43 MM 6591.

44 MM 6591.

45 MM 6407.

CHAPTER 11

LANGUAGE AND NAMES

Language and names in the borough of Leicester

In the twelfth century, the languages of written records within boroughs consisted of triglossia: Latin as the highest register, the most formal language of writing, and two vernaculars, French and Middle English, the former perhaps a higher register than the latter. To some extent, the written records also reflected the diglossia of the speech community, French and Middle English. It seems fairly clear that the French of the written records did not simply reflect the predilection of the clerks or *scriptores*.[1] Sufficient material has been digested from other boroughs of the twelfth century — King's Lynn, Canterbury, Winchester and the new borough of Battle — to allow a context for considering the use of language within Leicester.[2]

As a provincial, inland pre-Conquest borough, Leicester differed from the former capital, Winchester, the new borough of Battle, the new port of Lynn, and Canterbury, the seat of the Metropolitan and dominated by the Cathedral Priory. By comparison, however, there are no rentals for Leicester in the twelfth century, so that what can be discerned of language must be recovered from the gild merchant rolls commencing in 1196.[3] These records are formal to the extent that their incipits and headings are in Latin, as is any syntactical matter within the text of the rolls.[4] On the other hand, the description of bynames is triglossic, in Latin, French and Middle English. For the purposes of understanding the relationship between these languages, occupational, nickname and topographical names are the most significant. Assessment is undertaken here of the language of bynames from the inception of the gild merchant rolls in 1196 through to 1250 inclusive. During this period, 139 burgesses with occupational bynames were admitted to the freedom and 130 with nickname bynames.

Unlike at Battle, occupational bynames were not completely Latinized.[5] A considerable corpus was expressed in French and, moreover, some of the Latin forms may have concealed real French descriptions in the speech community. By comparison, Middle

English occupational bynames remained consistently low in number. Nevertheless, ME forms may be considered to have been more vital, for, whilst most French forms were uncompounded, ME names contained a very high proportion of compounds. Thus, whilst French was the language of commerce, ME largely displaced French for complex descriptions.

Twenty-eight occupational bynames were rendered in Latin in the rolls, accounting for 78 freemen admitted, but some Latin terms may have been synonyms, such as (*Auenarius*) and (*Auenator*) and *Aquarius* and *Ouarius* (*Owarius*). Moreover, although seven bynames for baker assumed the Latin *Pistor*, *Pestur* may have represented a French rendition. The Latinized occupational bynames are aggregated in Table 11.1.

Table 11.1

Latinized occupational bynames in admissions, 1196–1250[6]

Byname	No. of bearers	Byname	No. of bearers
Albus Tannator	1	*homo*	3
Aquarius	3	*Medicus*	1
Auenarius	1	*Mercator*	1
Auenator	4	*Molendinarius*	2
Aurifaber	6	*Ouarius*	2
Burgens	1	*Parmentarius*	1
Cancellarius	1	*Pestur*	1
Carpentarius	5	*Piscator*	2
Carnifex	1	*Pistor*	7
Caretarius [sic]	1	*Presbiter*	1
Clericus	2	*Rotarius*	5
Cocus	4	*Sacerdos*	1
Faber	13 .	*Textor*	1
Ferrator	2	*Tinctor*	4
		Vinator	1

In fact, French synonyms were consistently used in the rolls instead of these Latin forms: auener; le carpunter; le ferur; furnur; le keu (ko); le marcant; le muner; le roer (for *rotarius*); and parmunter. Consequently, several of the Latinized bynames seem likely to conceal French equivalents. Indeed, the number of different French occupational bynames considerably exceeded the Latinized forms, amounting to 39 names, as revealed in Table 11.2.

Table 11.2
French occupational bynames in admissions, 1196-1250[7]

Byname	Byname	Byname
auener	granger	paumer*
caperun	hoser	plummer
carpunter	keu/ko	potter
corder	liur de dras	precher
cotiler	macun	roer
coruiser	marcant	seinter
[curlewache]	mercer	seler
cuureur	muner	sopere
ferur	mustarder	specer
flauner	quareur	taillur
furnur	paneler	tanur
gardener	parcheminer	teler
geliner	parmunter	turnur

* Possibly a nickname byname.

Few of the French occupational bynames in twelfth-century Canterbury were replicated in Leicester, the two boroughs having a seemingly different environment. Selier, which occurred in Canterbury in 1163/7 and c.1206, might have been consistent with seler (saddler) in Leicester.[8] At Lynn, teler existed in the twelfth century, reflecting the importance of the cloth industry, perhaps explaining its occurrence in Leicester.[9] Although somewhat tenuously, some of the nominal evidence of occupations confirms that the language in use in the borough of Leicester was northern French. For example, gelinier (poulterer) is possibly indicative of northern France by comparison with southern galinier.[10] Suggestive of Picardie is marcand, as is caperon, macun and teler.[11] Nevertheless, other forms of occupational byname are not consistent with northern French usage, as, for example, mercer, corder, and potter.[12]

Whilst the corpus of early French occupational bynames contained few compounds, syntactical constructions formed a considerable proportion of the ME stock, although the construction usually consisted of the addition of a common suffix: halleknaue; huniman;

maltmongere; sereman; gresmongere; and spitalman. To these can be added a metonym (wetebred) and some syntactical constructions (hombaken and cocunbred), whilst le panne betere might have been diglossic. Whilst the compounded forms thus accounted for about 10 bynames, the simplex forms added another seven (dubbere, reue, cupere, feltere, packere, and combere).

Another principal contrast between the two linguistic corpora results from their occupational composition as well as syntax. Although the French names included fabric-making and use (parmunter, mercer, hoser, taillur, caperun, teler), the terms for the woollen cloth industry were almost exclusively ME (dubbere, feltere, packere, combere). There may have been a demarcation in the linguistic register for terms for commerce and retailing, for, whilst mercer and marcant may have belonged to a higher register, the compound -mongere was associated with more specific products.[13]

Similar patterns can be observed with respect to nickname bynames in the borough between 1196 and 1250. Of the 130 burgesses with nickname bynames admitted to the freedom in this time, only 35 bore Latinized forms of byname. Indeed, the corpus comprised only 10 Latinized bynames: *longus*; *cum barba*; *bonus*; *blundus*; *niger*; *ruffus*; *crassus*; *albus*; *caritas/karitas*; and *largus*. As with the occupational bynames, however, some of these bynames were barely concealed Latin equivalents of French bynames prevalent within the borough, such as blund and cras(set). Others may have imputed more obliquely French equivalents, such as Pite for *Caritas/Karitas*, for, whilst William *Caritas* was received into the freedom in 1225, the same privilege was conferred on Hugh Pite *filius Willelmi Pite* in 1262 and previously William Pite had been admitted in 1211. Nonetheless, the hereditary surname *Caritas* continued to be used, as when John *Caritas filius Willelmi Caritas* (sic) and Simon *Caritas filius Willelmi Caritas* (sic) were both granted the freedom in 1265.[14] The largest corpus consisted of French bynames, which greatly exceeded ME *cognomina*.[15] Between 1196 and 1250, about twice as many burgesses were admitted with French as with ME nickname bynames, some 80 against some 40.[16] In terms of different bynames, the rolls of admission recorded 35 French and as many (34) ME. The comparable nature of the range accords with the position in Canterbury, where the number of French and ME nickname bynames was similar.[17]

By contrast with the occupational bynames, a larger proportion of

French nicknames were compounded.[18] In this category fell folebarbe, curlewache (but possibly a metonym or occupational byname), maudit, plantefene (but possibly with occupational implications), vinttesdeners (but which may have had a ME equivalent), daubedame, belhoste, pikenot, and dismars. Pikenot, however, was ambiguously compounded, since it has been interpreted, in its existence in Canterbury, as a variant of *picavet*, 'faggot', current in Arras in 1224.[19] As with occupational bynames, a linguistic connection with northern France can be tentatively suggested, for Folebarbe and Plantefene/Plantefèue may be forms associated with Normandy and Crasset is dialect which is suggestive of north-eastern France.[20]

At least two 'Shakespeare' or 'imperative' forms in French were employed in the borough, plantefene and daubedame.[21] Such forms, combining the imperative of a verb with a noun, were, however, only slightly more numerous in ME, as described below, and thus Leicester's corpus cannot really contribute to the debate whether this compounded form had French or ME origins.[22] 'Bahuvrihi' types, which, combining an adjective and noun denoted personal characteristics, included particularly folebarbe, defined by Morlet as someone whose beard has become out of hand or unkempt.[23] Possibly to this category should be attributed the nickname consisting of a sum of money, vinttesdeners or vintesisdeners — whether reflecting personal wealth or assessment in a subsidy.

At Battle in the twelfth century, one of the inhabitants was described as Ælric Curlebasse, an unexplained byname.[24] A similar problem confounds the analysis at Leicester in the form of the important kinship group designated le Curlewache or Curlevache, of which Simon existed before the commencement of the gild merchant rolls in 1196. Additionally, Robert was admitted to the freedom in 1199 by patrimony, confirming the prior status of the family, whilst Simon's son, Alan, entered the gild merchant in 1214. By 1225, Simon had been elevated to the status of alderman of the gild, the principal officer of the borough. In 1242, Geoffrey and Henry Curlewache achieved the freedom. Despite its obscurity, one possible explanation of the nickname is an association with tanning, so that it might imply either curing cowskins or be a metonym for leather of cows.[25]

In comparison, the large proportion of the French nicknames were monothematic, even monosyllabic, and rather conventional, so that their significance for the use of French speech is ambivalent. It has been inferred, for example, that Curteis had 'no necessary bearing . . . on the currency of French speech . . .'[26] Indeed, there is a possiblity that curteis was also employed as a personal name ('forename') and certainly russel may have developed from the use of Roscelinus locally as a personal name, reflected in the Roscelinus with no byname who was admitted to the gild merchant in 1198.[27] Some of these nicknames in Leicester had, it seems, also become inherited before 1250, at least over one generation or represented a kinship. Curlevache is an important example, representing the French presence in the borough, but it is possible that vintesdners or vinttesisdeners were also inherited, for Simon, who entered the gild merchant in 1225, was followed by the admission of William in 1252. Less certainly hereditary, Folebarbe was listed in the entrants to the gild in 1196 and 1225.[28]

By contrast, a much higher proportion of ME nicknames comprised compounded forms, 21 out of a total of 34. Only three, however, appear to have been 'Shakespeare' compositions: spillecorn; makepa(i)s; and kepegest.[29] Accordingly, 'Bahuvrihi' compounds were more frequent: brokinhevid; smalestones; longstaf; smalbon; louelẻs; berdles; leftant; prudfot; rutefot; and possibly nutemuche.[30] In general characteristics, therefore, the ME compounds were more vigorous in formation, but also perhaps with a greater sense of irony, derogation, and sexual connotations. In the last category, for example, might belong smalestones and, much less certainly, longstaff and smalbon.[31]

Nonetheless, ambiguity exists in the language of the nicknames. Whilst gresgod was the single diglossic compound in nicknames, combining French grâce and ME god, its relationship to the ME compound encountered in the admissions before 1250, godesbest, is unclear.[32] Similarly, Simon Vinttesdeners was admitted to the freedom in 1225 and William Vintesisdeners in 1252, but in 1253 reference in the gild rolls was made to Simon Sixandtwenti and by 1258 William Sixandtwenti had been co-opted onto the informal council.[33]

In complete contrast, the language of topographical bynames was radically different, since few were constructed in French. In twelfth-century Canterbury, these types of byname were mainly constructed in ME, a different situation from that which obtained in Leicester, where topographical names were Latinized consistently before *c.*1250 and Latin forms predominated until 1293.[34] Nevertheless, topographical bynames were not prevalent in boroughs and certainly not in Leicester. Moreover, the admissions to the gild merchant are likely to under-represent topographical bynames in the borough, since this type of byname might have been associated with townspeople not of burgess status or of the lower ranks of urban inhabitants. Thus, before 1250, only seven burgesses with Latinized topographical bynames were received into the freedom, bearing six different bynames: *de Cymeterio*; *de Fraxino*; *ad Fontem*; *in Angulo*; *in Fossato*; and *de Marisco*.[35] The last might have been synonymous with the two forms of French topographical byname to occur in the freemen's lists, Maraz and de le Mire.[36] ME forms were conspicuously absent, unless the asyndetic *ston* was topographical, which seems unlikely. A matter of debate, however, is whether ME de le Woodgate and de le Hey were either minor urban placenames or topographical.[37] In 1253, the portents of ME were represented in the admission of John Cruke (reflecting habitation near a cross) *filius Hugonis Cruke*, but in 1254 Geoffrey *sub muro filius Walteri sub muro* was admitted, confirming the persistence of Latin.[38]

Between 1250 and 1293, Latin forms still predominated, with *sub muro*, *ad lacum*, *de marisco*, *de aula*, and *ad portam*, although *de aula* may equally have been occupational like *de la bracina* which occurred contemporaneously.[39] In this period, French topographical forms were entirely absent, unless de la chaumbre is thus interpreted. Equivalence was being established between Latin and ME topographical bynames during this period, but from 1293 Latin was completely supplanted by ME constructions, as some 45 burgesses with ME topographical bynames attained the freedom from then until 1505. Grene and Abouetun were the most frequent bynames of this type, but the range of 38 different bynames was fairly wide.[40]

It seems apparent, however, that into the thirteenth century, both French and ME were the spoken languages in the burghal community and that, although some French lexis had become conventional loan words in ME, French words persisted in their use in this environment. In particular, some compounded French nicknames, whilst becoming hereditary, contributed to the diglossia of the borough's speech community. Associated in some cases with prominent burgess families, such as Curlevache, French may have acted as a higher vernacular register, although it is clear from a wider understanding of linguistic change that it was rapidly becoming a learned language.[41] Furthermore, families seemingly of insular origin, such as Leveric, also advanced within the borough 'community'.[42]

In different boroughs in the twelfth and early thirteenth century, although triglossic use of language was characteristic of the local written records, different types of bynames were constructed in different languages. Whilst in Winchester Latin was the norm for occupational bynames in the survey of 1148, in late twelfth- and early thirteenth-century Leicester, French and ME were more dominant. Whilst ME was the language of topographical bynames in Canterbury, Latinized forms were comprehensive in Leicester. Different registers were assigned to different forms of byname, it seems, but the two vernaculars, French and ME, might have reflected quite closely the higher and lower registers of the urban speech community.

Language and names in rural places

Whilst some of the influences on the language of names in written records in the borough operated equally in the rural environment, there were differences between the two spheres. Although it is clear, for example, that the urban speech community was diglossic in the twelfth and early thirteenth century, there is less evidence for the employment of French as a vernacular language, even of a high register, in the rural environment, except as a literary language. Consequently, the individual predilection of *scriptores* assumed more importance in written records relating to rural settlements, with an increased importance on the possibility of code-switching by the compiler of the record, exhibiting learning. Particularly might this have been important after French became a learned language from the early thirteenth century.[43]

Additionally, there exists the possibility of different domains of people, free and unfree, and whether French might have been more frequently attributed to the names of free peasants rather than the unfree.[44] Whilst a similar division might have prevailed also in boroughs, between burgesses and non-burgesses, the non-burghal townspeople remained largely invisible in the records. Moreover, the suggestion has been advanced that French names might have been more readily accorded to burgesses than to the rural peasantry.[45]

For the rural context, perceiving the use of language in bynames and surnames is almost entirely dependent on nicknames, since French occupational names were mainly confined to urban places. The comparative employment of French and ME in nickname bynames and surnames can be most appropriately assessed from compounded nicknames, which, more than uncompounded forms, reflect at least some lexical and syntactical knowledge. Accordingly is raised the question of the linguistic origin of certain types of compounded nicknames, particularly whether 'imperative' ('Shakespeare') forms emanated from a French or ME *milieu*.[46]

It is appropriate then also to consider first the lexical contribution of French to ME. Recently, Coleman has demonstrated that French loans to ME became significant from the early thirteenth century, with a peak of borrowing in the late thirteenth century rather than Dekeyser's suggestion of maximum infusion in the late fourteenth century. Moreover, in the century after the Conquest, loans were unstable, with a high turnover, reflected in a quarter of loan words failing to persist. From the late thirteenth to the late fourteenth century, stability ensued, but followed by an era of maximum disappearance of loaned words.[47] That instability between the eleventh and early thirteenth century has been demonstrated in the context of nickname and occupational bynames in the borough of Leicester.

By comparison, however, French bynames appear to have been scarce amongst the peasantry of Leicestershire and Rutland in the twelfth century, although due consideration should be allowed to the paucity of records as also to the later development of bynames amongst the peasantry than amongst burgesses. Before discussion of the detailed perspective of language acquisition and use, however, an overall impression of compounded nickname bynames and surnames of the peasantry is necessary.

From the record sources relating to the peasantry from the twelfth to early sixteenth centuries can be accumulated about 130 different compounded nickname bynames and surnames, of which 76 were recorded in sources of the early sixteenth century. By the early sixteenth century, the corpus was predominantly ME, including only five French surnames, and only two exhibited codeswitching or combining (for example, Magdaunce/Makedans/Makedaunce). At that time, the 'bahuvrihi' forms (such as Pybodye) consisted of 21 surnames and 'imperative' (such as Makedaunce) eight. Assuming these two forms to represent, alongside unusual other compounded forms, the most vigorous and vital constructions, the corpus of compounded nickname surnames in the early sixteenth century, whilst predominantly ME, was still resourceful.[48]

The composition of the corpus at an earlier time can be assessed from the sequence of taxation records as in Table 11.3, although these excluded a considerable proportion of the peasantry.

Table 11.3

The characteristics of compounded nickname bynames in Leicestershire and Rutland, 1296–1381[49]

Date:county	'bahuvrihi'	'imperative'	other	French*
1296:Rutland	8	8	14	6
1327:Leicestershire	8	6	26	7
1377:Rutland	3	0	10	2
1381:Leicestershire	8	2	7	1

Notes: * French is not exclusive of other forms, but derived from all three.

It seems apparent that the proportion of French compounded nickname bynames declined during the later middle ages, although the numbers are rather too small to be conclusive. The linguistic composition of compounded nickname bynames can be further compared during the late thirteenth and early fourteenth centuries with adjacent counties, as in Table 11.4, which reveals the numbers of different compounded nickname bynames in the two vernaculars.

Table 11.4

The linguistic characteristics of compounded nickname bynames in Leicestershire, Rutland and adjacent counties, 1296–1332[50]

Date:county	ME	code-mixing	French
1296:Rutland	24	0	6
1327:Leicestershire	33	0	7
1332:Lincolnshire	72	7	18
1327:Warwickshire	93	3	30
1327:Staffordshire	36	2	7
1327:Derbyshire	12	0	1

Notes: Lincolnshire, comprising only the parts adjacent to our two counties (the parts of Kesteven and Holland).

In the Derbyshire lay subsidy, compounded nickname bynames were scarce, not only in ME, but also in French, especially since the only construction in the latter language was a gentry name.[51]

Moreover, many of the ME forms were common, such as barfot, greteheued, wyldebor, wysman and proudfot, although less usual were truselove *alias* trusselove, spychesach, romesheued (ram's head) and lithelad.[52]

The small corpus of French bynames of this kind in Staffordshire contains an element of common forms, such as saunfayl, beusire, malerbe, maveysyn, and durdent.[53] Whilst the French names contained no 'imperative' constructions, the ME contingent included the ubiquitous schakespeare and schakeloke, but also the less usual turnehare (two taxpayers), brekedish and turnepeny, fairly vital compositions.[54] In Lincolnshire, the ME 'imperative' forms consisted of ledelady, schakelock, drynkdregges, drynkwater and louegod, but were almost equalled by wastpayn, passeauaunt, bislaunce (*sic*) and the frequent parleb(i)en, borne by at least 10 taxpayers, particularly at Milnethorp, Pointon and Claypole.[55] Similarly in Warwickshire, French and ME 'imperative' compounds were in equilibrium, comparing pallehare, schakedon, schakeloc, sporehard, tornepeny, tredefen, and tredegold with daunceproud, passelewe, persehay, and placedeu.[56]

Conclusion

During the later middle ages, languages of speech communities varied, reflected in the construction of some forms of byname and surname. With literary texts, the use of language might involve simply the predilection of the author or might be informed by the prospective audience. In the case of locally-produced as well as centrally-enrolled records, the identity of the clerk again is an important aspect, but the language employed in names might also have been informed by the information communicated by the local speech community. At the very least, these records, it is contended, illustrate that local communities had a comprehension of some French vocabulary to the extent that compounds with some syntactical and lexical content were constructed.

References

[1] C Clark, 'The myth of the Anglo-Norman scribe' and 'People and languages in post-Conquest Canterbury', in P Jackson, ed., *Words, Names and History. Selected Writings of Cecily Clark*, (Cambridge, 1995), 168–78, 190, 197.

² C Clark, 'People and languages' (as n.1), 'Some early Canterbury surnames'; Battle *c*.1110: an anthroponymist looks at an Anglo-Norman new town', and 'The early personal names of King's Lynn: an essay in socio-cultural history', all in Jackson, ed., *Words, Names and History*, 179–279; O von Feilitzen, 'The personal names of the Winton Domesday' in M Biddle, ed., *Winchester in the Early Middle Ages*, (Winchester Studies, I, Oxford, 1976), 143–229.

³ *RBL*, I, 12 et seqq. by cross-reference with H Hartopp, *Register of the Freemen of Leicester 1196–1770*, (Leicester, 1927).

⁴ G H Martin, 'The English borough in the thirteenth century', repr. in R Holt and G Rosser, eds., *The Medieval Town. A Reader in English Urban History*, (London, 1990), 37–9, describes the first roll.

⁵ Clark, 'Battle', 227.

⁶ *RBL*, I, 12–64.

⁷ *RBL*, I, 12–64.

⁸ Clark, 'Some early Canterbury surnames', 213; G Fransson, *Middle English Surnames of Occupation 1100–1350*, (Lund Studies in English, 3, Lund, 1935), 214.

⁹ Clark, 'The early personal names of King's Lynn', 268.

¹⁰ M-Th Morlet, *Dictionnaire Etymologique dess Noms de Famille*, (Paris, 1991), 452.

¹¹ Morlet, *Dictionnaire*, 661, 646, 920.

¹² Morlet, *Dictionnaire*, 239, 685, 802.

¹³ Clark, 'People and languages', 193.

¹⁴ *RBL*, I, 23, 29, 106, 140.

¹⁵ See, in general, C Clark, 'Thoughts on the French connection of Middle English nicknames', *Nomina*, 2 (1978), 38–44.

¹⁶ Some nickname bynames are too ambiguous to classify or, in the case of a very small number (such as sturdi) could be equally French or ME. Clark suggested that sturdi was French, because of its occurrence in Arras: 'People and languages', 191. She made a similar observation about the obscurity of some apparently ME nicknames: 'People and languages', 192.

¹⁷ Clark, 'People and languages', 191.

¹⁸ Contrast with Clark, 'People and languages', 193, 197.

¹⁹ Clark, 'People and languages', 192.

²⁰ Morlet, *Dictionnaire*, 255, 419, 792.

²¹ Morlet, *Dictionnaire*, 792, has an interpretation as plantefèue/plantefol in Normandy rather than Bateson's plantefene, intimating someone who works arid land and thus has a reputation as being

'fol'. Alternatively, however, it might be considered as one who plants (seeds) hay?

22 B. Seltén, *Early East Anglian Nicknames: 'Shakespeare' Names*, (Lund, 1969); C Clark, 'People and languages'; J Jönsjö, *Studies on Middle English Nicknames: I. Compounds*, (Lund, 1979), 38-40, 43; G Fellows-Jensen, 'On the study of Middle English by-names', *Namn och Bygd*, (1980), 107-9.

23 B Seltén, *Early East Anglian Nicknames: 'Bahuvrihi' Names*, (Lund, 1975); Morlet, *Dictionnaire*, 419 ('barbe peu soignée').

24 Clark, 'Battle', 239, no. 86.

25 See above, 116, 119, 321-2.

26 Clark, 'The early personal names of King's Lynn', 275.

27 *RBL*, I, 16; T Forssner, *Continental-Germanic Personal Names in England in Old and Middle English Times*, (Uppsala, 1916), 220-1.

28 *RBL*, I, 13, 27, 65, 67, 74, 77-9. For Curlevache, see above, n.25.

29 *RBL*, I, 13, 20, 23, 24, 45.

30 *RBL*, I, 14, 17, 21, 22, 23, 27, 45, 62-3, 65.

31 E Partridge, *A Dictionary of Historical Slang*, (Harmondsworth, 1972), 915 (stones meaning testicles from the twelfth to twentieth centuries), 900 (staff has no clear sexual meaning, for the erect penis, until the nineteenth century, according to Partridge) and 96-7 (bone too only has a later popular interpretation as the penis).

32 *RBL*, I, 14, 62, 64.

33 *RBL*, I, 27, 65, 67, 77, 112, 143, 145, 209, 357, 383, 385-90, 399.

34 Clark, 'People and languages', 193.

35 *RBL*, I, 20, 22, 26, 27, 33, 35, 62, 67.

36 *RBL*, I, 27, 63, 211.

37 *RBL*, I, 63.

38 For Cruke, Clark, 'People and languages', 193; *RBL*, I, 28, 31, 67, 170.

39 *RBL*, I, 67, 77, 94, 97, 112, 121-2, 133, 136, 143, 144, 174, 202, 203, 208-11, 215, 217-19, 220, 222, 239, 256.

40 *RBL*, II, 29, 38, 46 (Abouetun) and see above, 222-5, for Grene.

41 I Short, 'On bilingualism in Anglo-Norman England', *Romance Philology*, 23 (1980), 467-79; Short, 'Patrons and polyglots: French literature in twelfth-century England' in M Chibnall, ed., *Anglo-Norman Studies XIV. Proceedings of the Battle Conference 1991*, (Woodbridge, 1992), 230, 242, 246-7; R Lodge, 'Language attitudes and

linguistic norms in France and England in the thirteenth century' in P R Coss and S Lloyd, eds., *Thirteenth Century England. Proceedings of the Newcastle upon Tyne Conference 1991*, (Woodbridge, 1992), 73-83; H Rothwell, 'Language and government in medieval England', *Zeitschrift für Französische Sprache und Literatur*, 93 (1983), 258-70; Rothwell, 'From Latin to Anglo-French and Middle English: the role of the multilingual gloss', *Modern Language Review*, 88 (1993), 581-99; M T Clanchy, *From Memory to Written Record. England 1066-1307*, (Oxford, revised edn, 1993), 197-223.

[42] *RBL*, I, 21, 23, 35, 72, 77, 84, 90, 143, 304, 311, 322, 338, 343-4, 347-9, 352-3, 356.

[43] See above, n.41; for the later middle ages, L E Voigt, 'What's the word? Bilingualism in late medieval England', *Speculum*, 71 (1996), 813-26.

[44] Fellows-Jensen, 'On the study of Middle English by-names', *Nomn och Bygd*, (Uppsala, 1980), 107-9.

[45] Fellows-Jensen, 'On the study of Middle English by-names', 107-9.

[46] B Seltén, *Early East Anglian Nicknames: 'Shakespeare' Names*, (Lund, 1969); C Clark, 'People and languages'; Fellows-Jensen, 'On the study of Middle English by-names', 107-9; J Jönsjö, *Studies on Middle English Nicknames: I. Compounds*, (Lund Studies in English, 55, Lund, 1979), 38-40, 43.

[47] J Coleman, 'The chronology of French and Latin loan words in English', *Transactions of the Philological Society*, 93 (1995), 95-124.

[48] PRO E179/133/104-110, 112-118, 121-122, 124.

[49] PRO E179/165/1, 21; *AASR*, (1888-9); PRO E179/133/35.

[50] PRO E179/135/14-15; I Hjertstedt, *Middle English Nicknames in the Lay Subsidy Rolls for Warwickshire*, (Acta Universitatis Upsaliensis, 63, Uppsala 1987); Jönsjö, *Studies on Middle English Nicknames: I. Compounds*, lists compounded nickname bynames in Lincolnshire without differentiating by the different Parts. G Wrottesley, 'The Exchequer lay subsidy roll of A.D. 1327', *Collections for a History of Staffordshire*, (William Salt Archaeological Society), 7 (1886), 195-255; J C Cox, 'Derbyshire in 1327-8: being a lay subsidy roll', *Transactions of the Derbyshire Natural History and Archaeological Society*, 30 (1908), 23-96 [but defective]. Foleiaumbe, a gentry name, at Tideswell and Wormhill: S Wright, *The Derbyshire Gentry in the Fifteenth Century*, (Derbyshire Record Society, 8, 1983), 197. Chisquare analysis would be inaccurate, since there are too many cells with the value below five. The figures relate to different bynames, not numbers of taxpayers.

[51] For Foliaumbe, Cox, 'Derbyshire in 1327–8', 59; for the other forms, 42 (trus(s)elove), 47, 67 (barfot), 50 (greteheued), 68 (spychesach), 74 (romesheued), 77 (wyldebor), 82 (lithelad), 88 (wysman), 95 (proudfot).

[52] The prototheme of trusselove is more likely to be ME trusse (pack, bundle) than OFr trousser (to pack).

[53] Wrottesley, 'Exchequer lay subsidy roll', 197, 205, 223–4, 228, 232. Maveysyn is equivalent to mal voisin, lacking neighbourliness.

[54] Wrottesley, 'Exchequer lay subsidy', 199, 204, 209, 216, 230, 248.

[55] PRO E179/135/14, mm. 1, 8, and E179/135/15, mm. 1, 3–4, 18, 20, 28. Bislaunce is assumed to be briselaunce.

[56] Hjertstedt, *Middle English Nicknames in the Lay Subsidy Rolls for Warwickshire*, 97, 149, 151, 154, 158–9, 176–7, 184, 193–4.

CHAPTER 12

PERSISTENCE OF SURNAMES

The persistence of surnames in a rural society in the late middle ages: Barkby

Analysis of the persistence of bynames and surnames on a Merton manor in Leicestershire, Barkby, is complex. The College's manor was only one of several in the parish, alongside the lands of the Pochin family and Leicester Abbey and a small property of Langley Priory.[1] Consequently, analysis of the College's records does not provide a comprehensive account of bynames and surnames in the parish. A principal problem, therefore, is whether bynames and surnames migrated between lordships within Barkby. It cannot be categorically stated that bynames or surnames disappeared from Barkby, for example, since it is possible that they simply migrated to another lordship within the parish. Similarly, it cannot be conclusively stated that new surnames, for example in the later middle ages, derived from outside the parish since they might have emanated from another lordship in the vill. To some extent, this problem is mitigated by taxation records, such as lay subsidies, which comprehended all lordships within the township and parish.

A further caveat is inherent in the type of records employed, particularly the manorial court rolls of the College. It is not always certain that litigants in the manorial court were resident in Barkby. A sufficient number of cases exist in which the litigant was specifically described as from another place, to suggest that most other litigants were resident in the parish, if not on the College's manor. Some fleeting bynames and surnames may, however, be explained by this phenomenon.

The data collection from court rolls was extended to 1544.[2] Surnames introduced into the College's manor in the 1530s and 1540s will thus be exhibited in Figure 19 as having only a short existence, but the explanation is simply the end-date for data collection. More problematically, however, the transformation of surnames in the later middle ages may give an illusion of the changes in kinship

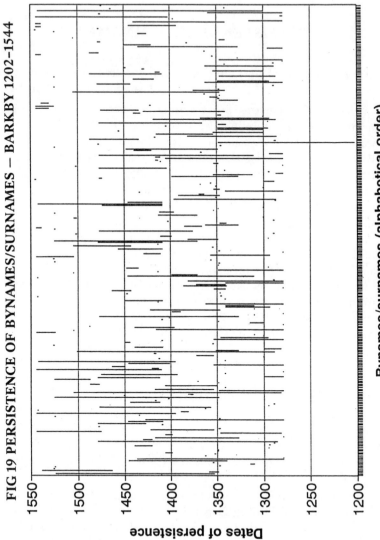

FIG 19 PERSISTENCE OF BYNAMES/SURNAMES – BARKBY 1202–1544

Dates of persistence

Bynames/surnames (alphabetical order)

structures.[3] The persistence of surnames represents continuity only through the male line of inheritance. Discontinuity of surnames does not conversely nor necessarily represent discontinuity in kinship structures. Low male replacement rates (below unity) whether through low fertility or emigration, may be reflected in changes of the structure of surnames, but continuity of kinship through female inheritance is not represented in surname data. Some displacement of surnames in the later middle ages may have resulted from female inheritance and marriage rather than disappearance of the kinship.

Finally, Figure 19 is only approximately accurate before the 1330s, because of the instability of bynames. As explained above, whilst the bynames of a core of families of the unfree peasantry became established as hereditary surnames in the late thirteenth century, that final transformation did not happen amongst all unfree families until later. Much of the loss of bynames before the 1330s may thus be as much a consequence of the instability of bynames as the failure of family names to persist.

Figure 19 represents the longevity or all bynames and surnames encountered in all records relating to Barkby from 1202 to 1544 — charters, court rolls, rentals, and lay subsidies. The total number of different bynames and surnames occurring within these records is suggestive of the caveats mentioned above; the aggregate number is 291, far too many in relation to the small size of the College's manor. A very large number of the fleeting occurrences, particularly in court rolls, must thus not represent resident individuals or kinships, although some will reflect short term residences of individuals. Figure 19 does reveal, nevertheless, the fairly high level of continuity of some bynames and surnames into the 1350s and then the rapid transformation of the stock of surnames on the manor therafter.

Those changes are confirmed by analysis of the names of the tenants of the College rather than all appearances in manorial and fiscal records, but again there are some problems. The rentals of *c*.1300, 1311, 1312 and 1315, seem to represent a wider structure of the tenantry, including small tenants and perhaps even under-tenants, since many fragmented holdings are included. The subsequent rentals of 1354/5, 1450 and 1475, show a more consolidated tenantry. Thus, whilst 60 holdings were enumerated in the rental of *c*.1300, only 28 were listed in 1354, 20 in 1450 and 19 in 1475 (although the number of tenants is even smaller, because of multiple holdings in

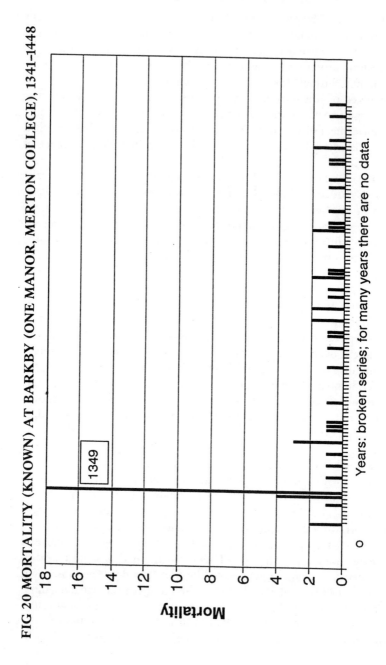

FIG 20 MORTALITY (KNOWN) AT BARKBY (ONE MANOR, MERTON COLLEGE), 1341–1448

Mortality

1349

Years: broken series; for many years there are no data.

the later middle ages). The difference in the numbers of holdings may have resulted partly from consolidation and engrossment of tenures in the later middle ages, but it does also seem that the earlier and later rentals comprehended different levels of tenants.

From the rentals of *c.*1300–1315, some 54 different bynames can be elicited. One customary tenant, Sampson, was listed without a byname, but his heirs assumed the byname Sampson. Of these names, about 10 or 11 persisted to the rental of 1354/5, some 20%. The absolute number is uncertain, because *Faber* existed in 1300x1315 and *Faber* and Smyth in 1354/5. About half of the 23 different surnames in 1354/5 had existed on the manor in the earlier rentals. Some are sufficiently distinctive to suggest that the cause of their continuity was not simply their commonplace nature rather than survival of a kinship: Arnold; Sampson; Hamelton; Playtour (Pleydour); Tante; and Styword.[4] About half of the surnames of 1354/5 thus existed on the manor about 40 years earlier. Only one or two, however, persisted from 1354/5 to 1450. Of the 16 different surnames in 1450, only Johnson, and possibly Jakson as a variant, had occurred in the rental of 1354/5, in the Latin form *filius Johannis*. At least 14 of the 16 names in 1450 had been introduced to the manor over the previous century. By the next rental, 1475, only four of the names of 1450 survived: Braunston; Beregh' (Beveryge); Jakson, and Bocher (Bowcher). Thirteen of the 17 names had been introduced during the 25 years — perhaps a little less than a generation — which had elapsed and only 25% had persisted from 1450.

The transformation of the naming stock of Barkby during the later middle ages, particularly after the 1350s, had thus been profound, although the turnover did not occur before the 1350s. Replication of this pattern occurred in the small, but developing, town of Loughborough, in the north of Leicestershire.

The persistence of surnames in a small town in the later middle ages: Loughborough

The composition of toponymic bynames and surnames in Loughborough changed quite radically over the later middle ages, in line with the general turnover of surnames.[5] Only four toponymic bynames from the rental of *c.*1370 (less than 4%) recurred in the rental of 1526 and only some five (about 20%) from the rental of 1526 into that of 1559. The total numbers of toponymic bynames and surnames declined from 42 in *c*.1370, to 24 in 1526, and subsequently to only 14 in 1559. All this analysis excludes the small number of complex names, including generic toponymic names (Irelonde, Breton) and French toponymic names (Bretuill'). The problem is, however, compounded by toponymic names of some local families which assumed gentle status in the later middle ages (Digby). Finally, the most complex problem, which cannot really be addressed, is the seignorial and territorial geography of Loughborough. Loughborough comprised an urban nucleus within a very large parish, the parish itself divided into several lordships. It is always possible that bynames and surnames migrated backwards and forwards between town and rural parish and between lordships. It is not possible fully to take account of that issue.

The overall transformation of names in Loughborough in the later middle ages was significant and radical. The rental of *c*.1370 enumerated some 230 different bynames or surnames, whilst that of 1526, 121 and that of 1559, 102. The reason for some of this discrepancy is that the rental of *c*.1370 included rural holdings as well as urban, whilst the rentals of 1526 and 1559 concentrated on the urban. Only 26 names (11%) from *c*.1370 survived into the rental of 1526 and in many cases they were common forms of name (Andrew, Bell, Browne, Cooke, Ellott, Fox, Grene, Irlande, Marchall, Page, Smyth[e], Ward and Wrighte). A higher number of names (44 or 36%) survived from the rental of 1526 to that of 1559. The namestock was thus almost completely transformed in the later middle ages and, allowing for the short span between 1526 and 1559, an incipient stability restored in the early sixteenth century, although a very small number of the names of tenants in the rentals of the sixteenth century pertained to families of gentle status (Digby, Pegge, Villers) who were not necessarily resident. Merely 10 names persisted from *c*.1370 through to 1559, almost all common (Andrew, Bell, Browne, Grene, Marshall, Smythe, Ward and Wrighte) and one gentry (Pegge).

The persistence of surnames in Rutland, 1665–1851

Surnames, used circumspectly, are one possible indicator which allows a perspective of secular persistence or change within the county.[6] Nevertheless, they can be no more than an approximate indicator of persistence and change, since they present numerous *caveats*. These problems are considered in more detail in the relevant places in the discussion, but it should be indicated that numerous surnames in Rutland were common ones, not distinctive to the local area, and so considerable caution is necessary in their analysis. Comparison is made here between the nominal evidence in the census of 1851 and the Hearth Tax of 1665, from which aggregate data are presented in Table 12.1. The data from the Hearth Tax cover the whole administrative county, whilst the data from the census relate to two registration districts covering the predominant part of the county, leaving a small amount of geographical discrepancy between the two datasets. Moreover, the 'urban' components of the data from 1851 have been separated to allow some further considerations. The advantage of this procedure is that the two 'populations' for 'rural' in 1851 (male and female heads in rural parishes) and for the Hearth Tax (those responsible for hearths assessed) are thus approximately equal.[7]

Table 12.1

Aggregate data on surnames in Rutland in 1665 and 1851[8]

Dataset	Size of population	No. of surnames
1665	2920	1033
1851 rural	2863	783
1851 Oakham	568	301
1851 Uppingham	411	224

The aggregate data suggest that a slightly greater concentration in the surnames occurred between 1665 and 1851 (the level of isonymy). The extent of that continuing concentration may be more exactly assessed by considering the numbers of different surnames which were borne by more than the mean number of heads of household (Table 12.2). For example, the mean number of heads of household per surname in rural parishes in 1851 was 3.645; allowing for the total size of the population, it was considered that a ratio of 10 heads per household was a significant level.

Revealed in Table 12.2 is an increase in the number of surnames above the mean in 1851 by comparison with 1665, reflecting a further concentration in surnames in relation to population. The level of concentration was greater in rural than urban communities, presumably because of higher levels of endogamy and more circumscribed migration in rural areas whereas urban communities were more volatile, if in these two cases only slightly moreso given their nature as small towns closely related to their rural hinterlands.

Table 12.2

Numbers of surnames borne by more than the mean number of heads[9]

Dataset	Level of significance	No. of surnames at this level	
		N	%
1665	10	54	5.3
1851 rural	10	72	9.2
1851 Oakham	5	20	6.5
1851 Uppingham	5	11	4.9

Table 12.3

Distributions of surnames in the population in 1665 and 1851[10]

Dataset	No.	mean	standdev	median	min	max
1665	1033	2.8	3.722	1	1	37
1851 rural	783	3.7	2.940	2	1	57
1851 Oakham	301	1.9	1.886	1	1	14
1851 Uppingham	224	1.8	1.845	1	1	20

Notes: Means are given to one decimal point. Interquartile ranges are omitted as being of no real significance because of the low numbers.

Further aggregate calculations comparing the actual surnames in the different datasets illustrate the extent of social endogamy through the persistence of surnames. Crudely, 42.7% of the 1,033 different surnames of 1665 still existed in rural Rutland in 1851; the 57.3% which disappeared did so at the rate of 5.9 (6%) per generation (21 years).[11] In fact, the percentages are probably too precise for the analysis. The difficulties involved in the method are several. First, there is the problem of matching orthographical differences in surnames between the two lists, which is, in fact, not too onerous. More complicated is accounting for the genitival -s, which may have been inorganic (not a real inflection) or simply a variant spelling in many cases. Thus, was the occasional Hills more than a variant of Hill? In such cases, discretion has been used in conflating the list of surnames, so that, in this case, for example, Hills was included with Hill. In many other cases, the context provided a reasonable explanation. Nevertheless, some problems remained, especially with toponymic surnames (see further below); for example, was Munton in 1851 a variant of Manton? In that case, it was decided to allow them to remain different surnames, although the distribution suggests that Munton was a variant of Manton, for they occur together in several parishes in 1851 (the distribution is shown in Figure 21).

The final problem, the most serious of all, revolves around inferences to be drawn from entirely common surnames. In both lists, these common, polyphyletic surnames ranked amongst the highest, as the following examples illustrate: Allen/Allyn/Allin borne by 27 assessed in 1665 and 18 heads in 1851 (figures for 1851 here relate to rural and urban communities); Brown(e) 36 in 1665 and 43 in 1851; Clark(e) 32 in 1665 and 56 in 1851; Smith 37 in 1665 and 68 in 1851; Wright 18 in 1665 and 32 in 1851; and Tailor/Taylor 12 in 1665 and 23 in 1851. Those surnames would not necessarily be distinctive in local society and their significance as crude indicators of persistence is thus ambivalent. In mitigation, however, the problem involves only a small number of extremely common surnames, no more than a dozen. The problem is then partly resolved by counting different surnames rather than bearers, so that all surnames have an equal weighting.

More ambivalence, however, is contained within surnames which are not unusual, but may be slightly more diagnostic of local society, such as Sharp(e), which seems unusually high in Rutland, borne by 34 in 1665 and 32 in 1851, or Green(e), again higher than might be expected at 15 in 1665 and 19 in 1851, reflecting back on local topographical conditions. Again, counting numbers of different surnames provides some corrective. The number of adjustments and difficulties, however, must not be exaggerated.

Close analysis of the extinct surnames revealed that they consisted, by and large, of those which in 1665 were borne by fewer than five persons throughout the county in the Hearth Tax assessment, thus indicating first that core surnames tended to persist and, conversely, that marginal surnames were the ones which disappeared and so may, in any case, have been transient even in 1665. The pattern was slightly more nuanced, however, since some localized, diagnostic surnames did exit: Faulkner declined from 16 in 1665 to seven in 1851 (rural and urban); Bun(n)ing from 13 in 1665 to two in 1851; Barker from 11 to no incidence; Cole(s) from 21 to only six;[12] Dracot(t), a diagnostic toponymic surname, from 11 to merely one; Ireland from 11 to two; Pitts from 12 to three; and the intensely localized toponymic surname Wing from 15 to only one. Others

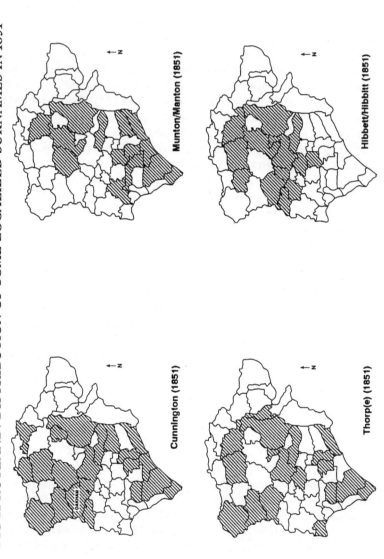

FIG 21 RUTLAND: DISTRIBUTION OF SOME LOCALIZED SURNAMES IN 1851

remained fairly stable in numerical incidence: Baines at 17 in 1665 and 24 (rural and urban) in 1851; Christian/Christain at 11 and 15; Royce at 15 and 17; and Sewell at 14 and 18. Yet others, however, expanded to form the new isonymic surnames: Bilsdon (local toponymic) from no incidence in 1665 to 12 in 1851; Chamberlain from four to 16; Cunnington (toponymic) from two to 30; Ellin(g)worth from one to 18; Fawkes and variants (Faulks, Faux) from five to 22; Goodliffe from none to 13; Healey from none to 17; Hibbett/Hibbitt similarly from zero to 27; Kettle[13] from two to 12; Kirby (local toponymic) from three to 19; Manton and Munton (local toponymic) from respectively eight and four to 13 and 23; Rawling(s) from seven to 23; Stafford from one to 12; Towell from seven to 16; Tyers from three to 20; Tyler (distinctively local occupational) from two to 22;[14] and Wiggin(g)ton from two to 13. A small number which had a very high incidence in 1665 maintained that level in 1851: Beaver (localized toponymic)[15] 11 in 1665 and 14 in 1851; the significant, but slightly ambiguous Thorpe,[16] from 20 to 41; and Tomblin from 10 to 30. Whilst the corpus remained substantially the same, the distribution of surnames did change internally. The geographical distribution sometimes also changed, as with Beaver, which was substantially rural in incidence in 1665, but had become concentrated almost entirely in Oakham by 1851 (12 of 14 male heads who bore the surname).

By 1851, those newly advancing surnames had contributed strongly to the slightly higher level of isonymy in the county. An attempt to ascertain the statistical level of relationship between social endogamy and isonymy in 1851 is, however, only partly successful.[17] The results suggest that, despite pockets of concentrations of surnames in parishes and communities, social endogamy within parishes is only one influence and that social endogamy within the county as a whole is just as important. More detailed qualitative examination does reveal, however, specific concentrations, which will be illustrated by a purposive sample of the distinctively localized surnames borne by heads of households in 1851.[18] Hibbett (*alias* Hibbitt) is an excellent example of a surname which was seemingly absent in 1665, but profuse in 1851 (Figure 21). Seven heads in the closed parish of Exton bore this name, with five more in each of Cottesmore and Edith Weston, two each in Whitwell, Greetham and Empingham, and others in Brooke, Egleton and South Luffenham. The toponymic surname Kirby — of which the precise toponymic origin is ambiguous, since the placename is locally prolific — was similarly concentrated: 10 heads in Barrowden, four in Morcott, others in Bisbrooke, and North and South Luffenham (thus extremely localized if the origin was Kirby Hall in Northamptonshire). Equally concentrated was Rawling(s), represented by 11 heads in Braunston, two in each of Teigh, Cottesmore and Market Overton, and another in Wing. Nine heads in Langton were called Sewell, with three in Barrowden and others in Lyddington, Hambleton, South Luffenham and Edith Weston. In Braunston was concentrated the isonymous surname Atton, held there by nine heads, with only one other example at Hambleton. These surnames were further diffused, however, by localized movement of male servants, so that another Hibbett was employed in Wing, a Rawlings in Market Overton and two servants called Sewell in Langham. Male lodgers of local extraction also facilitated localized diffusion, extending Hibbett to Hambleton, although the two Atton lodgers were also in Braunston.

This type of evidence confirms too the close relationship between the two market towns and their rural environs. Of the different surnames in Oakham in 1851, almost 60% (59.9%) were represented too in rural Rutland; the equivalent figure for Uppingham was 61%. Again, qualitative examples help to illustrate this phenomenon. The surname of Beaver apparently migrated from rural communities in the late seventeenth century to become virtually confined within Oakham by the middle of the nineteenth, but leaving a few residual examples in rural areas. Cunnington was heavily concentrated in Oakham too, held by 15 heads, but it was equally held by the same number of heads in rural parishes, in Seaton, Cottesmore, Egleton, Braunston, Horn, Whissendine, Hambleton, Lyddington, North Luffenham, Empingham and Market Overton (Figure 21). In Oakham there were also 12 heads whose surname was Ellingworth, represented in rural Rutland by four heads. By far the most significant surname in Uppingham was Thorpe; this name's origins are potentially ambiguous, because of the profusion of the placename, but Thorpe-by-Water is extremely close to the town. Twenty heads in Uppingham bore the name, exceeding the 15 in rural Rutland and the six in Oakham. It occurred in 11 rural parishes (25%) considered here as well as the concentration in Uppingham (Figure 21).

Perhaps a further diagnostic element of surnames is the character of toponymic ones in the county in 1851.[19] Whilst the corpus of very localized toponymic surnames had been greater in 1665, even in

1851 considerably more than half were of a similar nature.[20] Nevertheless, several problems are encountered in defining the terms of analysis. First, the forms of some surnames require interpretation because of phonetic and local dialectal characteristics: Musson is undoubtedly Muston (Leicestershire) and so equally Syson (Syston), and Cro(w)son (Croxton), rather than being patronymic forms. Similarly Wormall is probably Wormhill (Derbyshire) and Beaver Belvoir (Leicestershire). Cliffe is probably King's Cliffe (Northamptonshire) rather than a topographical form. Secondly, several placenames are ambiguous because they are prolific: Thorpe (as above) is one obvious example; Barrow is another (Rutland or Leicestershire); so too Belton (Leicestershire or Rutland); Orton (Overton) is more widely profuse; Corby might derive from that placename in either Lincolnshire or Northamptonshire; Floar is probably Flore (Northamptonshire); Islip is probably from the settlement in Northamptonshire, but might (remotely) derive from Oxfordshire, since Westminster Abbey had held that manor in Oxfordshire as well as the rectorial manor in Oakham; Laxton probably also has its origin in Northamptonshire, but might be from Nottinghamshire; Kirby too is probably from Northamptonshire, but is another ambiguous placename, as is Burton (but with good candidates in both Lincolnshire and Leicestershire). Appelbee (Appleby) occurred only once amongst the rural male heads, introduced by one born in Surrey, but is an entirely ambiguous placename, with settlements in Westmorland, Leicestershire, Lindsey and Hertfordshire. Wigginton, a surname held by 12 heads in 1851, may have origins in Hertfordshire, Oxfordshire, Staffordshire or Yorkshire North Riding.[21]

The analysis is thus not entirely free of ambiguity, but the corpus of toponymic surnames does help to confirm persisting localization: 16 such surnames from places within Rutland; 39 from those in Leicestershire; 22 from Northamptonshire; and 16 from Lincolnshire; and thus *in toto* about 93 localized forms. Paradoxically, the forms from places within the county were, with significant exceptions, held by few male heads; for example, Ashwell by two, Pickworth two, Casterton by three, Eagleton (Egleton) by one, Exton by three, Stretton by one, and Wing by one. More exceptionally in evidence were Munton/Manton (as above, some 32 male heads), Preston six, Seaton five, Stokes (an ambiguous form) 10, and Thorpe (15) (Figure 21). The surname Bra(u)ns(t)on (that is variously Branson, Braunson and Branston) was held by nine heads concentrated as noted above; it seems more likely to represent Braunston in Rutland than Branston or Braunstone in Leicestershire.

Surnames derived from places in Leicestershire followed a similar distribution as well as, in the main, geographical proximity. From east Leicestershire, derived the surnames Barsby (six male heads), Beaver (two), Beebe (Beeby, one), Bilsdon (10), Broughton (either Leicestershire or Nottinghamshire, but both places of origin contiguous, five), Busby (Bushby, two), Cro(w)son (four), Dalby (seven), Draycott (one), Frisby (but possibly Lincolnshire, eight), Glen(n) (probably Great Glen, but possibly the more distant Glen Parva, four), Harby (one), Musson (four), Hose (one), Lowseby (one), Owston (one), and Wartnaby (two), as well as forms from other parts of that county, in particular, from the south, Saddington (nine male heads), as also from the south and other parts of the county the less prolific Arnsby (one), Barwell (five), Belgrave (two), Bosworth (two), Gruby (Groby, one), Horsepool (one), Knighton (one), Sapcote (one), Mesham (one) and Seal (one). These surnames derived predominantly from within a distance of 15–20 miles.

Those originating from placenames in Northamptonshire travelled a much more circumscribed distance, mainly from within the Welland valley. Examples of such surnames, born by male heads, are Aldwinkle (two), Barfield (metathesis for Brafield, 12), Cliffe (seven), Kirby (17), Laxton (10), Middleton (two), and Welland (one), whilst more slightly distant settlements provided, for example, Floar (three), Rowell (Rothwell, four) and Saxton (one). Surnames from Lincolnshire, by contrast, travelled greater distances, reflected in the generic Lindsey (one male head) and Winterton (five), but equally from relatively closer settlements such as Claypole (one), Lowth (two), Scotney (two), Sculthorpe (one), Springthorpe (eight), Tailby (Tealby, one) and Tidd (six). Moreover, some surnames derived from other counties also travelled only short distances, such as Hickling (one male head), Blaisby (Bleasby, one) and Kellam (Kelham, one) from Nottinghamshire. The most important of this category of surnames was Cunnington, held by 15 male heads in rural parishes as well as 15 in Oakham, and which had its etymology in one of the Coningtons in either Huntingdonshire (eight miles south of Peterborough and 21 south-east of Oakham) or Cambridgeshire (six miles south-east of Huntingdon and 38 miles south-east of Oakham).[22]

Nevertheless, toponymic surnames from more distant places

were intruding into the county by 1851 such as, for example, Braithwaite (Yorkshire, West Riding, one male head), Buxton (Derbyshire, one), Hatfield (ambiguous, possibly Yorkshire, West Riding, one), Pickering (Yorkshire, North Riding, two), Stafford (12), Wigginton (ambiguous, 12), Rimington (Yorkshire, West Riding, six), Hallam (ambiguous, possibly Derbyshire, Yorkshire West Riding, or, less likely, Nottinghamshire, in the latter case Halam), Wakefield (Yorkshire, West Riding, two), Warrington (Lancashire, two), and Wormall (Derbyshire, two). Some of these persisted from an earlier time, represented in the Hearth Tax of 1665 (Peniston from Penistone, Yorkshire, West Riding, two male heads in 1851), or Sneath (from Snaith, Yorkshire, West Riding, nine male heads in 1851, one assessed male in 1665). Others, however, were newly introduced, mostly borne in 1851 by small numbers of male heads; some, indeed, were evidently introduced only in the mid-nineteenth century, such as Applebee, held by a male head in 1851 who had been born in Surrey, or Buxton by a male head born in Yorkshire, Dalton by one born in Surrey, Hustwick by another born in Yorkshire and Tinsley by one born in Warwickshire.

The relative importance of the different origins of toponymic surnames can, to a small extent, be assessed by their distribution amongst the rural population (male heads). Surnames from Rutland were, on average, held by more male heads, with those from Northamptonshire a close second, followed by those from Leicestershire, then non-local counties and finally those from Lincolnshire. The most localized toponymic surnames thus tended to be held by more male heads.[23]

Conclusion

Although surnames can and have been used to reflect the persistence of local populations, they remain an ambiguous indicator, perhaps useful only *faute de mieux*. The relationship between their persistence and the continuity of local cultures is an enticing but unproven hypothesis. Surnames, moreover, merely represent continuation through the male line, ignoring transmission through the distaff members of the family. In the late middle ages, familial continuity might have depended on the female line and, indeed, the turnover of surnames in local 'communities' was extensive. Stability was only re-established in the sixteenth century, when a long-term persistence of surnames returned. The identification of persistent surnames and core families in those local societies and settlements is a feature most closely associated with the early modern period. In the case of Rutland, social endogamy existed at the level of the county, artificial as this unit might seem, so that persistence of surnames was a characteristic into the nineteentn century, although there were losses and expansions of individual surnames.

References

[1] See S Postles, 'Barkby: the anatomy of a closed township, 1535-1780', unpublished MA thesis, Leicester University, 1979.

[2] MM 6556-6629. For a similar analysis on the College's other manor in the county, Kibworth Harcourt, C Howell, 'Peasant inheritance customs in the Midlands, 1280-1700' in J Goody, J Thirsk and E P Thompson, eds., *Family and Inheritance. Rural Society in Western Europe 1200-1800*, (Cambridge, 1976), 124.

[3] Z Razi, 'The erosion of the family-land bond in the late fourteenth and fifteenth centuries: a methodological note' and C Dyer, 'Changes in the link between families and land in the west midlands in the fourteenth and fifteenth centuries', in R M Smith, ed., *Land, Kinship and Life-cycle*, (Cambridge, 1984), 295-312.

[4] MM 6556, 6568.

[5] The sources are: HAM Box 20, flders 1-9, Box 21, flders 1-3, Box 24, flders 2, 4, 6, 7.

[6] For similar approaches using surnames as an indicator: E J Buckatzsch, 'The constancy of local populations and migration in England before 1800', *Population Studies*, 8 (1911), 62-9; R Watson, 'A study of surname distribution in a group of Cambridgeshire parishes, 1538-1840', *Local Population Studies*, 15 (1975), 23-32; M T Smith and B L Hudson, 'Isonymic relationships in the parish of Fylingdales, North Yorkshire, in 1851', *Annals of Human Biology*, 11 (1984), 141-8; and the summary in G Lasker, *Surnames and Genetic Structure*, (Cambridge, 1985), 56-61; N Evans, 'The descent of dissenters in the Chiltern Hundreds', in M Spufford, ed., *The World of Rural Dissenters 1520-1725*, (Cambridge, 1995), 296-8; P Spufford, 'The comparative mobility and immobility of Lollard descendants in early modern England', in M Spufford, ed., *The World of Rural Dissenters*, 313-324; contrast with M Zell, *Industry in*

the Countryside. Wealden Society in the Sixteenth Century, (Cambridge, 1994), 25–6.

7 *Rutland Hearth Tax*. It should be emphasized that the Hearth Tax data do enumerate the exempt or poor, who are indicated by either 'not chargeable' or 'ex''. For problems of the Hearth Taxes, C Husbands, 'Hearths, wealth and occupations: an exploration of the Hearth Tax in the later seventeenth century' in K Schürer and T Arkell, eds., *Surveying the People. The Interpretation and Use of Document Sources for the Study of Population in the Later Seventeenth Century*, (Oxford, 1992), 65–77 ('in principle socially comprehensive' at 65), and also T Arkell, 'Printed instructions for administering the Heart Tax', *ibid.*, 38–55. PRO HO107/2092–2093.

8 *Rutland Hearth Tax*; PRO HO107/2092–2093.

9 *Rutland Hearth Tax*; PRO HO107/2092–2093.

10 *Rutland Hearth Tax*; PRO HO107/2092–2093.

11 Compare these data with Buckatzsch's findings for Shap (Westmoreland) and Horringer (Suffolk) between the late seventeenth and late eighteenth centuries: in Shap 35% of the surnames of the late seventeenth century still persisted at the end of the eighteenth, but only 3% at Horringer ('The constancy of local populations'). In four Northumberland parishes over more or less the same period, Dobson found that 47–53% of surnames 39–41% persisted (résumé in G Lasker, *Surnames and Genetic Structure*, (Cambridge, 1985), 58–61).

12 In most cases, diagnostic status is attributed by reference to number of incidences, but Cole, for example, may have had a local etymology from the Anglo-Scand personal name Kolí or Kolr, for which see above, 242.

13 Another Anglo-Scand personal name.

14 The context is probably the stone slates of Collyweston and its area.

15 That is, Belvoir, for which, see above, 144–8.

16 Thorpe is a profuse place-name in areas of Scandinavian influence and especially here in the area of the Five Boroughs.

17 The statistical test was run on the following equation: first, the extent of social endogamy was calculated at parish level — for which, see the Appendix and Figure 21 — expressed as the percentage of resident male heads actually born in the same parish; the second stage was to establish a crude coefficient of isonymy at parish level by dividing the number of different

surnames in the parish by the number of male heads (producing a value between 1.0 and 1.9); next, Spearman's rank correlation coefficient was produced by correlating the surname coefficient with the value for social endogamy, the result of which is that C=0.566, that is positive, but not at a high level of p. Using Rank Regression in Minitab, with surname coefficient as the dependent value and social endogamy as the predictor produces tau=0.173 and least squares s=0.1669.

[18] For a recent qualitative statement about the function of surnames as a variable of a localized society, R Moore, *The Social Impact of Oil: The Case of Peterhead*, (London, 1982), 78 ('a few surnames appear again and again in the town and like any small isolated population it is heavily intermarried').

[19] The data for 1851 considered here relate only to the rural parishes of Rutland, although many of the surnames discussed recurred in the two towns.

[20] The problem is compounded by forms which may be toponymic, but are more likely topographical, which renders difficult an unambiguous total of different toponymic surnames in 1851. A working figure of 160 is suggested here, based on further observations in the text below.

[21] For these reasons of ambiguity, no attempt is made to produce descriptive statistics of distances moved by surnames; the margins of error are too great and more qualitative statements follow below.

[22] Male servants named Cunnington were also enumerated at Stretton, Edith Weston, Langham, Seaton (farm servant), Glaston, North Luffenham, and Oakham (two), as well as female servants in various parishes, but whose surnames may not have persisted.

[23] The values are as follows:

county of origin	mean	standdev	median
Rutland	6.19	7.930	3
Northamptonshire	5.00	5.040	3
Leicestershire	2.72	2.438	2
Non-local	2.65	2.895	1
Lincolnshire	2.38	2.071	1

It should be noted, however, that Cunnington is included in the non-local category.

CONCLUSION

Situated in central England, the two counties of Leicestershire and Rutland were surrounded by other shires, comprising Derbyshire, Nottinghamshire, Lincolnshire, Northamptonshire, Warwickshire and Staffordshire. Whilst Rutland received a legacy of an ancient discrete territory with distinct boundaries, which might have influenced social organization later, Leicestershire had both strong and weak borders.[1] The south-western and western boundary of Leicestershire, moreover, was located at the conjunction of two political influences: the meeting point of the regions of Scandinavian and West Saxon predominance. Both counties were contained within the region of the Five Boroughs, which had experienced Scandinavian control, but Leicestershire was open on the south and south-west to the penetration of West Saxon influence.[2] Whilst both shires comprised part of what has been considered East Midlands ME, Leicestershire was not secure from the infiltration of West Midlands ME and into both counties were introduced aspects and items of Northern ME through Lincolnshire. Leicestershire in particular, but also Rutland, thus exhibited the signs of a mélange of influences.

Both counties were contained within the area of the so-called Midland Plain of Lowland England, although Leicestershire included upland pre-Cambrian physical relief and areas of woodland and wood-pasture (reduced 'forest'), whilst Rutland contained a 'forest' (that term used here in the legal sense). Although regional diversity and contrasts thus existed within the two counties, the influence of ecology and geography on naming patterns was mostly informed by characteristics of the Midland Plain, by the predominance of nucleated settlement.[3]

Consequently, some principal aspects of naming included the intermixture of dialectal items. Northern Walker was accepted into the lexis of naming in preference to eastern Fuller. The genitival -s, prolific in Warwickshire, only expanded in Leicestershire and Rutland over the late middle ages. By contrast, the French diminutive

351

suffix -en in bynames and surnames derived from personal names, so predominant in Warwickshire and some other West Midlands counties, made little impact at all in the two counties. In Rutland in 1665, the -en diminutive was rare and even in 1851 its presence was negligible, as reflected in Uppingham and Oakham, in which towns Jonathan Gibbons and Sarah Gibbons represented the form, but only amongst half a dozen others with this form of surname.[4]

Hereditary surnames developed within the two counties at a similar time as in other central counties, by contrast with the later formation in more northerly shires.[5] Exceptionally, some occupational bynames retained their lexical content later, that is the bynames represented the actual trade of the bearer. By the middle of the thirteenth century, none the less, the free peasantry predominantly bore hereditary surnames, followed by a core of the unfree peasantry by the late thirteenth century and finally all the unfree peasantry by the early fourteenth.

In a similar vein, as a result of predominantly nucleated settlement, the proportion of taxpayers with toponymic bynames and surnames was consistent with other counties with a similar settlement pattern, by comparison with those which contained a higher element of dispersed settlement.[6] Overwhelmingly, therefore, toponymic bynames reflected migration of people rather than habitation in dispersed hamlets. The consequent migration of surnames was intensely localized, but wider dispersion was effected by the influence of medieval lordship.

Conversely, as a consequence of the limited nature of dispersed settlement, topographical bynames and surnames never achieved a significant influence on bynames and surnames within the two counties. Indeed, the topographical items remained largely conventional, particularly in comparison with the wider variety in adjacent Lincolnshire.[7] In particular, topographical bynames and surnames had little impact on the naming of burgesses in the borough of Leicester, although in small towns, if Melton Mowbray is representative, topographical bynames were not excluded. As elsewhere in Midlands counties, topographical bynames and surnames might have been associated more with unfreedom before the later middle ages.[8]

Despite the position of the two counties within the area of Scandinavian influence, the impact of pre-Conquest Anglo-Scand personal names on bynames and surnames was restricted, because of the profound effect on naming processes and patterns of the

Conquest. The persistence of this Scandinavian influence was perhaps stronger in Rutland than in Leicestershire, perhaps associated with its proximity to Lincolnshire. The peasantry of Nottinghamshire and Lincolnshire may have retained this influence more significantly than in Leicestershire and possibly Rutland, but in Derbyshire the impact was seemingly as low as in Leicestershire.[9] Survivals existed in Warwickshire, perhaps either through seepage from Leicestershire or through those earlier migrations identified by Insley.[10]

Although the two counties were not as sealed as some, nor did they contain many remote or isolate areas as some other counties, none the less the localized persistence of surnames appears to have maintained a high level. During the later middle ages, an extensive turnover of surnames occurred at the level of the local 'community', vill or parish, but probably drawing on the persistent stock of the two counties. By the middle of the sixteenth century, stability resumed at the intensely local level of parish and vill, which extended into the nineteenth century.

The ambiguous and ambivalent evidence of one distinctive form of surname — toponymic — intimates, moreover, the persistence of established areas of social organization.[11] Whilst surnames from Leicestershire and Rutland placenames in other counties predominantly clustered close to the boundaries of the two counties, some patterns of distribution were so defined as to suggest the influence of river valleys as funnels for the migration of surnames — the Trent and Welland/Nene valleys especially.

The variety of influences within the two counties was perhaps remarkably illustrated by the apparently different patterns of naming in Loughborough, the market town in the north of the county. There, although toponymic surnames in the later middle ages principally derived from other places in the two counties, there was nevertheless a large contingent from more northerly shires, especially from the Trent valley, but also more northerly. In complete contrast, shires to the south of Leicestershire provided little name material. In this town too, occupational bynames appear to have retained their lexical meaning for much longer, into the fifteenth century. Exceptionally, the suffix -man assumed a particular characteristic here, with the full implication that bearers of such bynames were servants in the wider, historical sense of that term. Naming in the town exhibited further distinctive features, the effect of which is to emphasize the diversity

within the two counties of this study as they were located at the
confluence of competing influences.

References

[1] C V Phythian-Adams, 'Introduction: an agenda for English Local
History' in *idem*, ed., *Societies, Cultures and Kinship, 1580–1850.
Cultural Provinces and English Local History*, (London, 1993), 1–24;
C V Phythian-Adams, 'Rutland reconsidered' in A Dornier, ed.,
Mercian Studies, (Leicester, 1977), 63–84; B Cox, 'Aspects of early
Rutland', a paper read at the Twenty-third Annual Study Conference
of the Council for Name Studies in Great Britain and Ireland,
Leicester, 5 April 1991.

[2] P Stafford, *The East Midlands in the Early Middle Ages*, (Leicester,
1985), 135–43.

[3] N Pye, ed., *Leicester and its Region*, (Leicester, 1972).

[4] I Hjertstedt, *Middle English Nicknames in the Lay Subsidy Rolls for
Warwickshire*, (Acta Universitatis Upsaliensis, Studia Anglistica
Upsaliensia, 63, Uppsala, 1987), 28–9; R McKinley, *The Surnames
of Oxfordshire*, (ESS, III, London, 1977), 219–32. In Leicestershire,
the following numbers of bynames and surnames with the suffix
-en are encountered: in 1327 two; in 1381 one; in 1524 five; and in
Rutland: in 1296 none; in 1377 three; in 1522 seven (Dicons/
Dikons, Gibbon/Gybbon (three) and Hochyn); in 1524 11
(similar content): *AASR*, (1888–9); PRO E179/133/35, 104–110,
112–118, 121–122, 124; PRO E179/165/1, 21; *Tudor Rutland*; PRO
HO107/2093.

[5] McKinley, *Surnames of Oxfordshire*, 7–40 by comparison with
R McKinley, *The Surnames of Lancashire*, (ESS, IV, London, 1981),
9–76.

[6] Compare D Postles [and R McKinley], *The Surnames of Devon*, (ESS,
VI, London, 1995), *passim*.

[7] PRO E179/135/14–15.

[8] McKinley, *Surnames of Oxfordshire*, 43–5.

[9] F M Stenton, *The Free Peasantry of the Northern Danelaw*, (repr.
Oxford, 1969); PRO E179/135/14–16.

[10] J Insley, 'Regional variation in Scandinavian personal nomenclature
in England', *Nomina*, 3 (1979), 52–60.

[11] Phythian-Adams, 'Introduction', *Societies, Cultures and Kinship*, 1–24.

INDEX LOCORUM

INDEX NOMINUM

A Barow, 52
A Dalby, 52
A Grene, 52
A Leke, 52
A Sybsdon, 52
Abbacia de, 221
Abbotes, 263
Abram, Habraham, 117
Ace, 117–18, 258–60
Adecockes, 263
Agrene, 52
Ailmer, Ailmore, 250, 253
Alan, Aleyn, 236, 259
Albus tannator, 318
Aldith, Aldyth, 118, 258–9
Aldwinkle, 346
Alexandri filius, 115
Alferd, 101
Alisaundre, 115
Allynson, 277
Alselin, 102
Alsi, Alsy, 118, 260–1
Alurici filii, 108
Alwin, 250
Ameson, Amyson, 70, 272
Amice, Amys, 116–17, 258
Amyssone, 273
Andrew, 55, 259, 338
Annesley, 203
Anotesson, 273
Anstey de, 138
Appelbee, Appulby, 50, 347
Aquam ad, 218
Aquarius, 255, 318
Arketil, 243
Arnold, 310–11, 316, 337
Arnsbee, Arnsby, 162, 346
Arsar, 55
Arwesmith le, 191
Ashbrenner, 200
Ashwell, 345
Asmund, 248
Astel, 73
Asteyn, 73, 95, 243
Asty, 243–4
Atte Abbotes, Atteabbotys, 217
Attechyrche, 42

Attecros, 220, *see ad Crucem*,
   Crosse atte
Attehall, Attohall, 217
Atteparsons, Attoparsons, 217
Atteprioris, 217
Atte Syrhwys, 217
Atte vikerus, 217
Atton, 344
Att(e)well(e), 51–2, 218
Aubigny d', 308
Auenarius, 318
Auenator, 185, 318
Auener le, 185, 319
Aula de, 111
Aurifaber, 191, 318

Bacstere, 187 *see* Baxtere
Baddesley de, 50
Bailiff, Baillyfes le, Balis, 179, 263
Baines, Banes, Banys, Baynes, Bane,
   81, 297, 303, 343
Baker, Bakar, Bakere, 31–2, 73, 179,
   187
Balle, 93
Banastre, 309, 315
Banckes, 55
Barba cum, 116–17
Barber, Barbour, 55, 187
Bardon, 49
Barfield, 346
Bar(e)fote, 295
Bark' de, 115
Bark(e)by de, 53, 64–5, 138, 313
Barker(e), 179, 187, 341
Barkeston' (de), 153–4, 160
Barre a la, 218
Barre, (atte, Barre, orientale), 218
Barton, 55
Barwell, 160, 162, 346
Barsby, 346
Basset, 126, 308
Bate, 71, 259
Batesone, 271
Baudwine, 259
Baxtere, Bauxter, 31–3, 200–4, 210,
   see Bacstere

INDEX RERUM

369